Spain

The Modern Nations in
Historical Perspective

ROBIN W. WINKS, *General Editor*

The volumes in this series deal with individual nations or groups of closely related nations throughout the world, summarizing the chief historical trends and influences that have contributed to each nation's present-day character, problems, and behavior. Recent data are incorporated with established historical background to achieve a fresh synthesis and original interpretation.

RICHARD HERR, *the author of this volume, is Professor of History at the University of California, Berkeley and author of* The Eighteenth Century Revolution in Spain.

ALSO IN THE EUROPEAN SUBSERIES

The Balkans *by Charles and Barbara Jelavich*
France *by John C. Cairns*
Italy *by Massimo Salvadori*
Poland and Czechoslovakia *by Frederick G. Heymann*
Scandinavia *by John H. Wuorinen*

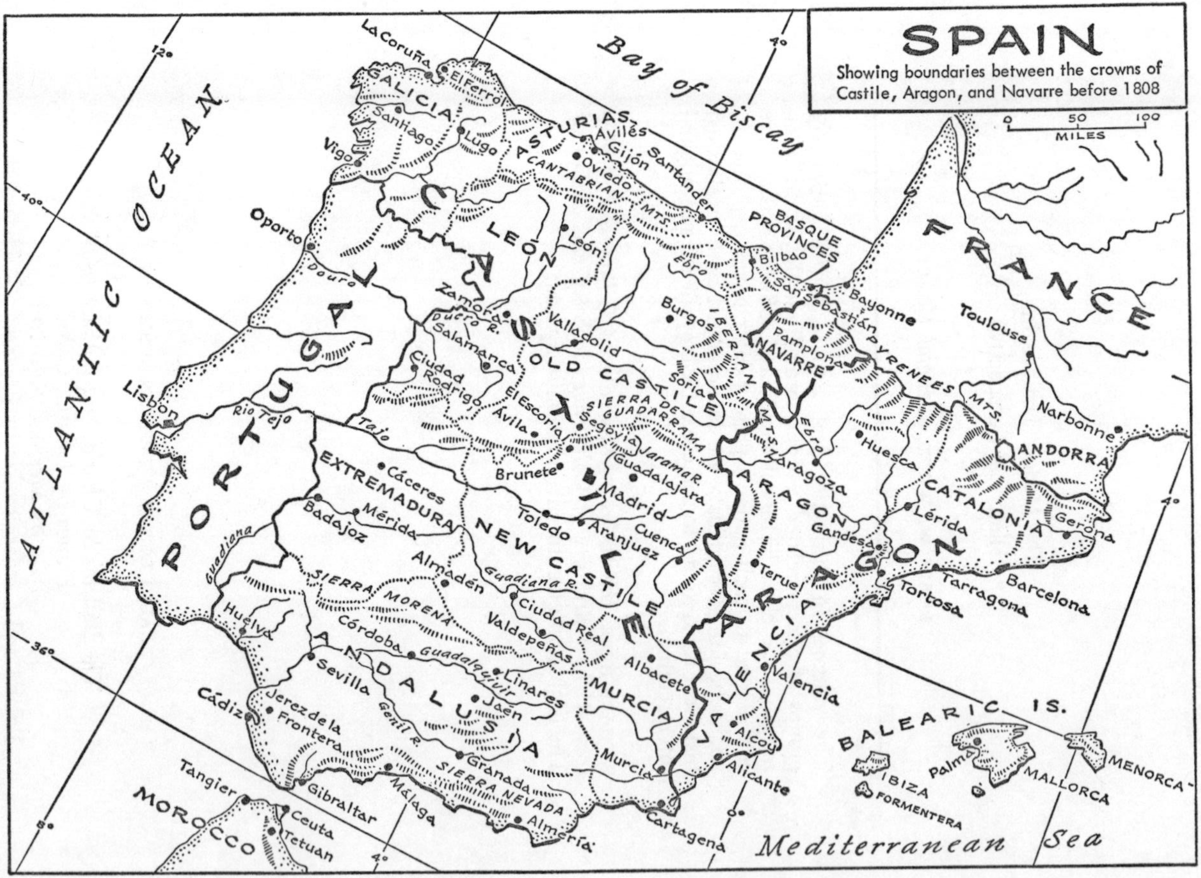
SPAIN
Showing boundaries between the crowns of Castile, Aragon, and Navarre before 1808
0 50 100
MILES
Bay of Biscay
ATLANTIC OCEAN
Mediterranean Sea
FRANCE
PORTUGAL
CASTILE
ARAGON
GALICIA
ASTURIAS
LEÓN
OLD CASTILE
NEW CASTILE
EXTREMADURA
ANDALUSIA
MURCIA
VALENCIA
CATALONIA
NAVARRE
BASQUE PROVINCES
ANDORRA
BALEARIC IS.
MENORCA
MALLORCA
IBIZA
FORMENTERA
MOROCCO
CANTABRIAN MTS.
PYRENEES MTS.
IBERIAN MTS.
SIERRA DE GUADARRAMA
SIERRA MORENA
SIERRA NEVADA
La Coruña
El Ferrol
Santiago
Vigo
Lugo
Avilés
Gijón
Oviedo
Santander
Bilbao
San Sebastián
Bayonne
Toulouse
Narbonne
Pamplona
León
Oporto
Douro
Zamora
Duero R.
Valladolid
Burgos
Ebro
Soria
Salamanca
Ciudad Rodrigo
El Escorial
Ávila
Segovia
Jarama R.
Guadalajara
Madrid
Brunete
Toledo
Aranjuez
Cuenca
Lisbon
Rio Tejo
Tajo
Cáceres
Mérida
Badajoz
Guadiana
Almadén
Guadiana R.
Ciudad Real
Valdepeñas
Córdoba
Guadalquivir
Linares
Jaén
Sevilla
Huelva
Cádiz
Jerez de la Frontera
Genil R.
Granada
Málaga
Gibraltar
Almería
Tangier
Ceuta
Tetuan
Albacete
Murcia
Cartagena
Alicante
Alcoy
Valencia
Teruel
Zaragoza
Gandesa
Huesca
Lérida
Tortosa
Tarragona
Barcelona
Gerona
Palma
4°
8°
12°
0°
40°
36°

The Modern Nations in Historical Perspective

SPAIN

RICHARD HERR

PRENTICE-HALL, INC. *Englewood Cliffs, New Jersey*

 C–13-824094-9. *Library of Congress Catalog Card Number 70–126814*. Printed in the United States of America.

Current printing (last number):

10 9 8 7 6 5 4 3 2 1

PRENTICE-HALL INTERNATIONAL, INC. (*London*)
PRENTICE-HALL OF AUSTRALIA, PTY. LTD. (*Sydney*)
PRENTICE-HALL OF CANADA, LTD. (*Toronto*)
PRENTICE-HALL OF INDIA PRIVATE LIMITED (*New Delhi*)
PRENTICE-HALL OF JAPAN, INC. (*Tokyo*)

Preface

More than anything else, this book is an extended essay which points out some of the problems that have been dealt with by historians of modern Spain and seeks to provide credible explanations for that country's evolution over the last two centuries. Since I first taught the history of Spain fifteen years ago, my ideas have evolved continually, and the interpretations put forward here represent only my current thinking on the subject. Tentative though they are, I hope they will be of use to others who share my interest in Spain.

A number of Spaniards have given me precious help. Don José Luis Cano, of the review *Insula,* and Professor José Montesinos, of Berkeley, have broadened my scanty knowledge of literary currents. Doña Gimena Menéndez Pidal, director of Colegio Estudio of Madrid, discussed contemporary education and cultural activities with me, and the author and editor Don Arturo del Hoyo gave me insights into various aspects of Spanish life since the thirties. Don Aniceto García Villar, professor at the School of Ceramics of Madrid, furnished most of my information on rural dress and culture in the early twentieth century. Professors Luis Monguió and Rafael Pérez de la Dehesa, of Berkeley, and Antoni Bernalte, of Barcelona, read critically an early version of the manuscript; and so did Professor Joan Connelly Ullman, of the University of Washington, who if not Spanish by nationality virtually is by her knowledge of the country and empathy for its people.

It would be impossible to recall all of the students who in discussions or in their writing have helped me formulate my ideas, but certain persons stand out. David Fogarty helped bring up to date my information on the period before 1700. I have drawn on the seminar papers of Edward James Blakely, Jane Alice Dawson, John R. Levenson, and

Robert H. Richheimer. In her doctoral dissertation "The Moderado Party in Spain, 1820–1854" (University of California, Berkeley, 1965), Nancy A. Rosenblatt provides a new and clearer picture of the early years of Isabel II, on which I have relied heavily in describing the origins of the Moderado order.

Because of the general nature of the book, I have used footnotes only for direct quotations and when I wished to call attention to unusual or especially helpful studies. Much of the information on the eighteenth century and Napoleonic period has come from my own research, some of it not yet published. Standard works, including those recommended at the end of the book or cited in the notes, have been my major source for the period 1814–1939. Since the end of the Civil War, I have turned to newspapers, the accounts of Spaniards and foreign observers, and official government statistics and other publications. Many of these last I obtained in the libraries of the Ministry of Education and the Ministry of Information and Tourism. I am grateful to their head librarians, Doña Vicenta Cortes Alonso and Dona Celina Iñíquez, for their enthusiastic help in ferreting out the kinds of publications I needed.

I was in Spain for extended visits from 1950 to 1952, in 1959–60, in 1963–64, and in 1969 for research on topics in Spanish history in the eighteenth and early nineteenth centuries. During these occasions I kept notes on my observations of the current situation, which proved of great use for the chapters on Spain under Franco. The general lines of my interpretation, not only of recent developments but of the last two centuries, originated as much in these personal observations as in written sources. The reader may judge how successful this approach has been.

Richard Herr

Contents

Spain

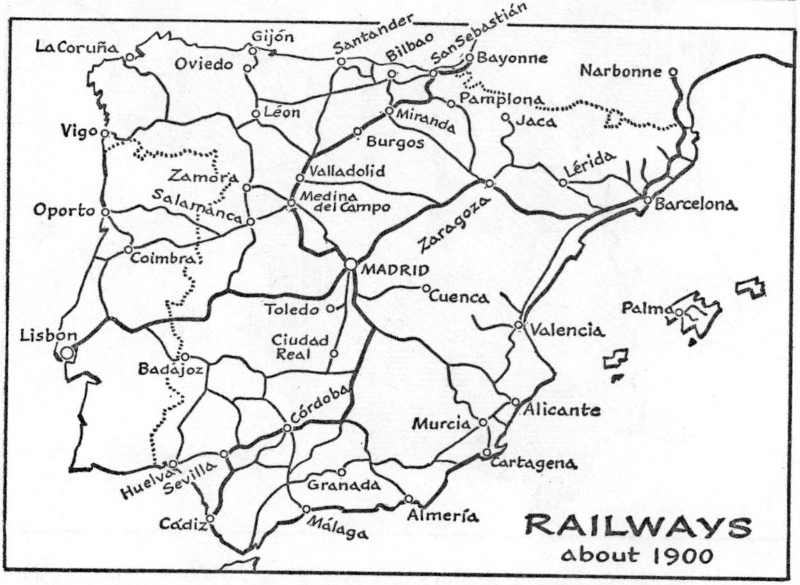

Based on stars radiating out of Madrid, both highway and railroad networks originally reflected political considerations more than economic, but their patterns eventually facilitated the recent industrialization of Madrid.

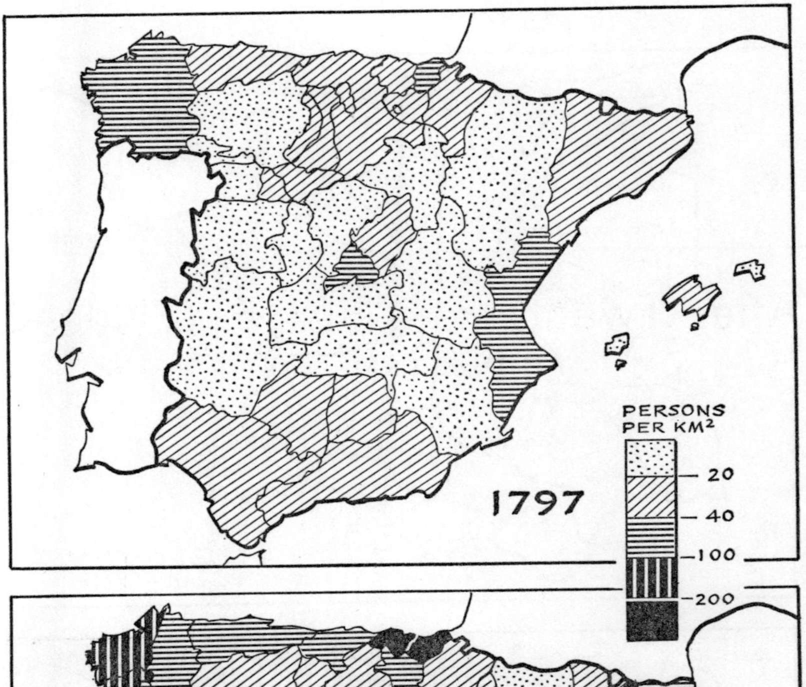

While the population rose sharply between 1797 and 1960 in almost all areas, the pattern of sparcity in the central plateaus and denser population in the periphery and in Madrid remained constant. Note, however, the faster growth of the main industrial regions: Barcelona, two Basque provinces, and Madrid.

1

After Twenty-Five Years of Peace

1

On April 18, 1963 a slight, pale fifty-two-year-old Spaniard named Julian Grimau faced a military court in Madrid. The state accused him of having personally tortured and executed political and military prisoners in Barcelona during the Spanish Civil War in 1937 and 1938, when he was head of the local Communist-dominated Criminal Investigation Brigade. Furthermore, the prosecution asserted, after fleeing to Russia at the end of the war, he had returned secretly to Spain in 1959 to become a leading member of the central committee of the outlawed Communist party, and he had directed subversive activities until his arrest in November 1962. The prosecution produced no witnesses, and Grimau, by rules of the military court, could not call any of his own. His counsel pointed out that evidence of his activities during the Civil War was all hearsay, and that there was none that he had plotted rebellion since his return in 1959. The military judges sentenced the defendant to death. In a final statement, Grimau proudly proclaimed, "I have been a Communist for nearly twenty-seven years, and a Communist I shall die." A few days later in Paris, lawyers from France, Britain, and Italy who had witnessed the trial described it as a tragic farce.

On the day after the trial, the Spanish cabinet and the Head of State, General Francisco Franco, reviewed the sentence. During the meeting an aide brought Franco a personal telegram from Nikita Khrushchev, prime minister of Russia, urging clemency. Despite some voices of moderation, the majority of the cabinet angrily rejected this plea and demanded execution of the sentence, a position with which

Franco concurred. At dawn on April 20, Grimau was led out to his prison courtyard, given a last cigarette, and shot by a firing squad.

Although this was the first known execution in Spain for political crimes since 1950,[1] it excited violent protests abroad. In London, Rome, Copenhagen, Stockholm, Moscow, and other cities, crowds denounced the Franco government. Police had to break up a violent demonstration outside the Spanish embassy in Paris, and in Brussels a mob assaulted and sacked the embassy.

One year later, on April 1, 1964, Franco officially proclaimed the beginning of festivities to celebrate "Twenty-Five Years of Peace." The date was the anniversary of the final surrender of the Republican army in Madrid in 1939. In the cities and smallest towns, large signs on public buildings proclaimed "25 años de PAZ" in modernistic letters. The press extolled the achievements of the quarter century under Franco, the first time since Roman days that Spain had been so long without war. During the next months different cities commemorated the occasion with folk dances, theater performances, and light opera (the nineteenth century *zarzuelas*). On Sunday, June 21, the Spanish soccer team met Russia's in the Madrid stadium to decide the European cup. When Franco arrived to preside over the encounter, a hundred and twenty thousand spectators gave him a prolonged standing ovation. All over Spain, wherever they could get to a television set, Spaniards tensely watched the game, and close plays called forth simultaneous shrieks from one end of the country to the other. Late in the game the Spaniards scored a goal to break a tie and win 2 to 1.

Much of what Spain was in the mid-1960's is revealed in the execution of Grimau and the celebration of 1964. A quarter of a century after the Civil War, mature people throughout Europe and America could not speak of Spain without reviving emotions from the thirties. At the same time, twenty-five years had so transformed Spain that in a very real sense it no longer was the country where the forces of communism, fascism, and democracy had staged a dress rehearsal for the Second World War. A new generation, more devoted to current sports than past politics, was rapidly replacing those who remembered the conflict (by 1964, 43 percent of the population had been born since the war). Spain's industry had grown, its cities expanded, its countryside been revolutionized in the most rapid transformation the country has ever known. Memories of the civil conflict were now hardly relevant, and yet they hung on, influencing political decisions at home and abroad.

Since classic times Spain has caught the imagination of other peoples. Stretching out toward the Atlantic from southwest Europe, reaching a fingertip toward a fingertip of Africa, it is a land unto itself. A

[1] *Time Magazine*, June 22, 1962, p. 28.

long coastline on the Mediterranean and another on the Atlantic have made it a fishing, seafaring, imperial country, yet next to Switzerland it has the highest average altitude in Europe, an arid land of sheep and goats, wheat, rye, and barley, vineyards and olive groves. In the north Galicia, Asturias, and the Basque Provinces hide from the rest of Spain behind the Cantabrian Mountains, turning their green hills toward the ocean winds. To the east a line of sierras cuts off the Mediterranean lowlands, Catalonia, Valencia, Murcia, and Malaga, from the high plateaus that form the heart of Spain. Jutting out from this eastern dorsal column, other ranges run like ribs to the west, slicing Spain further into Old Castile, Navarre, and Aragon in the north, New Castile and Extremadura in the center, and the low-lying valley of Andalusia in the south. Mountains impede communication and encourage regional characteristics. Only to the west does the peninsula open gently on the sea, but centuries ago the inhabitants of this fertile, moist zone broke off and formed Portugal. Beyond the seas, since the Middle Ages the Balearic Islands of the Mediterranean and the Canary Islands off the coast of Africa have also belonged to Spain.

Mountains and the sea have isolated Spain from the rest of Europe. Leaving the green plains and humid hills of France, the traveler who crosses the Pyrenees seems carried by magic to a faraway land of dazzling sun, clear dry air, and turquoise seas; of snow-crowned granite peaks, and gray rocky hills where sheep graze on fragrant herbs, partridges steal garbanzo beans, and bees gather exquisite honey; of silvery-green oak and olive trees outlined against the ochres and crimsons of the earth. Today the traveler can still see why Louis XIV is supposed to have said that Africa began at the Pyrenees, and why Romantic authors set their tales in Spain. Even man seems different, torn between the past and the present. Primitive towns all but disappear into the hillsides whence came the stones to build their houses. Mules still pull Roman plows and peasants harvest grain with sickles, while more prosperous farmers drive tractors and run gasoline threshers. At intervals new geometric apartments rise abruptly out of the fields like fortified rings built to protect medieval cities from some unknown danger the traveler may bring. Ragpickers with donkey carts collect the garbage from metropolises of a million people, and country priests in long black cassocks ride motor scooters to their scattered parishes. The clash of ages and cultures is that of present-day Spain itself.

2

Ruling over Spain since the Civil War has been one of the most remarkable political figures of the twentieth century. When the junta of officers who had risen against the government of the Spanish Republic named General Francisco Franco Bahamonde Jefe del Estado (Head of State) on October 1, 1936, few outsiders had heard the name, and even in Spain other generals were more prominent. His supporters assumed the title would be temporary, and his enemies saw in him only a cat's-paw for Hitler and Mussolini, who were aiding the Nationalists, as the insurgent side was called. Three decades later Hitler and Mussolini were only figures in history, but Franco was still Head of State and even his bitterest foes had come to recognize his diplomatic acumen and his success in controlling his turbulent country.

Self-discipline, an iron will, tremendous energy, and a keen ability to judge and manipulate persons with whom he dealt enabled him to reach his position. He was born in 1892 in the port of El Ferrol in northwestern Spain. Family tradition would have made him an officer in the navy, but he was not accepted as a naval cadet. The army infantry academy at Toledo admitted him instead. Here he suffered the quips of his classmates because of his short stature—he is five feet three—and his stiff asceticism, more typical of a peasant or a monk than a soldier. He was commissioned in 1910, and two years later he volunteered for duty in Africa. Service in Spanish Morocco provided his first chance for recognition. Spain was conducting an intermittent and unpopular war with the Moorish tribes. Franco asked to join the newly formed Foreign Legion, which included some of the toughest mercenary soldiers in the world. He rose to become its commander in 1923. A story is told that one day an obstreperous legionnaire threw the contents of his mess kit in Franco's face as he was inspecting the troops. Franco betrayed no emotion and calmly finished the review. After dismissing the soldiers, he wiped his face and ordered the soldier to the firing squad. Years later he would show the same cold ruthlessness toward those he considered insubordinate on a national scale.

In 1926 France and Spain cooperated in an amphibious assault on the coast of Morocco that finally crushed the Moorish guerrillas. The plans were the work of Franco. In recognition, he was promoted to general at age thirty-four, the youngest general in Europe. The following decade saw him gradually achieve the position from which he could become master of Spain. In 1927, the king named him head of a new military academy at Zaragoza. From this post he witnessed the municipal elections in 1931 which led to the flight of the king and the proclamation of the Second Spanish Republic. The Republic closed the academy and assigned Franco to a military command in the provinces. After a conservative electoral victory in 1933, his fortune revived. The new minister of war admired his abilities, and when revolutionary miners captured Asturias in October 1934, Franco took charge of the counterattack, bringing troops from Africa that crushed the uprising. Eighteen months later senior generals considered his support vital to the revolt they were planning against the Republic, for he could lead the forces in Morocco.

The ensuing months revealed his units to be the only disciplined and successful force on the Nationalist side. Despite his youth and inferior rank, the other leaders agreed in proclaiming him Generalísimo and Head of State. Soon he added the title Caudillo or "Leader," a title once worn by medieval warriors, and, in a characteristic style which reveals an almost mystical communion with Spain's rulers of old, the qualifying phrase "by the grace of God." In 1947 a plebiscite re-established the monarchy, and at the same time confirmed Franco as Caudillo and Head of State and gave him the authority to select the future king, or a regent in his place. For over twenty years he named no king, and in lieu of a monarch Franco dominated Spain in regal solitude and majesty, a curious cross between a successful medieval pretender and a modern dictator, king in all but name and more than king in power.

He chose to reside in a former palace, El Pardo, on the small Manzanares River a few miles above where it flows into Madrid. To receive foreign diplomats he journeyed to the vast royal palace in the capital, and the ceremony invariably involved pomp and uniforms that recalled the nineteenth century. Like Louis XIV retiring to Versailles, Franco avoided the turbulent city that long opposed his rule, but in the austerity, piety, and sobriety of his life he has imitated a different Bourbon king, the eighteenth-century enlightened ruler of Spain, Charles III. He shared that king's love of hunting, though Franco had to settle for partridge rather than royal deer.

He has had few intimates, and most of these are close relatives; his wife, his daughter, an only child, her husband and children—he is a devoted grandfather. Only one or two persons not of the family could be called close friends. Except on rare occasions he has remained aloof from his ministers, his subordinates, and all others. He does not smoke or drink, and until his health began to fail in the late sixties he could spend interminable hours at meetings of the ministry, outlasting younger ministers. He has invariably kept his thoughts to himself until he is ready to announce his policy. The Sun King of Versailles never more effectively embodied his office in his personal bearing.

3

Franco's chief instrument for ruling Spain has been the ministry or "Government." From the outset he assumed the position of President of the Government, that is, prime minister. In most European countries one person—king or president—represents the state in diplomatic and official functions and another, usually the prime minister, heads the working government. Franco took advantage of the title Head of State to fill both functions, thus allowing no one to rival his authority in any sphere.

The ministry has consisted of the heads of the different branches of government and the armed forces, each individually selected by the Head of State to advise him and carry out his decisions. Its numbers have varied; after 1962 it had nineteen members. Such political history as Spain had after the Civil War consisted in the changes that Franco made in the ministry. At first it included leading representatives of the three main groups on whose support he rested his regime—army, Catholic Church, and Falange (since 1937 the only legal political party)—which Franco successfully played off against each other so none could challenge his position. After 1957 his tendency was to name youthful ministers chosen for their abilities, not their association with any group. Among these technocrats, as they were called, several leading figures belonged to the Catholic lay organization Opus Dei. Many observers saw in the appointment of Opus Dei ministers a seizure of power by this body, but Franco's decision to use them appears to have been aimed primarily at eliminating old rivalries and instituting much-needed changes in policy.

In 1962 Franco created the office of Vice-President of the Government, to become President of the Government (prime minister) automatically if Franco were to die. The man he chose was General Agustín Muñoz Grandes, who ranked directly below him in the army. In 1967 he replaced Muñoz Grandes by Admiral Luis Carrero Blanco. A younger man of great energy, Carrero Blanco had long been one of Franco's closest collaborators, having been in the ministry since 1951 as subsecretary to the President. Long overshadowed by ministers with specific portfolios, he came more and more to public attention in the sixties. His appointment as Vice-President meant that for the time being, at least, he was the man Franco wanted to take over direction of the government if he were to be incapacitated.

Other government institutions existed more for show than for work. The vacant throne long had various claimants. Most conspicuous were Don Juan, the son of the last king, who lived in Portugal, and his son Juan Carlos, apparently Franco's favorite. Franco invited Juan Carlos to be educated in Spain, and in the sixties the young prince moved into a palace near El Pardo with his Greek wife and their children. A third claimant was Hugo Carlos de Borbon Parma, heir to the Carlist pretenders of the nineteenth century who denied the legitimacy of all reigning Spanish monarchs after the death of Ferdinand VII in 1833. Hugo was born in France and married a Dutch princess, but he had a strong following among the Carlists of northern Spain. Franco, in typical fashion, used his authority to name the next king to keep all parties and their followers courting his favor.

Foreseeing the possibility that Franco would die without naming a king, the plebiscite of 1947 which proclaimed the monarchy also established a three-man Council of Regency to rule temporarily in the event of Franco's death. The Council of Regency was to call at once a meeting of a thirteen-member Council of the Realm appointed by Franco from among the leaders of the most influential bodies in Spain. Meeting with the ministry, the Council of the Realm would select either a king or a regent. Until such an eventuality, however, neither the Council of Regency nor the Council of the Realm had any meaningful function, and they existed more on paper than in fact.

Final approval of the next king lay with the Cortes, which were the Spanish parliament. (The name is traditional, going back to the estates of the medieval kingdoms of Spain.) The Cortes were the major political institution in the constitutional monarchy before 1923 and in the Republic, with the powers of other Western parliaments. Franco's victory eliminated parliamentary government, and in 1942 he revived the Cortes in much different form. Part of their five-hundred-odd deputies represented the municipal councils, part the official unions of employers and employees called syndicates, part were ex-officio deputies from the universities and other educational and cultural bodies, and fifty deputies as well as the president of the Cortes were named personally by the Head of State. No opponent of the regime could filter through the system, and for years the Cortes were but a rubber stamp for legislation drawn up by the ministry.

While officially the syndicates sent representatives to the Cortes, these deputies in fact represented the official political party, the Falange (Phalanx), which controlled the syndicates. Founded during the Republic in imitation of foreign fascist parties, the Falange became the official party of the Nationalists during the war. Franco named himself its head and outlawed all other parties. Long considered a major pillar of the regime, the Falange declined drastically in power and prestige after 1955. Even its name fell into eclipse; official statements referred to it as the *Movimiento* (Movement), a term that had been applied vaguely to the entire Nationalist cause during the war and now suggested that the Falange was not a political party at all but a union of all Spaniards. The leaders of the Falange worked steadily after 1960 to get Franco to "institutionalize" it, that is, to give it constitutional recognition by making its governing body, the National Council of the Movimiento, an integral part of the Cortes. More radical Falangists, worried by its decline, sought to turn it into a genuine labor party. They wished it to oppose the threat of capitalism, which they found in the alleged control by Opus Dei of the ministry and key sectors of the economy.

After years of anticipation, Franco provided an Organic Law of the State that revised the structure of the Cortes. After submitting it to a plebiscite he issued it on January 10, 1967. This was the last of a series of fundamental laws establishing the constitutional structure of the regime, the earliest of which had been promulgated during the Civil War. The new law created 108 elected "family representatives" to sit in the 563-member Cortes. Chosen by male heads of families and married women, they were to be the first directly elected deputies in Spain since 1936. The law also granted the wish of the Falangists by raising the National Council of the Movimiento to the position of an upper house of parliament, with the power to rule on the constitutionality of laws. It was to be composed of 113 members, forty of them appointed by the Head of State and the others chosen in part by the Cortes and in part by the syndicates. The law also empowered the Cortes to elect a majority of the Council of the Realm, which in turn was now to propose three candidates for President of the Government to the Head of State for his final selection.

These changes turned out to be more liberal on paper than in fact. Franco did not name a President of the Government and continued to fill the position himself. In June 1967 the Cortes stipulated that all candidates for deputy must swear allegiance to the principles of the Movimiento and made difficult the nomination of independent candidates. Nevertheless, in the first election in October 1967 many independent candidates defeated those supported by the Movimiento. For several years, some deputies had been questioning official policies in the sessions of the Cortes, and younger ones more openly in committees. When the new Cortes met early in 1968, a large number of the family representatives began to attack directly the economic policies of the government. While still under Franco's control, the Cortes had become an institution that could easily be transformed into a true parliament if the regime should change.

Beneath the central organs of government, laws are enforced and policy carried out by appointed officials who receive authority from above, from the ministers and ultimately from the Head of State. Each of the fifty provinces has a civil governor responsible to the minister of *gobernación* (interior). The minister of *gobernación* also appoints the *alcaldes* (mayors) of the municipalities of more than 10,000 population, and the civil governors name those of towns below this size. All but the smallest towns have *ayuntamientos* (municipal councils) chosen in part by the heads of families, in part by the syndicates, and in part by the civil governors, but real authority—control over the police—lies with the *alcalde* and civil governor. As a representative of the state, the *alcalde* is vested with a status of his own. Once in a small Castilian town I observed that the *alcalde* had his head in a bandage. An outsider who wore a tie and felt hat, out of keeping with the peasant clothes of the townsmen, he was an unpopular ruler and had been beaten by some local citizens in a fit of anger. These were now in prison awaiting arraignment for attacking "an authority" (*una autoridad*). If the *alcalde* got well in two weeks their crime would be minor (*leve*); if not, it would be serious (*grave*). I did not learn the outcome.

To assist the civil governors and *alcaldes* in keeping order, the state has various police forces. In the cities are the Armed Police, known familiarly as the *Grises* (Grays) because of their dull gray uniforms, in the countryside the Civil Guard, famous for their green uniforms and shiny black broadbrimmed hats with the brim turned up in the back—the better to be stood against a wall and shot, their enemies say. All sizable towns of rural Spain have barracks of the Civil Guard, typically a heavy stone building with strong sentry boxes at the corners near the end of the main street. Towns too small for barracks can expect regular visits by two guards on patrol, the famous *parejas* (couples) often seen walking beside country roads. Once the civil guards were tough veterans of war, but in the sixties young recruits who had shed no more blood than that of the family pig became numerous. The guards have their own hierarchy of officers, and the local lieutenant of the Civil Guard shares with the *alcalde* the distinction of being *una autoridad*.

In a crisis the minister of *gobernación* or a civil governor can appeal to the local military commander. Spain has eleven such officers, known as Captains General, a term that goes back to colonial days. After the war military forces were stationed not only where they might repulse a possible invasion but where they could swoop down rapidly on a city in revolt. Army barracks were a conspicuous feature of the highways leading out of Madrid. The regime also relied on the army in a more subtle way. Acts of sabotage and such political offenses as subversion and circulating illegal political tracts were placed under military jurisdiction, where the rights of the accused were limited to a weak plea by a court-appointed attorney. The court martial of Grimau was but the most spectacular of such cases. Until 1963 a law made the spreading of "false or tendentious news" an act of military rebellion. Even those guilty of minor offenses, such as students caught throwing stink bombs in university buildings, were tried by military courts. Partly bowing to the world outcry over Grimau, in November 1963 the regime established a civilian Tribunal of Public Order to try such nonviolent political offenses as spreading false rumors and subversive propaganda. Here defendants could call witnesses, but the new court did not become known for its leniency. Acts of force against the state remained under military jurisdiction.

For the army to be the most trustworthy pillar of the regime was a new phenomenon. In the nineteenth century generals frequently rose against the government, they failed to defend the king in 1931, and they took the lead in overthrowing the Second Republic. However, the generals have been devoted to Franco, whom they admire for his success in the Civil War. Nevertheless, they control the most powerful force in the country. They are in the best position to take over Spain in a crisis—if civil turmoil were to place in doubt the form of government after the death of Franco, for instance. Significantly, the two men named vice-president since the position was created have been high officers in the army and navy.

For over a century the army has played an important role in forming Spanish society. In the sixties only a minority of its 200,000 men were career soldiers. Every year some 100,000 recruits were drafted for eighteen months. They came largely from the countryside, where the annual departure of the *quinta*, as the group of conscripts is traditionally called, was the occasion for local festivities. Sent to different regions of Spain, mixed together with men from other provinces, taught some reading and writing as well as military skills, the conscripts returned broadened and molded by the experience. They departed local boys and came back Spaniards, ready for marriage and adult life. At a higher social level, male university students had to go into the university militia. They received training for two summers and six months and came out either sergeants or *alferezes*, the lowest rank of officer. In the process their political and religious beliefs were closely supervised.

4

Franco has also delegated the formation of Spaniards to the church. The present union of church and state was worked out during and after the Civil War and embodied in a concordat in 1953. The church received surveillance over all education in Spain, public and private. After the war Catholic doctrine became a required subject in all schools from primary grades through the university, and the church received the authority to censor textbooks. Most children went to state elementary schools, but schools run by religious orders provided five-sixths of secondary education. Once in an elementary school in a *cabeza de partido* (county seat) of Castile I witnessed the celebration of the Festival of the Book, April 23, anniversary of the death of Cervantes. The pupils were standing lined up in a long hall, boys at one end and girls at the other (the law require the sexes to be separate in elementary and secondary schools), while the principal delivered an interminable speech to them and to a small number of local dignitaries. He informed the children that the occasion should be kept as a saint's day. He encouraged them to read good books but to shun bad ones. Lest they inadvertently read a bad one, he told them always to ask their parents or a teacher or their priest before beginning a book. The best book to read, he said, was *Don Quixote*, except, of course, for the catechism. (He obviously meant the children's edition of Cervantes' classic, expurgated of "dangerous passages.")

In ways like this the state and the church have reinforced each other. Benjamin Welles, long the *New York Times* correspondent in Madrid, obtained figures that in the early sixties about half the men in rural Spain went to church regularly, but only 5 to 10 percent of the workers in the cities.[2] In small towns the priest, who frequently had tended his flock for years, had strong moral authority. But everywhere Spaniards, with rare exceptions, must be baptized, married, and buried by the church. Baptismal certificates are needed to go to school. In return for the authority accorded the church, Franco obtained by the concordat the right to nominate candidates for bishoprics, submitting three names from which the Pope would select one. Spanish rulers traditionally had such a right, but no other European power now enjoys it. Like Napoleon, Franco has tied the church to the state as a spiritual police force.

The alliance of the state, the church, and the army is marked time and time again in public ceremonies. In many cities the processions of Holy Week are the greatest festival of the year. The most famous at Valladolid, Seville, and Granada attract thousands of tourists. Members of the lay confraternities march silently in long robes, hooded faces, and peaked hats reminiscent of the victims of the Inquisition. In their midst rise carved images representing the Passion of Christ and the sorrows of Mary, many of them marvels of baroque sculpture, borne aloft on platforms by penitants who stagger forward in slow rhythmical motions not unlike the rowing of chained galley slaves. Instead of the mallet of the galley captain, however, trumpets and muffled drums of military bands beat out a deathly march. The church finds nothing incongruous in the scene. The presence of the army signifies not Caesar's troops who arrested Jesus but the secular power that protects the Christian faith.

Nevertheless, the church is not a branch of the government, and within it a strong element of opposition to the regime has emerged. In the 1950's some prelates became critical of official policies. Encouraged by the example of Pope John XXIII, they urged the church to demand greater social justice. Younger priests became even more outspoken. Some of them helped organize poor parishioners to improve their condition even when such activities brought them into conflict with the civil governors. Such was the case of a young Catalan priest I met in a remote parish in central Spain. He had been trained for social work in the Leo XIII Institute in Rome and on his return had organized the inhabitants of a slum in a provincial capital to bring in their first running water, in conflict with official plans for the growth

[2] Benjamin Welles, *Spain, the Gentle Anarchy* (New York: Frederick A. Praeger, Inc., 1965), p. 143.

of the city. Under his leadership they contributed money and labor to install the water main. When the *alcalde* and the civil governor objected, his bishop transferred him to the mountain parish where I met him. The incident exemplified the tensions within the church, where young priests challenged older, state-selected bishops.

It was not accidental that many of the restless priests were Basques and Catalans. Catalonia in northeastern Spain and the Basque Provinces at the other end of the Pyrenees have languages and cultures of their own and a long tradition of opposition to rule from Madrid. In the Civil War both peoples fought against Franco, and since then they have sullenly resented his iron rule, exploding sporadically into acts of violence. Because of the church's independence from direct civilian authority, the clergy could demonstrate their opposition with relative impunity. Priests conducted services in the local languages, which had been banned for official usage, and in this simple way helped keep alive a sense of local patriotism. Resistance movements in both regions had the support of the lower clergy. In 1960 about 350 Basque priests signed a letter to their bishop protesting police brutality and the violation of human rights. In 1965 the government brought several Basque and Catalan priests to trial in Madrid. Over two hundred priests came from their regions to attend the trials and demonstrate their support. More than one hundred priests and monks marched in a group to police headquarters in Barcelona on May 10, 1966 to protest the mistreatment of an arrested university student. They refused to disperse and were beaten and kicked by the police. Priests were active in the underground organization Euzkadi ta Akatasuna (the Basque Nation and Liberty), which was responsible for acts of terrorism in 1968.

The church displayed its disenchantment with the regime in an official capacity by organizing Catholic workers' brotherhoods known as the Hermandades Obreras de Acción Católica (HOAC). Cardinal Enrique Plá, archbishop of Toledo and primate of Spain, founded them in 1947, as an organ of the Spanish branch of the society of laymen called Catholic Action. The activities of the HOAC were justified as a form of religious proselytizing.

In the 1950's the HOAC made little headway. Workers suspected their motives and for opposite reasons so did the more conservative bishops. Their big opportunity came in April 1962 with a series of strikes. The coal miners of Asturias in the north had a long history of militancy. Recently they had protested the failure of their wages to rise along with those of workers in the nearby government-controlled steel plant at Avilés. They petitioned through the official syndicates, but as Spaniards say, "*las cosas de palacio van despacio*," affairs of state move slowly. On April 6, workers in one mine struck for several hours. Since the war, strikes have been illegal, and seven leaders were arrested. The next day between fifty and sixty thousand Asturian coal miners walked out in protest. Although official censorship kept news of the strike out of the press and off the air, knowledge of it flew through Spain, helped by the broadcasts of Radio Free Spain (Radio España Independiente) from Communist Czechoslovakia. Workers in shipyards and metal trades in the Basque port of Bilbao, miners in the Sierra Morena and Andalusia in southern Spain, industrial workers in Barcelona and elsewhere, perhaps a hundred thousand in all, staged walkouts in sympathy. Although the government decreed martial law in Asturias and sent in four thousand soldiers, it hesitated to use force against so massive and peaceful a demonstration. Partly it feared foreign reaction. The Asturian strike lasted two months. In the end the government conceded most of the workers' demands for wage increases. Although police arrested two hundred and fifty miners after the strike, Franco could not hide the fact that for the first time under his rule workers had conducted a successful strike. Spanish labor was recovering its prewar position as a powerful and independent force.

Official publications blamed foreign agents led by Communists for instigating the strike. In truth, once the strike had begun labor unions and socialist parties in Western Europe and the United States sent funds to support the strikers, and Communists came from abroad along with others to encourage and direct them. But the strongest Spanish force behind the strike, besides the anger and determination of the miners themselves, was the young priests who headed local branches of the HOAC. During the strike police arrested the president of the HOAC and the president and vice-president of the affiliated youth movement, the Juventud Obrera Católica (JOC). The HOAC denied taking part in the strikes, and Cardinal Plá personally protested the arrests to Franco. Nevertheless, the HOAC gained wide favor among workers for the actions of their local leaders. This event belied the church's reputation as a monolythic bastion of the Franco regime.

5

The demonstration of proletarian power in 1962 was a direct threat to the syndicates, one of the major instruments of the regime. Originally established during the Civil War on the model of the state corporations of Fascist Italy, the twenty-four syndicates are vertical labor-management unions. Some of them group together workers and employers in an industry, others cover the professions, agricultural workers, and even university students. In 1962 their membership both male and female was about 3 million industrial workers, 3 million employers, and 5.5 million in other categories including agriculture. (How inclusive their membership was can be judged from the fact that the total active labor population in 1960 was calculated at 9.5 million men and 2.1 million women.) The syndicates collected and disbursed retirement, sickness, and other social insurance funds, and acted as employment agencies. In theory they provided a channel for collective bargaining of labor disputes, but in effect they were the institution through which the government enforced its control of wages and working conditions. In 1957 Franco named a new minister responsible for the syndicates, José Solís Ruiz. The latter instituted a policy of enlarging workers' control over the syndicates. He multiplied the number of *enlaces*, representatives to the syndicates elected by the workers, and encouraged independent candidates to run for the office. As a result in 1963 various leaders of the 1962 strikes were elected, whereupon the government, violating Solís' objectives, tried them for their previous activities. Since higher syndical officials were elected indirectly and since strikes were illegal, the syndicates did not become a viable representative of the interests of labor. During the 1963 elections the HOAC and the JOC demanded free unions and the right to strike as prerequisites for fulfilling the social doctrines of the church. Strikes and slowdowns continued to be the most effective means of protest. Official figures recognized 777 "labor conflicts" in 1963 and 484 in 1964, most of them in Asturias, the Basque Provinces, Catalonia, and Madrid—the industrialized areas of Spain.

A new form of labor opposition developed in the middle sixties. Within the structure of the syndicates, the *enlaces* could communicate officially only with the local headquarters of the syndicates. There was no provision for *enlaces* of different companies in the same industry to discuss grievances together or to formulate joint proposals. In various industries independent-minded *enlaces* began to meet together to do just this, and from here it was an easy step to planning active labor opposition to achieve their objectives. About 1966 these informal groups of workers' representatives became known as "workers' commissions."

In the elections for *enlaces* held at the end of 1966 the workers returned the activists in force. Solís Ruiz reacted energetically. The government declared the workers' commissions illegal and sought to arrest their leaders, but it was unable to destroy them. The commissions had become so well organized that they called work stoppages, walkouts, and demonstrations at a moment's notice, paralyzing key industries. In April 1967 at their instigation five thousand workers fought police in open battle in Bilbao, and in October in Madrid and Barcelona police had to use force to break up demonstrations which chanted, "Liberty!" "Unity!" and "Workers' Commissions, yes; Franco, no!" [3] In July 1967 the workers' commissions clandestinely held their first

[3] *The New York Times*, Oct. 29, 1967, p. 24.

national congress in Madrid. Some seventy deputies from forty-six provinces attended representing local commissions.[4] Much of the credit for the ability of the commissions to defy the government and avoid the police belonged to radical priests, who permitted the associations to hold secret meetings in church buildings.

Violent active opposition to the regime was not a monopoly of the proletariat. Beginning in 1956, many students at the University of Madrid, followed less daringly by those of Barcelona and the smaller provincial universities, protested vociferously the regulations that governed their academic lives. A small number of courageous professors supported them. The major objection of the reform-minded students was to their enforced membership in the student syndicate, the Sindicato Español Universitario (SEU), which was controlled by the Falange. The students wished to elect syndicate representatives of their own choice who would have authority over the SEU, with the ultimate objective of obtaining freedom from censorship and from state control of the courses taught at the universities.

The opposition of the students to the structure of their official syndicate made them sympathetic to the demands of the workers for their own syndicates, although university students by and large came from professional and employers' families. Many students also openly favored some kind of socialist state, accepting the view of the left-wing political opposition that the regime furthered capitalist exploitation of the masses. On May 5, 1962 about one thousand students in Madrid demonstrated in favor of the Asturian strikers until dispersed by the police. Trouble continued intermittently thereafter. In the winter of 1964–65, Madrid students organized a series of lectures on the cultural situation in Spain. When the rector prohibited one of the lectures, on February 20, 1965, students responded with a petition for academic freedom. A silent march by some 5000 students (of 32,000 enrolled in the university) was dispersed by police and some students were seriously injured. The protests continued, backed by a few professors. In Barcelona 17,000 students boycotted classes and strikes spread to the smaller universities. Eventually the government conceded the demand to recognize freely elected syndicate delegates, but it refused absolutely to allow freedom of expression, specifically maintaining censorship of student newspapers. The professors received much more severe treatment. Despite the time-honored sanctity of the university chair in Spain, three were expelled and two suspended. Among those expelled were José Aranguren, professor of philosophy in Madrid, a liberal Catholic, and Enrique Tierno Galván, professor of political science at Salamanca and a leading spokesman for socialism in Spain, both of them men of the highest reputation.

[4] *Ibid.*, July 17, 1967, p. 8.

Student resistance continued unabated. Agitation spread in the following winter to Barcelona, where students demonstrated against the SEU, were beaten by police, and eventually went out on strike. The government responded by closing the university on April 27, 1966. In May, as noted above, over one hundred priests and monks marched to protest police brutality and in turn were clubbed. Madrid students conducted a sympathy strike and again demanded the right to associate freely outside the SEU. The reaction of the government was once more a compromise between repression and concessions, the same tactic employed with the workers, but it was unable to establish peace. Student strikes were worse than ever in the fall of 1967.

The opposition of students, priests, and workers to the regime was a spontaneous reaction to the situation under Franco. As one could expect, those who had fought Franco during the Civil War tried to attract these forces of active resistance. The three largest parties on the Republican side in the war were the Socialists, the anarchists, and the Communists. Almost all their leaders left the country after their defeat and thereafter sought to maintain a following in Spain from abroad. Within Spain the parties had to operate clandestinely, so that none had a large organization, but they hoped to win sympathy and support for their ideologies among the large numbers of people who had become disenchanted with the regime and thus prepare a following for the day when they would come out in the open, presumably after the death or retirement of Franco.

Of the three groups, the anarchists had the least success. Before 1936 the center of their strength had been the industrial workers of Catalonia, and they sought to preserve this base, encouraging strikes and other forms of protest. They were not part of a well-organized international movement which could provide financial help, and as a result, even in Catalonia, they lost ground among the proletariat to the Communists and Socialists. Elsewhere the anarchists were blamed for acts of terrorism, such as placing small bombs in Madrid streets and public buildings in 1963 and succeeding years in an attempt to scare away tourists, but such activity was ineffectual and was evidently the work of a dissident minority organized from France.

After the Civil War the Communists broke with most other Republicans in exile and operated on their own out of Paris. They were the most militant party and eventually penetrated the syndicates, the Falange, and the student movement. They supported strikes along with the other parties, but they did not seem bent on violent upheaval. (The prosecution could produce no evidence that Grimau had plotted rebellion.) Since Spaniards remembered Russia as the sole power to aid the Republic in the Civil War and since they saw the United States form a military alliance with Franco, the cold war enhanced the popularity of the Communist party. Radio Free Spain in Prague effectively exploited the connection between the international situation and Spanish developments. The split between Russia and Red China hurt the Spanish Communists after 1960, however, for their followers by inclination admired China's uncompromising stand against the United States (an understandable sympathy for Fidel Castro's Cuba also contributed to their sinophile leanings), while the source of their foreign support was the European Communist parties, which remained loyal to Russia.

Most successful of the three parties in winning sympathy in Spain were the Socialists. Democratic and reformist in spirit since the end of the Civil War, they alone gained a significant following in professional circles. Lawyers and university professors became prominent among their leaders. Abroad they were long headed by Indalecio Prieto, remembered as a forceful middle-of-the-road minister of the Republic. But Prieto died in Mexico in 1962, and his successor, Rodolfo Llopis, although also a minister of the Republic, lacked Prieto's reputation. Within Spain the police repeatedly penetrated the Socialist organization, arrested its leaders, and sent them to long terms in prison. That the Socialists continued to make headway testified to a deep desire among many Spaniards to transform Spain peacefully along Western European lines.

These parties presented no real threat to the regime, for there was no danger of the government falling into their hands. They depended for financial help on foreigners and Spanish refugees, many of whom were motivated by romantic memories of the Civil War. They could also thank the regime. The press continually reminded Spaniards that Franco saved Spain from the Republic, which, it said, had fallen into the hands of international Marxist Communism and godless freemasonry. By parading the specter of the Republic, Franco encouraged his enemies to turn to its defenders. On the whole, however, Spaniards did not take enthusiastically to direction from abroad, feeling that their struggles were no longer those of the Civil War and that men who lived and suffered in Spain were more qualified leaders.

This spirit helps account for the success of the Christian Democrats, who could trace their ancestry not to the Republican cause but to the moderate Catholic and monarchist parties who at the time supported the Nationalists. Under the Republic a young lawyer named José María Gil Robles brought these parties together into an alliance called the CEDA (Confederación Española de Derechas Autónomas). The CEDA was banned in 1937 along with all other parties except the Falange. Gil Robles was in France at the outbreak of the war, and he did not return to Spain permanently until 1954. Two years later he publicly proclaimed his opposition to the regime by defending four young men accused of inciting university students to rebel. Thereafter Gil became recognized as the leader of the Catholic opposition, which took the name of Christian Democracy, with a vague program in favor of constitutional monarchy, religious freedom, and unity with Europe. For some Catholics he was too moderate, and a radical left wing of the Christian Democrats grew up under Manuel Giménez Fernández, a professor of canon law in the University of Seville.

By 1960 the active opposition within Spain was a vital force arising out of the contemporary situation, not a morbid attempt to fight the Civil War over again. Many leading figures who were once associated with Franco broke with him, took public stands against the government, and as a result suffered loss of position, prison, or exile. Probably most of these considered themselves Christian Democrats or Socialists. In either case they were guided by a desire to merge Spain with Western Europe. Among the Christian Democrats one could include Professor Aranguren of Madrid, who lost his chair in 1965, and Pedro Laín Entralgo, rector of the University of Madrid in the 1950's. In the Socialist camp were Dionisio Ridruejo, once the leading theorist of the Falange and now an outspoken enemy of Franco and protagonist of a genuinely democratic system, and Antonio Tovar, rector of the University of Salamanco before 1965, who left Spain in disgust at the dismissal of Aranguren and his colleagues and went to teach in Germany. All of these men were leading Falangists in earlier days and became disillusioned with what they felt was a betrayal of their ideals. They were the real leaders of the opposition among students and intellectuals, who could identify with their aims and fate.

So far the regime has been able to deny political freedom to the opposition parties. After the reform of the Cortes in 1966, the Christian Democrats, Socialists, and Communists considered presenting candidates for family representatives. The subsequent official prohibition of all candidates who would not swear to the principles of the National Movement caused them to drop their plans, convinced that they could not give their candidates effective support.[5] Nevertheless, like any political authority, the regime must recognize the demands of the forces that provide the sinews of society. This is why it has had to meet the protests of students and workers with concessions as well as force. Since the beginning of the century industrial workers on one hand and engineers, technicians, and professional men on the other—the latter group represented in recent conflicts by the university students—have struggled to wrest control of the country from those classes that have been dominant—landowners, manufacturers, conservative clergy, the military. The recent evolution of Spain, which has more and more

[5] *Ibid.*, Sept. 21, 1967, p. 18.

rapidly followed the economic and social course of the Western world, has been achieved by the owners of special skills and knowledge as much as by those who control capital and more than by military men. This evolution has provided the basis for the successful defiance of the regime by the new groups.

6

In the 1960's Spain experienced the most rapid transformation in its history. From a country that had been primarily rural, backward industrially and in agricultural methods, it was evolving into an industrialized, urbanized, mechanized society. Peasant costumes and local dances died out in the first half of the century; and now the quaint old ways of plowing and threshing with mules and oxen, of charcoal fires and oil lamps, of wagons and pack animals, were retreating into the remote, hilly areas, preparatory to disappearing altogether. The generation that has grown up since the Civil War will be the last to recall much of what has been the famed charm of Spain. Their memories will be of an old way of life vanishing before the spread of modern civilization, as Spaniards everywhere seek to raise their standard of living.

A few figures will suggest the magnitude of the transformation. In 1950 Spain had under 90,000 registered passenger automobiles. In 1957 the figure had doubled, and by 1966 there were 1,050,000. In addition Spain had in 1966 almost 500,000 commercial vehicles (as compared to 60,000 in 1950) and 1,200,000 motorcycles; in other words, one motorized vehicle for each eleven persons. Traffic jams and smog had come to plague the cities. Returning to Madrid from a Sunday in the mountains, a family could spend four hours in bumper-to-bumper traffic along a new four-lane highway to make the fifty-mile drive. In 1953 Spain did not produce automobiles—in 1958 it built 33,000, in 1965, 156,000, plus 93,000 commercial vehicles. The same growth took place in other areas. Thanks to a vast plan for constructing dams for irrigation and hydroelectric power inaugurated early in the century and pushed energetically after the war, the output of electricity doubled every seven years. In 1950 Spain produced 7 billion kilowatt hours, in 1966, 37 billion. There were 650,000 telephones in 1950, 2,800,000 in 1965. In 1958 Spain inaugurated a national television network and by 1962 transmitters covered the entire peninsula. From 50,000 television sets in 1960 the figure rose to 1,750,000 five years later. To understand the significance of these figures the imagination must translate them into more rapid and efficient transportation for farmers and manufacturers, into weekends in the countryside, into the spread of factories and workshops run by electricity, of dwelling places and storefronts with electric lights, telephone conversations for business and pleasure, and into hours spent in front of television sets watching activities hitherto not accessible to the vast majority.[6]

Perhaps the most expressive statistics are from the census. The population of Spain has grown steadily in the twentieth century, and accompanying this growth has been a migration from the countryside to the cities. These developments are not new, and they are a feature of the modern history of all Western countries. By comparison with the rest of Europe, Spain's growth in the twentieth century has been rapid. From 18.8 million in 1900, its population has risen to 30.4 million in 1960, a rise of 62 percent. In the same period France and England grew 21 percent and Italy 49 percent. (The United States grew 135 percent.)

Another striking feature in Spain's growth is the migration to the cities. About 600,000 Spaniards abandoned the countryside between 1960 and 1966. What was once a stream has become a torrent, increasing as time passes. In 1900 only eighteen cities had reached 50,000 population, and they accounted for 15 percent of the total population. In 1965, sixty-eight cities had 50,000 or more people, and they had 41 percent of the total. To visualize the development better, one can look at the growth of these sixty-eight cities relative to the rest of Spain since 1900. In 1900 they had 3.8 million people, 22 percent of the total Spanish population. Between 1900 and 1950 they grew 5.3 million, while Spain as a whole was growing 10.8 million; that is, the cities accounted for almost half of the nation's growth in those fifty years. Between 1950 and 1960 the same sixty-eight cities grew 2.1 million, while Spain grew 2.5 million; 85 percent of the growth of the decade was accounted for by the larger cities. Figures for 1965 based on estimates rather than a census show that the cities grew 1.8 million since 1960, while Spain grew only 1.5 million; that is, they absorbed all the growth of Spain and some 300,000 in addition. Between 1900 and 1950 these sixty-eight cities grew 19 percent per decade while the rest of Spain grew 7 percent per decade. The available figures show that between 1960 and 1965 they grew 35 percent per decade and the rest of the country, including the smaller cities as well as the countryside, was losing population at the rate of 6 percent per decade. According to these recent data, which are indicative of trends even if not fully reliable, all of central and southern Spain lost population between 1960 and 1965 except for those provinces with rapidly growing capitals: Madrid, Valladolid, Seville, Cadiz, and Malaga.

[6] On recent Spanish economic development, in addition to official government publications, the following works provide much valuable information and interpretation: Ramon Tamames, *Estructura económica de España* (3rd ed., Madrid: Sociedad de Estudios y Publicaciones, 1965); *L'Espagne à l'heure du développement, Revue Tiers-Monde,* Tome VIII, No. 32 (Oct.–Dec. 1967).

That urbanization should accelerate so rapidly after 1960 can be explained largely by the expansion of industry. Appreciable growth in industrial output began about 1953, and it became remarkable after 1959. In that year the government instituted what was known as the Stabilization Plan, which freed trade and industry from many state controls and attracted foreign loans and investments. Inflation in the following years encouraged industrial expansion while it set the stage for the labor strife of 1962. The gross national product rose about 5 percent per year.

In 1963 the government announced a four year Development Plan (Plan de Desarrollo) to go into effect the following January. Copied after recent French four-year plans, it aimed to direct the economic development of the country toward Spain's eventual integration with the rest of Europe. The plan called for a 6 percent per year growth in the national product based on a massive investment program of 5.5 billion dollars over four years. Sixty percent was to be provided by private investors, most of it from abroad. To end the concentration of industry in the north and northeast and in Madrid, the plan offered lower taxes and easier credit to industries that would move into seven secondary cities, or "poles of development" as they were called, four in central Spain (Valladolid, Burgos, Zaragoza, and Seville) and three on the Atlantic coast (La Coruña, Vigo, and Huelva.) The government's share of investment was to go into the expansion of programs already under way whose usefulness had been demonstrated by the achievements of the twenty-five years of peace. Mostly these were in the areas of agriculture, utilities, and transportation. They included the redistribution of farmlands by collecting small scattered plots into efficient holdings ("parcelary concentration"), the mechanization of agriculture, and the extension of irrigation. The plan called for 75,000 hectares of new irrigated land per year; since 1950 the extension of irrigation had averaged 40,000 hectares per year (250 hectares equal one square mile). The plan projected 120,000 hectares of reforestation per year; slightly higher than the 114,000 per year achieved since 1953. Construction of more hydroelectric installations and the building of two atomic power plants would increase the output of electricity, while 1.3 million telephones would be added to the 2.3 million in service. The government would build roads, railroads, and facilities for maritime and air transport. Finally the plan called for government subsidies and direction for social and cultural progress. Industrial expansion would produce 340,000 jobs, to be filled by persons leaving the countryside, whose emigration, along with the improvements planned in agriculture, would raise the average rural income. To house the new arrivals in the cities, 180,000 dwelling units were to be built each year, 155,000 of them with government subsidies. Spain had built about 70,000 per year from 1951 to 1960. And to educate Spaniards for better living and better jobs, schools would be expanded and teachers trained to handle more students at all levels, from elementary to university and technical.

The development plan is worth describing in such detail because it summarized the objectives of those in command of Spain in the 1960's and indicated the progress being made. Partly because of a favorable world situation, Spain reached most of the goals more rapidly than anticipated. Industrial output grew 9 percent per year from 1964 to 1966. In 1960 the average annual income per person was under $300; by 1966 it had more than doubled, to about $640.[7] Early in 1967 the government made public a second four-year plan for 1967–71, which was to emphasize the improvement of agriculture, transportation, and education.

Faced with such economic growth, observers spoke of a "Spanish miracle." Much of the explanation for Spain's success lay in the appearance of a new breed of Spaniard. Hitherto its wealthy classes had been timid and skeptical, lacking an orientation toward investment in industry. Those responsible for the recent expansion have been industrial and governmental technocrats who have come of age in the hard years since the Civil War. Some of them obtained posts in the cabinet in 1957 and were able to use the authority of the government to achieve their ends. These included the minister of commerce, Alberto Ullastres, a professor of economics; the minister of finance, Mariano Navarro Rubio, previously a director of the Banco Popular; and the technical secretary general in charge of drawing up the four-year development plans, Laureano López Rodó, a professor of administrative law. All three belonged to the lay Catholic organization Opus Dei. Although the religious objective of Opus Dei is to proselytize for the church, within Spain those of its members who reached positions of authority in government, business, and banking worked to modernize the economy by encouraging private activity. They hoped to bring Spain into the European economic orbit through membership in the Common Market, most of whose members have economically progressive Catholic governments.

Within Spain the technocrats, both inside and outside Opus Dei, have appealed to the interests of those Spaniards who have capital to invest, lands to improve, or industries to modernize and who are willing to use their resources actively. Landowners, merchants, manufacturers, and persons with capital (which includes the religious orders) stand to reap more than their fair share of the benefits of this new progress. En-

[7] Fernández Díaz, "Annexes statistiques," *L'Espagne à l'heure du développement*, p. 964 (see above, note 6). United Nations, Statistical Office, *Yearbook of National Accounts Statistics*, 1967, gives slightly higher figures for per capita income. For goals see Spain, Commissioner for Economic and Social Development, *Economic and Social Development Program for Spain, 1964–1967* (Baltimore: Johns Hopkins Press, 1965).

gineers, technicians, and skilled workers have also been favored groups. Although the expanding economy has also improved the condition of the other professional and laboring classes, they have lagged behind and therefore struggle forcefully for better treatment. Worst off have been the small farmers and agricultural laborers, and their young people have reacted by fleeing the countryside.

The institutional link that unites the advantaged interest groups has been the great private banks of Spain. Their directors cooperate with the government in formulating economic plans and directing investment. They float stock issues and have a controlling influence over many industries. Their power spreads out of the cities through the countryside. Any *cabeza de partido* will boast large modern buildings in its center. Invariably most of them are local branches of the great banks. In 1962 six major Spanish banks joined four Portuguese banks to form a consortium to promote the financial and industrial expansion of both countries, approaching foreign banks for funds for investment. The consortium was apparently the achievement of young Opus Dei bankers. One of the banks was the Banco Popular, known to be controlled by the Opus Dei, of which Navarro Rubio, the minister of finance, had once been a director.

After 1957 the technocrats set out to attract foreign investments and promote policies that would bring foreign exchange in order to purchase needed machinery and other supplies. In this they had the backing of the United States government and international monetary agencies. For two decades Spanish policy had been based on the principle of economic autarky inherited from fascist doctrines of the thirties. A fear of economic subjection to foreign interests existed, expressed in trade restrictions and a rigid limit on the share of stock in Spanish corporations owned by foreigners. In the 1950's Spain had sought and obtained aid for its lagging economy in the form of grants and loans to the Spanish state by the United States government. By 1959 the United States refused further direct aid of this kind, and Spain had to change its policies. This was the background for the Stabilization Plan of that year. In addition to reducing economic restrictions, Spain encouraged foreign investment by permitting foreigners to own up to 50 percent of the total capital of corporations, and facilitating the repatriation of profits. In the next three years 200 million dollars in investments came from abroad. The four year plan hopefully called for further foreign capital, again offering better conditions. Led by the United States firms, foreigners answered the call. By 1967 foreign investments in Spain totalled 1.25 billion dollars. Of this, 500 million dollars came from the United States, which in 1958 had only 68 million dollars in Spain.[8]

[8] *The New York Times*, June 13, 1967, p. 75.

An even greater source of foreign exchange in the 1960's was an extraordinary flow of tourists into Spain. The Civil War, the Second World War, and subsequent international ostracism kept away tourists while other Western European countries began to fatten on their expenditures. In 1950 only 75,000 persons from abroad visited Spain. By 1957 the figure was 3.2 million. After 1960 it rose dizzily: 6.1 million in 1960, 14.1 in 1964, 17.9 in 1967. Some drove across the French border for only a day, but three quarters stayed for longer periods. The largest number were French, followed by other Western Europeans. Tourism became Spain's main export industry. National income from tourists rose from 297 million dollars in 1960 to 1.16 billion in 1965. Private hotels and elegant state-owned *paradores* (inns established in historic buildings) sprang up to meet the need; restaurants, souvenir stores, travel agencies, air and bus lines, all expanded rapidly in one of the most successful economic ventures in Spain's history. At a time when private spending in industrial countries is being directed more and more to leisure activities, Spain has discovered a resource of inestimable value in its rugged landscape and sunny coast, its bullfights and flamenco dancing, and the artistic and architectural legacy of its complex Roman, Moslem, and Christian background.

A third source of foreign capital came from an exodus of skilled and unskilled workers who sought employment in northwestern Europe. Between 1959 and 1963 700,000 Spaniards went abroad, to Germany, France, Switzerland, and in lesser numbers to other countries. They included industrial workers from Madrid, Barcelona, and other cities, whose trades were in demand abroad. Many more were young people leaving the small towns—both men and women—finding work in construction, transportation, and domestic help, where supply was growing short in advanced countries. These emigrants sent home money and visited Spain as tourists, thus helping to build up its foreign exchange. Later many returned, bringing their savings and new skills to the further benefit of Spain's economy.

These sources of foreign exchange were essential to Spanish development, for they counterbalanced what would otherwise have been impossible trade deficits. Since Spain's economic progress began in the early 1950's, imports far outdistanced exports (Spain had 500 million dollars of exports and 900 million of imports in 1958). Each year its holdings in gold and convertible currencies declined until early in 1959 it had a balance of only 65 million dollars, while its foreign obligations stood at 68 million dollars. The stability of the peseta was in serious danger. Tourists and the 1959 Stabilization Plan saved the day. Although the trade deficit continued to rise (it was 1.2 billion dollars in 1963), Spain had piled up 1 billion dollars in reserves by 1962, 1.4 billion by 1964, and the peseta had become one of the soundest currencies in Europe. The technocrats felt confident that Spain's future lay in further economic integration with Europe.

7

The Spanish government was unable, however, to match its economic achievements in the diplomatic field. The memories of the Civil War have had their most permanent effect on Spain's foreign relations. Because Hitler and Mussolini aided the Nationalist side, European and American liberals and leftists reacted with strong emotional support for the Republican cause, and they later looked upon Franco's rule as another fascist dictatorship whose overthrow was a prerequisite for the completion of the democratic victory of 1945. After the Second World War, the Allied governments refused Spain membership in the United Nations and recalled their ambassadors from Madrid, and France closed the Spanish border to trade. During these years Spain's only friend was Portugal, whose dictator, Antonio de Oliveira Salazar, shared Franco's outlook. Cut off from Europe, Franco developed ties with the Arab states, claiming for Spain the role of "bridge" between Africa and Europe. He also looked to Latin America, playing up the concept of *Hispanidad,* the bond that a common language, religion, and culture gave the Spanish-speaking nations.

Early in the 1950's international developments put an end to Spain's isolation. The cold war, followed by the Korean War, made the United States look with new favor on regimes that claimed to be stoutly anti-Communist. Spain fitted the description, and furthermore its geographic location was strategically ideal for air and naval bases needed to control the Mediterranean. American leaders swallowed their liberal feelings and signed a pact with Franco in 1953, which gave them the coveted bases. By then Spain's appeal to Latin America had succeeded in placating all but its most bitter opponents (Mexico has still not recognized the Franco government). Together the United States, the Latin American nations, and the Arab states obtained Spain's entry into the United Nations in 1955.

This was the high point of Spain's diplomatic recovery. European memories proved much more impervious to military expediency than American. The United States and Spain foresaw Spain's rapid entry into the North Atlantic Treaty Organization, the defensive alliance formed by the United States and Western European countries against Russia in 1949. The British Labor Party and continental Socialist parties, however, had a violent ideological revulsion against admitting Spain to an organization whose charter said it was "founded on the principles of democracy, individual liberty, and the rule of law." Belgium, Denmark, and Norway, where socialist and Protestant sentiment was strong, successfully blocked Spain's entry.

After the change in ministry in 1957, Spain's technocrats turned their attention to penetrating various European economic groupings, hoping to use Spain's military ties with the United States and its improving economy as magnets to attract reluctant governments. At first their success seemed assured. Charles de Gaulle became president of France in 1958 and started courting Spain's favor, and West Germany now also backed Spain's entry into NATO. The next year the Organization for European Economic Cooperation, which was founded 1948 by the countries receiving Marshall Plan aid, took part in drawing up Spain's stabilization plan and admitted Spain to full membership. But this was a technical rather than a political body, and Spain's entry wounded no sensibilities.

Despite all efforts, Spain has advanced little beyond this stage. In 1962 it applied for membership in the Common Market, the tariff union of six Western European countries. Great Britain was also seeking entry to it, and the Spanish government felt economic union with its best customers was essential to Spain's future, even if for the moment its industries could badly stand the competition of more advanced countries. But Spain's application fell on deaf ears. Liberal and socialist parties in the Common Market countries blocked Spain's entry as they had to NATO. Rebuffed by the Common Market, Spain managed to expand its trade by negotiations with individual Western European countries, and it went in search of customers in Communist east Europe. But its major diplomatic associates remained Portugal, most Latin American countries, and the United States. To offset its failure in Europe, Spain was able to point to its new bosom friend across the Atlantic. The United States renewed the bases agreement in 1963 for five years with the flattering but not very meaningful proviso that it would consult Spain regularly on military questions.

In many parts of the world—notably central Europe and the Orient—the provisional status quo achieved in the decade after the Second World War has solidified, often along irrational lines. Spain attained its postwar position with the United States treaty of 1953. Despite untold efforts, it has had little diplomatic success since then. The clouds of the Civil War still hang on.

The failure of Franco to break his diplomatic isolation indicates that many Europeans still questioned the permanence of his regime. On the surface their doubts appeared unjustified. Despite worker and student unrest, most Spaniards were apolitical, far more interested in soccer results than in protest movements. The economic transformation was making them more conservative. Many who never owned anything before were now proud of a transistor radio, a television set, or a motor scooter, while better-off people had new four-door cars or apartments with modern kitchens, even summer cottages in the mountains or by the sea. They had steady jobs and they feared that violent change might deprive them of what they had. Spain was, in fact, becoming middle class.

Nevertheless, Spain's future is still wrapped in mystery. Like every country that has been ruled recently by a strong man, it is subject to the question, "After *he* goes, what?" For Spain this anxiety is especially keen because it has a long history of political instability, going back to the beginning of the nineteenth century. Spaniards have appeared by nature rebellious and politically mercurial. Indeed their recent striving for economic betterment has been interpreted as a sublimation of the energy they would normally devote to political agitation, a sublimation forced on them by the ban on politics.[9] Should the ban end, many persons, both friends and enemies of Franco, anticipate that Spaniards will return to their former habits. Clearly, in order to understand Spain today, one must place recent developments in historical perspective.

[9] Welles, p. 312; Stanley G. Payne, *Franco's Spain* (New York: Thomas Y. Crowell Company, 1967), pp. 76–77.

2

Historical Explanations of Contemporary Spain

Anxiety over Spain's political instability began long before the Civil War. Already in the nineteenth century, the nation's political turmoil suggested to thoughtful Spaniards that their country was somehow unsuited to a modern parliamentary system, while its failure to match the industrial revolution of other Western European countries made them question its capacity for economic progress. Why the inability of Spain to adopt modern civilization? Explanations were legion.

The troubles of the nineteenth and early twentieth centuries arose ostensibly from a continuous conflict over the form of the political constitution and the relations between church and state. Spain became divided between liberal anticlericals and conservative Catholics. For Spaniards of either camp, the simplest explanation for the dissension was to blame it on their opponents. By the end of the nineteenth century many conservative patriots and devout Catholics found the cause of Spain's troubles in the secret plotting of freemasons, who they believed had been working since the Enlightenment to instill anti-Christian and anti-Spanish doctrines among the people and the rulers. On the other side liberal Spaniards blamed the machinations of reactionaries, in particular the Jesuits and other militant clergymen. Both sides, that is, were satisfied with a simplistic plot theory of history.

More profound thinkers sought less artificial explanations. Among these Miguel de Unamuno, then a young professor of classics at the University of Salamanca, set the stage for later theories in a series of articles he published in 1895 entitled *En torno al casticismo* (*On the Essence of Spain*). In his childhood in Bilbao, Unamuno had lived through the violence that accompanied the Revolution of 1868 and the

First Republic of 1873. During his adolescence he was dismayed, as many Spaniards were, by the ineffectual parliamentary monarchy that was reestablished in 1875. In 1895 Cuban patriots rebelled against Spanish sovereignty, initiating a dismal struggle that ended with the United States intervention in 1898 and the loss of the few colonies that still remained of Spain's once glorious empire. Moreover, Catalan and Basque regional movements were threatening the unity of the homeland itself. Spain indeed appeared constitutionally unsuited for the modern world.

Unamuno struggled with the problem. He denounced the facile explanation of the conservative chauvinists:

> Every day Spain hears the bitter complaint that a foreign culture is invading it and submerging the pure Spanish element [*lo castizo*]. Little by little, the malcontents say, this European invasion is undermining our national character. Like a river that never runs dry, its level is rising and at present is in flood stage, to the consternation of the millers, whose dams are overflowed and whose flour has most likely been rotted.[1]

According to Unamuno, the trouble with the lamentations of Spain's traditionalist millers was that their traditions were no more essentially Spanish than were the European ideals of their liberal opponents. The medieval institutions they glorified were as much the product of historical accident as the modern constitutions they decried.

The true tradition of Spain, Unamuno maintained, was in the lives of the mass of people, who went on plowing and reaping at the end of the nineteenth century as they had before, back to Roman times. This "intimate character of the people" or "intrahistory," as he called it, was expressed in their language. Spaniards spoke various tongues, but Unamuno recognized Castilian as the national language because Castile had unified Spain. Although born among the green Basque hills facing north to the sea, he had come to love the harsh landscape of Castile which surrounded him at Salamanca. Spain's national character he found revealed in Castilian literature, especially that of the masters of the Golden Age of the sixteenth and seventeenth centuries, Santa Teresa, San Juan de la Cruz, Cervantes, and Calderón. Their works revealed Spaniards to be both mystical and practical by nature, and democratic in their instincts. What was wrong with the country in his day, Unamuno felt, was that its leaders, both conservatives seeking models in Spain's past and liberals copying foreign countries, had lost sight of its intrahistory, with disastrous results. Spain needed another rising of the common people, the *pueblo*, as it had risen against

[1]Miguel de Unamuno, *En torno al casticismo* ("Colección austral," Madrid: Espasa–Calpe, 1943), p. 15.

Napoleon in 1808, to eliminate its effete ruling class of both political persuasions.

Unamuno's call for the discovery of the true Spanish character fell on eager ears, especially after Spain's defeat by the United States in 1898 revealed how incompetent its leaders were. Intellectuals searched their history for their national character, hoping they would learn how to reconcile it to the demands of the contemporary world. One of these was the young philosopher José Ortega y Gasset. Ortega had studied in Germany, where he experienced the ideological current stemming from Nietzsche which held that every society needed authoritative leaders. According to Ortega, European societies were divided between the lower classes, whose ancestors had been present under the Roman Empire, and a directing elite, descended from the Germanic tribes who overthrew that empire. Unfortunately for Spain, he believed, the barbarian migrations had brought to this corner of Europe the weakest, most corrupt, most Romanized of all the Germanic peoples, the Visigoths. Unlike the Franks in France, they did not establish a proper feudal system and inculcate the relationship of lord to vassal. Therefore Spaniards never developed the art of commanding, and their descendants could not provide Spain with a true elite. Spain had no backbone and was able only in spurts to engage in great endeavors, like the conquest of America. *España invertebrada* (*Invertebrate Spain*), Ortega entitled his book (1921).

Since the Middle Ages, and especially since the sixteenth century, Ortega argued, Spain's history had been one of decadence. Its empire had gradually broken away, and now even the periphery of the peninsula seemed destined to fly from the Castilian core. This was logical in Ortega's eyes, for without a common goal every country would disintegrate, and Spain's lack of leaders meant no one was pointing out its proper goal. Particularism had taken over, not only the political particularism of geographic regions like Catalonia and the Basque Provinces, but the selfish particularism of social groups: the army, industry, the church, the crown itself. No one was interested in the common good, everyone only in his private aims, which he sought to achieve by direct action. Deprived of leaders, the masses took over authority which in a properly constituted society would belong to their superiors.

> In Spain the "people" have done everything, and what the "people" have not done has been left undone. But a nation cannot be only "people"; it needs an eminent minority, just as a live body is not only muscle but also nervous system and cerebral center.[2]

[2] José Ortega y Gasset, *España invertebrada* (Madrid: Revista de Occidente, 1948), p. 126.

Thus Ortega's explanation of Spain's misfortunes was opposed to Unamuno's. For Ortega the lack of an elite was the cause; for Unamuno the cause had been the stifling of the common people.

Unamuno and Ortega spoke as philosophers, familiar with the past of their country and concerned with its future. They were not primarily historians. Since the Civil War two younger members of their generation have written major historical works aimed at discovering the origin and nature of Spain's modern character. The first was Américo Castro, a student of literature before turning to history, who published *España en su historia* in 1948 (an English version appeared in 1954: *The Structure of Spanish History*). Castro, following the pattern of existentialist theory, believes that the history of every nation is determined by the unconscious inbred thought processes of its people, what he calls its "functional structure." This can best be discovered through a close study of its national literature. "It is . . . desirable, when we wish to write the history of the existence of a people to listen to the people as they feel themselves existing." [3] One is reminded of Unamuno.

Castro concludes after a lengthy study of the literature written in Spain that the functional structure of Spaniards was the product of the nine-hundred-year-long interaction of the three peoples who inhabited the peninsula in the Middle Ages: Christians, Jews, and Moslems. Three characteristics stand out in the Hispanic consciousness, according to Castro: an ever-present feeling of insecurity; a passionate religiosity; and a characteristic that he calls "integralism," which consists of an inability to isolate oneself from the world in which one lives in order to observe it objectively, that is, rationally and scientifically. The calculating rational spirit behind modern Western culture is so alien to Spaniards that they cannot adopt modern political forms, economic drives, or scientific methodology except in a forced and superficial way. What he finds wrong with contemporary Spain is that it has tried to mold itself to foreign rational ideas and institutions. Castro feels Spaniards should parade their own qualities with pride, not shame. They alone of modern Europeans have a culture that holds that "the only calling worthy of a man is to be a man, and nothing more." [4] Castro left Spain after Franco's victory and long refused to set foot in the country. Nevertheless he provided strong intellectual support for the traditionalist position that accused the liberals and revolutionaries of trying to impose foreign political systems on Spain. His conclusion that Spain's character is incompatible with modern forms of life seems to exclude his country forever from contemporary Western life.

[3] Américo Castro, *The Structure of Spanish History* (Princeton: Princeton University Press, 1954), p. 46.

[4] *Ibid.*, p. 630.

Another outstanding medievalist who accepted exile after 1939, Claudio Sánchez Albornoz, denounced Castro's fatalism. In his *España, un enigma histórico* (1956) he affirms the existence of a Spanish national character, much as Castro does, but he finds it in existence long before Castro does. For him it goes back far beyond the Christians' interaction with Jews and Moslems during the Reconquest. The Spanish character was already distinguishable when the first Romans arrived. It had been formed by Spain's ecology, the barren land and harsh climate of Castile. Later history slowly modified it; the Romans tempered it, the Visigoths sharpened it, the Jews made it intolerant.

Sánchez Albornoz does not find Spain's character fundamentally alien to the modern world. Three historical accidents account for Spain's failure to follow Western evolution: the Arab invasion and conquest of the peninsula, Colombus' discovery of America, and the accession of Charles V in 1517. The first was responsible for the birth of Spanish particularism because it destroyed the unity of Spain that Romans and Visigoths had labored for nine centuries to achieve. The other two events prolonged the sense of honor and scorn of manual work that was typical of the Middle Ages, America by filling Spanish minds with the dream of easy wealth and Charles V by destroying the budding industry of Castile through taxes to pay for his European wars. After Charles, Philip II's crusade against the Protestants forged chains which Spanish thought was subsequently unable to break. Sánchez Albornoz, although a devout Catholic, traces the rise of contemporary civilization to the appearance of the bourgeois ethic and Cartesian rationalism. Because Charles V stunted the middle class and Philip II used the Inquisition to kill the spirit of inquiry, Spain did not develop the worldly outlook of modern times.

According to Sánchez Albornoz, an intellectual minority has admired European ideas since the eighteenth century, but they have been unable to spread them to society at large. The result has been civil conflict. In sum, Sánchez Albornoz sees much the same reasons for Spain's troubles as Castro does, but he finds the origin of the Spanish character earlier. And he is more optimistic. He foresees Europe eventually reunited in a *universitas christiana,* and then Spain will take its place in the new order as an active and dynamic partner.

Despite the diversity of these four interpretations, they have much in common. All of them seek the explanation for Spain's modern difficulties in its national character. Spaniards, they maintain, are different from the rest of Western Europeans. There is a *homo hispanus,* as Sánchez Albornoz says, who is proud, antirational, mystical, violent, and individualistic, and therefore unsuited to modern science and modern political and economic forms. Their explanations are not materialistic (although Sánchez Albornoz finds the major cause of the Spanish character in the austerity of the geography), or based on class conflict (although Unamuno desires a popular rising and Ortega laments the lack of a virile elite). They derive in part from German thinkers like Nietzsche and Wilhelm Dilthey, who were in revolt against French rationalism, but they seem strangely out of touch with modern historical thought. They all agree that the Spanish character was formed before the seventeenth century, and they all find its most characteristic expression in the people of Castile. For them Castile is Spain and Spain is what it is today because of factors present before the Enlightenment and the rise of modern industrial societies and parlimentary governments. In the end they all belong to the same intellectual generation, the "Generation of '98." Spain's apparent incompetence in the world of their day, which the defeat at the hands of the United States and the later collapse of the Second Republic highlighted, filled them with anguish. But the belief that Spaniards have a unique character that accounts for their troubles is not limited to one generation or even to Spanish writers. It has become a commonplace in analyses of modern Spain.

Since the end of the Civil War, the best Spanish historians have turned from the *Kulturgeschichte* of Germany to the French positivistic school of history founded by Lucien Febvre and Marc Bloch. Febvre and Bloch called for the study of the factors affecting the lives of a people, geographical surroundings, economic conditions, social structure, and popular psychology. The center of Spanish historical activity moved from the University of Madrid, where the dead hand of political orthodoxy was stifling imagination, to that of Barcelona. The man primarily responsible for this development was Jaime Vicens Vives. Already an accomplished historian before the Civil War, he was forced to teach in obscure schools after the war because of his presumed support for the Republic. In 1948 he won the chair of modern history at the University of Barcelona. A man of tremendous energy, in the following year he founded a Center of International Historical Studies, through which he undertook to spread the lessons of Febvre and Bloch. Around him he formed a group of historians devoted to revising Spanish history, free from the concept of an unchanging national character and the prejudice that limited the history of Spain to that of Castile. At the end of his life—he died prematurely in 1960—Vicens Vives had turned to the history of Spain since the eighteenth century, writing almost single-handed the section on this period in the five-volume *Historia social y económica de España y America* (1957–59), which he edited.

For Vicens, the problems of Spain were to be studied in the distribution of property, in poverty and hunger, and in the relations between lord and vassal, bureaucrat and subject, priest and believer, employer and employee, capital city and province, Castilians and Catalans. These are factors, he says, "which are not so different from those experienced by neighboring Mediterranean countries, and for this reason it is doubtful that Spain is an historical enigma, as Sánchez Albornoz believes, or a constant soul-searching, as his opponent [Castro] affirms." [5]

Vicens Vives has inspired a reconsideration of Spanish history. As he says, Spain is part of Europe and shares its evolution. We must try to place Spain within the broad patterns of modern history: the industrial and technological revolutions of the last two centuries and the appearance of popular sovereignty. But European developments react in Spain in ways determined by local realities, both geographic, that is physical, and human, that is historical. We cannot ignore the question of Spain's setting and heritage posed by Unamuno, Ortega y Gasset, Castro, and Sánchez Albornoz. Such a study will show, I believe, that the instability of modern Spain has been the product of contemporary factors, not of an inherited national character.

[5] Jaime Vicens Vives, *Aproximación a la historia de España* (2nd ed., Barcelona: Editorial Teide, 1960), pp. 24–25. There is an excellent English edition: *Approaches to the History of Spain*, trans. and ed. Joan Connelly Ullman (Berkeley: University of California Press, 1967).

3

The Making of Spain

1

Wherever one wishes to start an historical account, one cannot dismiss what went before. In the case of Spain this is especially true not only because a society at any moment is the product of its past but because Spaniards have long been deeply conscious of their history. Intellectuals have pondered Spain's evolution, partly out of dismay at witnessing its decline as a world power, but even illiterate peasants are familiar with the main lines of their national epic. One cannot conceive of a Spaniard who does not know in a vague way that Spain once belonged to the Roman Empire, that it was conquered by the Moors, that the Christians drove out the Moors in the *Reconquista*, that under Ferdinand and Isabel Columbus discovered America where Spain founded a vast empire, that Spanish arms fought the heresy of Luther, or that Spanish guerrillas foiled Napoleon's conquest of their country. These are collective memories that make Spain a nation.

While avoiding the all-embracing views of an Ortega y Gasset or a Castro, let us look at the origins of the major features of present-day Spain. We have little precise knowledge about pre-Roman days, but there is a widespread belief accepted by such an eminent historian as Sánchez Albornoz that the original Iberians or Celt-Iberians who inhabited the peninsula had a definite character that has been passed on to this day. They were heroic and stubborn—witness the bitter defense of Saguntum on the Mediterranean coast against Hannibal in 219 B.C., and the even more tenacious resistance of Numantia in present Old Castile against the Roman armies from 143 to 133 B.C. The populace of Numantia burned down the city and perished in the flames rather than fall into Roman hands. Nowadays the Spaniard will say of a determined and stubborn person, "He is very Iberian."

To see a direct link between the heroism of these early sieges and Spain's fierce resistance to Napoleon or Republican tenacity in the Civil War seems far-fetched, however. Many peoples in highly emotional moments have demonstrated irrational self-sacrifice. What archeological and written evidence does show is that from earliest historical times the inhabitants of the peninsula were closely tied commercially to the major Mediterranean powers, whose traders came in search of its highly prized mineral and agricultural products. First Phoenicia and then the Greek states and then Carthage established political control over its eastern and southern ports. Finally Rome conquered eastern Spain from Carthage in the Second Punic War (218–201 B.C.). In the next two centuries the Roman legions slowly extended their authority over the hinterland until they pacified the entire peninsula, about the beginning of the Christian era.

For six hundred years, until the collapse of the Roman Empire, some or all of Spain was under Roman rule, longer than any other area outside Italy. The Roman legacy has marked the Spaniards more deeply than any other. The Romans spread urban life to the regions they conquered, founding cities, giving privileges to their ruling groups, and governing the countryside through them. Southern and eastern Spain have remained areas of urban agglomerations ruling over a more backward countryside. More important, Spain has inherited from its years under Rome both its language and its religion, the two characteristics that form the basis for the self-identity of modern European nations. "Hispanidad," the concept of a common Spanish heritage that Spain has used to attract its former American colonies to its cultural and diplomatic orbit, centers on the Spanish language and Catholic religion.

Although the Basques keep alive a pre-Roman language, the rest of the peninsula speaks Romance languages. Castilian is the tongue of the central region, from Asturias and Aragon south to Andalusia. The language of Galicia is Gallegan, closely related to Portuguese, which developed out of it. In the northeast Catalan is spoken, more akin to medieval Provençal than to Castilian. The local dialects of Valencia and the Balearic Islandis are variations of Catalan. Of the different languages, Castilian is spoken by the majority and was the one exported to America. It is the official language of Spain, and foreigners know it simply as "Spanish."

Tradition marks Spain as having received divine favor during the early propagation of the Christian faith under the Roman Empire and during the medieval defense of Europe against the encroachments of the heathen world. According to legend, James the Apostle, Santiago, whom medieval Spaniards believed to be the half brother of Christ, came to Spain to preach the gospel. The Virgin Mary appeared to him in person on top of a pillar of jasper at the site of the present Zaragoza, and the Virgen del Pilar has remained one of the country's most beloved patrons. Christianity had a wide following in the peninsula and had produced many martyrs before it became the official religion of the Roman Empire in the fourth century. Later, in the ninth century, when Christians were holding out against the Moslems in a small corner of Spain, the belief spread that some peasants had discovered the body of Santiago, which by miracle had been transported to Spain from Jerusalem after his death. Santiago became the patron saint of the Reconquest, and the site of his tomb at Compostela was the goal of the most famous medieval pilgrimage of Western Europe. Christian soldiers in battle with the Moslems believed he watched over them, and they spread accounts of his appearances in person at the head of the Christian host.

The Romance language and Christian religion penetrated Spanish society deeply enough to be preserved through defeat and domination by outside invaders in the millennium after the collapse of the Roman Empire. As in other parts of the Western empire, in the fifth and sixth centuries, Germanic tribes invaded and settled in the Iberian peninsula. The tribe that obtained lasting dominion of Spain was the Visigoths, who appeared across the Pyrenees about 414 A.D. on the heels of several other groups. The Visigoths had previously wandered through eastern and southern Europe and adopted the Aryan form of Christianity, which had been declared a heresy by the Council of Nicea. Because of the religious difference, their Spanish subjects opposed their dominion for over a century. Finally, to bring peace to the land, the Visigothic king Recaredo converted to Catholicism in 587, and soon the other Visigoths followed his example.

The inhabitants of Spain showed an even more tenacious devotion to their faith and their language under the next invaders, the Moslems or "Moors" who entered Spain in 711 across the Strait of Gibraltar. The Moslems conquered all but a corner of northwest Spain in seven years; the Christians fought intermittently for nearly eight centuries to drive them out. King Pelayo turning back the onrushing Moslems with divine help at the Cave of Covadonga in Asturias in 718; the capture of Toledo in 1085 by Alfonso VI of Castile, that of Zaragoza by Alfonso I of Aragon in 1118; the glorious Christian victory at Las Navas de Tolosa in 1212; the Catalan conquest of the Balearic Islands and Valencia under James I of Aragon and that of Andalusia by Ferdinand III of Castile (San Fernando) in the thirteenth century; and finally the triumphant entry into Granada of Ferdinand and Isabel on January 2, 1492 marking the expulsion of the last Moslem ruler from the peninsula—these are glories that every child learns in school. They represent the enduring assertion of European civilization against an alien culture imposed by the sword. The long centuries of perilous frontier life and intermittent warfare, carried on in the name of the Christian faith, imbued Spaniards with a crusading tradition that identified their existence as a people with the duty to defend and propagate Christianity by force of arms. In the thirteenth century one Spaniard, Santo Domingo, founded the Dominican order dedicated to rooting out heresy. In the sixteenth another, San Ignacio de Loyola, established the Society of Jesus (the Jesuits), which opposed the Protestant Reformation.

The Reconquest represented more than an armed conflict. Since Christian society was organized for war, a military and noble ethic spread through it. A powerful aristocracy emerged based on royal grants of land and jurisdiction in the reconquered territories, especially Andalusia, and beneath it grew up a numerous class of *hidalgos* or nobles, since everyone with a horse could seek fame, riches, and noble status by fighting the Moslems. It has been argued that Spain's later economic backwardness is due to a general aspiration to noble life and scorn of productive labor imbued by the Reconquest, a theory that is hard to test historically. The long contact with a different and in ways higher culture had other, more positive results. The Moslems developed a complex irrigation system which afterwards remained the basis of the prosperous agriculture of the Mediterranean and Andalusia *vegas*. They also brought to Spain classical learning that Europe had lost during the Dark Ages; Aristotelian philosophy penetrated Western Europe via Moslem Cordoba. Even the Christian concept of the crusade was largely a response to the Moslem holy war. Finally the Reconquest bequeathed to Spain a populace of mixed religions. When their rulers were driven out, most Moslems stayed behind, a good proportion of them descendants of Christians who had converted to Islam, and there were in addition many Jews, whose forefathers came even before the Moslems. Whether these three faiths could survive together after the Reconquest became the most critical issue in Spain.

In the fourteenth and fifteenth centuries, a time of political unrest and economic hardship, preachers aroused the Christian populace against the Jews. Some Jews converted voluntarily, but on repeated occasions Christians invaded the Jewish quarters of the cities and dragged Jews forcibly to baptism. In succeeding decades, the evident lack of enthusiasm for their new religion of many of these converted Jews or *conversos*, as well as their frequent economic and social success, roused suspicion and hatred among old Christians. Finally to bring order to the cities and to take justice out of the hands of mobs, in 1482 Ferdinand and Isabel obtained papal permission to establish an Inquisition in their realms, an ecclesiastical tribunal under close royal supervision whose duty was to discover and punish baptized Christians who accepted heretical beliefs or practiced non-Christian rites. It went promptly to work against the suspect *conversos*. There remained the Moslems and the unconverted Jews. No sooner did Granada fall than Ferdinand and Isabel ordered all Jews who would not accept baptism expelled from Spain. The decree resulted in driving out approximately 120,000 to 150,000 people, including some of the economically most valuable subjects, merchants and bankers from whose loss Spain never fully recovered. Ten years later the monarchs expelled from Castile the Moslems who would not become Christian, but this time most persons involved preferred conversion to exile. The Moslem converts became known as *moriscos*.

Despite the activities of the Inquisition, suspicion and jealousy of the *conversos* and *moriscos* remained. As the sixteenth century advanced, persons with Jewish ancestry, no matter how remote, were systematically barred from church and royal offices, from universities, and from other professions. Candidates for such positions had to prove their "purity of blood" (*limpieza de sangre*). Many a well-born Spaniard trembled lest someone discover a stain in his past that would disgrace him and ruin his family. The *moriscos*, most of whom were peasants or agricultural laborers, were not molested until the reign of Philip II (1556–98). When he threatened them with persecution for their Islamic practices, they revolted in Granada in 1568 but were defeated. Thereafter they were suspected of being secretly in league with Spain's enemy, the Turks. In 1609 Philip III (1598–1621) finally decided to eliminate this threat and cater to public feeling by expelling the *moriscos*. About 275,000 people were embarked for Africa, roughly 5 percent of the population of the country. But in Valencia they were 40 percent of the population, the main labor supply of its agriculture, and their departure left much of the region deserted.

With this history as a background, it is easy to understand why the Protestant Reformation found few converts in Spain, why the Habsburg kings of the sixteenth and seventeenth centuries could involve the country beyond its strength in wars to uphold the Catholic cause in Europe, and why Spaniards took seriously their duty to convert the inhabitants of the new world. The identification of Catholicism with Spanishness penetrated all layers of society. Even today most conservatives share Franco's feeling, "In Spain you are a Catholic or you are nothing." [1]

What Catholicism has meant for the character and history of Spaniards defies rigorous definition. Anticlerical Spaniards like to blame Spain's Catholicism for its economic backwardness, political instability, and social violence, but this is only a facile explanation for a highly complex problem. In the sixteenth and seventeenth centuries, the tests

[1] Quoted in Henri Massis, "L'Espagne qui renait; Franco nous a dit," *Candide*, August 18, 1938, p. 4.

for purity of blood and the activities of the Inquisition made Spaniards suspicious and secretive. On the other hand, a foreigner today gets the impression that their immersion in Catholic doctrine and practices makes Spaniards more tolerant of human frailty than north European Protestants, more willing to discuss their feelings with friends, more ready to accept others as equals regardless of their success or failure in life or their social or economic status. Yet even if such impressions could be proved, one cannot easily see how these qualities can account for the course of Spain's history.

2

The political unity of Spain has also been the product of a long-drawn-out process. Unity is usually traced back to the Romans, but in fact the peninsula was divided into three provinces under the empire. The economic and cultural centers and main lines of communication lay along the Mediterranean coast, present-day Andalusia, and through the western part of the peninsula, including Portugal. There was no administrative center to Roman Spain. The present form of unity, with Castile as the center of authority, first appeared under the Visigoths, when they set up their capital at Toledo in the middle of the sixth century.

The Moslem invasion destroyed the Visigothic achievement, and political unity was not reëstablished for a thousand years; of the whole peninsula, never permanently. The Christian Reconquest produced a variety of kingdoms. The earliest ones lay in a belt across northern Spain: Galicia, Asturias, the Basque Provinces, Navarre, Aragon, and Catalonia. They spoke different languages, had different customs, and developed different political systems. As the Reconquest proceeded and these kingdoms incorporated new territories, political boundaries changed in kaleidoscopic fashion until in the thirteenth century three major regions emerged: León and Castile (or simply "Castile"), geographically largest and most central, which incorporated the northern coast, the central plateaus, and the valley of the Guadalquivir; Aragon, which united with Catalonia and took over Valencia and territories beyond the sea, the Balearic Islands, and for a while parts of Italy; and finally Portugal, which broke off from Castile in the twelfth century and was able to maintain its independence with support from England and France, except for the period between 1580 and 1640.

The major step in the creation of the present boundaries was the union of Castile and Aragon, accomplished by the marriage in 1469 of the heirs of the two kingdoms, Isabel of Castile (ruled 1474–1504) and Ferdinand of Aragon (1479–1516). In many ways this momentous occasion was fortuitous. Had Ferdinand's rival for Isabel's hand, King Alfonso of Portugal, carried off the future queen of Castile, Spain as we know it might never have existed. Alfonso had many backers, but for reasons of state Isabel chose the handsome young Ferdinand, and together they defeated the Portuguese armies. After another war of ten years against the Moslems, they added Granada. Finally in 1515 Ferdinand conquered that part of Navarre that lay south of the Pyrenees.

The union of Spain was, however, purely dynastic. Ferdinand and Isabel and their successors maintained separate governmental institutions and legal systems in their kingdoms. Like other parts of Europe, every kingdom or province of Spain had its own rights and privileges which protected the authority of the local dominant classes and limited the powers of the king, especially in matters of taxation and military recruitment. Known as their *fueros*, these privileges were especially strong in the Basque provinces, Navarre, and the states of the Crown of Aragon (the kingdoms of Aragon and Valencia and the principality of Catalonia). Each of the states of the Crown of Aragon had a parliament known as the Cortes, meeting in separate chambers or estates representing the different legal classes. They had great authority in granting subsidies and voting laws. Liberal Spaniards who later looked back on the Middle Ages as a time of national greatness and public liberty liked to recall the legendary oath of allegiance of the Cortes of Aragon to each new king: "We who are as good as you swear to you who are no better than we to accept you as our king and sovereign lord, provided you observe all our liberties and laws; but if not, not."

Castile had very little of this kind of formal liberty. Here the Cortes had never obtained the power to approve laws. Since the clergy and nobility did not pay direct taxes, they took little interest in strengthening the Cortes, and the institution developed into an assembly of representatives of the leading Castilian cities. Never a strong body, by the sixteenth century it ceased to have any serious role in government. The individual cities had a more effective independence, but Ferdinand and Isabel established their own representatives in each city of Castile, the *corregidor*, who enforced royal authority. Thus the crown gained control of the formal institutions of Castile, and the only effective check on its power could come from the great aristocratic families, headed by the grandees, and from the church, both of whom had vast wealth in the form of extensive holdings of land obtained during the Reconquest. After Ferdinand and Isabel brought order to Castile, the clergy and aristocracy no longer posed a direct threat to the crown, but the kings did little to reduce the wealth of these groups or the income that they obtained from the commoners over whom the crown had given them seigneurial jurisdiction. Instead the rulers of the next two centuries used Castilian aristocrats and clergymen as advisers and administrators. It is not surprising that these two classes remained powerful, or that they were able to escape taxes while the commoners, both urban and rural, were more and more heavily burdened.

The only son of Ferdinand and Isabel, Juan, died in 1497. His premature death changed the course of history as much as did the marriage of his parents. (Sánchez Albornoz goes so far as to call the delicate Renaissance sarcophagus of Juan at Ávila the "tomb of Spain.")[2] The heritage of Ferdinand and Isabel fell instead to a daughter, Juana, whom for reasons of diplomacy they had married to Philip of Habsburg, heir to Austria and the Low Countries. After the death of Ferdinand and Isabel, Juana's son Charles, Duke of Burgundy, became the first Habsburg ruler of Spain in 1517. He inherited Austria in 1519 and was elected Holy Roman Emperor as Charles V (he was Charles I of Spain [1517–56]). When Charles demanded a grant to pay for the bribes involved in his election, the cities of Castile, angry at the demands of this foreigner, formed a league known as the Comuneros and rose in revolt in 1520. They fought briefly and unsuccessfully. The Castilian aristocrats turned against them when they threatened a social revolution, and provided arms for Charles to put down the rebels. The revolt of the Comuneros was the last time Castile seriously tried to resist its king.

The two centuries following the marriage of Ferdinand and Isabel brought Spain to the pinnacle of European power and subsequently saw it decline to be the plaything of England, France, and the Netherlands. This saga is the best-known part of Spanish history; it preoccupied Spaniards then and has ever since. The political unity and domestic peace achieved by Ferdinand and Isabel gave Spain the basis for European power, but its supremacy resulted from Columbus' discovery of the Antilles for the crown of Castile. When a generation later Spaniards extended their conquests to the mainland of America, they found in the Inca and Aztec empires territories that rewarded them beyond all expectations. The gold and silver mines of Peru and Mexico made the king of Spain the wealthiest ruler in Europe in the sixteenth century.

Unfortunately for Spain its rulers consumed this wealth in European wars. Charles V dragged Castile into the conflicts in which his central European lands involved him, against France, the Ottoman Empire, and eventually the German Protestants. Thus began a long bloodletting of Castile that marked the two centuries of Habsburg rule. Charles abdicated in 1556, leaving to his son Philip II Castile, Aragon, the Low Countries, provinces in Italy, and the empire in America. Charles' brother received the Austrian lands and became the next Holy Roman Emperor. The Spanish and Austrian Habsburgs re-

[2] Sánchez Albornoz, illustration facing Vol. II, p. 128.

mained close allies until the last Habsburg king of Spain died in 1700, and the alliance committed Spain to nearly continuous war in Germany and Italy. More serious was a revolt of the Low Countries against Philip II. They rose in 1566 to resist his attempts to stamp out the Protestant religion in their lands and to tax them to support his wars. The struggle continued intermittently for eighty years and hurt the rulers of Spain on the seas and in their colonies. Spain finally recognized the independence of the northern provinces, or Netherlands, in the Treaty of Westphalia in 1648, but it managed to keep the southern provinces (roughly present-day Belgium).

By the seventeenth century, Spain's wars were proving to be a drain to which its resources were unequal. After 1600 the output of the American mines declined while armies got ever costlier. The Peace of the Pyrenees between Spain and France (1660) marked the temporary end of Spain as a great European power. Henceforth France under Louis XIV took its place at the head of Europe. The treaty gave to France the portion of Catalonia lying north of the Pyrenees, and in the next decades Louis XIV gradually nibbled away at Spain's remaining territory in the Low Countries.

The domestic history of Spain during these centuries centers on a gradual process whereby the crown sought to extend to the rest of the peninsula the control it had over Castile. The process was not consciously planned but resulted from the need of the kings to seek money wherever they could for their armies. Under Philip II the difficulties of running an empire made up of kingdoms with different laws and privileges became evident. In 1591 the Aragonese nobility incited a rebellion in Zaragoza because Philip proposed to infringe their liberties. A Castilian army quelled the revolt. Philip was legally minded enough to maintain most of the Aragonese *fueros,* but he insisted on the right to name Castilians as viceroys. The gradual extension of Castilian personnel into the administration of the other territories was, in fact, to be the most successful method of the monarchs for increasing their control over their non-Castilian subjects.

The next major incident was far more serious. After 1635 Philip IV (1621–65) was engaged in war with France both along the Pyrenees and the Rhine, where the French enjoyed the alliance of the Dutch and other Protestant states. Fearing the invasion of Catalonia, Philip and his minister the Count-Duke of Olivares sent a Castilian army to the Catalan frontier, which they billeted on the countryside in the winter 1639–40. Olivares also proposed to change the Catalan constitution in order to allow the king to levy higher taxes in support of the war. In May 1640 Catalan peasants rose against the Castilian troops, and the rebels captured Barcelona and murdered the viceroy. The Catalans declared themselves at first an independent republic and then subjects of the king of France. Peninsular unity had been destroyed. After a long struggle Philip IV recovered control of Catalonia in 1652, but only at the expense of reaffirming all its *fueros*.

Accompanying the revolt of the Catalans was another by the Portuguese. Philip II had inherited Portugal in 1580, thereby completing the long-dreamed-of unity of the peninsula. As was the case in Aragon, he promised to maintain the local Cortes and liberties, but his successors violated his promises. They named Castilians to Portuguese offices and sought ways to raise Portugal's contribution to their war chest. In December 1640 a rebellion began in Lisbon which declared one of their own aristocrats to be king of Portugal. Despite efforts lasting twenty-eight years, Spain never recovered the land to the west. Help from France and England, Portugal's traditional allies, provided the margin needed to resist the Spanish armies. The natural desire of Spain's rulers to reestablish Iberian unity as it had been in Visigothic days had been thwarted by the Habsburgs' commitment to fight in central Europe.

Half a century later, effective unity of the remainder of the peninsula did come about as the result of a change of dynasty. Charles II (1665–1700), the only surviving son of Philip IV, was mentally retarded and failed to beget children. On his death he willed his lands to the grandson of Louis XIV, the Duke of Anjou, who had a claim to the throne through Louis XIV's marriage to a daughter of Philip IV. The Duke of Anjou mounted Spain's throne as Philip V, the first Spanish king of the House of Bourbon, which was to reign in Spain until 1931. The Bourbons did not obtain Spain without a struggle, however, for the Habsburgs of Austria put up a rival claimant to the throne in the Archduke Charles, a great-grandson of Philip III. Charles found allies in Great Britain and the Netherlands, who feared the combined maritime and colonial power that would result if France and Spain should be united.

The War of the Spanish Succession which ensued turned into a major European and colonial conflict. The Peace of Utrecht that terminated it in 1713 was a compromise. Philip V kept the crowns of Castile and Aragon and with them the overseas colonies, for despite Spain's many defeats in Europe, it had preserved its empire virtually intact; but he gave up to Austria Spain's remaining possessions in Italy and the Low Countries, and to Great Britain the island of Menorca and the fortress of Gibraltar. The British navy had captured Gibraltar, which was weakly defended, in the name of the Archduke Charles in 1704. During the war, the British came to realize its possibilities as a naval base at the mouth of the Mediterranean Sea and, when peace was negotiated, they insisted on keeping it for themselves. Spain recovered Menorca in 1783, but Gibraltar has remained British to this day. The occupation of this corner of the peninsula by a foreign power has been a thorn in the side of Spaniards, embittering relations between the two countries and helping to keep alive in Spanish minds an image of England as the primary national enemy.

Domestically the war put an apparent end to the problem of unifying the kingdoms of Aragon with Castile. After some hesitation at the beginning of the war, the Cortes of Aragon, Valencia, and Catalonia recognized the Archduke Charles as their rightful king, placing more confidence in a Habsburg than in an heir of Louis XIV to respect their *fueros*. Even with the help of Britain and Austria, however, these kingdoms proved no match for the armies of Castile who fought for Philip V, partly because, as on earlier occasions, they did little to help each other. The Castilians conquered Valencia and Aragon in 1707. Catalonia held out alone, even after Britain and Austria recognized Philip. In the summer of 1714 Barcelona withstood a glorious but futile siege, hoping to the end for British help that never arrived. Philip V retaliated for the disloyalty of these kingdoms by abolishing their *fueros*. The cortes of the three kingdoms disappeared. In the future their major cities would be instructed to send representatives to the Cortes of Castile. Military officers directly subordinate to the king called captains general replaced the viceroys, and the king sent *corregidores* to the cities. The tax systems were altered so that the crown would get a proper amount from each territory. Only the Basque Provinces and Navarre now preserved their traditional privileges.

Catalans were particularly bitter over the outcome. Twice in the past century they had fought valiantly to maintain their *fueros* against the encroachment of Castilians, whom they looked upon as foreign conquerors, and twice they had been abandoned by their non-Spanish allies, while the kingdoms of Valencia and Aragon failed to come to their support. Forgetting the essentially aristocratic nature of the *fueros* they had lost, Catalans who opposed the policies of Madrid in the future would excite the resentment of their fellow citizens by recalling the heroic resistance of their forefathers against Castilian tyranny in 1640–52 and 1705–14.

At last the crown had achieved the institutional unification which was the logical result of the marriage of Ferdinand and Isabel. Centralization was the objective of every European monarch in the sixteenth and seventeenth centuries, for it was a vital necessity for self-defense in this age of increasingly expensive wars. The states that failed to centralize became the pawn of their powerful neighbors. The most obvious example was the Holy Roman Empire defeated by France in the seventeenth century, but Spain also suffered from its disunity. Now Philip V's achievement made it the first major nation to achieve a unified government. Louis XIV has the reputation for creating a centralized absolute authority, yet long after Philip V abolished the Cortes of Aragon large areas of France kept their local estates and voted their own taxes. Britain achieved unity similar to Spain's by the Act of Union of 1702, which incorporated Scottish representatives into the English parliament, but here constitutional power was divided between crown and parliament, and the central government lacked effective control over local authorities.

3

Because of internal conflicts and foreign wars, the country that Philip V finally managed to unify was vastly different from the kingdoms of Aragon and Castile brought together by Ferdinand and Isabel. In 1500 Castile had been a flourishing land of wealthy and populous cities, while Catalonia, which was the economic center of the crown of Aragon, had declined from its earlier greatness as the dominant power in the western Mediterranean. The wealth of Castile rested on its production of wheat, wine, and olive oil, but most especially on the export of its fine merino wool. The city of Burgos, which monopolized this trade, had a prosperous merchant class, while the fairs of Medina del Campo attracted traders from throughout Europe.

All this changed in the next centuries. Because Castile was taxed more heavily than Aragon, the continual warfare of the Habsburg kings exhausted its economy. In 1610 the French ambassador estimated that Castile paid fifty times as much in taxes as Aragon, although its population was only six times greater. Besides heavy taxes, the rural Castilians suffered from the royal policy adopted by Ferdinand and Isabel of encouraging sheep grazing at the expense of agriculture. The export of wool brought valuable foreign exchange, and the annual migration of the flocks of sheep along the royally protected sheepwalks made them easy to tax. The rulers took the facile expedient for increasing their income of favoring the official guild of owners of migrant sheep, the Mesta. They gave it a perpetual guarantee of its sheepwalks and of the use of any pastures it had ever rented, and the right to try disputes with peasants in its own courts. Attracted by such conditions, large landowners preferred to turn their lands over to grazing.

Many of the Castilian peasants, who were heavily taxed, frequently in debt, and threatened with the loss of their lands, turned to careers in the church or the army or fled to look for jobs in the cities. They migrated south to Andalusia, where production for America offered employment. Many young men of marrying age joined the armies and went to central Europe, and less than a third returned. Large numbers of people perished in the epidemics which swept through Spanish cities in 1596–1602, 1647–52, and 1676–85. By the seventeenth century New and Old Castile were losing population and their once flourishing cities were becoming deserted. (Burgos fell from 13,000 to 3000 population during the first half of the century.) Castile could no longer furnish the men needed for its armies, any more than it could pay them. Little wonder that in 1640 Olivares sought desperately to tap the resources of Catalonia and Portugal.

Most lacking of all was a middle class engaged in commerce and manufacture. Whereas the aristocracy and the church kept their lands, Castilian manufacture was in decline by 1600, except for artisan production that furnished the needs of local markets. Persons who amassed wealth preferred to invest it in government securities (*juros*) or to buy land and a title. "There are but two families in the world, the haves and the have-nots," Sancho Panza's grandmother said. Castile had become a land of rich and poor and little in between.

The decline of Castile produced a lasting revolution in the human geography of Spain. In the sixteenth century the Castilian heartland dominated the peninsula by the weight of its population. In 1550 the crown of Castile probably had over 6 million inhabitants, that of Aragon and Navarre only about 1 million. This means that Castile, with 77 percent of the area of Spain, had about 86 percent of the population; it had a density of seventeen persons per square kilometer, Aragon and Navarre only nine. After rising to around 7 million inhabitants at the end of the century, Castile lost population after 1600, dropping to perhaps 5 million in 1715. While Castile was being humanly exhausted, the economy of eastern Spain began to revive in the late seventeenth century, headed by the once famous Catalan woolen industry. Improving economic conditions in Catalonia lowered mortality rates among the population and attracted immigrants from France and southern Spain. The population began to rise and continued to do so at a more rapid pace in the eighteenth century. Other regions in the north and east experienced similar developments. It is an ironic fact that when Philip V finally asserted Castilian sovereignty over the kingdoms of Aragon, the economic and demographic position of Castile vis-à-vis Aragon was growing progressively weaker. By the end of the eighteenth century, for which we have reliable figures, Castile had 7.6 million people, only 75 percent of the 10.2 million population of peninsular Spain. (The Balearic and Canary Islands had 360,000 more.) Furthermore, within the area of Castile, half the population was located in the northern coastal provinces and Andalusia. Aragon itself was barren by comparison with Catalonia and Valencia. Except for the part of Old Castile running north from Valladolid to the sea, the Castilian mesetas and Aragon had less than twenty inhabitants per square kilometer, despite a steady growth in the eighteenth century, while the coastal regions and Andalusia averaged over thirty. In direct contrast with the sixteenth century, Spain now presented the phenomenon of an empty center ruling politically over heavily peopled areas looking outward to the sea. In the eyes of the world, which was used to looking at Castile as if it were Spain, the country appeared in dismal decline, as its recent series of military defeats seemed to prove. The eighteenth century was to show that appearances were misleading, for Spain was to experience a revival in which the forgotten lands of the periphery were to take the lead.

4

Looking back at the Habsburg centuries, Spaniards naturally fix their attention on their country's great colonial expansion and its dominance in Europe. They are dismayed by its subsequent decline, in part confusing Castile with all Spain, as did contemporaries. That a country of between 7 and 8 million people should find it impossible to remain the dominant power in Europe, where France had over 15 million and the Germanies perhaps 20 million, is hardly surprising. The great miracle was Spain's power in the sixteenth century, attributable as much to domestic peace in a time when other countries were suffering civil wars as to its American treasure.

Spain's preeminence in these years was not only military and political. The Golden Age (Siglo de Oro), from the reign of Philip II through that of Philip IV, saw a flowering of Spanish art and letters which has seldom been equaled in any country. Whether one looks at religious art like the *Interior Castle* of the mystic Santa Teresa of Ávila, El Greco's paintings of apostles and saints, and Zurbarán's portraits of elegant friars, or whether one prefers worldly art like the picaresque novel *Lazarillo de Tormes, Don Quixote,* and the theater of Lope de Vega, one can choose from universal masterpieces. The spirit that dominates most of this art is an exhalted realism. Painting does not idealize saints, martyrs, or classic deities, but renders them as ordinary people with their flaws and passions; for instance, the paintings of Mary Magdalen and Saint Bartholomew by Ribera or Vulcan's forge by Velázquez. Velázquez's official portraits of Philip IV reveal not an arrogant lord or distant ruler but a sorely troubled and vacillating man. In Don Quixote and Sancho Panza, the *hidalgo* and the peasant, Cervantes fashioned opposite sides of the same coin.

In art Spaniards seemed to express a deep subconscious conviction that beneath the everyday distinction between social classes, between past and present, and between human and divine lies hidden the ultimate unity of creation. In El Greco's painting, "The Burial of the Count of Orgaz," Saint Augustine and Saint Stephen, dressed as dignitaries of the church, are burying the body of the count and Saint Francis and Saint Dominic mingle with the real living nobles who watch as mourners, while in the top half of the canvas an almost naked Saint John the Baptist pleads with Christ and Mary for the acceptance of the count's soul. Half the mourners are looking down at the body, the others upward to heaven, for the two realms are intimately joined together in their consciousness as in the artistic representation. Or another case—the palace of El Escorial built by Philip II to be his residence. It is a massive, harshly geometric granite structure in the form of the gridiron on which Saint Laurence, to whom it is dedicated, suffered martyrdom. At its center is a vast Renaissance church, and most of the rest houses a monastery. The royal quarters are a few rooms in one wing, and the king's bed was placed so that, through a small window, he could watch mass being said at the high altar. The king lived like a monk, a simple servant of God, though ruler of the largest empire in the world. Finally, one can look at Velázquez's painting, "The Spinners" ("Les Hilanderas"). In the foreground the women of a tapestry factory are spinning. Through an arch one sees aristocratic ladies who have come to buy a tapestry. Beyond them the figures of Minerva and Arachne are visible in the tapestry on display, painted to appear no less real than the living persons. Yet Velázquez put the common women in the foreground and the goddess at the back, purposely inverting the normal hierarchy. It is this mystical union of the supernatural with the natural, of king and monk, of ladies and spinners that marks the artistic creations of the time, gives them their greatness, and permits us to sense through them an age when fortune and poverty, and heaven and earth, were inseparable in everyday consciousness.

By the end of the seventeenth century the Golden Age had passed. It bequeathed to later generations a legacy of human creativity that has formed the minds of educated Spaniards ever since. As with so much of Spain's legacy to modern times, however, it was a mixed blessing. In art, in war, in trade and industry, and in empire building, Spain's present was to seem forever dwarfed by its past. The enduring sense of anguish that Américo Castro finds in Spaniards must have come largely from a feeling of inadequacy instilled by their history. It became easy for Spaniards to say with Sánchez Albornoz that the Habsburgs had brought about the ruin of Spain, or with Américo Castro that the national character was not suited for modern times, and thus to wash their own hands of responsibility for their fate. And yet they could have realized that the seventeenth century had changed the domestic structure of the country and its international position to such an extent that henceforth its problems would differ greatly from those of the Habsburg period. Had they done so, they would not have searched for the explanation of its subsequent history so exclusively in the past.

4

Enlightened Despotism and the Origin of Contemporary Spain

1

However great a legacy Spain inherited from earlier times, its contemporary history begins in the eighteenth century. This was the age of Enlightenment in Europe. A new spirit was abroad, a skeptical approach to accepted beliefs and a widespread concern to improve material conditions. Looking back at the Habsburg period, for instance, Spanish writers and statesmen of the eighteenth century condemned the expulsion of useful subjects because of their religious beliefs. In 1797 the minister of finance even proposed readmitting Jews if they would undertake to liquidate the royal debt. The idea was premature, but it illustrates how royal policy was now being discussed in terms of economic utility rather than religious unity. Reformers of the seventeenth century had anticipated many of the attitudes and innovations of the new age, but they had received scant attention in their day. Now royal councilors and men of letters read their works assiduously, saw to it they were republished, and put their ideas into effect.

Spain made a remarkable recovery in the eighteenth century. The loss of its European possessions and the break with the Austrian Habsburgs proved to be disguised blessings. Spain remained involved in wars in Italy under Philip V, who fought successfully to obtain the kingdom of Naples for his second son Charles, but after 1740 its major efforts were directed against British threats to its empire in America. In the Seven Years War, Spain signed an alliance with France in 1761 against their common enemy. The war was disastrous for the French empire, but Spain managed to escape without serious damage. It lost Florida to Britain, but France gave it the Louisiana Territory to compensate for this loss. The next conflict, the American War of Independence, was more successful. Spain won back Florida and also Menorca in the Mediterranean, which had been lost in 1713. Despite a strenuous siege, however, it failed to recapture Gibraltar.

In Spanish America the century saw a burst of territorial expansion, administrative reform, and economic progress. Pushing out from Peru, Spanish colonists developed the Plata basin and the northern coast of South America; while from Mexico they went north, especially into California. These areas flourished, bringing new wealth to the mother country; but most prosperous of all was Mexico, whose silver mines became the greatest producer of precious metals in the world.

In Spain itself the same spirit of daring optimism took hold of the royal government and the leading classes. It owed much to the two sons of Philip V, who ruled for nearly half a century after his death; Ferdinand VI (1746–59) and Charles III (1759–88). On the surface they were not imposing figures. Ferdinand VI's mother had died in his infancy, and he had suffered under Philip V's second wife. His own marriage was childless, and he made his wife the center of his existence. When she died in 1758, he retired to a palace outside Madrid in a state of pathological melancholy and there died himself a year later. As king, he sought to keep Spain at peace and build up its economy. He had the gift of choosing good ministers, of whom the most outstanding was the Marquis de la Ensenada, who undertook to strengthen the army and navy, reform the provincial administration, and introduce foreign technological advances in industry and agriculture.

Charles III, Ferdinand's half brother, was a rigorous ruler, the most successful monarch of Spain after Ferdinand and Isabel. He deserves a high rank among the enlightened despots of the eighteenth century, for in many ways he accomplished more than such famous rulers as Frederick the Great of Prussia and Joseph II of Austria. Charles did not reveal a brilliant mind, but like Ferdinand VI he recognized talent in his servants, and his ministers are among the best Spain ever had. A widower within a year after his accession, he lived modestly, his main diversion being hunting deer. It is in the simple costume of a hunter, with a musket in his hand and a dog at his feet, that Goya painted his official portrait. He is anything but handsome in the portrait—his face is too narrow and his nose far too prominent—but his eyes show warmth and kindness. Goya, who like Velázquez could be merciless in his portraits of royalty, clearly liked and respected this king. Such devotion was widespread. Charles' subjects admired his simple life and his religious spirit. The tale is told that once he gave up his carriage in Madrid to a priest who was carrying the last sacrament. After walking beside the carriage to the house of the dying person, the king received an ovation from a crowd of common people who had gathered to follow him.

2

After the War of the Spanish Succession Spain enjoyed almost a century of domestic peace. Not until the nineteenth century were Spaniards again at each other's throats. Yet looking back at the reigns of Ferdinand VI and Charles III, one can see that major issues which were to dominate Spain's subsequent history had their origin at that time. Although these issues were interrelated, they affected three distinct areas of Spanish life. Each had its roots in earlier times, but each assumed new features as it underwent the interaction of royal policies, the new intellectual ferment, and the expanding economy of the country.

The conflict which was to break the peace first was mainly ideological. Although the Enlightenment differed from country to country, everywhere in the Western world it brought a break with traditional values and accepted beliefs. Many of the new ideas it made popular had originated earlier in England and the Netherlands, but most Europeans learned of them through the writing of the French *philosophes* of the eighteenth century, Montesquieu, Voltaire, Condillac, Rousseau, and others. The accession in Spain of a French dynasty opened up its court to French cultural influences, artistic and architectural as well as intellectual. (Philip V tried to create a miniature Versailles at the summer palace of La Granja in the mountains near Segovia.) Before 1750, the economist Jerónimo de Uztáriz echoed the lessons of Louis XIV's famous minister Colbert on the need to increase agricultural and industrial production; an Asturian monk, Benito Jerónimo Feijóo, spread the skeptical attitude of the Enlightenment in philosophy and science in a series of widely read volumes attacking popular superstitions; and a Valencian doctor, Andrés Piquer, publicized recent discoveries in medicine. By the time of Charles III many writers had joined in the effort to bring modern thought to their fellow citizens.

Various French *philosophes* pointed to the story of Spain's decline in the seventeenth century as a practical lesson of the bad effects of religious intolerance and exploitation of colonial peoples. They painted a picture of Spanish history full of wickedness and deceit which has since been known as the "black legend." Enlightened Spaniards were tormented by this reputation of their country, believing it to be partly true, and they were determined to bring Spain abreast of the rest of Europe in learning and economic well-being. The new ideas that they found most appealing concerned natural science, political and moral philosophy, and education. The *philosophes* were skeptical in matters of religion, but this aspect of the Enlightenment did not make noticeable inroads in Spain, in part because of the censorship exercised by the royal government and the Inquisition, but mostly because few Spaniards were prepared to doubt their religious doctrines. Spanish partisans of foreign ideas showed instead a fascination for ways to improve industrial and agricultural techniques, to make education more useful and up to date, and to make the legal system more equitable for all classes and regions. They looked to the royal government to effect the needed changes, but they also sought to spread the spirit of reform to the educated public.

There were various ways in which the new ideas, the *luces* (lights) as they were called, reached the public. One was through local societies known as Amigos del País (Friends of the Country). A group of Basque noblemen founded the first society in 1764. After 1775, when residents of Madrid established another under the aegis of the king, societies were founded rapidly in many cities, receiving royal charters. Their members included aristocrats, high and low clergy, and interested commoners. Some joined, no doubt, seeking social prestige, but many were truly moved by the desire to bring prosperity to their provinces. The societies publicized new methods of agriculture and manufacturing and made surveys of local resources. They set up trade schools and published memoirs. The most successful, such as the Basque society, and those of Zaragoza, Segovia, Valencia, Palma de Mallorca, Seville, and Madrid, became focuses of local enlightenment.

After 1780 the periodical press of Madrid provided another medium for the *luces*. Periodical papers had come and gone intermittently for decades. Now many appeared within a few years and their circulation spread through the country. The *Correo de Madrid* (1786–91) and the *Espíritu de los mejores diarios literatos que se publican en Europa* (*The Spirit of the Best Literary Journals That Are Published in Europe*) (1787–91) translated or summarized for Spanish readers the latest articles on economics, science, and political theory appearing in France and elsewhere. Here Spaniards could learn the theories of Newton on the universe, Montesquieu on the forms of government, Rousseau on education, Beccaria and Filangieri on legal reform, and Condillac on the psychology of learning, even though many of the original works of these authors had been prohibited by the Inquisition. Other papers, such as *El Censor* (1781–87) and the *Semanario erudito* (*Erudite Weekly*) (1787–91), criticized Spanish society directly, drawing their ammunition both from foreign sources and from Spanish writers of the Habsburg era.

Although few progressive Spaniards questioned religious doctrines, the Spanish Enlightenment produced conflicts that involved religion and the church. The *luces* found opposition among conservative clergymen, in part because they conflicted with the traditional teachings of scholastic science, but even more because they became associated with a movement for reform within the Spanish church. Those persons who favored new ideas tended to demand devotion to the common welfare of the state, and many of them felt that the Spanish church had grown too worldly and was a burden on society. After 1750, reformers began more and more overtly to criticize the clergy, especially certain monastic orders, accusing them of leading useless, lazy lives, and of encouraging extravagant forms of worship and religious display, like street pageants and self-flagellation, instead of devotion to the unadorned, simple teachings of Jesus. Many of these critics were clergymen themselves. Naturally a majority of the clergy rejected these attacks. They labeled the reformers Jansenists, the name of a French sect of the previous century whom the Pope had condemned for wanting to make Catholicism too forbidding and puritanical.

The French Jansenists had aimed their criticisms at the teachings of the Company of Jesus, the Jesuits, calling them morally lax and casuistic. For a hundred years the Jesuits had fought Jansenistic tendencies in the church while championing the supreme authority of the Pope. Their reputation as agents of the papacy led the kings of Spain to look upon them with suspicion. Just as the kings sought to abolish provincial privileges, they attacked the authority of the papacy over the Spanish church in worldly matters. In 1753 Ferdinand VI signed a concordat with the Pope which gave the king the right to nominate two thirds of the bishops and to tax church lands. Charless III in 1768 prohibited papal pronouncements from circulating in Spain without royal approval. Royal councilors and reform-minded clergymen accused the Spanish Jesuits of being ultramontane, that is supporting the prerogatives of the papacy over the claims of the crown in the government of the Spanish church, in order to defend abuses from which they profited. The Jesuits who taught in the universities were suspected of forming an alliance with sons of aristocratic families to favor their mutual interests against royal encroachment. In Spanish America the Jesuits were rumored to be fomenting disloyalty to the king among the Indians of certain areas who were devoted to them.

In 1766 serious riots shook Madrid and other Castilian cities. Though the disturbances were largely a reaction to the momentarily high price of bread, a trial behind closed doors declared the Jesuits guilty of inciting the common people. Charles III determined to suppress them within his dominions, a step already taken by the kings of Portugal and France. He gave charge of the task to a capable and stubborn Aragonese grandee, the Count of Aranda, who effectively carried out the measure in 1767, deporting the Jesuits to the papal states. In 1773, pressure from the Bourbon courts led the Pope to dissolve the order. Charles rewarded José Moñino, who successfully negotiated in Rome to obtain their dissolution, with the title of Count of Floridablanca.

In 1776, Charles made him foreign secretary, and henceforth he was the king's leading minister.

The end of the Jesuits was a triumph for the so-called Jansenists and other reformers. In the next years they began a concerted attack on the backward education of the universities, which had been a Jesuit stronghold. The Council of Castile, the highest administrative and judicial body in Spain, encouraged university faculties to revise their curricula in order to introduce new theories of natural sciences and medicine and a modern study of law, including Spanish law and the doctrines of natural law. The first to undergo thorough reform was the University of Seville, in 1769. A struggle ensued with the more conservative members of the faculties, especially in the University of Salamanca, Spain's oldest and most renowned. Professors dedicated to Aristotelian and scholastic science and philosophy, many of them monks, defended their theories as both more correct and more in keeping with Christian doctrine. Nevertheless by the time of Charles III's death, students in most universities were using up-to-date, though fully orthodox texts.

Although Jansenists and partisans of the *luces* were not necessarily the same persons, they joined hands in the reform of the universities. They had in common the desire to see Spain progress by breaking the grip of the institutions that defended conservative thought, and by eliminating useless privileges and wasteful displays of wealth, whether in church ceremonies or in the lives of the aristocracy. Both groups saw their hope in the activities of Charles III and his ministers. Their opponents, unable to count on the king, sought the aid of the papacy and the Spanish Inquisition, hoping to stem the influx of new ideas by having them declared heretical. Thus the penetration of enlightened and so-called "Jansenist" thought created the basis for a serious ideological conflict. The conflict did not break out into the open at this time because the crown encouraged the reformers and the conservatives were not prepared to challenge the royal authority directly.

The position of the king was crucial. Charles III revised the regulations of the Inquisition in 1768 to assure a fair trial to writers and publishers accused of spreading heretical ideas, he reformed various monastic orders, and he nominated partisans of strict discipline within the church for bishoprics. But Charles was no friend of heresy. Although the Inquisition hesitated to act against high officials, the king allowed it to investigate and from time to time condemn university professors, editors of periodicals, and even royal servants. The most telling case was that of Pablo de Olavide, named royal intendent of Seville in 1767. He was responsible for the plan of reform of the University of Seville, and he antagonized influential clergymen by limiting the activities of the church in some new agricultural settlements the king founded in Sierra Morena. In 1776 the Inquisition arrested Olavide after collecting sufficient evidence that he doubted Catholic dogma to convince even Charles III. In a ceremony attended by high aristocrats and royal officials, it condemned him to eight years of confinement in a monastery and other forms of penance. After two years, however, he managed to escape to France, perhaps through the connivance of well-placed friends. But his case received wide publicity and served as a warning that the opponents of reform still had power.

Ideological differences affected only a small proportion of the population, for only the literate could appreciate the issues and not all of these were interested. Divisions appeared within the higher social groups. Many aristocrats supported the *luces,* although the spirit of economic reform could become a threat to their own privileges. The better writers were enlightened, but others fought the new ideas bitterly. Royal servants tended to support innovation because of the spirit infused in the government from above by Charles' leading ministers, but at the lower levels, local administrators frequently frustrated royal wishes. Many professional people and merchants favored reform, but many others were indifferent.

Most significant for the future, the Enlightenment and Jansenism split the clergy into opposing factions. Far from being monolithic, the church of Spain was racked with dissension. Some religious orders, notably the Augustinians, favored educational reforms; others, led by the Dominicans, resisted the *luces* and were ultramontane. There were Jansenist bishops and conservative bishops, holders of ecclesiastical benefices who supported university reform, wrote poetry, and read the French *philosophes,* and professors of philosophy who stuck by Aristotle and condemned the trend of the century. The Jansenists were a minority within the clergy, but a growing and influential minority who flourished with the support of the crown. Thus the first signs of a coming crisis was an ideological conflict centering in the church.

3

The spirit of reform did not produce a struggle between social classes, but the case of Olavide revealed that the ideological conflict involved social issues. He was feared and hated not only for his reform of the University of Seville but because he proposed changes that threatened the large landowners of Andalusia. In this instance also he was carrying out royal policy, for the ministers of Charles III were engaged in an attempt to reform the Castilian countryside. The second major issue which the eighteenth century would bequeath to the future involved the condition of agriculture in central and southern Spain.

Since the Middle Ages a landowning oligarchy of aristocrats and religious institutions dominated the more fertile areas of New Castile. During the Reconquest from the Moslems of the Mancha, Extremadura, and Andalusia—the southern third of Castile—the kings had awarded extensive territories to the noblemen who participated in the wars, in many cases giving them both ownership of the land and jurisdiction (*señorío*) over the inhabitants. As *señores* they carried out justice, collected certain dues from the population, and in many towns appointed or confirmed the municipal officials. Much of Old Castile was also ruled as *señoríos*, but here the Reconquest was earlier and peasants and *hidalgos* already owned much land when the king gave away or sold the jurisdiction over them, so that the *señores* usually did not have large properties within their *señoríos*. The Dukes of Alba were *señores* of a fourth of the province of Salamanca, 168 towns and villages, but they were the largest landowner in only thirteen of them, almost all very small; whereas in the province of Jaén in Andalusia, in over half of the towns under *señorío* the *señor* was the largest owner, and these were sizable places. Most aristocratic property, including lands, seigneurial rights, and movable goods, had been constituted as *mayorazgos* or entailed estates, which by law could never be broken up and were passed on by primogeniture, growing steadily by acquisition or by union through marriage.

Besides being the largest landowners, in central and southern Spain the aristocracy dominated many *ayuntamientos* or city councils, whose membership, in theory elective, had mostly become hereditary in practice. The *ayuntamientos* controlled the communal lands, which were often extensive. Instead of sharing the use of these lands equitably among the townsmen, many councilors appropriated the best tracts for their own use or that of their aristocratic patrons.

Closely associated with the aristocracy were the leading churches and monasteries and the military orders founded during the Reconquest. They owned vast tracts of land and controlled others that had been willed to them as endowments to support charitable and other religious activities. Like the entailed aristocratic estates, their properties could never be alienated and were known as *manos muertas* or mortmain. Some religious bodies and the military orders also had *señorío* (jurisdiction) over towns and villages. The various types of income went partly to finance the religious and charitable activities of the church, but much of it also ended in the pockets of the more privileged secular and regular clergy and the aristocratic *caballeros* (knights) of the military orders.

The aristocrats and religious institutions farmed most of their lands with overseers or leased them out in parcels to tenants. Their large holdings, to which the old Roman term *latifundia* is applied, formed the basis for great social inequality, with a class of opulent landlords living from the suffering of a mass of exploited renters and destitute hired hands. In Seville province, the most extreme case, only 4 percent of the men engaged in agriculture owned land, 10 percent rented land,

and 86 percent were landless laborers. For both geographic and historical reasons, in the more mountainous areas of central and southern Spain and in most parts of Old Castile, greater equality and more rural democracy existed. This was true also of the northern coastal areas, where there was an abundance of rain, and major portions of the east, where extensive irrigation dating from Moslem days supported a prosperous peasantry and earlier social struggles had established laws and customs that protected peasant farmers from excessive rents and eviction.

Social inequality was also fostered by a complicated and inefficient system of taxes dating in part back to the Middle Ages, which hit the farming, laboring, and merchant classes of Castille, and thus hurt economic growth. When Philip V destroyed the liberties of the kingdoms of Aragon, he introduced a single tax, called the *equivalente* in Valencia and Aragon, and the *catastro* in Catalonia. These taxes were cheaper to collect and more equitable than those of Castile.

Since the days of the Habsburgs, social critics had lamented conditions in arid Spain. Under Ferdinand VI, the Marquis de la Ensenada undertook to reform the tax structure of Castile. In 1749 the king extended to all Spain local fiscal officials, called intendants, after the French officials on whom they were modeled. Their first major assignment was to carry out under Ensenada's direction a survey or *catastro* of all the property and income of the inhabitants of Castile preparatory to introducing a single tax on property. The vast undertaking was successfully completed in the early 1750's. Its thousands of massive tomes, virtually unique in Europe, are only now being investigated by social historians. The accomplishment was too successful: it showed how much property the church and aristocracy owned and how heavily an equitable tax system would weigh on them. Ferdinand dismissed Ensenada in 1754, and the single tax was never instituted, although royal councilors kept the issue alive during the rest of the century.

Under Charles III, the attempt to reform rural conditions took a different tack. Bad harvests led to famine conditions in 1766 that produced the riots for which the Jesuits were blamed. To meet the need for more grain, Pedro Rodríguez de Campomanes, Charles III's leading adviser in economic questions, urged the government to increase the number of small farmers. He believed, as did many enlightened thinkers, that small, individually cultivated farms provided the soundest basis for productive agriculture. Campomanes had the support of other reformers like Aranda and Olavide. In 1767, Charles III ordered the intendants of New Castile and Andalusia to report on local agrarian conditions and to advise the best measures to take, and soon he instructed the *ayuntamientos* of the cities and towns of these areas to distribute municipal lands to indigent farmers on long-term leases.

These measures posed a threat to the dominant group in arid Spain.

Under the Habsburgs the high aristocracy of Castile held considerable influence in the royal government, as councilors, generals, and viceroys. The Bourbons ended this power, preferring like their ancestor Louis XIV to use men of lower origin, university graduates and provincial *hidalgos*, many of them from other areas than Castile. At the center of the state, they built up a loyal and progressive bureaucracy. Those who headed it, like Floridablanca (who came from Murcia) and Campomanes (from Asturias), received titles of nobility to raise their social position. The only grandee in Charles III's administration was the Count of Aranda, and he came from Aragon.

Ousted from the central government, the aristocracy could still find political and social power in its control of rural Castile. Just as it defeated Ferdinand VI's attempt to establish a single tax, it doomed Charles III's projects to create small farmers. In western and southern Spain the oligarchy simply refused to carry out royal orders to distribute the common lands; indeed it sometimes used them as a pretext to take over more land for itself. The king lacked local officials dedicated and powerful enough to enforce his reforms. After seven years of sullen conflict, he found it expedient to send Aranda to Paris as ambassador in 1773. Three years later the Inquisition arrested Olavide, and the period of active reform in agriculture came to an end. The inequality posed by the latifundia of Castile and Andalusia was to remain the greatest social problem to plague modern Spain.

Although Charles III failed to add significantly to the desired class of independent farmers, he did bequeath a program of reform to future generations. Many intendants submitted the reports on local conditions that he had ordered. The best was a detailed and penetrating study of Seville province written by Olavide. In 1780 the crown commissioned the society of Amigos del País of Madrid to study their recommendations and propose general agrarian legislation. The society asked Gaspar Melchor de Jovellanos, a member of the royal councils who was one of the most profound economists of the period, to draft its reply. Jovellanos did not finish his report until 1794, and the society published it as its *Informe de ley agraria* (*Report on the Agrarian Law*). Upholding the right of property and the doctrine of economic laissez-faire put forward by the economists of the Enlightenment as well as the eighteenth-century belief in the desirability of small landowners, Jovellanos found the greatest cause for the backward condition of Spanish agriculture in the entail of church and aristocratic properties. He recommended that the king prevent further entail and encourage the owners of entailed estates, both lay and ecclesiastical, to sell their lands or rent them out on permanent leases to small farmers (neither of which they could do under the current laws of entail). The towns should do the same with common lands. This was basically the policy that Charles III had tried to follow, except that Jovellanos placed more emphasis on the desirability of giving small farmers their own private property. His *Informe de ley agraria* formulated the issues clearly and provided easily understood solutions. It was to become almost a bible for nineteenth-century liberals, who would try to use the authority of the state to put its recommendations into effect.

On one policy the royal government and the landowners had been able to agree. This was to further the output of foodstuffs for the market. Because of the profit involved in the export of wool, royal policies had for centuries encouraged sheep grazing. In the eighteenth century the situation changed. Partly as a result of expanding population throughout Europe, the demand for food was growing everywhere. In Spain the price of wheat rose faster than the price of wool. Owners wanted to turn their lands over to food crops in order to raise their income, while the crown wanted more grain to feed the cities—this was the major objective of aiding small farmers. Both interests coincided in favoring agriculture at the expense of sheep grazing. In their way stood the privileges of the Mesta, the guild of owners of migrant sheep, which could prohibit owners from putting pastures under the plow. After 1780 Campomanes succeeded in abolishing this privilege, and he obtained for owners the right to enclose their lands and plant whatever they wanted. He hoped to help the peasants, but large landowners became the major beneficiaries, as they abandoned wool for wheat, wine, and olive oil as their source of wealth.

4

The third future conflict adumbrated in the eighteenth century was between geographic regions, the Castilian heartland and the periphery of the north and east. It arose from the different economic and demographic evolution of the two regions already evident under the Habsburgs. The relative decline of the population of the central plateau vis-à-vis the coastal zones which began in the seventeenth century continued in the eighteenth. While Castile and Andalusia were witnessing the expansion of large-scale agriculture, the northern and eastern coastal regions experienced the rise of industry. Three regions were involved: the Basque Provinces, Catalonia, and Valencia. For centuries these regions had had local industries based on their natural resources, the manufacture of iron and copperware in the Basque lands, weaving of woolens in Catalonia, and silk and linen weaving in Valencia. Now the peaceful conditions in Spain and new legislation facilitated the expansion of these industries. The markets of Europe and Spanish America were easily accessible by sea. Habsburg policy had kept the colonies closed to direct trade with northern and eastern Spain, but the Bourbon kings reversed this policy. Meanwhile the export of locally produced iron ore, nuts, fruits, and wines to Europe brought capital for investment in industry, while meat, fish, and grain could easily be imported to feed growing urban populations.

Until the eighteenth century, Seville and then Cadiz, southern ports which were outlets for Castile, held a monopoly on legal trade with America. Castilian manufacturers had proved unable to exploit the monopoly. Foreign agents in Seville and Cadiz loaded the exports of their own countries onto the Spanish convoys headed for the colonies, and north European shippers also smuggled their wares directly into Spanish American ports. Although the manufacturers of the north and east of Spain had been edging into the colonial market by shipping via Cadiz, the privileged position of Castile hindered their expansion. Philip V began to break the monopoly by establishing a trading company in the Basque port of San Sebastián in 1728 with an exclusive right to the commerce of Venezuela. In 1755 a royally chartered company in Barcelona took over the commerce with the smaller islands of the Antilles. Finally Charles III, influenced by Campomanes, abandoned the concept of trading privileges for special ports. Between 1765 and 1778 he opened up trade between all major Spanish ports and the colonies (except Mexico, which remained a monopoly of Cadiz for another decade). At the same time he made stricter the regulations against foreign interlopers in Spanish America. These measures helped the manufacturers of the north and east, whose trade with the colonies shot upward in the 1780's.

Charles III also encouraged manufacture directly by abolishing restrictive laws. Until this time industrial production was regulated through guilds, which maintained local monoplies of their products and discouraged innovation. Campomanes hoped to encourage production among vast numbers of independent artisans and women by allowing persons to engage freely in the trades. Royal edicts broke the monopolies of the guilds. The effect, however, was not so much to stimulate small producers as to make possible the growth of factories hiring nonguild workers. Merchants now also extended the practice of putting out, that is of financing small craftsmen, supplying their materials, and marketing their products. The putting-out system became common in weaving and metal work. The northern and eastern coastal regions with a history of local manufacture benefited most from the new laissez-faire legislation. In Catalonia one of the fastest-growing cotton industries in Europe developed beside the older woolen industry. Catalan *indianas* or printed cottons became a major export to the colonies and the interior of the peninsula.

By the 1780's the Basque lands with their forges and shipyards and Catalonia and Valencia with their looms were among the most flourishing regions in Europe. The Bourbon kings were not being purposely partial to the peripheral areas, but they no longer feared the rebelliousness of the non-Castilian lands, and they desired to strengthen Spain in every way possible to meet the challenge of colonial rivalry with England and other European powers. They struggled to revive Castilian industry as well, and established a number of royal factories in central Spain. Geography was opposed to their efforts here, for the cost of transportation across the mountains impeded exports. The kings built a series of roads radiating north, east, south, and west from Madrid to France, the major ports, and Lisbon. Charles III was even optimistic enough to begin a network of canals. Despite these efforts the heartland remained without significant industry or any large cities except Madrid, which flourished as the seat of the royal government.

At the end of the century one could distinguish two vastly different regions of Spain: the central and southern areas, characteristically arid, thinly populated, with large landholdings, and the coastal provinces of the north and east, which were territories of prosperous small farms and growing industries, oriented toward the sea. Each had its own privileged class. One was the landowning aristocrats and religious institutions, whose wealth rested on the production of agricultural crops for the market, either by direct exploitation or by renting lands to peasants. The other was the merchants, shipowners, and manufacturers of the periphery. Campomanes had hoped to create numerous small farmers and small craftsmen, not only to increase production but also because they would be loyal subjects. Economic forces that were common to all Europe, the effect of better communications and widening markets, favored larger and larger units of production, however, both in agriculture and industry. Once the governments removed trammels, large, not small, farmers and manufacturers multiplied everywhere, and Spain was no exception.

Despite the differences in the two regions, there was no immediate tension between them. The new prosperity of the periphery, partly the result of royal policies, partly the product of extraneous forces, had the effect of calming the former tensions between the crown and the non-Castilian regions. When war came with France after the outbreak of the French Revolution, almost all Basques, Catalans, and Valencians remained loyal to Madrid. The conflict which the Castile-oriented Habsburgs had been unable to resolve was ended by the broader vision of the Bourbons. Yet if one were to draw a line separating the two regions, the northern and eastern coastal areas from the center and south, and if one were to stretch the line westward from Catalonia and Valencia to include Madrid, the center of enlightenment and royal government, the result would coincide roughly with the front lines during the first year of the Civil War in 1936–37, with the Republican forces in the north and east and the Nationalist forces to the west and south. The phenomenon is more than coincidental; it shows that the geographical differences developing in the eighteenth century were to mold the future history of Spain. Because Catalonia had been the leading opponent of Castilian supremacy under the Habsburgs, one is tempted to see in the budding geographical division a continuation of the old struggle between the kingdoms of Castile and Aragon. To do so is to ignore a fundamental distinction in the periods. When Catalan hostility to Madrid reappeared in the nineteenth century it was to arise primarily from new economic conflicts rather than from memories of earlier political differences.

5

These three tensions—between ideological conservatives and progressives, between landowners and agrarian reformers, between rural center and industrial periphery—were soon to become crucial domestic issues. The eighteenth century left a related heritage that was less obvious and has hardly been noted by historians. It involved the difference between urban and rural life. Since Roman days the Mediterranean world has been a civilization of cities. Urban centers have carried forward the evolution of Western culture, while the agricultural countryside has lagged behind, tied to local traditions and customs. The dichotomy was never absolute, for there could be no sharp distinction between a small city and a large rural town, and the countryside was also evolving under the impact of the cities. Yet the difference was always clear enough to contemporaries.

In most of Spain the rural population has lived in small towns or *pueblos,* as a general rule increasing in size toward the south. Throughout most of history the *pueblos* have been dominated by local concerns, their horizons hardly stretching beyond their territorial limits. In the eighteenth century, as before, the royal government did little more than collect taxes and enforce conscription in the *pueblos,* and this through local townsmen. Only rarely did a royal official appear in all his imposing authority to make a survey of property for the Marquis de la Ensenada or to take a census for the Count of Floridablanca. From time to time the bishop would come to scrutinize the fulfillment of religious duties, including the payment of tithes. Such events hardly troubled the normal course of life.[1] Those who lived in the city, on the other hand, had a broader outlook. Through the press, officials of church and state, and travel of the upper classes, the higher sectors of urban society were in contact with a world that stretched beyond national frontiers. Madrid had foreign diplomats, French and Italian shopkeepers, and royal academies whose members corresponded with

[1] Some social anthropologists have described this situation, contrasting it with the present. See Carmelo Lison-Tolosana, *Belmonte de los Caballeros, a Sociological Study of a Spanish Town* (Oxford: Clarendon Press, 1966), pp. 212–14, 259–60: J. A. Pitt-Rivers, *The People of the Sierra* (Chicago: University of Chicago Press, 1961), pp. 213–18.

their foreign counterparts. In university cities like Salamanca, Valladolid, and Seville, professors and students discussed current philosophical and theological issues. Manufacturing centers like Barcelona were experiencing technological change common to all Europe, and in the ports, of which Cadiz was the most important, all classes were in frequent contact with persons who visited the outside world. Perhaps a tenth of Spain's population lived in the cities.

In the eighteenth century, the distinction between city and countryside began to take on new significance. It had hitherto been a question of culture—city folk mocked the country oaf in literature and the country people replied by accusing the cities of sin and corruption. The Enlightenment gave it an ideological content. The *luces* found a welcome among some people in the cities; they had no one to welcome them in the *pueblos*. The cities had centers of learning and societies of Amigos del País. The division between Jansenist and ultramontane, progressive and traditionalist, was an urban phenomenon, present in little islands of culture dotting the vast sea of illiterate rural Spain. Outside these islands only an occasional priest or councilman who subscribed to a periodical or a university student on vacation was aware of the issues. It was as if two different peoples were germinating, an active political Spain in the cities and a dormant apolitical Spain in the countryside.

This distinction was to underlie the national life of the next century and a half, as significant for the history of this period as Spain's fierce physical geography has been throughout all time. Besides its effect on the ideological conflict in the eighteenth century, it was also related to the other two budding issues. Agrarian reformers were educated urbanites trying to enforce their policies against the will of those who controlled the countryside economically and politically. The peasants did not know enough to help the reformers. The relationship of the urban-rural dichotomy to the tension between geographic center and periphery was less apparent. Most universities were in central Spain and both areas had active societies of Amigos del País. However, because of recent demographic changes, the largest cities except Madrid were located near the sea, where there was manufacturing and commerce. The importance of this fact would become evident in the next century.

5

The French Explosion and the Birth of Political Controversy

1

Charles III died in December 1788 of a cold caught while hunting. His son Charles IV (1788–1808), already forty years old, was heavyset and easygoing. He announced that he would keep the Count of Floridablanca on as his first secretary, thus reassuring the progressive Spaniards who mourned his father. Soon, however, he was to break sharply with the policies of the late king. His wife María Luisa of Parma was a wilful, thin, unattractive woman, with a strong hold over him. She had hated the austere life of her father-in-law and frequented the social functions of the more extravagant aristocrats. She rapidly changed the atmosphere of the court. Even more important, Charles IV's accession coincided with the beginning of the French Revolution. For the next quarter century, events abroad would largely determine the course of Spanish history. Gradually the impact of the Revolution and the character of the new monarchs combined to destroy the conditions that made enlightened absolutism possible, bringing in its place modern political conflicts.

In 1789 Europe followed with excitement and anxiety the news of mobs rioting in Paris and a National Assembly at Versailles declaring the people sovereign in France. The National Assembly soon remade the political structure of the country. It proclaimed religious freedom, closed the monasteries, put the properties of the Catholic Church up for sale to pay the royal debt, and provided for popular election of the clergy. The Civil Constitution of the Clergy, which embodied the legislation on religion, brought a rupture with Rome and was soon to be the cause of civil war in France. In 1791 the assembly forced Louis XVI, virtually a prisoner in Paris, to accept a written constitution which established an elected legislature and reduced the king from divinely appointed lawgiver to executive officer of the nation.

Floridablanca, now in his sixties, grew increasingly alarmed at these developments. For the French assembly to question royal authority horrified him. He tried to suppress all news coming from France and called on the Inquisition to help in collecting any French or Spanish writings that mentioned the revolution. All in vain, for interested Spaniards learned of the French achievements from one source or another, such as French papers smuggled in by merchants and the reports of refugees who crossed the Pyrenees. Almost in a panic, Floridablanca in 1791 stopped publication of Spanish periodicals and suspended the activities of the Amigos del País, the two main agencies of enlightenment in Spain. The Revolution had scared the veteran minister into abandoning the spirit of reform.

Because Floridablanca's attitude was weakening France's traditional friendship with Spain, and perhaps also because María Luisa found him too puritanical, Charles IV dismissed him in February 1792. His successor was the Count of Aranda, long famous for taking command of the expulsion of the Jesuits in 1767. For several months Aranda tried to improve relations with the French government, evidently in the hope of taming the Revolution. But his hope was futile. France went to war with Prussia and Austria, and in August 1792 an uprising in Paris overthrew the monarchy. France elected a new radical legislature, the Convention, which proclaimed a republic. Aranda was discredited, and the king dismissed him in November.

Charles IV appointed to succeed him a far different person from those who had counseled his father. This was a dashing twenty-five-year-old guardsman Manuel Godoy, who was descended from a modest *hidalgo* family of Etremadura. The king, for unaccountable reasons, had recently made him a grandee with the title of the Duke de la Alcudia. Now he raised him to be his first secretary, above all men of higher rank and more experience in government. Why this sudden favor? Because, rumor said, Godoy was the queen's current lover; María Luisa had the reputation of indulging herself with handsome young men of the court. The circumstances of Godoy's advent antagonized most aristocrats and progressive intellectuals. He was to seek to revive Charles III's liberal policies but would do little to improve his image. Besides being an upstart, he was vain, tactless, and opinionated. He made an ostentatious display of his wealth, which came from exploiting his new position. Yet he had a certain canny intelligence. Both the king and queen remained devoted to him for the rest of their lives, and trusted his wisdom. Except for a couple of years, he was the directing force in government during the rest of the reign.

From the outset, Godoy had to deal with a war-torn Europe. The

French Convention, after guillotining the king, declared war on Spain in March 1793. Spain fought with a coalition of European monarchs against the Republic. In 1794 French Republican troops invaded Catalonia and the Basque Provinces. Knowing his own unpopularity and fearful of the effect of military defeat on public opinion, Godoy made peace in 1795, ceding half the island of Santo Domingo to France. To celebrate the end of the war, Charles IV granted him the sonorous title of Prince of the Peace, placing him officially above all grandees, almost equal to a royal prince, but hardly endearing him to either the aristocracy or common people. A year later Godoy led Spain into an alliance with France against England, convinced with some justice that the real threat to the Spanish monarchy came from British penetration of Spain's colonial markets.

The war against Revolutionary France brought into question the whole concept of domestic reform. Already Floridablanca had curbed the leading agents of progress. Now the conservatives, with clergymen in the forefront, who had been muzzled by Charles III, could voice their opposition to reform. Pointing to the French attack on the crown and church, they preached a crusade "For Religion, for King, and for Country" against the French, whom they called atheists and regicides. They argued that enlightenment and reform would lead to anarchy in Spain as it had in France.

Even though the progressives were also dismayed by much of the Revolution, they fought back. When the French Assembly established the Civil Constitution of the Clergy, many of them hoped Charles IV would take similar action. Enlightened men and Jansenists had smarted before 1789 under the threat of the Inquisition, and many of them wanted to weaken and eventually abolish it. In order to do so, they felt the need to loosen the Spanish church from the Pope's authority, as the French had done. In 1797 Godoy obtained the appointment of Jovellanos, author of the *Informe de ley agraria*, who was known to be a Jansenist, as minister in charge of religious affairs. Jovellanos encouraged reform in the church and universities and recommended giving to the bishops the power to censor books now held by the Inquisition.

Jovellanos' policies led to a showdown with the conservatives. After 1798, with Godoy temporarily in disfavor, the ultramontane clergy and their allies managed to gain the ear of the monarchs. They convinced Charles IV that reform of the church involved the danger of revolution. In 1800 the king gave his support to the Inquisition to rout out and silence Jansenist clergymen and liberal officials. Jovellanos, their leading figure, was arrested in his house, accused of plotting against the king, and transported like a common criminal to prison in Mallorca. For all Godoy's penchant for progress, he acquiesced in the new policy when he returned to power later in the year. The alliance of enlightened Spaniards with the crown, which had been the glory of Charles III's reign, lay in ruins.

On the other hand, the financial needs of the government, arising out of the wars, also led it into conflict with the clergy. The war with Britain after 1796 was especially harmful. The British navy intercepted trade with America, colonial revenues could not reach Spain, and Spanish exporters lost their main market. Suffering from the expenses of war and declining income from taxes, the crown issued redeemable bonds, called *vales reales*, that circulated as legal tender. They rapidly depreciated and the royal credit was threatened. To raise funds, Godoy recommended taxes on the unproductive classes. The king decreed new levies on landowners and municipal governments. These privileged groups, who already hated Godoy, were not amused, yet these measures were inadequate. As a last resort, the wealth of the church offered a tempting way out of the pressing financial plight. The church held extensive property, both urban and rural. Most of this belonged directly to cathedrals, churches, and monasteries, but a large amount represented endowments to support the church's charitable and educational activities, as well as benefices and masses for the dead. In 1798, while Godoy was momentarily out of favor, Charles IV heeded the advice of his ministers and decided to put up for auction the properties that made up religious endowments. The proceeds were to be used to pay off the *vales reales* and save the royal credit. The religious institutions which had held the properties would receive 3 percent government bonds equal to their sale price. Although the king maintained that the churches were getting a good bargain, most clergymen disagreed, being justifiably suspicious of the soundness of the government paper they had to accept. They could not fail to observe that the French revolutionaries had found a similar solution to their fiscal crisis. When Godoy returned to power in 1800, he continued the sales, earning the lasting hatred of many clergymen.

The forced disentail of church buildings and lands lasted until 1808. About one sixth of all real property of the church had been sold by then, a vast transfer of land that began to give a new structure to rural society. Men who had free money to invest bought land—merchants and landowners who had profited during the recent inflation, even many priests and canons with lucrative benefices who wanted to enjoy private estates and leave them to their relatives. Along with the wealthy were thousands of small buyers who acquired an irrigated plot or a field of wheat or a house to live in, where previously they had worked the land of others. It was only a beginning, but Charles IV's ministers, under the pressure of war, did what Charles III's had failed to do, distribute entailed land to private hands. Like Campomanes, they wanted to create a class of small landowners, but again the large exploiter benefited most from the end of old restrictions.

For different reasons Charles IV and Godoy had managed to alienate both progressives and conservatives. Both groups began to look elsewhere for leadership. Some liberal young Spaniards, excited by the happenings in France, eyed the forceful general, Napoleon Bonaparte, who headed the government of France after 1799. Others looked to the youthful heir to the Spanish throne, Ferdinand, whose heritage Godoy was suspected of coveting. Ferdinand might reestablish the alliance of crown and enlightened subjects. Little was known of his character, and conservatives too saw in him a hope of ridding Spain of Godoy and his policies. Charles IV became ill as he aged, and a sense of expectation gripped the public; the prospect of a new king was exciting, the fear that Godoy and María Luisa might somehow eliminate him, anguishing.

2

Outside events brought the tensions to a head. Spain and France signed peace with Britain in 1802. Nevertheless Bonaparte's insatiable quest for power led to renewed hostilities with Britain in 1803, and Spain was soon involved in another war. In 1804 Bonaparte had himself proclaimed Emperor Napoleon. A year later a British fleet under Admiral Nelson destroyed the French and Spanish navies off Cape Trafalgar, near Cadiz. In 1807 Napoleon obtained the consent of Charles IV for a French army to enter Spain and join in an attack on England's ally Portugal. After a brief assault that was hardly more than a parade, Portugal lay prostrate in November 1807. Nevertheless Napoleon continued to send troops across the Pyrenees in the ensuing months, asserting that they were to protect Spain against a British invasion. Suspicion grew among Spaniards that Godoy might be in league with Napoleon to deprive Ferdinand of his right to the throne and take it for himself. French troops arrived in Madrid in March 1808. Godoy, who was loyal to his king and feared Napoleon's motives, took the royal family south, out of reach of the French; but to the public he seemed to be arranging for the monarchs to sail for America, as the Portuguese rulers had done, abandoning the country to the mercy of Napoleon. On March 18 violent riots broke out at Aranjuez, where the royal family had stopped. After two days of shooting and pillaging, Charles IV, thoroughly frightened, dismissed Godoy and abdicated in favor of Ferdinand. The news of the accession of the young Ferdinand VII (1808–33) sent a thrill through the length and breadth of the country. Godoy was in prison, and Spaniards welcomed the end of fifteen years of ministerial despotism. Progressives and conservatives both looked to the new king to support their cause.

But Spain's joy was short-lived. Napoleon refused to recognize Ferdinand, Charles soon regretted his abdication, and both kings accepted the emperor's invitation to Bayonne in France to settle their rival claims. In one of the most treacherous cases of mediation in history, Napoleon pressured both father and son to abdicate in his favor and proceeded to name his brother Joseph Bonaparte to the vacant throne. He convoked to Bayonne a body of pliant Spanish notables—church dignitaries, grandees, and royal councilors—who in June recognized Joseph as their legitimate king and adopted a written constitution for their country drawn up under Napoleon's direction. Although the constitution provided for cortes, it left final power in the hands of the king. In Madrid the royal councils recognized the *fait accompli* and welcomed Joseph I as king of Spain in July, while Napoleon sent Ferdinand and Charles off to captivity in distant Chateaux.

The Spanish people, however, did not accept passively the abduction of their young prince charming. On May 2, 1808 crowds in Madrid attacked the French forces and were crushed savagely. (The day has since been a national holiday.) At the end of the month, when news of Ferdinand's abdication reached the provinces, simultaneous risings occurred in various parts of unoccupied Spain. Mobs drove out or lynched the royal officials who had dared proclaim Ferdinand's renunciation. To get control of the situation, leading citizens set up local governing juntas composed of respected clergymen, aristocrats, and loyal government officials which proclaimed Ferdinand VII legitimate king of Spain. The juntas raised troops and ran local affairs through the summer while they groped for a solution to the problem of a lack of a central governing body. Finally, at the proposal of the juntas of Murcia and Galicia, all the juntas sent representatives to form a Supreme Central Junta that met on September 25 at Aranjuez, in the very palace where all the trouble had started six months earlier. Most prominent among its members were Floridablanca, now eighty years old, who had lived quietly in Murcia since his dismissal in 1792, and Jovellanos, freed from prison by Ferdinand. The junta recognized Ferdinand VII as sovereign of Spain and itself as the depository of his authority until his return, thus legitimizing its own revolutionary origins with the name of the absent king.

The conflict with France that began in this fashion lasted five years and became one of the most bitterly fought wars in history, as Goya's stark etchings of the "Disasters of War" testify. Spanish armies inflicted surprising defeats on the French in the summer of 1808, forcing Joseph and his supporters to flee Madrid, but their victories were short-lived. Napoleon came to Spain in person and easily recaptured the capital in December. The Central Junta fled to Seville; on the way Floridablanca died, worn out by the tensions, the last figure who could command respect throughout the country. Much of 1809 was militarily indecisive. Rather than accept the "intruder king," Spaniards resorted to guerrilla warfare (the name originated here). They enjoyed the support of the British navy, for the common fight against Napoleon had made the two countries uneasy allies, and in Portugal a British army under Arthur Wellesley, the future Duke of Wellington, held back the French. Nevertheless, by January 1810 Napoleon's generals had overwhelmed organized resistance in Spain, and only parts of the periphery and the mountain areas of the center remained free.

Joseph Bonaparte ruled over most of Spain for the next two years, but he could never solidify his hold. The majority of the royal officials and inhabitants of the occupied areas who accepted his rule did so without enthusiasm, and French armies paid only lip service to the king as they lived off the countryside. A few Spaniards, who became known as *afrancesados*, were wholeheartedly devoted to Joseph, believing in the need to regenerate Spain from above and convinced of the futility of resistance to French armies. Some had been partisans of Godoy. The smallness of their numbers reveals how dead the ideal of an enlightened despot had become since 1789, for this was the role Joseph Bonaparte tried constantly to fulfill. He sold off monastic lands, abolished the Inquisition, and appealed to monetary interests by guaranteeing the *vales reales*. He set up Masonic lodges in the main cities, where his Spanish partisans could mingle socially with French officers and administrators and tingle to a forbidden freedom from religious superstitions. And he got thanks from hardly anyone.

3

Most Spaniards remained loyal to Ferdinand VII and the governments that defended his cause. Fighting a desperate struggle against Napoleon, these governments took measures that permanently changed the political atmosphere in Spain. The Central Junta, like most local juntas, was conservative in majority. While he lived, Floridablanca was its president. It assured the support of the clergy by ending the sale of ecclesiastical lands and supporting the Inquisition. Nevertheless, in order to justify their revolt, both local and central juntas had to assert that the people had sovereign rights which even their king could not transgress. He could not give his subjects to a stranger like chattel. The Central Junta announced to the king's subjects in America that they were no longer colonists but equal to Spaniards and would share in their government: "Your destinies no longer depend on ministers or viceroys or governors, they are in your hands." [1] Many progressive Spaniards, recalling the Cortes of the Middle Ages, felt the proper solution to the lack of a legitimate king was to convoke national cortes, which would assume sovereignty in his absence and write a constitution that would prevent a repetition of ministerial despotism

[1] Decree of January 22, 1809.

and irresponsible transfer of the crown. A minority of the Central Junta urged this action.

Their chance came when military defeats at the end of 1809 discredited the Central Junta. Fleeing from Seville to Cadiz in January 1810, the Junta issued a convocation of cortes representing the entire empire and then dissolved itself in favor of an interim five-man regency. A French army immediately laid siege to Cadiz. The city was filled with refugees, infested by yellow fever, and could communicate with the rest of free Spain only by sea. The war seemed lost. The cause of Ferdinand was at its lowest ebb, yet the Spanish armies and guerrillas fought on.

The regency, headed by the testy old Bishop Pedro Quevedo of Orense, was even more conservative than the Central Junta and hesitated to assemble the Cortes for fear of opening a Pandora's box. It was finally forced to act by news reaching Cadiz in the summer of 1810 that citizens of Caracas and Buenos Aires, after learning of the demise of the Central Junta, had established juntas that assumed local sovereignty in the name of Ferdinand. The regents set a date for the meeting of the Cortes as a desperate means of keeping the empire together.

The Central Junta, before dissolving, had agreed to call the Cortes in two estates, but they had failed to convoke the upper house of grandees and church prelates. In Cadiz the regents were surrounded by a radical populace which included the city's enlightened merchants and many government officials and others who had fled before Joseph's armies. The regents feared the effect of now issuing a call for a second estate for the Cortes, and never did so. They made another critical decision. Only in unoccupied Spain could any semblance of free elections be held. Not to leave the occupied provinces unrepresented, and also to have deputies from America (which the Central Junta had declared an integral part of the monarchy), the regency provided for temporary substitute deputies chosen among the citizens of these areas present in Cadiz. Many of them enlightened bureaucrats and clergymen, the substitutes formed nearly half of the Cortes when they met, and they insured that the body would have a radical orientation.

From the outset, the Cortes put conservatives ill at ease. At their opening meeting, on September 24, 1810, while proclaiming Ferdinand legitimate king, they declared themselves sovereign in the name of the nation, a step the Central Junta, although more revolutionary in its origins, had never taken. When Bishop Quevedo, head of the regency, refused to take an oath of loyalty to the Cortes unless he could qualify it by the proviso that it did not infringe on Ferdinand's ultimate soverignty, the Cortes ordered him to prison and kept him there for months until he took the oath without qualifications. In November 1810 the Cortes proclaimed freedom of the press in all matters except religious dogma and established lay juntas with jurisdiction in matters of the press. Within two months the Cortes had attacked both the concept of royal absolutism and inquisitorial censorship.

Many of the deputies who supported these measures were young and little known. They represented the appearance of a new generation at the head of Spain. In spirit they were heirs to the Jansenists and enlightened Spaniards of the previous century, but they had been formed in the days of Godoy and the French Revolution and were more extreme than their elders. They angered conservative clergymen and troubled even moderates. In the last months prior to his death in January 1811, Jovellanos, the leading reformer of the 1790's, was frightened by their measures. They were soon called "Liberals" (the first use of this term as a political label). Almost all the substitute deputies were Liberals, whereas a majority of the regularly elected deputies were of the other party, known as the "Serviles." The division was ominous for the future.

In December 1810 the legislators established a commission to write a constitution for the Spanish nation. Heading it were Agustín Argüelles and Diego Muñoz Torrero, the leaders of the Liberals. Late in 1811 the Cortes subjected their draft to extensive debate, enacted it, and proclaimed it on March 19, 1812, the fourth anniversary of the advent of Ferdinand VII. The Constitution of 1812, the first written constitution enacted by a European nation that was fighting the French, was a decisive document in the history of Spain. It declared the nation to be sovereign and defined Spaniards as all men of free birth in the realms on both sides of the Atlantic. It specified the civil rights of citizens as well as their duties, and it declared the religion of the nation to be Catholic, with none other allowed. It created a one-house legislature, the Cortes, to be chosen biennially by universal male suffrage with an indirect system of elections. The king, no longer absolute, held the executive power and had a suspensive veto over legislation. At the local level, the Cortes abolished *señoríos,* the feudal jurisdictions held by aristocrats. They replaced the *ayuntamientos* long controlled by hereditary oligarchies with freely elected municipal governments. Carrying to the extreme the process of centralization that had been going on under the Bourbons, they replaced the remaining local privileges and distinctions by a system of administration, taxation, and representation that applied equally to all Spain and the former colonies. A Council of State, in which ecclesiastics and grandees would make up only one fifth of the membership, took the place of the separate royal councils, including those of Castile and the Indies.

In other words the Cortes of Cadiz had turned Spain and its former colonies into a single vast democratic nation that bridged the ocean. Support for centralization and uniformity came from the deputies of the periphery. There was no fear of unity if Castile did not dominate the nation, and the incorporation of Spanish America into the nation and destruction of local oligarchic rule meant that in the future Castile would not.

In a lengthy preamble the Cortes sought to legitimize the new charter by finding a historical pedigree for it. They called the constitution a revival of Spain's medieval *fueros* and cortes. They explained the new uniformity as a return to the unity of Visigothic days. The unicameral legislature without privileged orders, so unmedieval, they called a necessary corollary to the new equality of all citizens. Many critics at the time and since have pointed out that the constitution resembled the French one of 1791 more than anything out of Spanish history; but in the daring simplicity of its egalitarian and unitary structure it was more radical than any constitution that came out of revolutionary Paris.

Unoccupied Spain initially accepted the constitution and began to carry out its provisions. From the start covert opposition was present, especially among the clergy. The troublesome Bishop Quevedo, back in his see in Galicia, refused to swear to it without the qualification that ultimate sovereignty lay with the king, and this time he escaped to Portugal to avoid arrest. For many he was a martyr to Ferdinand's cause.

A year later the Cortes, with a much smaller majority than usual, abolished the Inquisition on the grounds that its procedures violated the rights of the citizen proclaimed in the constitution. The Liberals thus gave a radical solution to the dilemma of the Jansenists and progressives of an earlier era. The conservative clergy, who had bit their tongues at earlier acts of the Cortes, found here an issue on which they could attack the Liberal majority. Many refused to read the decree in their churches as ordered by the Cortes and stated in their sermons that the Inquisition alone could guarantee the purity of Catholic worship promised by the constitution. Napoleon had abolished the Inquisition in December 1808. Were not the Liberals who repeated the measure really Frenchmen at heart rather than Spaniards?—That was the inference behind their sermons.

The Liberals were unable to silence their critics. A flourishing press in Cadiz eloquently expressed their position, and the Serviles did not have publicists to match them, but the clergy could get their message to a far wider audience through the pulpit. Furthermore the clergy had support among the large landowing class of Castile, for the Cortes had abolished seigneurial rights, and the free election of *ayuntamientos* threatened their dominance over local government. The Liberals even proposed to distribute monastic lands to veterans of the war, waking fears for the property of the church that the Central Junta and regency had carefully defended. Many Spaniards outside the centers of enlightenment like Madrid, Cadiz, and other main cities became suspicious of the Cortes and the Constitution of 1812. Elections for the first regular Cortes, which met in Madrid at the end of 1813, returned a much smaller Liberal majority than those present in the Constituent Cortes.

4

While the Cortes were remaking the political structure of Spain, the French armies, taxed by the constant harassment of the guerrillas, slowly lost their momentum. By 1812, the British and Spanish forces began to liberate conquered territory. In August Wellesley reached Madrid. Although Joseph Bonaparte soon reentered the capital, his success was brief. In 1813 Napoleon called his best troops in Spain to central Europe to salvage his position after his disastrous invasion of Russia, leaving Joseph defenseless against his enemies. Wellesley routed the French at Vitoria on June 21, 1813. Joseph fled to France, and the remaining French forces rapidly evacuated Spain.

The end of military operations did not bring calm to the war-torn country, racked now by the political conflict between Liberals and Serviles. The outcome rested on the position Ferdinand would take on his return. Ferdinand had spent his time in captivity writing sycophantic letters to Napoleon, but Spaniards knew nothing of this and still idolized him as their innocent young king, betrayed by the monstrous French tyrant. In December 1813, Napoleon got Ferdinand to sign a treaty of alliance against the British and sent him back to Spain shortly thereafter.

Ferdinand proved disloyal both to Napoleon and to the Cortes which had ruled in his absence. Once on Spanish soil he gave ready ear to Servile spokesmen who came to meet him. Ignoring instructions of the Cortes to come at once to Madrid, he went to Valencia, where he soon found army commanders who favored the overthrow of the Liberals. With assurance of their support, on May 4, 1814 he declared the original convocation of the Cortes illegal and all their legislation null and void. Spain would return to the status quo before the French attack. In Madrid Liberal deputies, caught by surprise, sought popular support, but only a few small disturbances protested the king's decree. Spaniards welcomed the return of Ferdinand as joyously as they had his accession six years earlier. Few questioned the motives of their beloved king. The Constitution of 1812 disappeared, local ruling groups resumed their authority, and the Inquisition hunted out Liberals and Jansenists. Some Liberals fled, but many were arrested, and their leaders, including Argüelles, went to prison in the garrisons of Africa.

It was twenty-five years since the death of Charles III. In one generation the nature of political authority had changed irrevocably. Before 1789 the figure of the monarch transcended internal divisions.

With the advice of his councilors, he determined the objectives of government and acted as ultimate arbiter for conflicting interests. After 1814 the king could no longer play such a role. The ministry of Godoy, replete with disasters for which he was only partly to blame, and the reputation of Charles IV as an ineffectual cuckold, discredited the crown. The French Revolution meanwhile revealed a new kind of political life, where sovereign citizens organized in parties around different political doctrines struggled for ultimate control of the country. The removal of the king from Spain in 1808 left Spaniards in a position similar to that of Frenchmen after 1789, lacking a supreme ruler. When the Cortes met at Cadiz and decided to write a constitution, they claimed to be returning Spain to medieval practices, and they doubtless were sincere, for they did not blindly imitate foreign examples. But they could not hide the fact that a written constitution which said "Sovereignty resides essentially in the nation" [2] was the symbol of a new age. Ferdinand on his return could abolish the constitution, but he could not erase the memory of these years from Spanish minds.

Into this new political bottle, the debates of Cadiz poured the old wine of eighteenth-century issues. The Liberals pushed the policies of the Bourbon kings toward their logical conclusion: uniform centralized government, destruction of local oligarchies, distribution of church properties to private owners, freedom of expression from religious authority in nonreligious matters. But the Cortes lacked the aura of royal majesty, and the Liberal constitution became a partisan program, not a national creed. Those who felt threatened, including in the end the king, denied the legitimacy of the new order. Taking the lead were clergymen, who stood to lose both income and moral authority. Thus the constitutional question came to center on the incipient ideological conflict of Charles III's day. Political and religious issues had become inseparable. Although they were loyal Catholics, Liberals saw the conservative clergy as their main enemy; while conservatives felt they were fighting antireligious doctrines imported from France.

Beloved on all sides, Ferdinand might have acted impartially and become a constitutional monarch. But he was a mean, short-sighted man, and on his return he treated the Liberals as traitors. Like most European rulers after 1815, he believed he was reestablishing royal absolutism, but that was dead beyond recall. He was only giving the crown a partisan role in the new political life, hardly different from other interest groups. Spain was entering a period of bitter civil conflict as it sought to adjust to the era of popular sovereignty that began for Europe in 1789.

[2] Article 3 of the Constitution of 1812.

6

The Search for a New Order

1

After Waterloo most legitimate rulers returned to their absolute, hereditary thrones. They sought to recover the orderly, tranquil structure they believed had existed before 1789, recognizing only where necessary the irreversible changes that had taken place in frontiers and legal institutions. As in Spain they relied heavily on their churches to oppose radical ideologies and revolutionary activities, the alliance of "the throne and the altar." Under the impetus of Alexander I of Russia most monarchs joined the Holy Alliance aimed at preserving the status quo. Louis XVIII, brother of the guillotined Louis XVI, who returned to France behind the victorious allied armies, was almost alone in attempting to establish a moderate monarchy. He granted his people a charter that provided for a two-house legislature with a chamber of deputies elected by a restricted property franchise. In such an atmosphere defeated partisans of the Revolution were driven throughout Europe to plot secretly to upset the conservative restoration.

Ferdinand VII's quashing of the Constitution of 1812 left politically concerned Spaniards divided between the partisans of absolutism and constitutionalism, both sides now believing that they might be justified in using extralegal means. This was not the only serious problem facing the country. After the revolutionary and Napoleonic wars it was exhausted economically as well as emotionally. Requisitions and plunder by opposing armies had laid waste both its agricultural and industrial resources. Stimulated by the wartime disappearance of civil authority, banditry and smuggling became a plague in the next decades. Most harmful was the disruption of the colonial empire, for the eighteenth-century economic expansion had rested largely on trade with the American colonies. After 1796, the British navy made such trade sporadic at best, and during the Napoleonic war, the French occupation of the manufacturing north and east cut them off from America. Peace might have brought recovery, except that the colonies were in revolt. They too had reacted to the collapse of legitimate government by setting up local juntas. Although the juntas remained nominally loyal to Ferdinand VII, their supporters disliked the unification with Spain imposed by the Constitution of 1812, partly because they felt it did not give the former colonies adequate representation in the Cortes. After the restoration of Ferdinand, some areas remained in revolt. The king sent armies to quell these rebellions, which spread rapidly after 1816 when Argentina declared its independence. As a result America now represented a drain on Spain rather than a resource. Not until after 1824, when the Creole armies dealt a final blow to Spanish hopes of recovering the colonies on the American mainland, was Spain freed from the millstone. The empire was reduced to Cuba, Puerto Rico, and the Philippine Islands, but in the next decades these proved to be valuable sources of income. Economic signs indicate that Spanish industry began to revive shortly thereafter, about 1827. However, civil war in the 1830's slowed the recovery, and prosperity did not return until the mid-1840's. Until then, Spain faced the task of adjusting to a vastly inferior economic and international position. In such a situation it was unlikely that any regime, whatever its merits, could win an enthusiastic following, but no government of real merit appeared.

When Ferdinand VII overthrew the constitution in May 1814, he promised to call legitimate cortes in the near future, and he talked of reinstating freedom of the press. He never carried out these promises. Instead he built his regime on the privileged groups that the juntas of 1808–1809 had represented: primarily the church and the landowing oligarchy. He also sought the support of the state creditors, reaffirming the guarantee of the *vales reales*. When the Pope reestablished the Jesuits in 1814, Ferdinand welcomed them in Spain. The Inquisition, brought back to life, hunted out the recent writings of Liberals and Jansenists, in 1817 prohibiting a list of four hundred publications of the war period. It tracked down the Spaniards who had joined Joseph Bonaparte's Masonic lodges and those who had been too vocal in support of the Cortes of Cadiz. But when the monasteries and churches in 1817 requested the return of their lands sold under Charles IV, Ferdinand refused to upset the new distribution of property, saying the sales had been legal. The purchasers of these properties were now part of the established order and belonged with those on whom the king rested his power.

2

Ferdinand's attempt to revive the old regime lasted less than six years. From the outset leading army officers of the war against Napoleon opposed the restoration, and various of them conspired unsuccessfully to restore the constitution. Working with them were members of Masonic lodges which had secretly remained in existence, offering centers for liberal plotting. On January 1, 1820 Major Rafael Riego, who commanded part of an army being staged near Cadiz for transport to the colonial wars, brought out his men in favor of the Constitution of 1812. Riego's *pronunciamiento*, as military coups such as this came to be known, found support among other garrisons of the peninsula. Finding no one ready to fight for him, Ferdinand accepted the constitution in March, and Spain had experienced its first successful revolution. Liberal juntas sprang up in various cities to take over local government, on the pattern of 1808, until the Cortes met in July.

The Liberals virtually monopolized the new Cortes. They proceeded at once to attack the old order, putting into legislation the old enlightened and Jansenistic objectives. They expelled the Jesuits and again abolished the Inquisition. They ended *señoríos*, as in 1811, and now also the *mayorazgos*, the entail of properties of the aristocrats. Finally they put up church lands for sale to pay off the national debt. This move was aimed to win confidence among governments abroad as well as domestic bondholders. Now of vast proportions because of the nearly continuous wars since 1793, the national debt had become a diplomatic issue, for much was owed to citizens of Britain and other countries.

The parliamentary monarchy lasted only three years. Again the Liberals failed to win general acceptance for constitutional government, and the king behind their backs found the means to overthrow them. The ease of their triumph blinded the Liberals to the dangers they faced. Almost at once they split into two groups which embodied different generations and political philosophies. On one side were those who had been active at the time of the Cortes of Cadiz, called *doceañistas* ("men of the year '12") or, soon, Moderados. These men, although representing the authors of the constitution, had been disillusioned by the failure of the common people to rally to it in 1814 and were beginning to look for restraints on absolute popular sovereignty, such as England and France found in limited suffrage and an upper house to the legislature. Their leader was the Romantic playwright Francisco Martínez de la Rosa. On the other side were younger men, followers of Riego and army officers, who took credit for the successful revolution of 1820. They were labeled Exaltados or extremists and believed in the democratic popular suffrage represented by the constitution. The Exaltados appealed to the urban lower classes by defending the abolition of the *consumos* or taxes on prime necessities, which the juntas had ended after the revolution and the Moderados sought to restore. Much of their strength was in provincial cities, where the radicals were becoming stronger than in Madrid. Control of these cities put them in a good position to influence the composition of the Cortes, for the constitution provided for locally chosen electors to gather in the capitals of the provinces to choose the deputies to the Cortes. The Exaltados and Moderados fell out not only in the Cortes but in the Masonic lodges that had grouped together the Liberals before the revolution and were now multiplying wildly. The Exaltados broke off to form a society known as the Comuneros, after the Castilian rebels of 1520.

The division became critical in 1822. In the biennial elections the Exaltados won a majority in the Cortes. Ferdinand chose to disregard their victory and named a ministry under Martínez de la Rosa, thus raising the issue, important in nineteenth-century European parliamentary evolution, of whether ministers were the servants of the majority in the legislature or of the king. The Moderados were prepared to let the ministry be responsible to the king, denying thereby the full sovereignty of the people. Furthermore, they wanted to revise the constitution to set up an upper house in the Cortes. The Exaltados defended the unicameral Cortes with supreme authority.

Events were not to allow the two parties to solve their differences. During these years the defenders of the established order had been seeking means to overturn the constitution. The clergy, especially the monks, saw their position threatened by the Liberal program, and they appealed to the common people. Rebel juntas raised guerrilla forces in the rural areas of the north, and a royalist regency was established near the Pyrenees, on the assumption that Ferdinand was not a free ruler. Meanwhile the king secretly negotiated with the powers of the Holy Alliance for help. Portugal and various Italian states had followed Spain with revolutions of their own in 1820, and the conservative rulers of Europe were eager to stamp out the new source of subversive doctrines. On their side, the Cortes could count on some loyal army commanders and the National Militia, which the constitution had established in each province and now served to put down local anticonstitutional movements. Here and there the army and militia shot reactionary priests and monks. Blood had now been shed in the constitutional struggle. Spain was rapidly degenerating into civil war when in April 1823 Louis XVIII of France, with encouragement from the rulers of Russia and Austria, sent an army across the Pyrenees to restore the absolute authority of Ferdinand. Organized Liberal resistance melted before these "Hundred Thousand Sons of

Saint Louis." They chased the Cortes to Cadiz and there forced them to surrender and free the king, on September 30.

These three Liberal years revealed more clearly than the Napoleonic period the disappearance of a commonly accepted authority. Distinct groups had reached the conclusion that they alone represented the true will of the nation, and that to establish this will they had the right not only to appeal to the king and to the public, but to intrigue, and if necessary to resort to force. Riego's *pronunciamiento* signified that army officers were assuming the obligation to modify the civil government if, in their eyes, it should become unworthy of governing. Similarly, the rising of the absolutists against the Cortes indicated that those tied to the old order, especially those who acted as spokesmen for a wounded church, would not rely on the vagaries of popular elections, where in the long run they could probably have controlled the majority, but felt justified also in taking up arms. Without a consensus on the nature of authority there could be no loyal opposition. Finally, foreign intervention revealed that Spain's divisions were depriving it of international respect. The nation that had withstood Napoleon was becoming the plaything of European politics, like the small Italian states.

3

This time Ferdinand took violent vengeance on those Liberal leaders who did not escape across the border, imprisoning and executing without mercy. He nullified the legislation passed since 1820, including the abolition of *mayorazgos* and *señoríos* and the sale of church lands. Only the opposition of the French commander prevented him from reviving the Inquisition. In Paris and London refugees kept alive Spanish liberalism, in contact with their foreign counterparts; but within the Spanish church the spirit of Jansenism, which had been active in 1820 as in 1812, was effectively stamped out. The ideological conflict nascent under Charles III and Charles IV had engulfed the nation, but within the clergy, which had first felt its ravages, the conservatives had at last succeeded in silencing the reformers.

Despite his severity, after 1823 Ferdinand was unable to satisfy the reactionaries. They were unhappy over his failure to revive the Inquisition and to incorporate the insurgents who had fought the Cortes into the regular army. Led by clergy and royalist guerrillas of 1823, these *opostólicos* began to group around Ferdinand's brother Carlos, who, since the king was childless, was heir to the throne. In 1827 Ferdinand crushed an *apostólico* revolt in the hills of Catalonia.

Besides this threat from the absolutists, the regime was faced with a desperate financial situation, due to the expenses of strife at home and in America and the depression of the economy. Ferdinand had little alternative but to seek support among the mercantile interests of the north and east. To attract them, his ministers began to consider liberal reforms, and he even made contact with exiled Moderados. In October 1830 Ferdinand's fourth wife, his young niece María Cristina of Naples, gave him his first child to survive, a daughter christened Isabel. During the queen's pregnancy, the partisans of Don Carlos, anticipating the possibility of a female heir, pointed out with satisfaction that a law promulgated by Philip V at the time of the Treaty of Utrecht prohibited women from inheriting the throne. Ferdinand's ministers discovered, however, that Charles IV and the Cortes of Castile in 1789 had secretly abrogated the law. Ferdinand published the act of 1789 before the birth of Isabel, but Don Carlos denied its validity.

Another event of 1830 darkened the hopes of the Carlists, as the absolutists were now called. In July, a revolution in France overthrew Charles X, who had tried to disregard the charter of 1814. In place of the Bourbons, the revolution gave the throne to Louis Philippe of Orléans, who sided with those desirous of an effective constitutional monarchy. Louis Philippe's accession disrupted the Holy Alliance. Spain's absolutists could no longer expect help from the rulers of France.

4

Ferdinand died in September 1833. His will appointed María Cristina regent for their daughter Isabel II (1833–68). Don Carlos, who had fled to Portugal, refused to recognize the king's final dispositions. His partisans proclaimed him Charles V and raised his standard in the north, where the pretender soon appeared to lead his forces. Domestic dissension had at last brought Spain to open civil war. The Carlists claimed a scrupulous concern for the legality of the succession, but they had stronger motives. Most ardent Carlists were firm Catholics who feared for the safety of the church's authority and property. Clergy were prominent among them, and the Pope sanctioned their cause by refusing to recognize Isabel II. Although Carlist sympathizers could be found throughout Spain, their strength lay in the rural areas bordering the Pyrenees: the Basque lands, Navarre, and upper Catalonia. The Basques and Navarrese were apprehensive of the loss of the medieval *fueros* of their territories, which eighteenth-century Bourbon centralization had spared but the Constitution of 1812 abolished. But more than the periphery's distrust of Castile, Carlism represented an ingrained fear of the cities and modern ideas among the well-off peasants of the north, where independent small landowners dominated the countryside. The industrial and mercantile cities of these areas remained loyal to Isabel: Barcelona, Bilbao, San Sebastián. A rural reaction against urban political and cultural progress appeared in the guise of religiosity and regionalism.

The Carlist War lasted seven years. It was pursued bitterly in the north and northeast, not with major engagements but with a series of skirmishes and futile Carlist sieges of the Liberal cities. To maintain order elsewhere, María Cristina's government in 1834 established an Urban Militia, similar to the National Militia of 1820. Although only those men who paid a certain level of taxes could enroll, the Urban Militia attracted politically committed residents of the cities like artisans and small shopkeepers, who tended to be radical in their outlook. Neither side gave quarter in the war, and both committed acts of savagery that shocked Europe. In 1837 a Carlist column got within sight of Madrid but did not attempt to attack it. The Carlists could hold out in the mountains, but they had no hope of conquering Spain without foreign support. In 1834, however, France and Britain signed an alliance with the government of Isabel, and the Carlists were diplomatically isolated. In Spain as in the rest of Western Europe, absolutism had become the romantic creed of a minority, able to disrupt national life but no longer able to take power.

During the war, the partisans of the regent María Cristina and young Isabel II sought a viable form of liberal monarchy to which they could rally all Spain. In 1834, under the advice of the Moderado leader Martínez de la Rosa, whom she had made first minister, María Cristina promulgated an *Estatuto Real* (Royal Statute) patterned on the French Charter of 1814. It provided for cortes but justified them by citing the ancient laws of Spain, thus avoiding the thorny problem of whether sovereignty belonged to the king or the people. It established a two-house Cortes: an Estate of Notables (*Próceres*) consisting of all bishops, archbishops, and grandees, and other leading Spaniards appointed by the crown; and an Estate of Procurators elected by a small proportion of citizens who paid a stipulated property tax. The Cortes voted taxes but could not initiate legislation without royal approval.

The Estatuto was María Cristina's concession to win Liberal support against the Carlists. It was a statement of classical nineteenth-century liberalism, which the Moderados had come to represent. It embodied the desire to limit royal absolutism through a parliament representative of the responsible elements of society, while at the same time providing by limited suffrage against the threat of rule by the uneducated, irresponsible masses, whom the Moderados believed too easily swayed by fanatical monks or raving radicals. The Estatuto did not recognize popular sovereignty, for moderate liberalism was not democracy. As in France and England, it might satisfy the established classes, but radicals could not accept it. In Spain these were the Exaltados, who remained loyal to the Constitution of 1812. Once again their strength lay in provincial cities, where they gained control of the Urban Militia and hunted out suspect Carlists with zeal.

The question of the church was as vexed as the constitutional one. Since many clergy were Carlists, the church became an easy target for Liberals, who could blame the ills of the country on the secret machinations of men in black. In July 1834 an outbreak of cholera was killing hundreds of persons daily in Madrid. When rumors spread that monks were poisoning the wells to produce the epidemic, an angry crowd of common people led by members of the Urban Militia set upon and killed a suspect Jesuit and went on to attack several monasteries. An orgy of violence and murder ensued that left some seventy regular clergymen dead. The next summer similar riots in Barcelona, Zaragoza, and other cities killed more monks and friars. Surprisingly, priests were not harmed. Even radical Spaniards had not turned against their religion, only against the monastic orders, who they believed were fighting the will of the nation in order to preserve their privileged positions. Antimonasticism, limited in 1812 to advanced literate Spaniards, had been spread by the appeals of the Exaltados to the lower class of the cities.

The monastic orders suffered more permanently at the hands of the Liberal government. Martínez de la Rosa resigned in June 1835, discredited by the continuing war. A few months later María Cristina named as first minister Juan Álvarez Mendizábal, a liberal financier of Jewish origins from Cadiz, who had been a refugee in London since 1823. Having made a fortune in England, he had a reputation as a financial wizard. His task was to defeat the Carlists and at the same time conjure away the royal deficit, which was as always threatening disaster. His ideas were hardly new, however, except in the magnificence of their scope. In October 1835 he passed through the Cortes a decree which closed all male and female religious orders except several minor ones dedicated to charitable works. The orders were easy scapegoats for the ills of the country, and in truth the number of monks and nuns had been declining for a long time. When Mendizábal failed to raise a loan in London to carry on the war, he put up for sale the property of the extinct orders to pay the national debt, and he proposed to sell all secular church property as well, thereby winning the lasting reputation among good Catholics as the archenemy of the church. To complete the restructuring of land ownership, the Cortes in 1836 abolished *señoríos* and *mayorazgos,* this time for good. Aristocrats lost the income from *señoríos,* but they kept their lands, which as has been noted were extensive in New Castile and Andalusia. Without the entail of a *mayorazgo,* a spendthrift heir was free to dissipate the family estate, but in fact few aristocrats were so unwise. The following year the Cortes also abolished the tithe, the main financial support of the secular clergy.

As in the days of Godoy, the hope was not only to bring solvency to the state but to build a body of small property owners who would be loyal to the new regime. The two aims were incompatible. Sales of church properties at auction were designed to obtain the maximum profit for the treasury, but they put the properties in the hands of the richest bidders. Although it took some time to implement the law, after 1840 ecclesiastical properties were auctioned off rapidly. Monastery buildings as well as lands were put on the block, with the result that some of Spain's finest architectural treasures fell into the hands of men who cared little for their artistic value and tore them down or used them as factories or farm buildings. Many were lost permanently; others were recovered by the monastic orders or the state in the late nineteenth and twentieth centuries, often sadly spoiled.

For some time the Exaltados, who were now becoming known as the Progresistas, had instigated uprisings in the provincial cities against Moderado rule and the Estatuto Real. To their dismay, María Cristina dismissed Mendizábal in May 1836. In August military men of their persuasion inspired the sergeants of the queen's guard to present María Cristina with an ultimatum. Caught by surprise in her summer palace at La Granja, she was forced to convoke constituent cortes, elected under universal suffrage according to the Constitution of 1812. These Cortes produced a new constitution in 1837, which offered a reasonable compromise between that of 1812 and the Moderados' Estatuto. The leading figure in drawing it up was Agustín Argüelles, who had been the principal author of the Constitution of 1812. The Cortes remained a bicameral legislature. There was not universal suffrage, but the lower house, called the Congress of Deputies, was to be elected directly by a wider franchise than that of 1834. The upper house or Senate consisted of men appointed by the monarch from lists proposed by the voters in each province. The constitution reestablished the National Militia and municipal self-government. So well worked out was the compromise document that Moderados as well as Progresistas accepted it, and a Moderado government ruled under it from 1837 to 1840.

By 1839 the Carlists, discouraged, had become divided among themselves. Those who were fighting for their local privileges turned against the partisans of a theocratic society. Baldomero Espartero, the leading Isabeline general, mounted an offensive that forced the Carlist commander to sign an armistice at Vergara on August 29. With Don Carlos in flight across the Pyrenees, the Carlists recognized Isabel II as their queen. In return Espartero promised a guarantee of the Basque and Navarrese *fueros*.

The Carlists had abandoned the church in order to obtain their political objectives. The Liberals had closed most monastic orders and taken their property, and they had abolished the tithe on which priests relied for their livelihood. The laws promised pensions to the former monks and nuns, but these were seldom paid, while priests had no assured income. The Pope had broken relations with Isabel, and half the sees in Spain lacked bishops as a result. Far from holding the nation in its powerful grip, as radical anticlericals accused it of doing, the church had become the prime victim of the advent of constitutional government.

With the Peace of Vergara, Spain seemed to have lived through the prolonged birth pangs of parliamentary government. It was the only major country on the continent besides France to have established a tradition of constitutional rule. The partisans of absolutism had surrendered, and the two Liberal factions had made up their differences behind a constitution that provided for parliamentary supremacy over both the crown and the clerical and radical extremists who appealed to the masses. The end of the Carlist War meant a lower budget and a chance to reestablish the royal finances. The government could attack the swarms of bandits and smugglers that hampered legitimate trade. Everything seemed to promise political peace and economic recovery.

Such hopes were at best precarious, however, for passions still ran high. Spaniards needed to recover a sense of loyalty to some symbol, such as the king had been before 1789, so that cooperation within an established framework would replace conflict and intransigence. Could the young Isabel or the Constitution of 1837 provide the needed symbol?

7

The Entrenchment of the New Oligarchy

1

They were not able to. The stresses in Spanish society were too strong for a compromise constitution to achieve a national consensus, and Isabel did not become a queen who drew her people round her. Eventually parliamentary monarchy became stable, but only when it had associated political authority with social power. The leaders who matured under Ferdinand VII and the Carlist War would have to give way to a new generation, more practical, more cynical, who would not let ideology interfere with peace and profits.

Except for the Carlist dissidents on the right and extreme radicals on the left, in the future the active forces of the nation would seek to achieve objectives by obtaining a satisfactory parliamentary constitution, even if at times this meant establishing a new constitution by force. Until 1923 Spain would never be without a written constitution and cortes. After 1840 the two parliamentary parties that had taken shape in the 1830's, the Moderados and Progresistas, who were both originally heirs of the Liberal cause of 1812, expanded their appeal to attract forces which had not been constitutionalist before, changing their own nature in the process. The Moderados became the party of the upper classes, the Progresistas of the more radical urban middle and lower-middle classes. As the century advanced other parties appeared with other constituencies. The social conflicts of Spain thus became expressed in political divisions.

Ambitious leaders appeared to take command of the parties. It was not pure coincidence that many of them were generals. Since the war against Napoleon, the army had participated in political conflicts.

In the reign of Ferdinand VII, most generals, brought up under the absolute monarchy, did not see themselves as political leaders. The *pronunciamiento* of Riego, a young officer, does not disprove the generalization. Under the turbulent minority of Isabel II, the ease with which María Cristina dismissed civilian leaders like Martínez de la Rosa and Mendizábal and the critical role of the army in defeating the Carlists convinced a new generation of generals that they were the best qualified persons to settle the ills of the country. Conversely, since force had proved the ultimate arbiter of the dynastic conflict, civilian politicians looked naturally for allies among the generals. The result was that for the next three decades, political parties usually had military leaders at their head. This did not mean that Spain had become the plaything of the army or that parliamentary government had ceased to exist. It meant that generals made better political leaders than most men. They could capture the popular imagination. In the reign of a young queen, they could embody masculine force and command respect. But the issues were between political parties based on different social groups, not between army and society. The army was not monolithic. Almost every shade of opinion found a general to turn to who could rally some troops to its side.

The new political structure of Spain took shape in the decade after the Carlist War. The first sign of this development came immediately after the Peace of Vergara. When the electoral system of 1837 established direct elections for candidates to the Cortes, it provided for entire provinces to vote for slates of candidates instead of for smaller districts with a single representative from each. The system thus enabled the provincial capitals to exercise a strong influence on the elections in their provinces. The Constitution of 1837 also provided for the qualified voters to elect the *ayuntamientos* or municipal councils, in line with the tradition of 1812. By 1840 the provincial capitals and major cities had set a pattern of electing Progresista *ayuntamientos*. Feeling their control over the Cortes threatened, in 1840 the Moderado majority passed a law, patently opposed to the spirit of the constitution, giving the crown authority to appoint the *alcaldes* in all provincial capitals, and giving the provincial *jefes políticos* (civil governors), the local deputies of the central government, authority to name the *alcaldes* of all other municipalities of more than five hundred population. By this law the Moderados planned to nullify the power of locally elected municipal councils. It made the question of centralized administration versus local self-government a political issue dividing them from the Progresistas. The issue was to remain one of the thorniest problems of Spanish political life.

The queen regent gave the measure her approval, for she had come to sympathize openly with the Moderados. They had answered Ferdinand VII's appeal against Don Carlos, and they had enacted the Estatuto Real, which gave the crown authority over legislation. María Cristina could not forget that the Progresistas had inspired the guards' rising of 1836 which forced her to accept a new constitution. She had other, more personal reasons for liking the Moderados. An impulsive and attractive young woman, within three months of Ferdinand's death she married a handsome guardsman, Fernando Muñoz. She kept the marriage secret, since it violated the terms of her regency, but she could not hide her pregnancies. By 1840 she had borne Muñoz four children. Carlists and Progresistas both whipped up the scandal, angering the regent, while Muñoz became closely allied with Moderado leaders. In giving her assent to the law on *ayuntamientos* in 1840, María Cristina let her passions outweigh her political wisdom.

First in Barcelona, where María Cristina was staying, then Madrid and other provincial capitals, popular uprisings encouraged by the National Militia and the Progresista *ayuntamientos* protested the law and established local governing juntas. The Progresistas found a champion in the victorious general of the recent war, Baldomero Espartero, the successful son of a muleteer of the Mancha, a rough and ready man of the people, reminiscent of Andrew Jackson. Since Espartero appeared to be the only person who could pacify the cities, the queen regent named him first minister. Thereupon she informed him of her resignation as regent. Despite a tearful protest on his part, she sailed for France on October 17, 1840, taking Muñoz with her but leaving Isabel behind. Many Moderado leaders followed her into exile.

Elections for new cortes produced a Progresista majority that named Espartero regent in her place. Espartero was a vain man, and new to the art of politics. He proved less astute as regent than as a general. He was unable to cooperate with the Cortes and repeatedly called for new elections at the first sign of opposition. Seeking the diplomatic support of Great Britain because Louis Philippe of France befriended María Cristina and the Moderados, he agreed to a tariff that opened Spain to English cotton cloth, thereby threatening the cotton industry of Catalonia, which was at last recovering from its collapse at the beginning of the century. In Barcelona, opposition to the new tariff brought on a serious rising in November 1842, involving the National Militia and industrial workers. Espartero ordered the army to bombard the city into submission, apparently forgetting that Progresista strength lay in the cities. The effect of this act was to turn Catalonia against Espartero and split the Progresista party.

The Moderado leaders in exile meanwhile were reorienting their party to attract conservatives who had been opposed to both Liberal parties in the 1830's. They found willing ears among the moderate Carlists, uncommitted military men, and most important of all, conservative clergymen. The Moderados, under the guidance of the aging Martínez de la Rosa and two young Catholic writers, Juan Francisco Donoso Cortés and Jaime Balmes, came to favor granting official recognition of the role of the church in Spanish society in order to end the conflict between constitutionalism and religion. While the Moderados had no desire to undo the sale of church properties carried out under Mendizábal's law of 1836, they felt the process had gone far enough and unsold properties should be returned. Papal recognition of the past sales, and of Isabel as queen of Spain, became major objectives. Since Espartero reactivated the sale of church lands, Catholic leaders who had hated the Liberals now grasped the hand proffered by the Moderados.

Meanwhile middle-class merchants and manufacturers were reacting against the repeated Progresista demonstrations that had shaken the cities since the death of Ferdinand. They began to fear lower-class violence. There had been the assault on monks in 1834 and 1835. Since the 1820's Barcelona had witnessed growing labor unrest, directed at the mechanization of the textile industry. In 1839 the Cortes permitted organization of worker's mutual aid societies, and next year a Mutual Association of Workers of the Cotton Industry was established in Barcelona. Illegal groups also existed. The rising of Barcelona in 1842 saw republican and socialist groups active for the first time in Spain, directed by craftsmen. Many maunfacturers began to look for a stronger, more conservative government, and they too turned to the Moderados.

The Moderados also cultivated a number of generals who had gone into exile out of opposition to Espartero. Most prominent was Ramón María Narváez, who had rivaled Espartero for command of the Isabelline armies during the Carlist War. The generals provided the immediate means for the Moderados to return to power. When Espartero dismissed newly elected Cortes in 1843 because the majority opposed his policies, army units rose in the name of the constitution. Landing in Valencia, Narváez gave unity to the rising. Espartero, deserted by the army, fled via Cadiz to England, and Madrid fell to Narváez after a weak defense by its militia.

To facilitate Moderado rule and prevent the reappearance of a strong regent, the Cortes declared Isabel II to be of age in 1843, capable of ruling in her own right. She was only thirteen, but already had a well-developed adolescent figure which foretold her later womanly sensuality. The Moderados also permitted María Cristina to return to Spain. No longer restrained by her position as regent, she now lived openly with her husband, Fernando Muñoz, to whom his stepdaughter granted a suitable title. The mores of the palace were becoming a political question, as they had been in the time of Godoy.

The Moderados rapidly established firm control over the country. Narváez became first minister in 1844. A harsh, despotic soldier, he ruled Spain with a firm hand until 1851. Both Progresistas and die-hard Carlists conducted half-hearted risings against him, but he put them down brutally, not flinching at frequent executions. When revolutions shook Europe in 1848, he squelched minor revolts in Madrid, and the country remained calm.

The Moderados used their power to create a new order, modifying or eliminating the institutions which provided support for the Progresistas. They reenacted the law of 1840 on *ayuntamientos*. They were not doctrinaire, however. Espartero, as punishment for an uprising in the Basque Provinces and Navarre, had abolished the local *fueros*. The Moderados now drew the Basques and Navarrese to their side by restoring the *fueros*, although they provided self-government inconsistent with the administrative centralization of the *ayuntamiento* law. The Moderados disbanded the National Militia, which though theoretically the defender of constitutional government had become the major support of the Progresista juntas that sprang up in every crisis. In its place, in 1844 they created a new armed police force, the Civil Guard, whose first task was to prevent political subversion. It also fought banditry, making rural Spain safe for travel and commerce. Later, when peasant revolts occurred, the Civil Guard put them down. Gradually it became a typical institution of modern Spain, well disciplined, humorless, cruel, and loyal to its superiors. The Civil Guard came to personify the law, the state, and the ruling classes throughout the small towns and countryside of Spain.

Although until 1840 the Moderados had worked happily under the Constitution of 1837, and overthrew Espartero in its name, the Moderado leaders now found it dangerously democratic. In 1845 an act of the Cortes reformed it sharply. The Constitution of 1845 revealed the new Moderado thinking. It strengthened the crown, and through it the ministry. The monarch appointed the senators for life from among grandees, bishops, generals, and other specified groups. A property qualification was established for members of the Congress of Deputies, and the constitution dropped the provision for automatic meeting of the Cortes if the king failed to convoke them annually.

In order for constitutional monarchy to give effective control to one group it was not enough to strengthen the executive, to have the support of the army, to hold down the common people with the Civil Guard, and to weaken the Progresistas by appointing the *alcaldes*. In the end elections must be controlled too. A subsequent electoral law provided for deputies to be elected by individual constituencies, not by provinces as a whole, thus eliminating the dangerous influence of provincial capitals over the voters in the small towns and cities. It also doubled the tax qualification for the suffrage from 200 reales in direct taxes to 400 reales, or 200 for men belonging to certain professions. In the future only about 12 percent of the adult males could vote.[1]

The Moderados had for some time realized the need, in addition to modifying the formal electoral structure, to plan for election victories. In the late 1830's they had formed a committee to select candidates and campaign for their elections. Under Narváez the corruption of elections became a regular practice, through bribery and falsification of returns, facilitated by the small electoral districts with few voters, easily known and influenced. In 1847 the Moderados elected their entire slate throughout the country. Gradually supervision of elections became a fine art, with the minister of *gobernación* (interior) as the main manipulator. Once the Moderados, or any other party in power, gained control of the electoral machinery, the only hope for a change of government became revolt. Furthermore, since the governing party often had a general at its head, the possibility of revolt had to rest on winning the prior support of army officers willing to break discipline and lead their men against the government. The system of manipulated parliamentary monarchy had as a corollary the necessity of the *pronunciamiento* as a form of political action.

2

The Moderados remained in power without interruption until 1854. Under them a new social and political ruling class came to the fore. It included those sectors of the old privileged groups which had successfully survived the Liberal onslaught of the first decades of the century. Beside them appeared new classes produced by contemporary economic and political developments.

One of the new provisions of the Constitution of 1845 declared, "the religion of the Spanish nation is the Roman Catholic Apostolic religion," [2] a statement that the Constitution of 1837 had avoided although it promised to support the ministers of the Catholic faith. The article embodied the Moderado determination to reestablish the alliance of church and state. Prolonged negotiations with Rome followed, helped by Narváez's astute move of sending troops to fight the revolutionary Roman Republic in 1848. In 1851 Pope Pius IX and the government of Isabel II signed a concordat, restoring the peace between the Spanish monarchy and the papacy that the accession of Isabel had

[1] In 1865 there were 481,271 qualified voters. In 1868 under universal male suffrage (men over 25) approximately 3,990,000 could vote. See Miguel M. Cuadrado, "La elección general para Cortes Constituyentes de 1869," *Revista de Estudios Políticos*, No. 132 (Madrid: Instituto de Estudios Políticos, 1963), pp. 65–93.

[2] Article 11.

broken. In the concordat the church recognized the sale of its properties; in return it received the right to acquire unlimited property in the future. Three religious orders would be supported by the Spanish government; two were specified, the third was to be named later. The concordat guaranteed that no other religion would be tolerated in Spain, and bishops were authorized to see that public and private education at all levels conform to Catholic doctrine.

The Concordat of 1851 was a momentous accomplishment. With it the wheel had made a full turn. Like enlightened despotism of the eighteenth century, the constitutionalism of 1812 attacked the authority of entrenched groups, notably the aristocratic landowners and the conservative clergy. Abolition of the Inquisition turned the latter into the bitterest enemies of constitutional rule. Liberals responded later by abolishing the religious orders and selling the church's properties. By 1840 they had stripped the church of much of its wealth and authority. Now, desirous of reestablishing peace and order, the Moderados tended to agree with the bishop of Barcelona, "Religion is the only guarantee of order." [3] The concordat reconciled the church and the constitutional monarchy, but the Moderados had not brought a cowed church to heel. On the contrary the concordat conceded a prerogative that both Charles III and the early Liberals had attacked, control over education. In addition, at a time when Western Europe was accepting religious tolerance, the Moderados promised to hold back history within Spain by using the authority of the state to prohibit other religions. In church-state relations, the Moderados' order represented a fundamental negation of the original Liberal ideals.

Aristocratic landowners had also felt the lash of the early Liberals. Liberal regimes abolished *señoríos* and *mayorazgos*, the mainstays of the hereditary aristocracy, and they attempted to break its control of municipal governments. But the Liberals did not destroy the oligarchy of landowners, they only succeeded in changing its composition. By auctioning off monastic lands to pay the national debt, a practice begun by Charles IV, they furthered a process of disentail that was to extend through the nineteenth century. Later governments would sell off royal and municipal lands. The process created a class of new landowners, made up of the most venturesome men in commerce and agriculture, as well as speculators, government contractors, and high civil servants, who could bid for land with government notes. These men joined the old aristocratic families in control of the countryside of Andalusia and the central plateau.

Commercial agriculture had grown in the eighteenth century. The new blood gave it new impetus, for recently purchased properties

[3] Quoted in V. G. Kiernan, *The Revolution of 1854 in Spanish History* (Oxford: Clarendon Press, 1966), p. 127.

lacked the sentimental association of the family *mayorazgo*. The buyers were not feudal lords of *señoríos*, they were investors who sought profits. They wanted products they could sell on the market at home and abroad, like wheat, olive oil, wine, ham, and wool. A new tariff in 1825 which effectively kept out foreign cereals helped them by forcing the coastal regions to buy Castilian wheat. The century saw an increase in olive groves in southern Spain, vineyards in most parts of the country, *dehesas* (meadows studded with live oaks which provided acorns to fatten hogs and cattle) in the center and west, and *cortijos* (large estates dedicated to wheat) in Andalusia. In 1836 the liberals finally abolished the Mesta, whose privileges were under attack in the eighteenth century. Sheep raising remained an important activity, however, encouraged by the expanding woolen industry of Catalonia. The central mountain ranges had important flocks, while sheep continued to migrate from north to south in the west.

The persons who gained most by the redistribution of land were tied by interest to the new regime. It was not pure accident that the only rural areas to support the Carlists were in the north and northeast, where small farmers were dominant. It was said that thirty thousand purchasers of monastic lands after 1820 lost money when Ferdinand revoked the sales in 1823. A Carlist victory posed the same threat. The new landowners might be good Catholics, dislike liberal legislation, and sympathize with Don Carlos, but they did not want to lose their acquisitions. After 1840 the Moderados knew how to cater to their wishes. By the concordat they obtained the church's recognition of the property transfer, while the law of *ayuntamientos* undid the main liberal threat to the rural oligarchies. Landowners who cooperated with the regime could get the government to appoint *alcaldes* who defended their interests against local reformers and used the Civil Guard against troublemakers. Like the clergy, the landowners discovered the benefits of the Moderado version of constitutional monarchy.

The long economic slump finally ended after 1840. The middle years of the century were a period of boom and industrial expansion, helped by Narváez's domestic peace. Catalan manufacturers introduced steam power and the latest spinning and weaving machinery. Modern textile factories appeared in Barcelona and the lesser cities of Catalonia, concentrating a growing number of workers in fewer and fewer establishments. In 1847 there were 97,000 workers in cotton factories, in 1860, 125,000. Catalonia made Spain the fourth cotton-manufacturing nation of the world, after Britain, France, and the United States. Iron production also expanded, driven by the demands of the first Spanish railroads. Blast furnaces rose in the Basque lands and at scattered points along the southern coast. Only Valencia, the third industrial area of the eighteenth century, did not join in the expansion. Having lost its American market, the local silk industry did not convert to modern machinery and was unable to meet competition from France. In the future the source of Valencian prosperity would be its agriculture.

Spain built its first railroads under the Moderados, about a decade after the more advanced continental countries. Spain's long depression, its wars, and the amount of private savings that had gone into the purchase of church lands left it short of capital to build railroads. Funds came from abroad, making railroad building subject to the forces of international finance. Only two short lines had been completed before a European depression halted construction in 1847. In the 1850's Europe enjoyed prosperity again. It was the age of the Second French Empire; under Napoleon III the French economy flowered as never before. Largely financed by French capital, the fever of railroad building spread throughout Europe. To obtain authorization for a line in Spain involved an act of cortes, but great rewards were anticipated. Two groups of French bankers, one headed by James de Rothschild, the other by the Pereire brothers, founders of the Crédit Mobilier bank and friends of Napoleon III, fought for the right to build the main Spanish lines, working through Spanish agents who could spread bribes in high quarters. Rothschild joined with the Spanish entrepreneur, José de Salamanca, himself closely associated with the husband of the queen mother, Muñoz. They built the Madrid-Zaragoza-Alicante railroad, which connected Madrid with Lisbon, Seville, Valencia, and Zaragoza. The Pereires obtained the more promising Company of the North, which held the concession from Madrid north to France. Catalan capital built the line from Zaragoza to Barcelona and on to France and Valencia; but a depression in the sixties forced the main Catalan railroad to merge with the Madrid-Zaragoza-Alicante. By 1868 the major trunk lines had been built, some 5000 kilometers radiating out from Madrid like the highways of Charles III, 80 percent of them owned fully or partially by French capital.[4]

Investors discovered in Spanish mines another source of profit. Spain had some of the best mineral deposits in Europe, exploited by backward techniques under royal monopoly. A law of 1839 encouraged private investment in mines, and in the next decades Catalan and foreign capital flowed into iron, zinc, and copper mines. The famous mines of Almadén, which had supplied mercury for the smelting of Mexican silver under the empire, now became a concession of Salamanca and Rothschild. Belgian bankers exploited zinc deposits in Asturias. In 1868 a further law allowed Spanish or foreign companies to obtain perpetual concessions to all Spanish mineral deposits. Thereafter foreign capital entered even faster. British interests obtained the Río Tinto mines in Andalusia, the largest source of copper in Europe, and iron

[4] Rondo E. Cameron, *France and the Economic Development of Europe, 1800–1914* (Princeton: Princeton University Press, 1961), pp. 263–64.

mines in the north. All the major industrial countries had placed money in Spain.

Throughout the Western world, the modern city took shape in the nineteenth century. In Spain enlightened governments of the eighteenth century had driven an occasional avenue through the crabbed and winding labyrinths of the old cities. To permit expansion, municipal governments now tore down medieval city walls and granted permits for new suburbs. Broad new streets in rectangular patterns spread out around the edges of the cities. José de Salamanca developed a suburb northeast of the heart of Madrid, close to the Paseo del Prado, which had been the center of elegant life at the time of Goya. When completed the Barrio (district) of Salamanca became the most aristocratic of the capital, dominating it until the age of Franco. In the 1850's a corporation in which the stock was held in equal parts by the crown, the city of Madrid, and private investors was established to provide water for the city. It built dams in the mountains north of Madrid and the "Canal of Isabel II" to carry the water to the city. After its completion, Madrid boasted the purest and most palatable water in the world. Similar developments took place in Barcelona and other cities. They all offered profits to smart investors.

New financial institutions provided for the needs of this age of expansion. The king gave his approval for a stock market in Madrid in 1831, but it did not become active until the forties and fifties saw waves of speculative investment. Acts of 1848 and 1856 facilitated the founding of corporations based on the public sale of stock. Modern banks made their appearance in Spain. Hitherto the only public bank was the Bank of San Fernando, originally founded by Charles III, closely connected with the state, which issued bank notes and facilitated the transfer of commercial payments. The ubiquitous José de Salamanca was instrumental in founding the Bank of Isabel II in 1844, aimed at raising capital and issuing credit to railroads, industry, and commerce. The economic collapse of 1847 forced it to merge with the Bank of San Fernando, and in 1854 the new institution was officially named the Bank of Spain, the name it still bears. It was in effect a state bank, issuing paper money and extending credit to private banks. It was not allowed to float stock for new corporations; private banks took over this function. First was the Bank of Barcelona founded in 1844, followed by the Bank of Bilbao and the Bank of Santander, both in 1857. Foreign bankers also entered the Spanish market. Rothschild and the Pereires founded subsidiaries in Spain. The Pereires' Crédito Mobiliario Español supervised their railway interests and controlled mining and other concessions as well. All these banking institutions mobilized private capital for investment in railroads and industry. Through the Bank of Barcelona, Catalan wealth, largely obtained from manufacturing, shipping, and trade with Cuba, was siphoned into the construction of railroads and the modernization of cities in all parts of the peninsula. The home of these banks is very revealing, for it shows the origin of the capital that developed Spain: the peripheral manufacturing areas and foreign countries, mainly France. In 1851 almost one third of French capital invested abroad was in Spain—more than in any other country.[5] Foreign entrepreneurs were finding the Iberian peninsula a highly attractive place to invest; their interest in its political developments was bound to grow accordingly.

3

Pedigreed aristocrats and newly arrived landlords, Basque and Catalan manufacturers, urban developers, railroad builders, and exploiters of mines—together these formed the new dominant class of Spain. The Moderados had drawn them into an alliance to hold down the country and exploit it. The Concordat of 1851 brought the church into the alliance. Concessions to foreign capitalists meant that it would have influential friends abroad, especially in France, who could pressure their governments to oppose any threat to the regime. Most Carlists were reconciled, the Progresistas powerless, the lower classes under the thumb of the army and Civil Guard. For the moment the new governing class had the situation well in hand.

The alliance was still new and uneasy. The agricultural oligarchy of the center and south had different interests from the industrial elite of the northern and eastern periphery. The issue appeared in connection with the tariff. Agricultural producers would benefit from free trade, which would help them to export their products to Britain and other industrialized countries, while Basque and Catalan infant industries cried out for protection. In 1845 the Moderado ministry proposed to abandon the rigid protective system inherited from the old regime. Catalan manufacturers protested bitterly and succeeded in obtaining a compromise in 1849. Henceforth no articles were completely excluded, but domestic manufacturers were still protected by high tariffs. The compromise kept the industrialists happy with the new order, but they were becoming suspicious of Castilian agriculturists. As in the days of Charles III, prosperity served to assuage social and economic conflicts.

In 1845 certain Moderados tried to establish the senate as a hereditary house, as it had been in the Estatuto of 1834. Their colleagues objected that the abolition of the *mayorazgo* had destroyed the basis of hereditary aristocracy, and that new men were appearing in the world

[5] *Ibid.*, p. 85. On the Spanish economy of the nineteenth century, besides the relevant sections in this work, the following works are particularly good: Jaime Vicens Vives, *An Economic History of Spain*, trans. F. M. López-Morillas (Princeton: Princeton University Press, 1969), Part VI, and Raymond Carr, *Spain, 1808–1939* (Oxford: Clarendon Press, 1966), pp. 264–77.

of finance, industry, agriculture, and the army who should be represented. This was the form that the senate took. The Moderado order recognized these men and gave them control of the country. The recognition was social as well as political. In 1845 the crown began to grant titles of nobility, even grandeeships, at a rate never known before. It would continue to do so until the fall of the monarchy in 1931. Generals received titles—Espartero was already Duke of the Victory, now Narváez became Duke of Valencia, and soon no leading general was complete without his title. Successful entrepreneurs joined them. José de Salamanca, Spain's first capitalist millionaire, was named Marquis of Salamanca. Through the new aristocracy, the crown drew to itself the powerful forces of the country, creating in them a vested interest in the conservative parliamentary monarchy.

In an age of speculation and quick riches for the smart and lucky few, the absolute monarchy had been replaced by a kind of vast joint stock company in which the monarch held some of the shares but not the controlling interest. At a gala ceremony before national and foreign dignitaries in 1850, Isabel II, twenty years old, fetchingly plump and resplendent in a white robe and crimson shawl, inaugurated an imposing building to serve as a meeting place for the directors of the corporation. It was the Palace of the Cortes. Built in the massive neoclassic style of official buildings everywhere in the nineteenth century, it still stands in Madrid, near the Paseo del Prado and the Barrio de Salamanca, across the old city from the royal palace, a monument to the Moderado order.

8

The Opposition to the Established Order: Revolutionary Period

1

The Moderado order lasted from the 1840's to the First World War and even a few years beyond. It was based on an alliance of minorities that held power over the strongest economic and cultural forces in the country, manipulating a parliamentary monarchy to maintain their positions. When they were not under serious threat they quarreled among themselves, but they managed to draw together in the face of danger.

Although they enjoyed an entrenched position, opposition had not ceased. There were Carlists and fervent Catholics who had not accepted parliamentary rule. At the other extreme, beneath the class of manufacturers, bankers, and speculators who supported the new order, in the cities a middle class of professional men, storekeepers, and merchants continued to desire a more democratic legislature and local self-rule. Many of them were anticlerical, so that their opposition was both ideological and political. They were the backbone of the Progresista party, which was defeated but not eliminated. Farther down the social scale, industrial and agricultural workers gradually became politically conscious.

The seventy-year rule of the Moderado order can be divided into two periods. In the first the enemies of the order made use of the *pronunciamiento*, an uprising of part of the armed forces which counted on the support of the dissatisfied groups in the cities. It was marked by two successful uprisings in 1854 and 1868 and by an unsuccessful one in 1866. The revolution of 1868 put the opposition into control for six years, but it was unable to establish a stable government. The second period began with the Restoration of 1875 and lasted until 1923. Defenders of the order tried more seriously to make parliamentary monarchy work successfully, but they did not end opposition. The army now became a reliable pillar of the system, so that *pronunciamientos* no longer took place. Opposition took other forms: regionalism, labor agitation, intellectual ferment, and appeal to voters.

In Europe the old order crumbled with the Revolution of 1848, which began in Paris and spread to central Europe, forcing German and Italian rulers to recognize revolutionary regimes and promise constitutions. Within a year the revolutionaries became divided and rulers regained power for themselves and the propertied classes. On the fringes of Europe, Russia did not succumb to the Revolution because the tsar was too strongly in control, nor did England because it already had representative government. Spain also avoided revolution, partly because it had a constitution and partly because Narváez employed his usual harsh methods against the first sparks of revolt.

The first successful challenge to the Moderados came in 1854. By 1851 their sense of security had created divisions in the party. In that year Isabel dismissed Narváez and replaced him by Juan Bravo Murillo, a civilian who believed in autocratic rule to enforce economic progress from above. Henceforth the government fell increasingly into the hands of a group allied to the financial world of Salamanca and Muñoz. The more liberal Moderados became estranged from their party and drew close to the more moderate Progresistas. At the same time the ministry's attempts to pare down the military budget in the interest of fiscal solvency angered many generals.

On June 28, 1854 several military leaders headed by General Leopoldo O'Donnell issued a *pronunciamiento* outside Madrid. Calling only for a new ministry, they failed to gain popular support. They were close to defeat and retreating southward when an astute young politician, Antonio Cánovas del Castillo, convinced them to issue a manifesto at Manzanares on July 6 which appealed directly to the Progresistas. It proposed to call new cortes, liberalize the press and electoral laws, establish municipal autonomy, revive the national militia, and create temporary municipal juntas to support the revolution. By now the main cities were in revolt, expressing their own grievances. Popular uprisings in Barcelona, Valencia, and other cities established juntas, and in Madrid barricades went up. Thoroughly frightened, on July 20 Isabel called on the Progresista idol of the 1840's, General Espartero, to be head of government. He entered Madrid in triumph, welcomed by both the left and the right. Seeking to restore peace, Espartero joined forces with O'Donnell, who represented the disaffected Moderados, making him minister of war. Out of their collaboration grew an uneasy alliance of Progresistas and liberal Moderados known as the

Liberal Union. They agreed to call unicameral cortes to write a new constitution.

The new Cortes proceeded to legislate the Progresista ideals into existence. A new constitution, enacted in 1856, provided, as could be expected, for direct election to both houses of the Cortes by provinces rather than single districts, a National Militia, elected *alcaldes,* and a brand new article: no Spaniard could be prosecuted for his religious views as long as he did not manifest public opposition to the Catholic Church. This was the first attempt to institute religious toleration in Spain, and the article was in opposition to the Concordat of 1851. Since the 1830's missionaries of the British Foreign Bible Society had been proselytizing for Protestantism in Spain, with some success, especially in Andalusia. The article legalized the situation; besides embodying a growing belief of liberal Spaniards in religious freedom, it was aimed to curry favor among British public opinion against a hostile Europe.

Reviving the Progresista policy of ending the entail of land, the Cortes voted on the proposal of the radical Barcelona lawyer, Pascual Madoz, to sell at auction not only the remaining properties of the church but also those of the crown and municipal lands that were not actually used in common by the townsmen. The proceeds, as usual, were to be applied to the national debt, in the hope of solving an acute fiscal crisis and gaining support among Spanish government bondholders at home and abroad.

Clearly many of these arrangements were unpalatable to the few Moderados who had been elected to the Cortes, but they went along with Espartero and O'Donnell. Carlists rose unsuccessfully in the north in defense of the church. The Progresistas soon lost power, however (before the constitution ever took effect), largely because the middle classes that normally supported them were frightened by the appearance of a new social force, the urban working class.

After the labor agitation in Barcelona under Espartero's regency, the Moderados had made workers' associations illegal. The movement did not die, however. Spanish writers who were familiar with European socialist thinkers like Robert Owen and Étienne Cabet provided the workers with knowledge of socialist and communist ideas. In March 1854 a weavers' strike in Barcelona inspired sympathy strikes by workers in other industries, leading to rioting and several deaths. Employees and manufacturers reached terms, but news of the June *pronunciamiento* led to renewed violence. Demanding the removal of new "self-acting" spinning machines, the workers burned factories and destroyed the machines. Order was reestablished at the end of July when responsible citizens of Barcelona took to the streets in armed patrols. A year later, in June 1855, the captain general of Catalonia banned all labor unions. Workers responded with a ten-day general strike of all industries.

Labor agitation spread to Valencia and then to central Spain. In Zaragoza, Valladolid, Burgos, and other places in Old Castile mobs attacked flour mills and other factories. Although the National Militia restored order, men of property were frightened.

In Madrid the working classes found leadership in a new party called the Democrats. It had been established during the European revolutions of 1848 by men who had become disenchanted with the Progresistas and looked back nostalgically at the Constitution of 1812. The party favored universal male suffrage and an end to conscription. Some Democrats without doubt wanted a republic, on the model of the Second French Republic, but they did not openly challenge the monarchy until 1854. At the time of the Revolution of 1854 their leading figures were José María de Orense, a marquis, and Francisco Pi y Margall, a young Catalan socialist and political theorist. These Democrats were close to the workers who manned the barricades, but they welcomed Espartero when he arrived and gave him their support. They elected a small vocal group of representatives to the Constituent Cortes, were suspected of complicity in the Barcelona riots, and to less radical Spaniards appeared to personify a grave social threat. Their existence cooled the enthusiasm for reform of many Progresistas.

Espartero felt his following slipping by 1856 as a result of continuing social disorder. In a dramatic gesture that he hoped would show how indispensable he was, he resigned in July. To his chagrin, Isabel accepted his resignation and named O'Donnell first minister. Sensing that Espartero's departure meant counterrevolution, the National Militia and workers revolted in Madrid, Barcelona, Zaragoza, and elsewhere, but the army, whose officers disliked the militia and were firmly in the hands of O'Donnell, stifled the uprising. The revolutionary period proved to be over, and the experience only strengthened the established order. O'Donnell brought back the Constitution of 1845 and the other Moderado institutions. In France Napoleon III rejoiced at the news.

2

Of the Progresista legislation only the Madoz law had a permanent effect, even though O'Donnell rescinded it in September 1856. It had made possible a new wave of land sales, for this time municipal and national lands were added to ecclesiastical lands. It has been estimated that by 1854 about half of the church lands had been sold. Another quarter were sold in 1855–56. O'Donnell negotiated with the papacy to recognize the recent sales. Eventually in 1860 the state took over the remaining lands of the church, giving their former owners 3 percent bonds. The part of the Madoz law applying to municipal and national properties was revived in 1858. Many towns managed to defend much of their property, especially the poorer land not fit for plowing, but the best land went into private hands in the next decades.

The process of disentail continued until the end of the century. In this way the vast extensions of church, crown, and municipal properties, which had been one of the characteristic features of the old regime, were at last liquidated. Little is known about this development. One suspects that municipal lands now passed legally into the hands of the local oligarchs who had controlled them anyway. There is evidence that speculators and entrepreneurs also invested part of their new wealth in land.[1] The final effect was to increase the concentration of landholding in a class of *neo-latifundistas* that was alienated economically and spiritually from the ragged hordes of *braceros* and *jornaleros* who labored in the fields, olive groves, and pastures. The hapless poor of southern Spain rose in protest sporadically in the decade after 1856, but the Civil Guard was there to meet such eventualities.

As before, the parliamentary conservatives compensated the church for its losses with other favors. Since the clergy was no longer financially independent, the state promised them a subsidy, although it was anything but munificent. Religious toleration disappeared along with the Constitution of 1856, and the government attacked Protestant converts. When in 1861 Austria accepted religious toleration, Spain became the only European state that enforced religious unity. In 1856 the clerical-minded minister Claudio Moyano fathered a law on education that was to remain in force until 1931. It called for state-supported primary education in towns of more than five hundred population, an article that was not fulfilled, and activated the article in the concordat which gave authority to the bishops to ensure that education in both public and private schools conform to Catholic doctrine. This part was carried out.

Narváez replaced O'Donnell in October 1856, but O'Donnell returned in 1858 and was head of the government until 1863, making an effective party of the Liberal Union of moderate Progresistas and liberal Moderados. He initiated a policy of importance for the future: he turned the attention of Spain's military forces outside the peninsula. In 1859 Spain declared war on Morocco to avenge an insult to the Spanish flag, and O'Donnell personally took command of the troops. The Spanish army defeated the Moors, and there was an outburst of national enthusiasm. The hero, besides O'Donnell, was the Catalan general Juan Prim. Two years later O'Donnell sent a Spanish army under Prim to Mexico to join a French and British expedition dispatched to

[1] See Francisco Quirós Linares, "La Desamortización, factor condicionante de la estructura de la propiedad agraria en el valle de Alcudia y Campo de Calatrava," *Estudios Geográficos*, XXV (1964), 367–407, esp. 396–402.

force that country to honor its debts. Despite orders from Isabel, Prim refused to cooperate with the French in setting up Maximilian as emperor of Mexico, thus becoming a hero for those Spaniards who opposed the opportunism of the Liberal Union.

The years of Liberal Union rule were the apogee of the reign of Isabel II. The easy prosperity of rapid economic expansion produced an extravagant society in Madrid and other major cities. The life of the court contributed to the atmosphere of moral relaxation. Isabel's mother and stepfather Muñoz were widely believed to be manipulating ministries and profiting from government corruption. The queen's own private life also caused scandal. She was married in 1846 for reasons of state to an effeminate cousin whom she hated all her life. Beginning shortly after her marriage she won the reputation, evidently deserved, of taking lovers among the generals and handsome men of her court. At the same time she became almost superstitiously religious. Her confidante was Sor Patrocinio, a nun who claimed to have the stigmata. Liberals felt that Carlism had triumphed in the palace after losing in the field. Isabel was discredited with the people of Madrid before 1854—many wanted her deposed during the revolution—but she remained popular in the provinces, and the birth of a male heir, Alfonso, in 1857 helped her reputation. Spaniards were torn between chivalrous loyalty to a woman ruler and disgust at her private life, which seemed even blacker than that of Godoy and María Luisa.

After 1863 Isabel's position deteriorated. Her reputation as a woman of easy virtue was spreading beyond Madrid, and her clerical camarilla dismayed the Liberal Union. In 1863 she named Narváez first minister, the general she called on whenever she felt the need to discipline her subjects. He remained the leading figure in government until 1868 and gradually restricted constitutional liberties. In 1864 a professor at the University of Madrid, Emilio Castelar, published an attack on the queen in the journal of the Democratic party. Narváez deprived him of his chair illegally, the faculty protested, students demonstrated, and the Civil Guard killed nine students and wounded a hundred in the center of Madrid. Narváez thereupon required all professors to take an oath of loyalty to the monarchy and the Catholic religion. Several refused and lost their positions. The episode was significant, for it revealed a new source of political activity: university students and faculties.

An economic crisis that began in 1866 worsened the position of the regime. It was part of a general European depression set off by a shortage of raw cotton from the United States during the Civil War. Catalan cotton mills were idle, and the flow of foreign capital into Spain dried up, ending railway construction. Workers grew restless, and the Democrats gained support in Barcelona and among the agricultural poor of Andalusia, who resented the loss of their common lands.

General Prim had by now become the recognized head of those

Progresistas who had remained aloof from the Liberal Union. In 1866 he attempted a *pronunciamiento* in Madrid, and when it was defeated, he fled abroad. In Belgium and Paris he negotiated with the leaders of the Democrats and Liberal Union generals also in exile. Meanwhile Narváez tightened his grip, and the queen ignored protests by the Cortes. Rule according to a constitution gave way to personal dictatorship, which was not to the liking of the Liberal Union or anyone to the left of it.

3

O'Donnell died in exile in 1867, Narváez while in office in April 1868, leaving Isabel without a strong general to defend her. Before the year was out, she became the victim of another military revolution. Prim, in alliance with one of Isabel's former lovers, the Liberal Unionist general Francisco Serrano, and Admiral Juan Bautista Topete, who controlled the navy, landed at Cadiz on September 18, 1868 and issued a *pronunciamiento* against the queen and in favor of "the reestablishment of constitutional monarchy." When Isabel discovered that the army would not respond to her appeal for support, she fled to France, while revolutionary juntas took over the cities. Reaching Madrid, Prim and Serrano found a junta in control that forced on them the Democrats' demand for constituent cortes elected by universal suffrage and the proclamation of freedom of religion and of the press. These events became known as the "glorious" September Revolution.

The strength of the different revolutionary forces was revealed in the electoral campaign for the Constituent Cortes. The major decision to be made was between a monarchy and a republic. Republican sentiment had spread among the Democrats in the last years of Isabel's reign, and now Orense, Castelar, Pi y Margall, and others broke away from the monarchist Democrats. Claiming that not just the "spurious race of Bourbons" but monarchy as a system was the cause of Spain's ills, they fought an active campaign in favor of a republic. The election was unusually fair. Sixty percent of the eligible voters went to the polls in a country where over two thirds of the adult males were illiterate. The largest group elected was 160 Progresistas. They fell almost squarely in the middle, for to the right of them were about 80 Liberal Unionists and 30 Carlists, and to the left 40 Democrats and 85 Republicans. The size of the Republican delegation surprised everyone. It came largely from the southern and eastern periphery and the provincial capitals of Castile, areas that had hitherto been Progresista strongholds.

The Cortes proceeded rapidly to draw up a new constitution. It was essentially a revival of the stillborn Constitution of 1856, a Progresista document, with a democratic flavor to satisfy the new left. Despite the vocal opposition of the Republicans, the monarchy was maintained. There was a two-house legislature, with both houses elected by universal suffrage, similar to the system of the United States. While promising to maintain the Catholic clergy, the constitution proclaimed religious freedom and, for the first time, allowed non-Catholic religious observances in public. Additional laws provided for elected *ayuntamientos* and a militia, this time called the Citizens' Militia. The latter was dissolved in the fall of 1869, however, for aiding Republican risings in various cities.

The revolution had thus been molded into a Progresista triumph. Its leading figure was General Prim, the most attractive of the military men who ruled Spain in the nineteenth century. A strong-willed Catalan and a sincere idealist, he looked upon Lincoln (whom he vaguely resembled) as his model. Had Spain become a republic with him as president, perhaps he could have established a stable progressive order, but he was convinced that Spain needed a king to provide a symbol for national unity. With Serrano as regent and himself as first minister, he set out to find a substitute for the hated Bourbon line. The search proved difficult, for Spain now had a reputation as an unstable country, and few royal families wished to furnish a candidate to replace a deposed queen, even a queen who was a disgrace to the profession. A nephew of the king of Italy declined, as did the ex-king of Portugal. A Catholic branch of the Prussian house of Hohenzollern appeared interested, but Napoleon III of France, fearing a revival of the empire of Charles V, opposed the candidacy so strongly that he led France into war with Prussia in July 1870. While the Prussians were conquering France and a rising in Paris was proclaiming the Third French Republic, Amadeo, second son of the king of Italy, quietly accepted the Spanish crown. Since the kingdom of Italy was taking Rome away from the Pope at this moment, Prim's choice of Amadeo was a gauntlet thrown down to devout Spanish Catholics. The Carlists increased their appeal, and in 1872 another Carlist war broke out in the north and northeast. Now that Spain had repudiated the direct Bourbon line, the Carlists hoped to put a handsome young grandson of the original Don Carlos on the throne. They plagued the Madrid governments for the next four years.

The reign of Amadeo seemed doomed from the start. Prim was the only person who might have kept the revolutionary parties cooperating, but on December 27, 1870, just as the new king was about to reach Spain, six armed men assassinated him in his carriage in a dark snowy street in Madrid. Who shot him no one ever learned. Two stormy years later, on February 11, 1873, Amadeo abdicated. Aristocrats and generals had snubbed him repeatedly, and the Progresistas, who had called him to power, had broken into two warring factions. He explained in a letter to the Cortes that he had been unable to bring peace to Spain. "If the enemies of [Spain's] happiness were foreigners, I would take the lead against them at the head of our valiant and long-suffering soldiers. But all those who, with their swords, their pens, or their words, aggravate and perpetuate the ills of the nation are Spaniards, all invoke the sweet name of our country. Among so many contradictory expressions of public opinion, it is impossible to decide which is right." Privately he said in Italian, "I don't understand anything; we are in a cage of madmen." [2]

Left without a king, the Cortes at last took the logical alternative. On the day of the abdication, ignoring constitutional procedures, the Cortes declared Spain a republic. They had the example of France to inspire them, but the republic proved to be less stable even than the democratic monarchy. Less than a year after its inception, it had become a cloak for military rule, and at the end of 1874 generals successfully pronounced in favor of the restoration of the Bourbon line in the person of Isabel's son.

The six years from 1868 to 1874 posed the most serious challenge of the nineteenth century to the established order. Yet the forces that brought about the revolution so easily in 1868 were unable to create a workable alternative. In the end probably neither Prim nor anyone else could have avoided the ultimate collapse; for while the entrenched groups had become fairly stable, those that supported the revolution were in rapid evolution. New forms of opposition that were to be typical of the twentieth century were making their appearance. The instability of the revolutionary forces proved their own undoing.

During these years demands for political decentralization, which the Progresistas had always voiced in a modest way, became far more radical. The movement had various manifestations, but in all of them Catalonia played a central role. One aspect of it grew out of an apparently harmless interest in the Catalan language as a literary medium, known as the Renaixensa or rebirth. In the first half of the century throughout Europe Romantic authors of subject nationalities were eagerly reviving the literary use of their languages, and Catalans were among them. In 1834 Buenaventura Carlos Aribau wrote an "Ode to the Fatherland" in Catalan, which sang of the love of the Catalans for their native tongue. Other local poets followed and in 1859 an annual contest for the best poem in Catalan was inaugurated. It was called the Jochs Florals or Floral Games, after a medieval festival. When Víctor Balaguer, a Catalan Progresista, began to publish a history of Catalonia in Catalan in 1860, the movement began to assume political connotations. In 1869 Catalans elected Republican deputies who, led by Pi y Margall, a Catalan, favored a federal republic with local self-government. Thus republicanism merged with literary regionalism to produce stronger movement than either was separately.

[2] Quoted in Fernando Soldevila, *Historia de España* (2nd ed., Barcelona: Ediciones Ariel, 1963), VII, 398 and 400–401.

During Prim's ministry, the Progresistas inadvertently strengthened the decentralist tendencies of Catalonia. Motivated by a doctrinaire acceptance of economic liberalism and a desire to encourage the national economy by furthering the export of foodstuffs and minerals, they reduced the tariff. They were following the rest of Europe, which had been moving toward free trade since 1846 and especially since 1860. The Figuerola Tariff of 1869 abolished import prohibitions and provided for duties to be lowered to a maximum of 15 percent on all objects, with gradual reductions from the present level to begin in 1876. Catalan manufacturers protested that their industries would be ruined. Since the loss of the American colonies on the mainland, they had found their fortune in a closed national market which included Cuba, Puerto Rico, and the Philippine Islands. They had sought to influence the central government to insure their protection, and had successfully fought the danger of lower tariffs in the 1840's. After the Figuerola Tariff, more and more of them began to consider the advantages of local autonomy.

The establishment of the Republic in February 1873 strengthened the revolt against central control in Catalonia and elsewhere. With great difficulty the first head of the Republican government, Estanislao Figueras, himself a Catalan federalist, prevented provincial officials from declaring Catalonia an independent state within a Republican confederation. Going in person to Barcelona, he urged the local leaders to await the convocation of constituent cortes. Since the monarchist parties boycotted the election, when the Cortes met in June 1873, the Republicans had an overwhelming majority. Their first acts were to proclaim a federal republic and replace Figueras with Pi y Margall, the leading proponent of federalism.

Very rapidly the move toward local self-government got out of control of the Republican leaders. In July a commission of the Cortes under Castelar presented a draft constitution for a federal republic. It divided Spain into thirteen peninsular and four overseas states, each to have its own constitution, legislature, and control over its public works, taxes, education, and the like. Beneath the states would be autonomous municipalities. Already, however, Cartagena, Valencia, Seville, Cadiz, Malaga, and city after city in southern and eastern Spain were declaring themselves independent municipalities or cantons ready to join in a confederation, but not in a federation such as that proposed in the draft constitution. Against Castelar's federalism of the United States type, the cantons stood for an alliance of independent municipalities on the model proposed for France by the Paris Commune of 1871. The cantonalists were extremist, or as they were called, "intransigent" Republicans, with their strength in the urban lower-middle class.

To add to the difficulties of the Republican government in Madrid, the cantonalist movement coincided with an organized worker's movement in favor of social revolution. Throughout the sixties, workers' associations had grown in Catalonia, despite government persecution. When the revolution came in 1868, the Russian anarchist leader Michael Bakunin, who was struggling with Karl Marx for control of the International Workingmen's Association founded in London in 1864, sent a representative to Spain to proselytize among the Spanish proletariat. This man, Giuseppe Fannelli, convinced the Catalan workers' groups to join the International and send deputies to its congress at Basel in 1869. Other labor organizations were forming in eastern and southern Spain, and a congress of ninety representatives of these groups met in Barcelona in 1870. It founded a Spanish branch of the International called the Spanish Regional Federation and adopted the anarchist doctrine of Bakunin of boycotting elections and other legal political activities, a doctrine that was to remain the hallmark of Spanish anarchism.

Frightened by the Paris Commune, for which the International claimed credit, the Cortes outlawed the International in Spain in 1872, although its Spanish members were more interested in setting up an organization that could bargain effectively for better labor conditions than in staging a revolution. Under the Republic, the Regional Federation again came out in the open, demanding municipal autonomy. In some towns of Andalusia and Extremadura its followers seized private latifundia and divided them among the peasants. On June 26, 1873 the Federation of Barcelona momentarily set up a Committee of Public Safety, as the Paris Commune had done, to organize resistance to the Carlists, who were threatening Catalan cities. In Alcoy, a textile town south of Valencia, the International declared a general strike for shorter hours and higher wages, the Civil Guard provoked the workers into an armed uprising, and on July 9 the strikers set fire to a spinning factory and killed some civil guards and the *alcade*. The press magnified the event with tales of murdered priests, the rape of young girls, and similar gruesome fictions. Horror swept through Spain, and the more moderate groups who had favored the Republic were frightened by the specter of social disintegration. The leaders of the Regional Federation did not favor the cantonalists, seeing in them only another group of capitalist exploiters, but in various cities organized workers fought for the cantons. The juxtaposition of the two movements in the public mind discredited the cantons. The government of the Republic had no choice but to take action against the cities in revolt.

The cantonalist movement proved fatal to the Republic. In eastern and southern Spain only Catalonia remained loyal to Madrid, for here Republicans had the sense to see the need for national unity. In the north the Carlists were making dangerous progress, while the southern cantons, following federal doctrines to their logical conclusion, abolished recruitment for the army and refused to collect taxes for the central government. Pi resigned in July, and in September the Cortes took the drastic measure of voting full power to Emilio Castelar, who criticized the doctrinaire republicanism of his colleagues and proposed to use all possible measures to save the Republic. He saw the only hope in collaboration with the army, ignoring warnings that the generals would be disloyal. He ordered Generals Manuel Pavía and Arsenio Martínez Campos, who had command in Andalusia and Valencia, to crush the cantons so that the army would be free to turn on the Carlists. The move worked, for by the end of the year all the cantons except Cartagena were suppressed. However, the majority of the Republican deputies were outraged by Castelar's harsh use of the military against the cantonalists, whom they considered wayward brothers.

On January 2, 1874, the Cortes met for the first time in three months to review Castelar's accomplishments. They listened to him defend his acts, debated all night, and finally defeated a motion of confidence. Upon learning of Castelar's fall, General Pavía, who was in Madrid, invaded the Palace of the Cortes with his troops and disbanded the deputies. Pavía instituted a centralized republic, and when the Republicans refused to cooperate with him, he gave the presidency to Prim's collaborator in 1868, General Serrano. The Republic, now lacking committed defenders, limped on for a year, while Pavía and Serrano strove in vain to crush the Carlist rising. Few persons lamented the change when Martínez Campos, victor in Valencia over the cantons, pronounced in December 1874 in favor of the son of Isabel II, Alfonso XII, a seventeen-year-old lad who was studying in England. Other generals rapidly followed, and Serrano resigned. Spain's most valiant attempt of the nineteenth century to set up a democratic system freed from control of oligarchic groups had ended in failure.

4

The failure is not surprising, if one compares Spain with other Western European countries. The European revolutions of the mid-century, those of 1848, had also been defeated. By the end of the century, France, Germany, and Italy had conservative regimes representing the propertied classes (which included the peasants in France), but functioning under more or less democratic parliamentary systems. It is ironic but in historical perspective understandable that the doctrine of popular sovereignty introduced in Europe in 1789 had the effect for over a century of strengthening the political power of the upper classes. The Spanish revolutions of 1854 and 1868 have been compared to the European revolutions of 1848. In both cases the revolutions suffered and eventually fell partly because the groups supporting them were divided. The unforeseen appearance of radical extremists and workers' groups preaching doctrines that threatened property frightened off many middle-class moderates.

Spain was not, however, simply repeating 1848 with delayed timing. The revolutions of 1848 were the product of a spirit which tied bourgeois liberals together across national frontiers. They still embodied the humanitarian ideals of the Enlightenment and the French Revolution. Conflict between revolutionaries in different countries did not seem possible in 1793 or in 1848. Nevertheless, during the revolutions of 1848 liberals of different nationalities and language groups discovered that their territorial objectives were incompatible. They ended up opposing each other even as they became frightened by the socialistic demands of the urban workers. Nationalism destroyed the international revolutionary spirit in the middle class. Liberal revolutions henceforth became local affairs, like the French revolution of 1870–71, nationalistic, establishing the propertied classes in political power. Only socialist proletarian movements remained international.

Spain was different. It had never really formed part of the "Liberal International," even if Spanish refugees in Paris or London mixed with those from other countries. In 1808 most liberal Spaniards rejected the constitution imported by Joseph Bonaparte. They wrote instead their own Constitution of 1812, against the French invaders, not under their auspices. After their experiences in 1808 and 1823 Spanish liberals were not inclined to follow France. Unlike other European countries in the nineteenth century, Spain had its own constitutional tradition to inspire its revolutions and did not need to look to Paris. Madrid became an independent focus of revolution; in 1820 Europe took its cue from Spain, not France. Thus except for France and England, Spain was ahead of the rest of Europe. Although it received influences from abroad, as did France and England, at the very outset it achieved the national stage of liberal revolutions. It is the inability to recognize this political independence of Spain, which after the eighteenth century led it to mold its own transition into modernity side by side with France and Great Britain, that has led historians to describe Spanish history as an ineffectual imitation of European developments.

Spain's constitutional struggles also produced a peculiar alignment of the groups which disputed the political structure of the nation. In 1812 the constitutionalists had embodied the ideals of eighteenth century enlightened despotism: political centralization and an end to the hereditary power of the privileged orders. They instituted elective municipal councils to destroy local oligarchies. By 1860 the old oligarchy and its new recruits had taken over both constitutionalism and centralism. Under the Moderados, privileged groups discovered that a properly organized constitutional monarchy provided them with far more effective power than absolutism had permitted. They could now control the court and the country both. In self-defense the intellectuls, professionals, and smaller merchants had to appeal to more popular groups. But an appeal to the people turned out to be an appeal to localism, for the artisans and shopkeepers who made up the strength of national militias and urban juntas had grown to suspect the influence of the crown in municipal government, and the workers and peasants had not been integrated by tradition or education into a unified Spanish state. It is hardly surprising that when Romantic writers revived visions of past glories of Catalonia, Catalan revolutionaries imagined themselves to be continuing the defense of Catalan independence against Castilian rule.

In this way the opposition to the established order came to embody the old particularism against which the crown had struggled for centuries. The conflicts were still much as they had been in the eighteenth century, large landowners against peasants and reformers, clericalism against modern thought, with added tensions arising from the early stages of industrialization. In the eighteenth century the crown had favored peasants and modern thought. The king could be centralist because he felt no need to base his authority on an appeal to the groups whom he favored. With the disappearance of his prestige and authority, centralism became the weapon of the descendants of the enemies of the crown. The defenders of the interests which the crown had favored had to fall back on popular support and hence on particularism. For democracy and particularism to be allies was different from the pattern in most Western European countries and the United States. Spain's unique situation was already producing different political conflicts from those common to other Western countries.

9

The Opposition to the Established Order: Evolutionary Period

1

The restoration of the Bourbon line at the end of 1874 inaugurated a fifty-year period of relative political peace. Alfonso XII (1874–85), the most attractive ruler of Spain in the nineteenth century, died prematurely of tuberculosis in 1885 at the age of twenty-eight. He left two daughters and a pregnant widow, María Cristina of Habsburg Lorraine, who gave birth to a boy in May 1886, the next king of Spain, Alfonso XIII (1886–1931). For the second time in half a century the country had a regent named María Cristina, but unlike her predecessor this one ruled with decorum until her son was declared of age in 1902.

The defeat of Spain in the war with the United States in 1898 and the consequent loss of its last colonies in America and the Pacific was a blow to the regime from which it was never able fully to recover. The opposition no longer made revolutions, but it was growing stronger, fed by the development of the industrial areas and the growth of the cities. By the First World War political and social tensions were reaching a point where the parliamentary system could not cope with them. Although the system was to limp on for almost a decade, its days were numbered.

The architect of the Restoration was Antonio Cánovas del Castillo, the man who had done most to popularize the idea of a return to the Bourbon line after 1868. After supporting O'Donnell in the Revolution of 1854, he had been one of the leaders of the Liberal Union, the party that had brought together moderates from both the Progresistas and the Moderados. Now he headed a party known as the Liberal Conservatives, or simply the Conservatives, which was heir to both the Moderados and the Liberal Unionists. Cánovas established an ad hoc commission in 1875 which, without legal standing, drew up a new constitution. Meanwhile elections for new cortes, held at Cánovas' insistence with the universal suffrage of 1869 but carefully manipulated by the minister of *gobernación*, Francisco Romero Robledo, returned a docile body of deputies that ratified the new document in 1876.

Cánovas' objective was to create a workable parliamentary system that would appeal broadly to the major segments of society, putting an end to violent civil strife. This he hoped to do by obtaining the cooperation of the successors to the Progresistas, the Liberal Party, led by Práxedes Mateo Sagasta, who had been Prim's minister of *gobernación* in 1869. Instead of reestablishing the Moderado Constitution of 1845 as many of his followers demanded, Cánovas sought to compromise between their ideal and that of the Progresistas. The individual rights of 1869 were preserved, including individual freedom of religion and the right to celebrate non-Catholic services in private houses. This article brought forth a storm from intransigent Moderados and other Catholic deputies, but eventually Cánovas quieted them by his firm stance and a promise to the church of continued state financial support and a monopoly of public religious functions. The few thousand converts to Protestantism would continue to exist legally.

On the other hand the constitution maintained the Moderado structure of 1845. In the bicameral legislature, the Senate would be made up of members by right such as grandees, archbishops, captains general, appointees of the crown, and members elected from specified categories of persons by official bodies and the highest taxpayers. The Congress of Deputies would once more be elected in single member constituencies. The suffrage was specified in a separate law and required the payment of a land tax of twenty-five pesestas (five dollars) per year or a tax on business activity of fifty pesetas per year (Cánovas considered peasant landowners more reliable than shopkeepers). In addition members of learned academies, generals and retired officers, priests, teachers, high bureaucrats, and members of similar groups received the vote. Property plus talent would rule the country, with emphasis on the former. With the experience of the Republic fresh in his mind, Cánovas would have no truck with democracy. He believed (as did many European liberals of his generation) that "universal suffrage means the dissolution of society. . . . It is the negation of the national will and the parliamentary regime." [1] To make doubly sure that the people would not dissolve society, the constitution gave considerable authority to the monarch: approval of legislation, command of the army and navy, the right to declare war and make peace.

The great achievement of Cánovas was to get the heirs of the Progre-

[1] Statement to editors of *Figaro*, 1883, quoted in Soldevila, *Historia de España*, VIII, 156.

sistas to work within his parliamentary system. This was partly because of his wisdom in refusing to dictate a vindictive settlement, "a lo Fernando VII," partly because of the difficulty of finding generals willing to make a *pronunciamiento;* but to a great extent it was because Alfonso XII and María Cristina acted as impartial constitutional monarchs, exercising a self-discipline that was beyond either Isabel II before them or Alfonso XIII after them. Periodically, as the political situation became difficult, the party in power resigned, and the monarch appointed a ministry of the opposition and then dismissed the Cortes and called for new elections. Thus the new minister of *gobernación* could insure the electoral victory of his party, but, inspired by the example of Cánovas, he was careful to allow the leaders of the opposition to be reelected and not to infringe on the strongholds of the Carlists and Republicans. By seeing that the Liberals were treated fairly, Cánovas made them part of the established order. Until an anarchist assassinated him in 1897, the only two parties that had nationwide organizations cooperated in maintaining the parliamentary monarchy. The system, which was known aptly as the *turno pacífico,* reached its apogee in 1885 on the death of Alfonso XII. Cánovas, who was first minister, fearing Republican and Carlist agitation and wishing to insure the loyalty of the Liberals, recommended to María Cristina that she give power to Sagasta, which she did. (The event is known, somewhat misleadingly, as the Pact of the Pardo, after the palace where the king had died.) Sagasta and the Liberals held the government for five years, during which time they legislated the remaining objectives of 1868, including the right of free association (1887), civil marriage (1889), and universal suffrage (1890). The last act caused the moderate Republicans led by Castelar to accept the regime. Since many Carlists had joined the Conservative party, Spain at last appeared to be approaching a political consensus, Cánovas' dream. After a century Spaniards seemed to have found again a common loyalty, the political legitimacy that had once belonged to the absolute monarch.

Unfortunately the political underpinning of the Restoration monarchy belied its respectable surface. The *turno pacífico* depended on a refinement of the system of controlled elections which originated under Isabel II. In Spanish history the system is known as *caciquismo,* from the word *cacique,* meaning originally an Aztec chief and later a local political boss in Spain. *Caciques* could be found in all parts, but they were especially powerful in Galicia and in the rural areas of central and southern Spain. They existed in a variety of forms. They could be the local agents of the large landowners; *alcaldes* or other local officials; or independent political bosses who ran entire districts. When the Cortes were dissolved, the minister of *gobernación* gave instructions to the local *jefe político* (civil governor of a province), who was his appointee, and the *jefe político* worked with the *caciques* to produce the desired majority. After 1890 under universal suffrage peasants and landless workers, many of them illiterate, voted when and for whom they were told to. There were many districts firmly in the hands of *caciques* where candidates ran unopposed. The elected deputies were often Madrid lawyers or bureaucrats who had no connection with the district they represented and little contact with life outside the capital. Since they supported the established groups, *caciquismo* allowed the parties to rotate without threatening the system. Democracy, as in many Western countries at the end of the century, including the United States in its larger cities, had become a travesty of its ideal and a way to keep an organized group in power. There was no true consensus, but the forces of discontent were powerless until after 1898.

2

Behind the political evolution of this period lay a transformation of the economy which had begun before 1850. Like the rest of Europe, Spain in the nineteenth century experienced a rapid demographic expansion. The population of the peninsula and the Balearic and Canary Islands went from 10.5 million in 1797 to 18.6 million in 1900, a rise of 76 percent. During the same century France's population grew 43 percent, England's 89, and Germany's 150. Spain's growth rate was behind that of the rapidly industrializing countries, but above France's. Within Spain the population of the periphery continued to expand more rapidly than in the center, as it had since the seventeenth century. If we divide the peninsula into four areas—north (Galicia, Asturias, Basque Provinces, and Navarre), east (Catalonia, Valencia, and Murcia), south (Andalusia), and center (Aragon, León, and Old and New Castile)—we find that the area of most rapid growth was the east, followed by the south, the north, and the center in that order. The central plateau continued its relative decline:

DISTRIBUTION OF POPULATION, 1797–1900
(excluding Balearic and Canary Islands)

	Percent Growth 1797–1900	Percent of Total Population 1797	Percent of Total Population 1900	Percent of Area
East	111%	20.4%	24.4%	16.5%
South	87	18.8	19.9	17.7
North	75	19.9	19.6	11.7
Center	57	40.9	36.1	54.1
Peninsula	78	100.0	100.0	100.0
Totals		10,114,000	17,937,000	492,000 km.[2]

Catalonia grew at a faster rate than any other area in the peninsula; 129 percent in the century. It went from 8.5 percent of the total peninsular population in 1797 to 11.0 percent in 1900. Part of this growth was the result of migration, as inhabitants of other areas of eastern Spain moved in to take advantage of the growing economy. The proportion of the population living in the northern provinces declined slightly, but the decline was mainly attributable to emigration to America in the last third of the century. Between 1882 and 1920 there was a net departure of 860,000 persons from Spain, and within the peninsula, the highest rate of emigration was from Galicia and Asturias. (The Canary Islands had an even higher rate.)

Urbanization was another feature of demographic growth. Throughout the West the expansion of cities in the nineteenth century herded vast numbers of people together in urban conditions. The population of Madrid rose from about 169,000 to 540,000 during the century, of Barcelona from 115,000 to 533,000. Rapid urban growth began in Spain only after 1860. At this date about 10 percent of Spaniards lived in cities above 20,000 in population, hardly more than in 1800. This proportion was slightly behind France (11 percent in 1851) and ahead of Italy (13 percent in 1881). By 1900 the proportion of Spaniards living in cities of over 20,000 had risen to 21 percent, which was somewhat behind both France (24 percent) and Italy (26 percent). Most of the seventy Spanish cities of this size in 1900 were scattered around the periphery; only eight were in the vast central region of the peninsula. The majority were not heavily industrial, since only ten were in Catalonia and the Basque Provinces while nineteen were in Andalusia, where urban agglomerations had always been large. But whatever the basis of the economy of the cities, this concentration of population brought people into contact with the world of modern civilization and politics. Inevitably it provided recruits for the opponents of the established order.

The completion of the railway system helped stimulate the expansion of the economy and the growth of cities. Prior to 1868 the trunk lines had been built. Between 1875 and 1900 branch lines were added, doubling the mileage and bringing all provincial capitals into the system. Where there were roads, stagecoach lines (*diligencias*) introduced early in the century carried passengers to points beyond the reach of the railroads. After spending the night in an inn by the station, the travelers would rise before dawn and set off behind four or six horses for a dusty ride over gravel roads. Most small towns, however, were still accessible only by mule path and relied as for centuries past on the mules and burros of the professional *arrieros* for a few outside supplies. Although their reach was limited, the railroads were the first means of transportation to cross Spain's rough mountain chains efficiently. Carrying people, mail, and agricultural and industrial products, they tied the country together as an economic unit and began to break down the isolation of vast regions of the center.

The new transportation encouraged agricultural specialization for distant markets. Since the eighteenth century farmers of arid Spain had broken pastures for grain crops. Wheat farming reached its greatest extension about 1860. Thereafter, despite tariff protection, the production of wheat declined, as marginal lands recently put under the plow became exhausted, American wheat began to flood Europe, and landowners turned to more profitable crops. After 1877 Spain was, as in the eighteenth century, again dependent on the importation of foreign grain. Wheat fields began to give way to vineyards and, in the region south of Madrid, where the climate permitted, to olive groves. Fruit orchards also expanded, especially where irrigation existed from previous times, as in the *vegas* of Mediterranean Spain, or was now introduced, as in western Catalonia, where the newly constructed Canal of Urgel brought life to a large deserted area around Lérida. After the loss of Cuba in 1898, sugar beets became another important market crop, especially in the zone along the Pyrenees, in Granada, and to a lesser extent in the central plateau. Common wine, unrefined olive oil, and oranges were the major export crops. Spain was the world's largest exporter of wine at the end of the century. During the First World War wine replaced iron ore as the country's most valuable export, only to give way in about 1930 to the oranges of Valencia.

The effect of this specialization was to bring new sources of income to the owners of land. In arid Spain the people to benefit most were large landowners, for the typical small peasant remained nearly as isolated as before or else became a day laborer in the olive groves or wheat fields of the rich owners. The latter, the "*señoritos*," frequently moved to the cities, leaving their lands in charge of overseers and returning only occasionally for hunting or relaxation. In the periphery, on the other hand, agricultural specialization for export went back to the eighteenth century. The economic advantage often accrued to the well-to-do peasant who had a vineyard, an orchard, an orange grove, or an irrigated field of his own. The evolution of agriculture tended to increase the difference between center and periphery.

This was also a period of industrial growth, in which the established areas, Catalonia and the Basque Provinces, continued to lead the way. Catalonia's major industry, as traditionally, was weaving. Catalan manufacturers had been frightened by the prospect of the free trade tariff of 1869, which was to go into effect after 1876, and they were found among the partisans of the Bourbon Restoration. In return the new government postponed introducing the tariff, without, however, rescinding it. When Sagasta moved to enforce the tariff in the eighties, Cánovas came to the aid of the manufacturers, who were, after all, important members of the system. In 1891, Cánovas put through a protective tariff, and thereafter Catalan textile manufacture advanced rapidly. However, the independence of Cuba was a severe blow to the cotton industry, which lost both a larger market than it had in Spain itself and its major source of raw material. After 1900 foreign raw cotton was far and away Spain's largest import.

The Basque Provinces were the center of iron and steel production. Prior to the middle of the nineteenth century, Spain had smelted little of its iron ore, but the demand for iron and steel for the railroads led to a rapid increase in domestic production. Fifty thousand tons of pig iron per year had been average before 1868. By 1900 production was 328,000 tons, and 422,000 in 1913. Steel production rose from 166,000 to 392,000 tons between 1900 and 1913. Still Spain, lacking abundant coal and capital, lagged behind the more industrialized countries in iron and steel production. It produced only 20 kilos per person per year at the turn of the century, while England produced 207, Germany 146, and France 62. Ninety percent of Spain's iron ore was still exported unrefined.

The need for fuel of the railroads, factories, blast furnaces, and growing cities stimulated the exploration of Spain's few coal deposits. Production of coal rose from 450,000 tons in 1865 to 2.7 million in 1900 and 4.3 million in 1913. The country's needs could not be met from domestic sources, however, and Spain imported about three quarters as much coal as it produced, mostly from England. Half of the domestic production came from Asturias, where coal had been mined in the valleys above Oviedo since the end of the eighteenth century. This now became a highly developed mining region, closely connected with the Basque industrial area.

Although Catalonia was the most industrialized part of Spain, the Basques were more rapid in adopting modern financial structures. Catalan manufacturing remained primarily a matter of family businesses, but the Basque iron-and-steel industry was organized in modern corporations, which attracted capital from Catalonia and Great Britain, as well as locally. In banking too the Catalans were backward. The future of banking lay in combining the role of deposit bank with promotion of investment in industrial and other corporations. Catalan banks continued to restrict their activities to handling deposits and transfers, with the result that they declined in importance.

The turn of the century saw the creation of the modern Spanish banking structure with the establishment of what became known as the "five great banks." Two of them were Basque, the others centered in Madrid. The first was the Banco de Bilbao, founded in 1857, which had already played a major role in financing Basque mining and smelting industries. The financial crisis following the Spanish-American War produced the next three. Capital repatriated from Cuba, Puerto Rico, and the Philippines went into founding the Banco Hispano-Americano in 1901. The Banco de Vizcaya, located in Bilbao, capital of the province of Vizcaya, appeared in the same year, and next year came the Banco Español de Crédito. The latter took the place of the Pereires' Crédito Mobiliario Español, which had been in trouble since the death of the last of the original Pereire brothers in 1880. Though it was incorporated in Madrid, the majority of its stock was owned by French and Belgian investors.[2] The merger of various regional banks in 1919 produced the fifth great bank, the Banco Central. These banks became the main agents for floating stock, and they therefore encouraged the growth of corporations. Under their leadership, the financial and industrial structure of the country began to assume the aspects of corporate capitalism.

This was the case, for instance, with electricity. The turn of the century saw the beginning of production of electricity in Spain, a development which was to have as far-reaching results as the railroads. Basque banks and Basque capital lay behind four of the five major electrical power corporations established at this time: in the north, the Madrid area, the Guadalquivir valley, and the southeast. The fifth, in Catalonia, was in the hands of a Canadian company known familiarly as "la Canadiense," which drew its capital from investors of various nationalities. Because of Spain's shortage of coal and ubiquitous mountains, three quarters of its electrical productive capacity in 1930 was hydroelectric. Electricity freed Catalonia and other manufacturing zones from dependence on scarce Asturian coal and made possible the mechanization of small shops and extension of industry into new areas.

The First World War provided the Spanish economy with a windfall. Spain remained neutral and suddenly found the warring nations and those cut off from normal suppliers begging for its foodstuffs, minerals, and manufactured goods. The Catalan textile industry was swarmed with foreign orders and the price of coal and iron shot up. Production and the number of industrial workers increased rapidly. After peace in 1918, however, Spain was unable to keep these new customers, and its manufacturers had to fall back on the domestic market, which had its limits because of the large proportion of the population living at subsistence level in the countryside. The letdown caused violent tensions in the industrial areas after the war which were critical in bringing the end of the constitutional monarchy.

Wartime profits made possible the buying out of foreign investors in some areas, most notable being the railroads. Still, foreign capital did not disappear from Spain. Having gone earlier into mines and railroads, much of it went after 1900 into public utilities, as in the case of

[2] See Nicolás Sánchez Albornoz, "De los orígenes del capital financiero: la Sociedad General del Crédito Mobiliario Español, 1856–1902," *Moneda y Crédito*, No. 97 (June 1966), 29–67.

Catalan electricity. In 1925 the Spanish government gave the International Telephone and Telegraph Corporation, a United States entity, a twenty-five-year franchise of the telephone services of the country. The company built Spain's first skyscraper, "la Telefónica," on the recently opened Gran Vía in the center of Madrid. Figures are not available for the extent of foreign investment in Spain, but even after the First World War, it was considerable in mining, smelting, and utilities.

3

The expanding economy thus benefited the three vested interests on which the established order rested: landowners, manufacturers, and foreign investors. The Moderados had turned the church into another ally, but the Revolution of 1868 and its aftermath had severely shaken it. The proclamation of religious toleration, the church's loss of control over education, and the end of state financial support under the First Republic had driven many Catholics to side with the Carlists. Most clergy had preferred, however, a restoration of the legitimate Bourbon line to a Carlist victory. After 1875 the church recovered from its setback, aided actively by Alfonso XII and María Cristina. Although the Concordat of 1851 had provided for state support of only three religious orders, the church registered many others under the provisions of the Concordat. By 1900 Spain had 597 male religious communities and 2656 female communities, with 55,000 monks and nuns. This was little more than half the eighteenth-century figure, but their influence was great, for over half of their houses were dedicated to teaching. Primary and secondary education of upper- and middle-class children was solidly in the hands of the clergy. And the clergy, impressed by the anticlericalism of the Third French Republic and the Italian monarchy, remained firmly aligned against the dangers of liberalism and republicanism.

The religious orders also rebuilt the independent wealth which they had lost by the confiscation and sale of their lands. Most orders preferred now to place their investments in industry and commerce rather than in real estate. The amount of their wealth is undisclosed, but in 1912 the secretary of the Catalan textile manufacturers association, who should have been well-informed, declared, they "control without exaggeration one-third of the capital wealth of Spain." [3]

The result was that the clergy in general remained tied to the established order. They did little to help the immigrants drawn to the

[3] Joan C. Ullman, *The Tragic Week, a Study in Anticlericalism in Spain, 1875–1912* (Cambridge, Mass.: Harvard University Press, 1968), p. 35. This work provides a good discussion of the position of the church, pp. 27–47.

industrial cities from the countryside. The alienation of the urban lower classes from the religious orders evident in the assaults on monasteries in 1834–35 was increasing, abetted after 1868 by the spread of socialism and anarchism. By 1900 the church was a symbol of an unjust social order to many of the lower classes, as it had been at the beginning of the century to liberals.

After its long history of political activism, the army turned into a reliable supporter of the entrenched groups. Just as the accession of Isabel II had coincided with the maturity of a generation of generals who would be active in politics, that of Alfonso XII saw their disappearance. O'Donnell, Narváez, and Prim had died in the previous decade, and Espartero followed in 1879. Serrano remained to welcome the new king, but he rapidly disappeared from the political stage. The new figures, of whom Martínez Campos was the leader, had been shocked by the anarchy of the First Republic. They were committed to order, centralism, and the monarchy. Cánovas contributed to their loyalty by working to keep the army out of politics. Martínez Campos was sent to Cuba, where in 1878 he succeeded in pacifying a revolt in progress since 1868. At the same time the officer corps became more homogeneous, a career for members of the middle and upper classes. Officers were trained in select academies, promotion was strictly by seniority except in theaters of war. Gone were the days of rapid rise of men of modest origins like Espartero. High officers were still convinced of their mission to save the country, but they ceased to lead political movements.

Spain's defeat by the United States in 1898 and the loss of its remaining colonies turned the thoughts of the officers back to the political arena. Having suffered the ravages of tropical disease and guerrilla warfare in Cuba and the Philippines, the surviving soldiers and officers returned to Spain to discover their services unappreciated. After 1900 many young officers felt underpaid in relation to their social status, even though the army received half the national budget and most of this went into salaries. The officer corps was a kind of cancerous growth that resisted all surgery: 500 generals and 24,000 lower officers for an army of less than 50,000 soldiers on active duty! The government called on the army repeatedly after 1898 to put down labor agitation in Barcelona and elsewhere. The officers as a caste hated Catalan particularism and scorned and detested the working classes. After 1904, the army was engaged in intermittent warfare in Morocco, which again lacked popular support. Many politicians and writers attacked the military forces as a useless expense. The officers, stung by what they considered national ingratitude, became alienated from the parliamentary system. They needed only a leader to prepare them for a new kind of *pronunciamiento*. After 1902 such a figure appeared, the young Alfonso XIII, who prided himself on his constitutional position as supreme commander of the armed forces, appeared regularly in military uniform, and looked on the army as his own property. Thus although the army had become a pillar of the social order, it posed a latent threat to the parliamentary regime. If the politicians should fail to maintain domestic peace, it was likely to step in. In the end, this is what occurred in 1923, because the forces of opposition eventually grew strong enough to threaten the system.

4

The collapse of the First Republic left the opposition groups disorganized and disheartened. Until the end of the century they were reorienting themselves, creating new institutions, and seeking new leaders. After the disaster of 1898 discredited the governing groups, the opponents of the regime were able to take the offensive, campaigning for political influence and resorting on occasion to violence.

Since the late eighteenth century, ideological conflict had never ceased to tear Spain apart. Although the persecutions of Ferdinand VII managed to stamp out the spirit of Jansenism among most of the clergy, the strict puritanical concept of devotion to the common good had lived on in other areas. Some of the societies of Amigos del País remained in existence, notably the society of Madrid, which had continued its activities during the dismal first half of the century and now found new life. Beside it there was the Ateneo de Madrid, a private association of intellectuals that had been founded in 1820, closed in 1824, and reopened in 1835. It presented courses of lectures to the public, bringing higher education out of the closed circle of the universities. After 1875 Cánovas befriended it and made it the leading center of intellectual life in Madrid, where members who opposed the regime were free to voice their criticisms.

The Restoration of 1875 saw the birth of a new center for educational reformers. It grew out of the revolt of university professors against the state system which began before 1868, highlighted by the violent reaction to Castelar's dismissal for insulting the queen. The inspiration for their revolt came partly from republicanism and at least as much from the teachings of Julian Sanz del Río, a professor of philosophy of law at Madrid. After studying law at Granada, Sanz del Río had gone abroad in 1843. Disappointed with the French rationalism he found in Paris, he moved on to Heidelberg. Here he became an admirer of a recently deceased disciple of Kant, Friedrich Krause. From Kant via Krause, Sanz adopted a philosophy which insisted on the primacy of morality in human relations but freed it, in the fashion of the European Enlightenment, from any particular religious faith. In 1854 Sanz obtained a chair at the University of Madrid, and in the last decade of Isabel II's reign many future republicans and other political radicals, including Castelar and Salmerón, listened to his lectures and accepted the doctrines of "Krausismo." Its emphasis on morality and probity appealed to the spiritual heirs of the Jansenists and fortified their opposition to church control of education. Sanz's most remarkable student was Francisco Giner de los Ríos, who succeeded him in his chair in 1868.

One of the first pieces of legislation of the Restoration was a decree authored by the minister of education, the Marquis of Orovio, in February 1875. Orovio had been responsible for the oath of loyalty of 1867 which led to the dismissal of various professors. His new decree required that all textbooks in use be approved by the state and that all university professors clear their lectures with their rectors to see that they did not conflict with Catholic dogma and morality or the monarchic system. The decree was a sop thrown by Cánovas to the intransigent Catholics. It raised again the question of freedom to teach. Castelar resigned his chair, while Salmerón, another president of the Republic, and Giner de los Ríos publicly protested the decree. Cánovas deprived the latter of their professorships and had Giner arrested and exiled to Cadiz.

While in Cadiz Giner conceived the idea of a private educational institution which would be free from government and church control. Upon his release, he and his associates established a corporation entitled the Institución Libre de Enseñanza (Independent Institution of Education) to be supported by private stockholders and under private control. Originally Giner conceived of a free university, but when this proved impractical, he turned to a secondary school, soon adding primary education.

Though never large in numbers, the Institución marked Giner out as one of the great educators of all time. In it he attempted to put his ideals into practice. Partly these were Krausist, partly inherited from domestic reformers like Jovellanos. Giner also admired the education offered by English and American schools and colleges and German universities. Discarding all textbooks, the professors taught by lecture and student participation. Frequent excursions to the countryside and to historic and artistic monuments stressed the importance of seeing and doing, in contrast to the education by rote commonly practiced in church schools. Giner and his staff taught the children to appreciate the music and culture of the common people. One of the novel features of the Institución was coeducation, with girls participating in activities, including outdoor sports, alongside boys. Teaching at the Institución or otherwise associated with Giner were many persons who had been active in the revolutionary period after 1868. Salmerón, Figuerola, and other reformers joined him, but Giner strove to keep the Institución out of politics, feeling, not unlike some army officers, that parliamentary strife was the ruin of Spain. A gentle man with sparkling eyes and a white beard, Giner had a powerful effect on associates and students alike. His idealism and personal magnetism and the upright character of his fellow teachers turned the Institución pupils into young men and women who felt themselves a small band of missionaries dedicated to the improvement of their country. Many of Spain's leading teachers of this century have been "Instituciónistas."

The spirit of educational reform inspired by the Institución Libre de Enseñanza leavened Spain in the twentieth century. Friends and associates of Giner were responsible for a series of new cultural and educational organizations. One of Spain's greatest modern intellectuals was Santiago Ramón y Cajal, who came out of rural Aragon to become an outstanding neurologist and Spain's first winner of the Nobel Prize in science. In 1907 he and Giner, convinced of the need for Spaniards to go abroad to study, founded the Junta para Ampliación de Estudios Históricos e Investigaciones Científicas (Committee for the Extension of Historical Studies and Scientific Research) to give fellowships for young Spaniards to go to foreign universities. To the consternation of conservatives the current Liberal government gave it official recognition and a subsidy. In 1910 Ramón Menéndez Pidal, one of the leading figures of the Junta and Spain's greatest medievalist, was largely responsible for founding the Center of Historical Studies, in which was trained Américo Castro, among other leading Spanish historians. The Residencia de Estudiantes (Students' Residence) in Madrid, established in the same year, offered lodging to Spanish and foreign university students and became a center for intellectual exchange that has been remembered with great warmth by many Spanish intellectuals. Finally disciples of the Institución established secondary schools in Madrid, Valencia, and Barcelona. A direct challenge to the schools of the religious orders, they nevertheless received state support. Known as the Instituto Escuela in each locality, they fostered the same kind of camaraderie and sense of mission among their graduates as did the Institución. The bodies which grew directly or indirectly out of Giner's inspiration, although more academic than the eighteenth-century Amigos del País, revived the latter's aim of reinvigorating Spanish society by working outside the established educational institutions. Once they proved their value, the royal government gave them encouragement and financial support, as it had to the Amigos.

In many areas intellectual activity was flowering by the turn of the century. The defeat of Spain by the United States in 1898 and the loss of its last colonies, in which the incompetence of the government and armed forces lay naked for all to observe, brought forth a flood of publications dedicated to analyzing the causes for Spain's disgrace among Western nations. Miguel de Unamuno, then professor of classics at Salamanca, had already begun the task in his *En torno al casticismo* of 1895, which cast the blame for Spain's decrepitude on the religious fanaticism and chauvinism of its ruling classes. Essayists like Angel Ganivet, Azorín, and Ramiro de Maeztu, novelists like Ramón del Valle Inclán and Pio Baroja, the poet Antonio Machado, the painters Ignacio Zuloaga and Joaquín Sorolla sought to capture the nature of Spanishness. In general they agreed with foreigners that Spaniards were a people apart, as different in character as in geography from other Western European nations. These men thought Spaniards should recognize the qualities of their existence, their passion, their individuality, their religiosity, but that they should regenerate themselves by participating in Western culture, science, and political philosophy. Although these thinkers spoke of Spain, most of them found Spain embodied in Castile, as we have already observed.

The Generation of '98, the name applied loosely to this group of intellectuals, was widely read at home and abroad. It gave currency to the idea that Spanish government was inefficient, corrupt, and unstable, running the country in the interest of the privileged few. Although most were not primarily political in their outlook, their criticism had obvious political connotations and inspired desires for reform. One of the friends of Giner de los Ríos who gave them inspiration did, however, labor directly in this direction. This was Joaquín Costa, like Ramón y Cajal of poor Aragonese origin, a self-taught lawyer and historian. In 1902, under the auspices of the Ateneo de Madrid, he produced a stinging indictment of the evils of *caciquismo*. He called for a "surgeon of iron" who could cut out the cancerous growth and remake Spain in the interest of the common people. He denounced the sale of the public lands in the nineteenth century and preached a return to communal farming as the salvation of Spain's rural masses. Agrarian reform and irrigation he made the objectives of personal crusades. He died in 1911 at fifty-five, but not before he had set in motion many currents of thought that would mature later. *Caciquismo* never recovered from his exposé.

5

Other protest movements were more directly involved in the collapse of *caciquismo*. The first to be effective was Catalan nationalism, the outgrowth of the Romantic cultural revival that had become a political force under the Republic. Until 1875 the Catalanist movement was politically radical, but the threat posed by the Figuerola tariff of 1868 made the industrialists of Catalonia susceptible to the appeal of regional autonomy. After 1880 they began to subsidize Catalanist newspapers and political parties, thus providing the regionalist intellectuals with bourgeois associates along with much-needed financial support. These same developments made Castilians suspicious of Catalan objectives. The enemies of the First Republic looked upon it as a Catalan creation, since Catalans were most prominent among its leaders. And Castilians began to consider high tariffs a subterfuge for Catalan exploitation of the pockets of other Spaniards. The tariff question pitted agrarian interests against manufacturing, splitting the coalition on which the established order rested. Despite Cánovas' efforts to pacify Catalan interests, the basis was present for a serious political conflict.

In 1879 Valentí Almirall, a former follower of Pi y Margall who had turned away from the latter's socialist ideas, began to publish the *Diari Catalá*, the first daily periodical to appear in Catalan since one of 1810, created by Joseph Bonaparte to woo Catalonia. Almirall soon headed a movement called the Catalan Center. Its objective was to group together all partisans of Catalan interests, and it urged Catalans to boycott both major parties, thus establishing Catalanism as a separate political movement. Soon a young law student, Enric Prat de la Riba, broke off and founded the Catalanist Union, with more directly political objectives. Representatives of the Union and other regionalist groups met at Manresa in 1892 and agreed on a three-point program: autonomy for Catalonia in all matters save defense, foreign relations, and interregional matters; a separate Catalan parliament which would rule the region according to its own laws, using its own language, and with only Catalans in local offices; and separate Catalan regiments in the army with their own officers and using their own language. The first two demands echoed the federalist position of 1873, but could also be presented as a revival of the *fueros* destroyed in 1714.

The war in Cuba and the Philippines served to strengthen the movement. The major market for Catalan textiles was in Cuba, and Catalan capitalists had invested heavily in Cuban sugar plantations. The loss of the colonies brought on a serious financial and industrial crisis in Catalonia, accompanied by labor agitation. Its bankers and manufacturers forgot Cánovas' recent favors and heaped blame on the ineptness and lack of political vision of the Madrid government, which they felt could not defend their markets in the world nor their interests as employers against the working classes.

In 1901 various Catalan parties united in a new common front called the Lliga Regionalista "to work by all legitimate means for the autonomy of the Catalan people within the Spanish state." [4] In that year the Lliga elected four deputies to the Cortes. After 1904 it was headed by Francesc Cambó, a leader of the powerful Fomento del Trabajo Nacional, the Catalan textile manufacturers' association. His leadership symbolized the new alliance of Catalan regionalists and industrialists.

[4] Quoted in E. Allison Peers, *Catalonia Infelix* (London: Methuen & Co. Ltd., 1937), p. 144.

In 1905 a group of military officers, who considered the regionalist movement subversive and were angered by a cartoon in a Barcelona periodical mocking the army's failures in Morocco, stormed the paper's office and smashed the presses. Catering to the demands of the army, the Cortes passed a "Law of Jurisdictions" which gave military tribunals jurisdiction over all offenses against the army and navy, including attacks in the press. Faced by this challenge, the regionalist movements from left to right regrouped themselves as the Solidaritat Catalana and won a resounding victory at the polls in April 1907. Catalans were thus the first to succeed in breaking control of elections from Madrid. The defection of the Catalan industrialists was a serious threat to the stability of the system.

The advances of Catalan regionalism found an echo among the Basques. The Basque Provinces and Navarre had been the only regions of Spain to preserve their *fueros* from the centralization of Philip V, and their support for the Carlists had been motivated to a considerable extent by fears that liberal centralism would destroy their local liberties. Navarre lost most of its privileges at the end of the Carlist War. After crushing the Carlist revolt of the 1870's, Cánovas took the opportunity at last to end Basque exemptions from military conscription and national taxes, but he permitted the Basques to keep a good amount of self-government. Nevertheless a regionalist movement arose to protest the loss of the *fueros*. Embodying the strongly clerical spirit of the Carlists, the Basque Nationalist Party, founded in 1894, aimed at preserving the Basque language and the local Catholic faith against the liberal centralism of Madrid. It was successful in electing a few deputies to the Cortes in succeeding decades.

6

Regionalist movements appealed to the upper and middle classes and to the peasants of the advanced areas. They had virtually no social program, and the urban proletariat developed its own independent organizations. The anarchist movement that took root after 1868 in association with the First International continued in existence despite the efforts of the Restoration governments to crush it. The anarchists became famous in Spain as elsewhere for spectacular individual acts of violence aimed at terrifying political leaders and the antirevolutionary public. In 1893 an anarchist bomb killed twenty people at the opening night of the Barcelona opera season. A Catalan anarchist threw a bomb at Alfonso XIII as he left his wedding ceremony with his bride in 1906, barely missing the couple and killing twenty-four others. Anarchist bullets killed Cánovas in 1897 and José Canalejas, the most capable Liberal leader, in 1912.

Anarchists also preached mass violence. In 1881 the clandestine followers of the defunct First International founded the Workers' Federation of the Spanish Region. It gathered in the remnants of the labor movement of Andalusia, but it could achieve little except to excite occasional fierce attacks on well-to-do landowners by agricultural workers whose lives were marked by poverty and despair. To them the anarchist organizers offered a millenarian faith in a better world, independent of the hated church. The Civil Guard carried out vicious reprisals and kept the movement in hand.

The expansion of Catalan industries attracted immigrants to Barcelona and other cities of the region. After 1880 they came in larger and larger numbers from Aragon, Valencia, and Murcia, areas which did not speak Catalan. These new recruits were not susceptible to Catalan nationalism, which in any case was becoming a middle-class movement, but anarchism did appeal to them. In Catalonia anarchism had been associated from the start with labor organizations, which usually had to operate clandestinely. The First International had expired in 1876 and Bakunin had died in the same year. Foreign concepts of labor organization, especially French, affected the Catalan workers in the following decades, replacing their primitive anarchism with anarcho-syndicalism. The anarcho-syndicalists believed in organizing the workers into syndicates or labor unions capable of industrial strikes, for they saw the strike as the prime weapon to achieve social revolution. Their ultimate objective was the general (or universal) strike that would paralyze the economy, forcing concessions and eventually bringing about the overthrow of the state (that is, the centralized government, which they conceived to be devoted to defending the interests of the bourgeoisie).

The Law of Associations of 1887 legalized workers' syndicates. During the depression following the defeat of 1898, syndicalism spread rapidly in Catalonia. When the metallurgical workers of Barcelona struck at the end of 1901 for an eight-hour day, they won the support of other labor groups, who voted for a general strike in February 1902. Some 80,000 workers (in a city of 500,000) went out on strike. The Civil Guard and the army moved in to break the strike, and there was some fighting, which lasted a week before the workers were defeated. The syndicalist movement suffered from this setback, but the workers continued uncowed. In 1907, when the regionalists and manufacturers established the Solidaritat Catalana, the anarchists responded by establishing a union of workers' groups called the Solidaridad Obrera (Labor Solidarity).

Meanwhile, under the leadership of a fiery speaker, Alejandro Lerroux, part of the Catalan Republican movement, which had been kept alive by Salmerón, broke off from the Catalanists and appealed to the workers with calls for a social revolution. Lerroux named his party the Radical Republicans, or simply the Radicals. He directed his strongest attacks against the church, which for him epitomized the evils of the existing economic system, and Catalan separatism.

By 1909 there was a high state of tension in Barcelona. Bombs had been thrown at leaders of the Lliga Regionalista; some claimed by anarchists, others by agents provocateurs of the industrialists or the Madrid government. An economic crisis and unemployment aggravated passions. In July 1909 the army decided to call up the military reserves to meet a critical situation in Morocco, and began with working-class men of Catalonia. Given the hatreds present among the workers of Barcelona, this announcement had disastrous consequences. The anarchists and Radicals joined in proclaiming a general strike, which began on July 26. Next day the army established martial law. The workers responded with barricades and, excited by agents of Lerroux's party, systematically set fire to churches and convents. Order was not reestablished for five days, by which time over fifty church buildings had been burned. The government, searching for a scapegoat, found him in the radical anticlerical Francisco Ferrer, a friend of Lerroux and a founder of a school associated with the anarchist movement, the Escuela Moderna. He was tried summarily and shot, causing an international scandal that blackened the name of Spain among liberals and workers throughout Europe.

The Tragic Week, as the event became known, added further discredit to the parliamentary system. Yet, like the nineteenth-century revolutions, it frightened the middle-class opponents of the established order into temporary quiescence, while the privileged classes drew back together. The Catalan industrialists and the Madrid government were ready to make peace. Solidaritat Catalana had collapsed, and Cambó's Lliga Regionalista pressed the ministry for home rule. In 1914 the king and ministry granted a common government for the four provinces that made up Catalonia, known as the Mancomunitat. It had authority over social services, communications, and education. Prat de la Riba was its first president. Dominated by the Lliga, it proved ready to cooperate with the central government against the proletariat of Catalonia.

The Catalan workers were disillusioned by the lack of success of the Tragic Week. Support for Lerroux declined among them. The Solidaridad Obrera held a congress in 1910 and established the Confederación Nacional del Trabajo (National Confederation of Labor) to coordinate anarchist activity in line with the French syndicalist doctrine of direct action and the general strike. The CNT was the first broad permanent institution established by Spanish anarchists, showing that the need to face the state in combat had forced them to give up the anarchist ideal of basing their activities on local organizations.

Anarchism was not the only revolutionary doctrine to take hold of the Spanish proletariat. In the First International Bakunin's party had been opposed by the followers of Karl Marx. Before it dissolved in 1876 the organization expelled the anarchists and established Marxist socialism as its official doctrine. From this conflict Spanish labor leaders learned of Marxism. Fleeing France after the Paris Commune, Paul Lafargue, Marx's son-in-law, went to Spain in 1871 and there sought to win over the workers' associations from Bakunin. He failed, but he left effective converts behind. The most important of these was a young printer named Pablo Iglesias, who was to demonstrate great capacities as an organizer and administrator.

Having fallen out with the anarchists, in 1879 Iglesias founded a clandestine Socialist Workers' Party in Madrid, and in 1888 an association of labor unions, the Unión General de Trabajadores (General Union of Workingmen). The UGT had little success in penetrating the anarchist stronghold of Catalonia, but it obtained followers among the craftsmen of Madrid and the Basque ironworkers. It conducted succesful strikes in Bilbao in the 1890's and the following decades. At the same time the Socialist party became active in the political sphere. Bilbao elected eight socialist municipal councilors in 1901, and Iglesias won a place on the *ayuntamiento* of Madrid in 1905. Four years later the Socialists joined the anarchists in the general strike of the Tragic Week in Barcelona, extending their appeal for support throughout the country. Shortly thereafter, through an alliance with the Republicans, the Socialists elected Iglesias to the Cortes, Spain's first proletarian deputy. By now the UGT was extending its membership among the workers of the north, Castile, and Andalusia, including miners of Asturias and the Sierra Morena, the copper miners of Rio Tinto, the railway workers, and other groups, many of them employees of foreign companies. A growing number of landowning peasants of Castile and Valencia also joined the Socialist unions.

Under the inspiration of Iglesias, the Socialist party and the UGT worked to educate the people for political democracy, believing that with the universal suffrage established in 1890 honest elections would ultimately bring reform and an end to capitalism. They established Casas del Pueblo in the cities and towns of central Spain, places where there were cafés and lending libraries and the Socialists could hold meetings and offer public lectures. By 1910 the Socialists found support among Madrid intellectuals, including Spain's greatest modern novelist, Benito Pérez Galdos, who became a friend of Iglesias. In these ways the Socialists spread Marxist doctrines to a large sector of Spanish thinkers and workers.

The labor movement was thus divided between the anarchists and anarcho-syndicalists, who believed in violent direct action and no compromise with the employing classes, and the Socialists, who strove for limited gains and a gradual evolution toward socialism through legislation. Spain was not unique. By the turn of the century, many European workers' movements had split into evolutionary and revolutionary wings. In most countries both wings were Marxist in their orientation. The Spanish anarchists never accepted the Marxist doctrine of the need of a dictatorship of the proletariat to establish the new society after the revolution, for they steadily opposed a centralized state in every form. Their rejection of political action meant that workers' parties had much less political strength in Spain than in other Western European countries.

Spanish socialism and anarchism developed in different geographic areas. The anarcho-syndicalist stronghold was Catalonia, and messianic anarchists found their followers among Andalusian peasants. The Socialists appealed to Castilian craftsmen and peasants, and to the miners and industrial workers of the north and Andalusia. The anarchist CNT and Socialist UGT rarely cooperated, but one instance was the Tragic Week, when the weak UGT of Barcelona feared for its following if it failed to participate in the insurrection. The division of Spain between the two doctrines was partly the result of historic accident, but there was also a deeper cause. Although Catalan anarcho-syndicalists and nationalists were bitter enemies, the one representing the working classes, the other the intellectuals and propertied classes, both movements opposed a strongly unified and centralized state organization. The same was true of the cantonalist movement and the First International in eastern and southern Spain during the First Republic. Socialist Marxism, on the other hand, which taught the need for tight political organization and a revolutionary dictatorship, appealed to the central region of Spain, accustomed for centuries to dominate the peninsula politically. The connection cannot be pushed too far, however, for the Socialists were strong among Basque workers, in an area which was traditionally regionalist.

Class divisions weakened the industrialized regions in their conflict with Madrid. Socialists and anarchists split the proletariat. Intellectuals could be found favoring most every form of opposition. After 1898 the order survived because its enemies were divided, but the existing parliamentary system was discredited and could find no way to reconcile its opponents. By 1914 Spain needed only a serious shock to disrupt the Moderado order.

10

The End of the Order and the Gentle Dictatorship

1

Like the rest of Europe, Spain had a passion for opera at the end of the nineteenth century. Its own contribution was to the genre of light opera, the *zarzuelas* which caught the spirit of the common people of the cities. Of the *zarzuelas*, the most popular was *La Verbena de la Paloma*, a joyous and witty tale of the old quarter of Madrid composed in 1894 by Tomás Bretón. In the opening scene Don Hilarón, the elderly pharmacist whose passion for attractive young Madrileñas is the spice of the tale, tells of the latest medical discoveries:

> ¡Hoy las ciencias adelantan
> Que es una barbaridad!

As the twentieth century advanced, the people of Madrid, along with their counterparts throughout the cities of Spain and the rest of Europe, could well agree with Don Hilarón that it was barbarous how science was advancing. They were familiar with the latest inventions: streetcars, automobiles, electric lights, telephones. By the second decade buses began to complement the railroad network to tie the cities together, slowly replacing the stagecoaches of an earlier era.

Spain was keeping abreast of modern civilization in other ways. Although ornate Easter processions symbolized the unity of church and state, religious freedom existed. There was virtually no censorship of public expression. In Madrid the quality of newspapers rose with the appearance in 1910 of *El Debate*, a liberal Catholic journal edited in the spirit of Pope Leo XIII, and in 1917 of the moderate *El Sol*, which rapidly provided the most reliable political news in Spain. A new generation of writers, educators, and artists was becoming famous throughout the West: the novelists Ramón del Valle-Inclán and Vicente Blasco Ibáñez, the historians Rafael Altamira and Ramón Menéndez Pidal, the genre painters Joaquín Sorolla and Ignacio Zuloaga, the cubists Pablo Picasso and Juan Gris, and the composers Enrique Granados and Manuel de Falla.

Progress still ended at the city's edge, however. The railroad had commercialized large-scale agriculture, but virtually all peasants lived without benefit of Don Hilarón's scientific advances. They still plowed with a Roman plow, cooked over open fireplaces, and never dreamed of using a telephone or electric light. A well-to-do peasant's kitchen was a veritable museum of ceramic pots and handwrought brass and copper pans. The peasants enjoyed their traditional songs and dances. They wore the dress of their ancestors, the woolen *calza* (breeches that stopped below the knees) and stockings or *polainas* (woolen leggings worn above the shoes tied on the outside of the leg). The major regions had their variations on this basic costume. For market days the peasants put on their best dress, which differed from the clothes worn daily in the fields only in being newer. As they walked around the market towns, they could tell which villages the other farmers had come from by the shape of their hats, the color of ribbon on their legs, or other distinguishing features. Joaquín Sorolla preserved for later generations the beauty and uniqueness of Spain's regional costumes in a series of paintings commissioned in 1911 by the Hispanic Society of America in New York.

In the nineteenth century, when peasants had migrated to the cities, they had kept their rural dress. This habit had died out around the turn of the century, and the city proletariat had put on the *gorra* (cap) and *blusa* (smock). In the Sunday promenades in the cities one could still recognize the members of the different trades by their dress—masons by their fresh white jackets, butchers by their striped aprons—but rural costumes no longer appeared. As Unamuno put it, "Between the city and the countryside, there is more distance than between the most different climes."[1]

Such in brief was Spain when Europe went confidently to war in 1914. Slowly as the war dragged on, Europeans began to realize that it might be destroying their nineteenth-century order, that progress toward a stable middle-class society and parliamentary government might not be so inevitable as they had believed. The war ate up their carefully accumulated capital and stimulated violent political movements which

[1] Quoted in Carmelo Lison-Tolosana, *Belmonte de los Caballeros, a Sociological Study of a Spanish Town* (Oxford: Clarendon Press, 1966), p. 15.

threatened constitutional democracy. Spain remained neutral, yet the effects of the war also destroyed its established order.

From the outset, news of the fighting and propaganda spread by agents of the two sides polarized Spain. By and large, the entrenched groups were sympathetic to the Central Powers. The liberal intellectuals, the Republicans, and the workers favored the Allies. The division of sympathies followed also a geographic line: most Catalans and Basques, regardless of social class, were "aliadófilos"; Castile outside of Madrid was generally "germanófilo." The ideological impact of the conflict culminated in 1917, the year in which the United States entered the war to make the world safe for democracy and two Russian revolutions overthrew the tsar and brought Lenin and the Bolsheviks to power. Spanish partisans of both causes—parliamentary democracy and revolutionary socialism—believed their hour had come.

The war had a strong effect on Spain's working classes. Foreign demand for Spanish goods drew rural workers into industries and coal mines and encouraged farmers to plant marginal lands. Some Spaniards went to France to replace Frenchmen mobilized for war. When they returned, they brought new ideas and customs. In place of the *gorra* and *blusa* the Spanish proletariat began to don blue overalls and black berets, the *mono* and *boina*. Cheaper and more practical, the new costume was to become the trademark of the urban working class in the next decade. As the effects of war multiplied the number of industrial workers and pushed up their wages, the syndicates of the UGT and CNT attracted many more members. Their leaders became more belligerent, strikes were frequent, and the organizations began to call jointly for a general strike.

Strikes had been common ever since the Tragic Week, but the army had always been available to restore order. Now, however, the virus of reform had infected the officer corps. The junior infantry and cavalry officers were angered by the level of their salaries, made proportionately lower by wartime inflation, and by the revival of battle promotions in Morocco, which disadvantaged those who stayed home with their families. In December 1916 the officers in Barcelona below the rank of general formed an association to further their demands, and early in 1917 similar officers' groups were established throughout Spain, known as Juntas Militares de Defensa. In May 1917 the minister of war ordered the members of the Barcelona junta arrested. The other juntas replied with threats of an armed rising. After releasing the prisoners and agreeing to negotiate, the ministry resigned. The king selected the Conservative leader Eduardo Dato to head the next ministry. His first act was to recognize the statutes of the infantry juntas, apparently giving in to the threat of force.

The press magnified the crisis, reminding Spaniards that the defection of the Russian army had precipitated the fall of the tsar. The discontented groups became excited. Noncommissioned officers and public servants also formed juntas to air their grievances. Political leaders and labor groups began to agitate. In June Socialists, Republicans, and Catalan nationalists demanded the convocation of constituent cortes, and the syndicates threatened a nationwide general strike. When Dato refused to bring the issue of reform before the Cortes, the Catalan Lliga invited dissident deputies to a parliamentary assembly in Barcelona. Seventy-one deputies met on July 19, 1917 representing the gamut of the opposition, from industralist Lliga under Cambó, through Republicans and Lerroux Radicals, to Socialists. Their common cry was "*¡Renovación!*" The assembly barely had time to back the call for constituent cortes when the police arrived and put the deputies briefly under arrest. Nonetheless, the assembly excited wide expectations. *Ayuntamientos* from all parts of Spain, as in times past, voiced their support. The moment was critical, for Institucionista intellectuals, regionalists, employers, workers, and army officers were all calling for "renovation," although they did not all agree on what it meant.

Almost immediately the parliamentarians lost control of the movement. Strikes were spreading among dockers, railroad employees, and metalworkers. The socialist and anarchist syndicates joined efforts, each fearful of dropping behind. Among the Socialists, a dynamic young figure, Francisco Largo Caballero, took the initiative away from the aging Iglesias and proclaimed a nationwide general strike in favor of a socialist republic on August 10, a few days before the assembly of opposition deputies was to reconvene in Madrid. The UGT and CNT together paralyzed the industrial districts of the north, east, and south. Trains stopped running, food shortages threatened in the cities.

At this point the army proved the decisive factor. The Juntas de Defensa had never intended to achieve more than an end to the grievances of army officers. Now, frightened by the specter of a proletarian rising, the officers gave their support to the government. Under their command the soldiers turned machine guns on the workers, killing about one hundred in various cities and arresting their leaders, including Largo Caballero. In three days the general strike was broken. Unlike the Russian army, the Spanish had not been ravaged by war and maintained discipline in a crisis. Neither Madrid nor Barcelona was to be Saint Petersburg.

Although the army had killed a revolution, the Juntas de Defensa continued to issue manifestoes demanding reform. The parliamentary assembly of opposition deputies finally met again in Madrid on October 30, 1917 and again called for constituent cortes to establish a workable democracy. This time, however, the opposition was no longer united. The general strike had scared the Catalan Lliga Regionalista. When Alfonso XIII on November 1 named a coalition ministry drawn from all loyal parties to face the threat, it was headed by a Liberal, Manuel García Prieto, and included representatives of both Conservatives and the Lliga. The social crisis had brought out the essential conservatism of both the Liberals and Lliga. The Catalan manufacturers preferred to deal with Madrid than with their workers. In Andalusia, the growing wave of strikes drove Liberal and Conservative clubs to coalesce into "Círculos de la Unión," united in the face of the restless lower classes.[2] The prolonged crisis of 1917 was Spain's best opportunity to replace the Moderado system with effective parliamentary democracy. It failed, as nineteenth-century revolutions had failed, because parliamentarians and revolutionary workers did not have common methods or objectives. The ruling groups had once again drawn together and saved the order.

2

A few days after Alfonso XIII and the loyal politicians had finally outmaneuvered the reformers, in Russia the November 1917 Revolution brought the Bolsheviks to power. The news aroused Spanish workers and revolutionaries, for Russia was a backward country like Spain. A year later, the end of the First World War caused the collapse of Spain's economic boom. Foreign orders for foodstuffs and manufactured goods dried up, and British coal flowed back into Spain, hurting the newly opened Asturian mines. Unemployed farm laborers flocked to the cities just as manufacturers dismissed many workers in an effort to keep solvent. Prior to the war emigration had offered an outlet for the under-employed, but the American nations now restricted this movement. In 1912 195,000 Spaniards had emigrated; only 20,000 did in 1918 and 62,000 in 1921. Conditions were ripe for a social upheaval.

The defeat of July 1917 caused only a brief letup in proletarian agitation. Since before the war anarchist organizers had been strengthening the agricultural syndicates of the south. Excited by reports from Russia, all through 1918 the landless workers of Andalusia, Valencia, and Murcia staged strikes, now in one town, now in another. Swept up in the movement, artisans and landowning peasants supported them. By the end of the year, the wave of strikes culminated in provincewide general strikes. Many landlords fled in terror, while the braver and wiser ones conceded wage increases and other workers' demands. In May 1919 the government at last responded to the pleas of the landowners and sent in the army and Civil Guard. The strike movement collapsed like a burst balloon, and order was restored.

[2] J. A. Pitt-Rivers, *The People of the Sierra* (Chicago: University of Chicago Press, 1961), p. 135.

Catalonia was the next scene of labor turmoil. In July 1918 the anarchists Salvador Seguí and Ángel Pestaña got a regional congress of the CNT of Catalonia to restructure its syndicates into "single" or vertical syndicates, grouping together all the different workers in each branch of industry. The objective was more effective strikes. The first test came in February 1919, when the workers of the Catalan electric power company, the "Canadiense," struck to force the reinstatement of some employees, higher wages, and an eight-hour day. The strike was spectacular; it threw Barcelona into darkness, forced factories to close, and brought thousands of idle workers out into the streets. Though a mediator from Madrid got the company to concede most demands, the captain general of Catalonia refused to release the strike leaders he had imprisoned. The CNT countered with a general strike at the end of March, which lasted two weeks and was broken only when the captain general declared martial law, ignoring the authority of the civil government. During the rest of the year the manufacturers and military forces cooperated to fight the syndicates, oblivious of the cabinet in Madrid.

By the end of 1919 the established order had survived two waves of attack typical of Europe in these years: the democratic offensive, encouraged by President Wilson, which had introduced or strengthened constitutional democracy in both victorious and vanquished nations, and the revolutionary socialist offensive which had triumphed in Russia and terrified propertied classes in Germany, Hungary, Italy, and elsewhere. By keeping Spain out of the war, the conservative forces had saved themselves.

Yet the days of the constitutional monarchy were numbered. Elections in February 1918 did not return a majority for either Liberals or Conservatives, and the number of opposition deputies rose from 55 to 89, including four Socialists who were in prison for leading the general strike of 1917. Only another coalition government, which brought together Conservatives, Liberals, and Lliga, was able to win a parliamentary majority and keep the army satisfied. Even this ministry lasted only until November 1918. Stable government was no longer possible. The average length of ministries in the next five years was five months, half what it had been from Alfonso XIII's coming of age until 1917. *Caciquismo* had collapsed, and in its place the only sure arm of the established order was the army. But the officers were disdainful of parliament and felt their first loyalty to the king, who used the agitation of the Juntas Militares to flaunt his concern for the army.

Although Spain's proletarian leaders admired the Russian Revolution, with few exceptions they did not become Communists. While large sectors of the French and Italian Socialist parties voted to join the Communist International, in Spain the Socialist party, after much debate, rejected this course by a sizable majority at a congress in 1921.

A few dissidents broke off and founded the Spanish Communist party. The following year the CNT also voted against affiliation with Moscow, remaining loyal to anarchist doctrines. Again a minority left to join the Communists. They included Andrés Nín and Joaquín Maurín, who were to become the leading figures of Spain's minuscule Communist party. In Spain the anarchists already offered an allegiance for the kind of revolutionary workers who became Communists elsewhere.

After the war the relative harmony that existed between the UGT and CNT in 1917–18 disappeared, the former reverting to evolutionary tactics, the latter more uncompromising than ever. The possibility of proletarian revolution dwindled, but middle-class fears continued, because as the syndicates became weaker, labor violence increased, particularly in Catalonia. After 1919 Catalan industrialists were out to destroy the CNT. They refused all concessions, used the lockout, and hired gangs of *pistoleros* or gunmen to assassinate syndicalist leaders. They encouraged the growth of rival Catholic Free Syndicates, which had been founded in 1916. From 1920 to 1922 they had a cooperative general as civil governor, Severiano Martínez Anido, who looked the other way when the army or Civil Guard shot anarchist prisoners "while trying to escape." The CNT hired its own *pistoleros*, not only to terrorize employers but to fight the Free Syndicates. The wave of assassinations rose until, in sixteen months in 1922–23, 230 persons were murdered in the streets of Barcelona.[8] The prime minister Dato was killed in Madrid in May 1922. In March 1923 it was the turn of the syndicalist leader Seguí, and the anarchists replied by shooting the reputedly reactionary archbishop of Zaragoza. To Catalan manufacturers the Madrid government seemed powerless and the army the only force that could save them. General Martínez Anido ruled Catalonia as an independent proconsul, scorning directives from Madrid but finding favor with Cambó and the Lliga.

When the Lliga called the parliamentary assembly of 1917, one of its hopes was to strengthen Catalan self-government. Wilson's ideals included autonomy for subject nationalities, and Catalans felt they deserved it as much as Czechs and Poles. The tensions of the postwar years revealed Cambó to be more concerned in preserving order by cooperating with Madrid and the army than achieving a satisfactory solution to the regional problem. Catalan nationalists among the intellectuals and lower-middle class became disenchanted with the Lliga. In 1921 a fiery Catalan in his sixties, Francesc Macià, founded a separatist movement, Estat Català. A year later others formed Acciò Catalana. They rejected the parliamentary monarchy and believed only a federal republic could solve Catalonia's problems, reverting in effect

[8] Gerald Brenan, *The Spanish Labyrinth* (Cambridge: Cambridge University Press, 1943), p. 73.

to the ideal of 1873. This revival of militant Catalan nationalism and the labor warfare made Catalonia the gravest problem for the monarchy at the beginning of the 1920's.

In the end, however, it was not the radical and revolutionary opponents of the system that succeeded in destroying it, but the king and the army. Neither believed in the supremacy of parliament. Alfonso XIII itched to exert authority, feeling that he, not the Cortes, was the true sovereign. He had frequently used his constitutional authority of choosing ministers and dissolving the Cortes to interfere with the normal functioning of the parliamentary system, to the distress of his loyal parliamentarians. He took literally the wording of the constitution that he was supreme commander of the armed forces; he kept in close touch with the generals, and trusted them more than the politicians to protect the throne from Republicans and Socialists. The officers responded by appealing to him against parliamentary and popular criticism.

Events in Morocco triggered the outcome. Since 1909 the Spanish army had struggled to pacify the Moorish tribes in Spain's sector of the protectorate. In 1921 a reckless advance led to a bloody and shameful defeat at Annual, with thousands of casualties. It seemed like 1898 all over again. The opposition groups jumped at the chance to discredit the regime and called for an investigation to determine responsibility. After a year of probing, the general entrusted with the task drew up a report indicating corruption among the officers and by implication involving Alfonso, who had egged on the generals against his ministers' advice. The contents of the report were secret, to be presented to the Cortes when they reopened on September 17, 1923.

On September 13, the captain general of Catalonia, Miguel Primo de Rivera, with the connivance of Alfonso XIII, pronounced against the government. While other military commanders vacillated, Alfonso assured the success of the *pronunciamiento* by naming Primo de Rivera prime minister. Four days later Primo appointed a "directory" under himself of eight brigadier-generals and a rear admiral and established local military delegates to rule the country. He proclaimed martial law, dismissed the provincial civil governors, abolished the *ayuntamientos*, and dissolved the Cortes. The presidents of the two houses of the Cortes went to Alfonso to remind him that the constitution required that elections be held within three months. The king dismissed them and Primo suspended the constitution; briefly, he assured everyone, pending return to normality.

The pattern of events was not unique. Threats to parliamentary government from the right and the left were general in Europe in the postwar years. The governments of Germany and Italy withstood serious attacks from the left, but the middle classes and manufacturers had been frightened, just as they were in Spain, encouraging right-wing militants to overthrow liberal democracy. Germany had a strong enough government to put down the militarist Kapp Putsch in 1920. In Italy, however, antiparliamentary and antiproletarian forces found a gifted leader in Benito Mussolini, recent founder of the Fascist party. After a wave of political assassinations reminiscent of Barcelona's and bloody street battles between the Fascists and the Italian Socialists, Mussolini demanded power to restore order. The king made him prime minister in October 1922, and a cowed parliament voted unlimited powers to him, which he used to terrorize his enemies, win the next elections, and abolish civil liberties. By an ostensibly legal process he established a dictatorship.

Primo de Rivera's *pronunciamiento* had many similarities. It too responded to a fear of proletarian revolution and established a dictatorship in place of a parliamentary government that was unable to curb disorder. Like Mussolini, Primo was patronized by a compliant king, ready to sacrifice parliament to save his throne. But Mussolini headed an organized party and had the craft to cloak his rule in parliamentary legality. Primo represented no civilian party, and his first move was to suspend the constitution. Reminiscent of the generals who had made nineteenth-century *pronunciamientos,* he justified his rebellion, or "technical indiscipline" as he called it in his manifesto, by the "true discipline owed to our dogma and the love of our country." [4] He was acting in a Spanish tradition that in the end was his undoing.

3

General Primo de Rivera was fifty-three years old at the time of his *pronunciamiento*. He came from an Andalusian army family and had been a career officer all his life, having served in Cuba, the Philippines, and Morocco. A bluff and open widower with six children, he had a reputation for enjoying life, especially wine, women, and flamenco music. He was proud of his literary style and angered when intellectuals mocked his flowery prose. Although a firm leader, he was not cruel and could not bear a grudge for long, a strange figure for a twentieth-century dictator.

Unlike Mussolini, Primo had to face little active hostility. Because they had failed to obtain reform, the opponents of the former regime had no tears to shed for it. Its beneficiaries welcomed a strong hand that would offer them more protection than the Cortes had. Primo's manifesto ordered the army to occupy Communist and revolutionary centers, and the Catalan Lliga Regionalista welcomed his advent. Ortega y Gasset, who in 1921 had condemned Spain's lack of authority

[4] Manifesto dated Sept. 12, 1923, in Miguel Primo de Rivera, *El Pensamiento de Primo de Rivera,* ed. J. M. Peman (Madrid, Sáez Hermanos, 1929), p. 24.

in his *Invertebrate Spain,* called the directory "those magnanimous generals, who generously and disinterestedly have realized the half-century-old aspirations of twenty million Spaniards without its costing the Spanish people any effort whatsoever." [5] Primo pictured himself as the "surgeon of iron" whom Joaquín Costa had prayed for. Hoping to ride the crest of the spirit of '98, he called to his banner all those who "loving our country, see no other salvation for it than to save it from professional politicians, the men who for one reason or another have displayed to us the sight of misfortunes and corruption which began in the year '98 and threaten Spain with an imminent end, tragic and dishonorable." [6]

His popularity continued for three years. Prosperity had returned to Europe after the postwar collapse, calming angry spirits. Primo de Rivera's greatest triumph was to end the war in Morocco, which had been draining Spain's energies since shortly after '98. He enjoyed better luck than the parliamentarians. Having withstood the Spanish forces, the Moorish insurgents made the error of attacking the French sector of Morocco. This led to a joint Franco-Spanish offensive in 1925 that quickly routed the tribesmen. Primo took personal command of the Spanish troops. In December 1925 he announced to a grateful nation that the African cancer had been excised.

From the outset the provisional nature of his rule posed difficulties for the dictator. He had suspended the constitution of 1876, not abolished it, and stated that the Directory was to be a "brief parenthesis" in the political life of Spain, at most ninety days, until honest civilians could come forward to restore constituional government. The days turned into years, however, without Primo's discovering the civilians to replace him. By what right did he rule? He pledged himself to his country, he called to his side all patriotic Spaniards, he had the approval of the king; but his rule, like that of every government, had eventually to be justified by commonly accepted principles. Since the defeat of the Carlists in the 1830's, sovereignty clearly resided with the Spanish people, not the king, and European events of 1917–18 had made popular sovereignty a universal dogma. But how to give the people sovereignty and keep them from exercising it? The dilemma had brought down the parliamentary regime. It faced all twentieth-century authoritarian rulers. Lenin and Mussolini had already met it, so Primo de Rivera was not entirely on his own.

Italy and Russia had outlawed all political parties except the one of the regime. Primo de Rivera from the start voiced a desire to replace Spain's parties with a new organization, an "apolitical party" that

[5] Quoted in Dillwyn F. Ratcliff, *Prelude to Franco: Political Aspects of the Dictatorship of General Miguel Primo de Rivera* (New York: Las Americas Pub. Co., 1957), p. 38.

[6] Manifesto of September 12, 1923, *loc. cit.*, p. 19.

would attract selfless, patriotic Spaniards to serve the state. He termed the organization the Unión Patriótica (UP). It held meetings in various cities from 1923 on, but was slow in taking shape. In 1924 Primo spoke vaguely of an association of all Spaniards who accepted the Constitution of 1876 as the basis of a new order, in which the intrigue, squabbling, and corruption of political parties would disappear. Those who joined the UP had to state: "I detest all sectarian or partisan politics because I wish to serve my country with a comprehensive ideology and personal independence without owing to any influence which represents favoritism the justice which is mine by right." [7] Civil servants, school teachers, politicians who had been unsuccessful under the parliamentary monarchy, indeed anyone who desired favors or a job from the government was likely to be found in the party. Despite Primo's intentions, incorruptibility was not its major characteristic. Neither was enthusiasm. Without achieving the emotional appeal of Fascism or adopting its strong-arm tactics, Primo nevertheless followed its concept of a one-party state.

Late in 1925, flushed with his Moroccan triumph, Primo de Rivera at last decided to legitimize his rule. He dismissed the military directory on December 3 and replaced it with a civilian directory, whose members held regular cabinet posts. (The generals had had no individual responsibility or authority.) The following September he conducted a national plebiscite. The Unión Patriótica ran the affair, its first major undertaking. It set up tables throughout all Spain, where citizens could sign a statement indicating their approval of the government. There was no way to indicate disapproval except by abstaining. Seven and a half million signatures were thus collected, almost two-thirds of the total adult population, male and female. The people had spoken, presumably spontaneously, and henceforth Primo could claim that his regime had a democratic base.

Nevertheless it still lacked a building over the base. Return to normality proved far more difficult than Primo de Rivera had imagined, for his capable, uncorrupted civilians failed to materialize. Only the old political leaders were present, urging the king to end the extraordinary rule. In the face of their protests, Primo convoked a National Assembly which Alfonso XIII opened on October 10, 1927. It met in the chambers of the Cortes to give advice to the dictator. Most of its four hundred members were appointed: local chiefs of the UP and representatives of administrative bodies. The public sessions were carefully regulated to provide efficient discussion. Members were allotted twenty minutes for speeches and ten for replies, and they could not call the ministry to account. It met again in 1928 and 1929, but no legislation ever emanated from it.

[7] Quoted in Ratcliff, p. 60.

A commission of the National Assembly drew up the draft of a new constitution, which it finally completed in 1929. The proposal reflected Primo de Rivera's views. It provided for a one-house Cortes elected by universal male and female suffrage. (Primo was the first ruler of Spain to give women the vote, on the assumption that they were less revolutionary than men.) The king and his ministers retained authority, however, for the Cortes could not overthrow the ministry. At first Primo planned to submit the project to the Cortes for ratification, but as political leaders, intellectuals, and professionals made their opposition patent, he decided to use instead another plebiscite. It was planned for 1930, but before the scheduled date Primo had resigned and the project disappeared with him. He never found his fig leaf of legality.

4

If Primo de Rivera failed to create a permanent political order, he had more success in effecting economic development. Since the beginning of the century reform and progress had been shibboleths of government and opposition alike. Joaquín Costa, with his cry for agrarian reform and irrigation, was the prophet, but others had worked at the practical day-to-day level. The government established the Institute of Social Reforms in 1903 to investigate labor conditions and recommend social legislation. Its governing board included representatives of agriculture, industry, and labor. In 1902 the government adopted a plan for irrigation drawn up by the minister of public works Rafael Gasset, uncle of Ortega y Gasset, and in the next decades began the construction of dams in Aragon and Castile. There had been plenty of plans but no government permanent or strong enough to carry them out effectively. Primo de Rivera pushed forward their realization, fulfilling dreams of the men of '98.

Irrigation and roads were his major achievements. To direct the former he appointed a brilliant engineer, Manuel Lorenzo Pardo, who rationalized Gasset's uncoordinated plans. Gasset had selected areas for irrigation indiscriminately. Lorenzo Pardo focused on three regions most likely to benefit from irrigation: the lower valleys of the Ebro and Guadiana Rivers (the latter near Badajoz), and the plains of Valencia, where water could be piped across the divide from the upper Tajo basin. Under Primo de Rivera much of the Ebro River complex of dams was completed, augmenting both the acreage under irrigation and the output of electricity. The other plans remained for future regimes to take up.

Although there were some automobiles in Spain before his time, Primo de Rivera introduced the age of motorized transport. He undertook to build a network of all-weather highways, many of them paved with blocks of granite, which followed the familiar pattern of a star radiating from Madrid. His regime built or improved 7000 kilometers of roads. The rural bus, the *coche de linea*, became a familiar sight, driving out the last of the stagecoaches. When Primo de Rivera fell, Spain had one of the best highway networks in Europe, but it hardly grew in the next twenty years because of economic restrictions and war.

In opening Spain to motor traffic, Primo set in motion a slow revolution in the countryside whose full effects have only been felt in the last decade. Gradually rural Spain was feeling the influence of urban civilization, a fundamental social development of the twentieth century which has been little studied. First to be affected was the regional dress. The heavy woolen cloth of the small Castilian factories could no longer compete in price with the products of Catalan mills, and the younger generation of peasants welcomed a change that would make them less conspicuous when they went to the towns. Men began to put on pants and a sleeveless jacket (*chaleco*) of brown or black corduroy (*pana*), which they wore with a wool waistband (*faja*) and cotton shirt. The women made themselves cotton skirts and petticoats (*refajos*) and over them put on an apron (*mandil*) and scarf (*pañuelo*). By the 1930s, in the typical Sunday promenades of the small towns, girls could even be seen in homemade versions of the latest city fashions. Not only the peasant dress suffered. Radio made its appearance in the twenties and reached as far as there was electricity. The larger towns began to hear popular modern music and their young people began to dance cheek to cheek, "*agarrados*." The old songs and dances retreated to remoter regions.

The transformation was gradual, spreading like grease stains from the provincial capitals and *cabezas de partido*. In the twenties and thirties vast regions could still be found, in Extremadura, for instance, or Cuenca, which still did not know the train, the automobile, the electric light, or the radio; and their dress and customs remained unchanged. Aware of what was going on, some artists, musicians, and teachers, who shared the admiration of the popular culture that the Institución Libre de Enseñanza and the Generation of '98 had inspired, went to remote towns to record the disappearing folklore. As the peasants gave up their ways to ape the cities, these intellectuals made it a labor of love to preserve and exhalt "*lo típico*."

The vast building programs of Primo de Rivera which accelerated these changes were only possible because of worldwide prosperity and because he dared use unorthodox fiscal policies. Construction was paid for out of loans, on the assumption that the resulting economic growth would more than repay the outlay. The government established special banks and credit agencies to finance industrial expansion, agricultural improvement, municipal public works, and railroad modernization.

Traditional politicians and conservative economic thinkers shook their heads as the public debt rose by a third. They pointed to the recent devaluation of the French franc and the collapse of the German mark brought on by the cost of the First World War and reconstruction.

Many of the dictator's economic policies originated with an intelligent but reckless young man whom he made minister of finance in his civilian directory, José Calvo Sotelo. Calvo Sotelo embarked on a concerted program of economic nationalism. The European nations that had suffered from the war were attempting to protect their economies by creating domestic self-sufficiency. They multiplied tariff walls and exchange restrictions, belying the rosy economic picture of the twenties. Under Primo de Rivera, Spain was in the forefront of the movement. It raised tariffs on both agricultural and industrial products and after 1926 virtually prohibited the importation of foodstuffs that competed with Spanish crops. The government set up a Banco Exterior de España to encourage exports and investments in Latin America, where Spanish capital had followed immigrants since the turn of the century. At the same time the regime sought to prevent foreign economic exploitation of Spain. In 1927 Calvo Sotelo established a state monopoly of the sale of petroleum products, on the pattern of the tobacco monopoly in existence since the seventeenth century. The state chartered a corporation to distribute petroleum called Compañía Arrendataria del Monopolio de Petróleos, S.A., or CAMPSA for short, which is still the only legal outlet for gasoline. This was economic nationalism but not socialism, for CAMPSA's stock and dividends went to private investors. When the international petroleum companies boycotted Spain in reprisal, Primo de Rivera obtained supplies from Russia. But it was dangerous to anger and frighten foreign investors, as Calvo Sotelo did with fiery speeches as well as acts, and they did not come to save Primo de Rivera when he ran into fiscal trouble.

Progress did not spread through the private sectors of the economy. Although iron and steel production continued to grow, textile manufacture and agriculture were stagnant. Beyond offering cheap credit and protecting inefficient production with high tariffs, the regime had no clear program for private enterprise. World agricultural prices steadily declined in the twenties, and declining profits, added to the difficulty of emigrating, slowly were creating an explosive situation in the areas of latifundia. Primo de Rivera in 1926 set up a Bank of Agrarian Credit, which could help the *latifundistas* but hardly anyone else. The dictator was sympathetic to the exploited rural laborers, but to have attempted serious reform would have meant an attack on the rural oligarchy, and Primo was not one to awaken sleeping dogs, especially if they were big.

Until the world depression of 1929, however, his regime was able to ride the wave of prosperity. He climaxed the decade with showy and expensive international expositions in 1929 in Barcelona and Seville. The latter was devoted to the Hispanic world and aimed at boosting Spain's cultural and diplomatic influence among its former colonies. Primo de Rivera was one of the first active prophets of Hispanidad. The expositions proved to be the swan song of the dictatorship, for at this very time the peseta, weakened by a decade of unbalanced budgets and capital exports, fell 30 percent on the world market, its lowest point since 1898. The dictator's economic policies were as discredited as his political ones, and his critics recalled their warnings.

5

Since Primo de Rivera came in with a promise to end the threat of labor strife, the problem of the proletariat was the most urgent domestic issue facing him. To solve it he created institutions whose inspiration came partly from Italian Fascism and partly from domestic reformers. Mussolini had forced the Italian manufacturers and workers into state-controlled vertical "corporations" which had sole authority to negotiate labor agreements. In 1926 Primo set up twenty-seven similar corporations for various industries and professions. At its lowest level each corporation consisted of a number of *comités paritarios* or arbitration committees empowered to negotiate labor conflicts on wages, hours, and other conditions. Conceived by the Institute of Social Reforms, the committees consisted of equal numbers of delegates from employers and workers (hence their name), with a chairman appointed by the government. Each corporation had a governing council representing employers and the committees, and each council sent an employer and a worker as representatives to a Delegated Commission of Councils. This last was the only nationwide representative body actually to function under the dictatorship.

The *comités paritarios* posed to the leaders of the proletariat the question of their attitude toward the dictatorship. For the anarchists of the CNT this was no problem. One of their dogmas was a refusal to cooperate with organs of the state, since they believed only direct action could lead to social revolution. Moreover, to Primo de Rivera they represented the forces of disorder that he had come to quell. He declared the CNT illegal and used the power of the state and the army to crush it. Driven underground, the anarchist leaders split. In the face of possible extermination by the government and loss of their followers to the Socialists and Communists, the more radical in 1927 created a centralized secret society, the Federación Anarquista Ibérica (FAI). FAI was a group of militants devoted to upholding the doctrines of direct action and revolutionary anarchism within the CNT.

Determined to destroy the anarchists, yet in need of the support of labor for the success of his corporations, Primo de Rivera appealed to the Socialists to cooperate with his regime. For the Socialists the invitation posed a real dilemma. Pablo Iglesias, the grand old man of Spanish socialism, died in 1925. For some time the younger leaders had been divided in their policies. After Iglesias' death, the conflict became more acute. The democratic spirit of moderation that he had championed now found voice in Indalecio Prieto, who had built up the Socialist following in Bilbao. He would have nothing to do with the dictatorship and convinced the party not to accept Primo's invitation to send delegates to the National Assembly.

The other strand of thought was embodied by Francisco Largo Caballero, who had come to prominence in the general strike of 1917. After the death of Iglesias, he took over the leadership of the UGT. Sensing the possibility of destroying the anarchist threat to the Socialist unions, he led the UGT to cooperate in the choice of worker members of the *comités paritarios* and he accepted a position of councilor of state in the government. The move brought momentary advantage to the UGT, but it left Largo Caballero with a stigma to live down, for the anarchists painted him and his followers as traitors to the working class.

If labor felt ill at ease in its new role as a pillar of the established order, for the church such a position had become almost second nature. From the outset Primo de Rivera courted clerical support. The motto of the Unión Patriótica was "Country, Religion, Monarchy." To some Carlists this must have sounded nostalgically like their old cry, "God, Country, and King," for among Primo's most committed supporters were Carlists, who found themselves in the strange position of cheering the man who had come to protect the king they called illegitimate. Republicans and Socialists had long opposed the article in the Constitution of 1876 which declared Catholicism to be the religion of the state. Primo de Rivera's draft constitution preserved the article with its guarantee of state support for the church. From the 1850's on, however, the real key to every regime's position on the church was its education policy. Under pressure from the Liberals and Republicans, in its last decades the constitutional monarchy had relaxed the requirement of religious instruction in public schools. Primo de Rivera cooperated closely with the church in this field. He enforced religious instruction and required teachers to go to mass, whether or not they were believers.

6

Primo de Rivera's clericalism was one of various policies that led him into conflict with the intellectuals. The cultural rebirth which occurred before the First World War was now coming to fruition. Gathered around the tables of the cafés in Madrid and other cities, politicians, writers, journalists, teachers, artists, and their associates discussed eagerly the latest world developments in all areas. At the Residencia de Estudiantes the young Andalusian poet Federico García Lorca exchanged inspirations with the Catalan surrealist painter Salvador Dalí and the fledgling movie maker Luis Buñuel. New monthly periodicals joined the daily newspapers in providing a vehicle for writers. The most famous of these was the *Revista de Occidente,* founded by Ortega y Gasset in 1923 to uphold a liberal political and intellectual outlook. Thanks to the spirit of '98 and more specifically to the activities of the Junta para Ampliación de Estudios, by the twenties remarkable men were to be found in university chairs. Unamuno was rector of the University of Salamanca; at Madrid Ortega was a professor of philosophy, Menéndez Pidal of philology, Américo Castro of history of the Spanish language, and Claudio Sánchez Albornoz of Spanish history; and in Barcelona Pere Bosch Gimpera held the chair of ancient history. Ramón y Cajal retired from the faculty of medicine of Madrid in 1922, but his young follower Gregorio Marañón was already adding luster to the school. These figures could rival those on any faculty in the world.

Such active intellectual ferment rapidly proved to be a greater threat to the dictatorship than the revolutionary forces from which it had set out to save Spain. Since Primo de Rivera's coup was timed to prevent the exposure of the Moroccan situation, he at once established censorship of the press. He continued to protect his government from adverse criticism, requiring the press to submit all copy to official censors before publication, and closing for a time the Ateneo de Madrid, the leading extra-university center of intellectual activity. Nor was he content to keep Spain silent. In 1924 an Argentine newspaper published a private letter of Unamuno sarcastically critical of the dictator. As punishment, Unamuno was exiled to the Canary Islands. Faced with a worldwide protest of intellectuals, among them Albert Einstein and Thomas Mann, Primo de Rivera allowed his enemy to escape to France. Unamuno settled just over the frontier in Hendaye, near his native Basque Provinces, and proceeded to direct clandestine propaganda into Spain. His was but the most dramatic case of the violation of academic freedom. Various other professors were arrested at one time or another, and several resigned.

Behind the professors, or even ahead of them, were many university students, especially in Madrid. They lampooned the dictator with insults scribbled on walls and circulated seditious leaflets. To protect the university system against his attacks, in January 1927 they organized a nationwide student association, the Federación Universitaria Española (FUE). Beginning in that year the students took to the streets in demonstrations against the regime, and all the efforts of the forces of order proved unable to control them. The student protest reached out from Madrid and embraced all the universities of Spain. In Catalonia the students were angered by Primo de Rivera's attacks on Catalan regionalism. The FUE took up their cause, bringing together into one movement a new generation of liberal Castilians and nationalist Catalans. It thus revived the alliance behind the First Republic which the Generation of '98, oriented strongly toward Castile, had neglected.

Next to the unrest of the working classes, Catalonia was the most obvious sore that Primo de Rivera had come in to heal. The postwar years had left Catalan nationalism in a state of flux. Cambó's participation in ministries had discredited the Lliga Regionalista with the committed nationalists, and the Lliga had made the further mistake of welcoming Primo de Rivera's coup because he promised to put down proletarian disorders. A few days later he prohibited the official use of the Catalan language and the display of the Catalan flag. He stopped the teaching of Catalan in schools and forbade the regional dance, the *sardana*. In 1925 he abolished the Mancomunitat, the modest regional government conceded to Catalonia in 1914. The army was unitary in outlook, and Primo de Rivera shared its spirit. Since even the country's prosperity seemed to avoid Catalonia, Catalans sullenly bore his insults and awaited the day of deliverance. Macià, the founder of the Estat Català, had gone to Paris, and from there he carried on an international propaganda campaign in favor of Catalan independence. In 1926 he made a comic-opera attempt to invade and liberate Catalonia with an army of 130 men. It ended with the participants in French prisons, but it achieved worldwide publicity for his cause. In 1927 Cambó publicly appealed to Alfonso XIII to lead a rapprochement between Castile and Catalonia. When he received no answer, Catalans of all classes, from anarchist workers to Lliga industrialists, had become the enemies of the dictator.

Primo de Rivera's destruction of the parliamentary system also lined up against him the leaders of the political parties. In 1926 Count Romanones, who had headed the Liberal party, led a conspiracy which aimed to overthrow the government by a kind of civilian *pronunciamiento*. It included several disgruntled generals, intellectuals like Marañón, Republicans, and even syndicalist leaders. Only the Conservatives, regionalists, and Socialists stayed out of this weird alliance. Primo learned of the plot, arrested its leaders, and treated them with contempt by releasing them with heavy fines adjusted to their means. Without prison sentences or executions, the plotters became butts of satire rather than martyrs.

But this year was the apex of Primo de Rivera's career. The politicians nursed their grudge and awaited better times. So far José Sánchez Guerra, leader of the Conservative party, had stuck by Alfonso, hoping he would dismiss Primo. When Primo convoked the National

Assembly, Sánchez Guerra lost faith in the king. He protested by going into exile in Paris. With his defection the remnants of both old established parties had entered active opposition.

Still Primo de Rivera had on his side the church and the army, and he knew Alfonso would not dare dismiss him. From the king down, however, his partisans felt more and more ensnared in a trap and they resented his autocratic airs. They tolerated him while he was successful, but as soon as his popularity began to wane, they hastened to disassociate themselves from him, like the proverbial rats of the shipwreck. As a result, he fell as rapidly and disappeared as unlamented as the constitutional monarchy had.

The agony of his dictatorship began in the spring of 1928, when he attacked the universities directly. Since the eighteenth century, the government had strictly controlled higher education. In the 1860's and 1870's, its restrictions on the content of lectures had led to faculty protests and eventually to Giner de los Rios' founding of the Institución Libre. But as part of state control, the universities had a monopoly of examinations leading to degrees and thus to professional careers, a monopoly resented by certain religious orders which offered independent higher education. In 1928, under pressure from the Jesuits, Primo agreed to permit the Jesuit college of Deusto to set up its own board of examiners consisting of two members of its faculty and one of a state university.

To faculties and students of the state universities this was the final violation of civil education in favor of the church. Several professors resigned, including Ortega y Gasset, and students began demonstrations, not only in Madrid but at virtually all provincial universities. The FUE was the moving force behind the protests. In Madrid students stoned the residence of Primo de Rivera, derailed streetcars, and fought the police. Primo closed the universities and prevented the giving of examinations, but the official censorship could not hide the disorders or disguise his growing unpopularity.

Student demonstrations continued into the next year, encouraging other groups to come out against Primo. Wise heads in the clergy worried about being caught in a collapse of the regime and began to shy away. Sánchez Guerra, the Conservative leader in exile in Paris, plotted a *pronunciamiento* that included Republicans and various generals. He landed in Valencia in January 1929, but he had been betrayed and the generals failed to back him up. He was arrested and tried at the end of the year by a military court, which acquitted him, a verdict that revealed serious disenchantment with Primo within the army.

Faced with desertion of the leading social groups, Primo fought to keep popular support by issuing the draft of his constitution. But he spoiled its effect by refusing to submit it to elected cortes. The peseta had collapsed, and Cambó publicly excoriated Calvo Sotelo's fiscal policies. The Wall Street crash of October 1929 destroyed all hope of reestablishing the government's credit. Alfonso XIII at last awoke to the danger to the monarchy of Primo's unpopularity. His one remaining prerogative was to dismiss his ministers. When Primo became aware that he was no longer welcome at the palace, in January 1930 he asked the captains general of Spain and Africa to declare their continued support of him. Their replies were evasive, pledging support to the monarchy but not to Primo. Demoralized and in bad health, Primo de Rivera resigned on January 28. He went to Paris, where so many had fled before him, and there he died within two months.

7

Thus ended Spain's first taste of modern dictatorship. Primo de Rivera had promised to restore constitutional rule and step down as soon as he had eliminated corruption. Only slowly did people realize that his *pronunciamiento* marked the end of the parliamentary monarchy. The order founded by the Moderados in the 1840's was dead. For eighty years, with brief interruptions, an alliance of the economically strongest groups had ruled under a cloak of parliamentary government. As a generation which had grown up under universal suffrage came of age after 1900, it proved no longer willing to vote according to the dictates of those in power but began to follow the critics of the regime, the intellectuals, the regionalists, and the proletarian leaders. After the First World War, *caciquismo* ceased to be a viable alternative to the parliamentary democracy advocated by Republicans and revisionist Socialists. Though the opposition never approached a parliamentary majority, the strains of the war and postwar years revealed the incapacity of the ministries to run the country. The cry for reform was becoming irresistible. Control was rapidly slipping from the parties of the established order; and the king and the army, who also had vested interests in the order, rushed in to grab control before it fell into the hands of the opposition.

The established groups were frightened enough to welcome an autocratic dictatorship disguised by a contrived plebiscite, even if in the process they lost the power to govern. They suffered attacks on their prerogatives but they were shielded from revolution. Having displaced the established groups, and unable to resuscitate the political structure inherited from the nineteenth century, Primo de Rivera ruled the country by relying on the institutions the Moderados had painfully tied to their order: the army, the church, and the crown. The army was essential. In the age of mass politics, if those in power could not keep the loyalty of the citizens, the only alternative to loss of power was to control their bodies. Control of their pocketbooks was no longer enough, for the people were learning not to vote according to the wishes of those who exploited them.

Ruling groups in other countries were finding similar answers to the dilemma of democracy. But the fascist dictatorships, though more cruel and violent, catered directly to the ideology of mass democracy, whipping up popular emotion, paying lip service to constitutional forms, and ruling through a single political party. Primo de Rivera's essay into mass politics, the Unión Patriótica, never roused enthusiasm, and he could not live down his unconstitutional advent. He offered Spain a *pronunciamiento,* not a nationalist ideology. He was misled by a Spanish tradition which the education of the electorate had outdated. In the nineteenth century *pronunciamientos* had been followed by constituent cortes; now freely elected cortes were precisely what Primo had come in to avoid. Unable to solve the dilemma, he watched the groups that had welcomed him drop away one by one, until at the end the defection of Alfonso XIII and his fellow generals left him defenseless. As an alternative to popular democracy his dictatorship had also failed.

Primo de Rivera also lacked the personal qualities needed for a modern dictator. He was too easygoing to be a match for Mussolini, much less Hitler. Although his rule was harsher than any Spain had had since Narváez, he never executed an opponent. This is why, when Spaniards experienced an infinitely fiercer dictatorship, the *dictadura* of Franco, they came to call the regime of Primo de Rivera, though in many ways the forerunner of Franco's, the *dicta-blanda*—the gentle dictatorship—by contrast to the later *dicta-dura*—the hard dictatorship.

11

The Second Republic

1

The dictatorship had ended, but the monarchy remained, sorely tarnished by recent events. The enemies of the old order blamed Alfonso XIII, with some justice, for the advent of Primo de Rivera and called for a republic as the prerequisite of parliamentary democracy. Of all the established institutions the monarchy was the most in danger, but if it gave way to a truly democratic republic, all the other groups that the parliamentary monarchy had shielded would also come under attack. The immediate question facing Alfonso was whether the privileged groups would stick by him and try to restore the system of Cánovas, or sacrifice him in the hopes of manipulating a new order. Alfonso's first move was to replace Primo de Rivera as the head of the Directory with a docile general, Dámaso Berenguer, one of his palace intimates. Berenguer relaxed Primo's controls, permitting Unamuno to return to Salamanca and Sánchez Guerra to speak in Madrid. Such events produced scenes of great public enthusiasm, but those who rejoiced no longer saw Primo de Rivera as the public enemy. He was dead; it was the king himself.

Alfonso struggled for over a year to get out of the impasse of ruling without a constitution and having to fall back on military men to head his governments. He obtained the support of Francesc Cambó, the leader of the Catalan Lliga, who as a manufacturer was alarmed by the increasing strikes of Catalan workers, who were excited by the CNT's vision of an imminent revolution. Support also came from the Count of Romanones, former leader of the Liberal party, himself a wealthy landowner. But the king was unable to attract all former monarchists. Early in 1931, the Conservative Sánchez Guerra rejected his request to head a ministry that would include parties of the opposition. The king had to make an admiral, Juan B. Aznar, the next prime minister, with Romanones as foreign secretary. Romanones conceived the project of restoring constitutional government by a series of elections, first for municipal councils, then for provincial councils, and finally for the Cortes.

The opposition, no longer forced to operate from abroad, now organized actively within the country. Niceto Alcalá Zamora, a Liberal minister in 1923, publicly declared himself in favor of a republic in April 1930 and founded a new party, the Liberal Republican Right. On August 17, 1930 at the summer resort of San Sebastián, leading opponents of the monarchy, Alcalá Zamora, Prieto for the Socialists, the timeworn Radical Lerroux, and leaders of the Catalan left reached an agreement to establish a republic, by force if necessary, to proclaim civil and religious liberties, to call constituent cortes, and to permit the regions of Spain to draw up plans for their autonomy. Out of this meeting grew a Central Revolutionary Committee, with headquarters in Madrid and secret branches in various cities.

The spirit of revolution was stirring in all sectors. As in 1917, junior army officers became involved, and two of them revolted in northern Aragon in December. The king had them executed, thereby gaining further public opprobium. Gentlemen did not shoot their enemies; even Primo de Rivera had not. In Madrid, the Central Revolutionary Committee was discovered and arrested for plotting rebellion, only to have the king soon come begging its members to form a ministry. They refused, but were freed by the court that tried them and greeted jubilantly by crowds in the street. Student riots broke out, the universities were closed, and intellectuals and professors, led by the philosopher José Ortega y Gasset and the professor of medicine Gregorio Marañón, formed a "Group in the Service of the Republic." In Catalonia Francesc Macià drew various left-wing Catalan parties together into a coalition called the Esquerra Republicana de Catalunya (Republican Left of Catalonia) to oppose Cambó's Lliga, which was still monarchist. The situation was hardly auspicious for the monarchy when Spaniards went to the polls for the first time in eight years.

Voting for municipal offices took place on Sunday, April 12, 1931. That evening returns were announced for the major cities. Every provincial capital except Cadiz (of all places!), voted for a majority of Republicans and Socialists. In Catalonia Macià's Esquerra won a resounding victory over the Lliga. April 13 was a day of hesitation; both monarchists and Republicans had been taken by surprise. The king's ministry resigned, convinced that the election was a national plebiscite against Alfonso. On the fourteenth the new municipal councilors took office in the major cities. In Seville, Valencia, and elsewhere they proclaimed a republic. Crowds thronged to the central squares of Madrid and Barcelona. From a balcony overlooking the multitude in Barcelona, Macià proclaimed a Catalan republic to be an integral part of an Iberian federation. In Madrid the Count of Romanones urged the king to leave Spain and personally negotiated a transfer of the government to the Revolutionary Committee. When General José Sanjurjo, commander of the Civil Guard, informed the king that the guard would not fight for the monarchy, Alfonso hastily agreed to leave and before sundown drove off to Cartagena to take ship for France. Abandoned by the traditional pillars of the crown, the monarchy, which counted its origin in the ninth century, had ended with hardly a whimper.

Late on April 14, 1931 Spaniards went to bed under the Second Republic and with a provisional government headed by Alcalá Zamora. Conservatives congratulated themselves on avoiding violence and liberals and Socialists relished the victory they had awaited since 1917. In the excitement most persons failed to note that the Republican victory was marginal at best. Of over 80,000 municipal councilors elected, Republican parties won about 34,000 and the Socialists 4900, or slightly less than half between them. The others elected were monarchists or members of other parties, or were unaffiliated local candidates often running unopposed in areas controlled by *caciques*. Monarchists dominated rural Galicia, Andalusia, and Extremadura, all classic areas of *caciquismo*. Republicans and monarchists divided the smaller cities and towns of Old Castile and Aragon. The Socialist strength was mostly in the cities, except those of Catalonia, which voted for the Esquerra Republicana. Although the picture is not entirely clear, the election that brought in the Republic was a victory for urban and peripheral Spain over those groups that controlled rural central Spain, of the heirs of the Progresistas and the First Republic over the heirs of the Moderados.

The advent of the Republic was marred almost at once by a painful event. On May 6 the provisional government decreed that religious instruction would no longer be mandatory in public schools. Cardinal Pedro Segura, archbishop of Toledo and primate of Spain, a testy defender of the monarchy and the rights of the church, replied with a pastoral letter calling upon Catholics to oppose attacks on religion. On May 10 in Madrid a street scuffle between monarchists and Republicans degenerated into an attack on churches and monasteries by a small mob. Six buildings were burned. Since lives were not evidently in danger, the government hesitated to call upon the hated Civil Guard to put down the disorders. On learning the news of Madrid, mobs also burned churches in various Andalusian cities. The disturbance lasted two days and was a shock to devout Catholics. Magnified by their press, the event gave the impression that the Republic was out to destroy religion. From the very start, the Republic and the church seemed to have declared war on each other.

Liberal Spaniards were too euphoric to let the event distress them. They had at last obtained the victory that they had been denied in 1917. For them April 1931 inaugurated the springtime of a new age. The century-long search seemed over for a popularly accepted form of government that could assume the legitimacy once enjoyed by the absolute monarchy. The miraculously easy advent of the Republic, the happy surging throngs in the cities on April 14, the mute disarray of the partisans of the monarchy, all promised that Spaniards as a people now wished to live under parliamentary democracy. Republicans and Socialists who trusted the wisdom of a free people scented the fragrant air of their promised land. Enthusiasm pounded in the hearts of university students, whose strikes and violence had been instrumental in overthrowing Primo de Rivera. Anticipation gripped older intellectuals of the stamp of the Institución Libre who had long fought the sham and pettiness of the monarchy and the oppression of the dictatorship. All these men of good will would at last be able to remake Spain and give it its proper place in the world as a country of progress and intellect. They foresaw using funds that had been lost through corruption and squandered on the army and the church to rebuild the country. They had visions of minds imprisoned by obscurantist teachings of the religious orders, or illiterate and uncultivated for want of schools, being trained for citizenship and rewarding lives. In their joy and hope they seemed to have stepped out of the Enlightenment, not the twentieth century. Wordsworth's greeting to the French Revolution never applied more fittingly than to Spanish Republicans in 1931:

> Bliss it was that dawn to be alive,
> But to be young was very heaven!

2

Unfortunately the dawn had come, not in 1917, when the Republic could have enjoyed a decade of prosperity, but fourteen years later, when the world depression was nearing its depths. Human problems would not be as tractable to idealism and good will as the Republicans hoped. Yet for two years they were free to apply idealism and good will, and they accomplished enough to bring Spain to world attention.

The provisional government represented the groups that had agreed to the Pact of San Sebastián. It was a coalition of Republican parties of various colorings, Socialists, and regionalists. Its president, Niceto Alcalá Zamora, was a former Liberal heading the Liberal Republican Right party; and it included Alejandro Lerroux of the old Radical party and Manuel Azaña, a writer and president of the Ateneo de Madrid, for the Left Republican party. The Socialists were represented by Francisco Largo Caballero and Indalecio Prieto, who had been rivals for control of the party since the death of Pablo Iglesias. The Catalan Esquerra sent secondary figures, for Macià preferred to remain in Barcelona. From the outset the success of the Republic depended on the ability of a coalition of Socialists and Republicans to stick together despite divergent economic and social doctrines.

The provisional government promptly called for elections to constituent cortes. Fearing *caciquismo*, it adopted the old Progresista tactic of making elections provincewide for a slate of candidates rather than in single member constituencies. It also provided that the party or coalition of parties that obtained a majority in a province should receive between two thirds and four fifths of its seats. It hoped to prevent the proliferation of splinter parties typical of the Third French Republic or the German Weimar Republic, and thereby to facilitate stable parliamentary government. In the process it enabled a coalition with a small popular plurality to obtain a commanding majority in the Cortes. This was not unlike the American and British systems, but it presupposed the loyalty and patience of defeated parties who saw their representation in the Cortes far below their percentage of the popular vote.

The elections, on June 28, fulfilled Republican hopes. The Left Republicans and Socialists had formed a coalition and together won 250 seats, over half, thanks to the new electoral rule. Sympathetic to them were the 30 deputies of the Catalan Esquerra and 20 Gallegan Republicans, and to a lesser extent the 100 Radical deputies who followed Lerroux. On the right but still Republican were some 30 conservative Republicans, mostly of Alcalá Zamora. Of doubtful loyalty were 14 Basque nationalists and 10 Lliga Regionalista deputies of Cambó. Scattered among the deputies were leading intellectuals who were elected with no party commitment: Unamuno, Ortega y Gasset, Marañón. *Caciquismo* had been emasculated, but the election figures were misleading. Supporters of the defunct monarchy had not had the time or the spirit to run a real campaign.

In honor of the French Revolution, the Cortes were inaugurated on Bastille Day, July 14. Their first order of business was to write a new constitution. A commission representing the various government parties presented a draft in August which the deputies discussed and finally proclaimed in December. In socialist spirit, it declared Spain to be "a democratic republic of workers of all classes."[1] It guaranteed the standard liberal civil rights: freedom of expression, of religion, from arbitrary arrest. The suffrage was given to everyone over twenty-three, regardless of sex, a step already proposed by Primo de Rivera. It also

[1] Article 1.

abandoned bicameralism, which even the First Republic had kept, and went back to the egalitarian pattern of 1812 of a single house. The Cortes would be elected for four-year terms and meet annually. To prevent possible abuses by an all-powerful legislature, the constitution provided for a president with more authority than in most European democracies of the twentieth century, and a Court of Constitutional Guarantees which could declare laws unconstitutional. The president would be elected for a single six-year term by the deputies of the Cortes plus an equal number of elected "commissioners." He would choose the prime minister ("president of the government"), who would then select the other ministers, all subject to approval by the Cortes. If the president judged that the Cortes were no longer functioning effectively, he could dissolve them and call for new elections. He was allowed to do this only twice, however, and after the second dissolution, the following Cortes was "to examine and decide upon the necessity of the decree of dissolution of the previous Cortes. The unfavorable vote of the Cortes shall effect the removal of the President."[2] The Constituent Cortes thus created a strong executive but precluded a return of the system whereby Alfonso XIII had made stable government impossible by dissolving the Cortes at will.

In the tradition of the Progresistas, the constitution established municipal councils and *alcaldes* to be elected by local citizens. It also provided for extensive regional autonomy on the model of the First Republic. A lengthy section allowed the creation of autonomous regions with "common historical, cultural, and economic characteristics."[3] The regions could establish statutes providing for their own self-government. The central government reserved to itself matters of foreign relations, armed forces, the monetary system, interregional communications and public works, and the regulation of cults. The constitution made possible a radical decentralization of Spain. Going far beyond the provisions of the Catalan Mancomunitat of 1912, it represented the fulfillment of the Republican commitment to the Catalan nationalists made in the Pact of San Sebastián.

Meanwhile during the summer of 1931 Catalan nationalists under Macià had drawn up a statute and submitted it to a local plebiscite, which endorsed it overwhelmingly. The project gave the regional government full authority over education and made Catalan the official language of the region. After acceptance of the national constitution, the Cortes took up the Catalan project, reworking it to fit the terms of the constitution. The Cortes eliminated absolute local control of schools and insisted that Castilian remain also an official language in Catalonia. Otherwise they accepted most of what the Catalans had

[2] Article 81.
[3] Article 10.

proposed. Under the statute Catalonia got a government known as the Generalitat with a president, prime minister, and a parliament, almost like the national government. The Generalitat had authority over local finances and communications. In effect Catalonia also got its own school system with classes in Catalan, even in the University of Barcelona.

Despite the qualms of Ortega and other Castilian centralists, the Cortes ratified the statute in September 1932 by a nearly unanimous vote. Manuel Azaña, who had been the prime minister since October 1931 and was largely responsible for the successful compromise, went in person to Barcelona. From the balcony where Macià had proclaimed the Catalan state eighteen months earlier, he presented the new statute to a vast throng, asking three times, "Now do you belong to the Republic?" Three times the crowd roared, "¡Si!" [4] Catalans were to show four years later how strongly they felt this commitment.

Other regionalist movements were encouraged to draw up their own statutes. On one occasion the Basque leaders of varying persuasions literally came to blows over the question. The strongly clerical Basque nationalists wanted to control religious questions locally; the Basque Republicans wanted to leave the matter to the central government. When the statute was proposed to the voters, Navarre rejected it, and the Basque provinces were only lukewarm. Before it could be brought to the Cortes, the Constituent Cortes had been dissolved, conservatives were in control, and the statute was buried until the outbreak of the Civil War.

Even in regions without traditions of home rule, the possibility excited local leaders. The Gallegan Republican party, under Santiago Casares Quiroga, drew up a statute, which was approved locally but unenthusiastically, but it also came to the Cortes too late for prompt action. Movements appeared in Aragon, Valencia, and Andalusia to establish autonomous regions. They did not have a serious following. Some Castilian liberals had hurt feelings, and monarchists were able to exploit the army's fear of decentralization. Nevertheless, by giving ear to the claims of the regionalists instead of trying to crush them, as the dictatorship had done, the Republicans had worked out an apparently successful solution to the long-standing conflict between Castile and the periphery.

The Cortes also had to deal with the enemies of the Republic. The king was safely out of the way. The Cortes, for added safety, wrote into the constitution that no member of the royal family was eligible for the presidency. They also convicted Alfonso of high treason for helping Primo de Rivera to establish the dictatorship, and sentenced him to banishment for life.

The last three decades had shown that Spanish parliamentary

[4] Salvador de Madariaga, *Spain* (2d. ed., London, Jonathan Cape, 1942), 307.

democracy had most to fear from the army. It had broken strikes by force and had opposed the nationalist movement in Catalonia. Alfonso XIII had used his authority over it to promote officers loyal to him. Ill equipped, poorly trained, the army was less a force for national defense than, like the old British Empire, an outdoor relief for the respectable classes. For many families a career as army officer had provided an honorable if not remunerative opening for a second son. Need for reform had long been recognized within the army itself, especially the need to reduce the excessive number of officers. The minister of war in the provisional government, Manuel Azaña, acting before the Cortes met, drew up a new table of organization which called for only one third the existing number of officers. To eliminate the excess, he offered army officers retirement on full pay, complete with the future raises they could expect if they remained on active service. Many officers hastened to accept such a fine offer, but others, monarchists and conservatives, saw in the move an attempt to emasculate the only force capable of resisting the follies of the new regime. Within the officer corps a sullen conflict developed between supporters of the Republic, who suspected and disliked the monarchists, and the opponents of the Republic, who felt discriminated against for political reasons. Dissatisfaction within the army was to remain a running sore, as it had been in the German republic after 1918.

The provisional government also destroyed the hegemony of the Civil Guard over the maintenance of public order. The church burnings of May 1931 showed the need for men specially trained to put down urban riots. Previous governments had called in the Civil Guard and the army in such contingencies, often with unnecessary bloodshed. The workers detested both bodies so heartily that the Republicans hesitated to use them and they were doubtful of their loyalty. Nineteenth-century revolutionary regimes had established the National Militia in such a situation, but it had been overly political and undisciplined. The Republican government's answer was to create a highly trained elite corps of urban police called the Assault Guard, on whose loyalty it could count. No longer needed in the cities, the Civil Guard returned to its original role as a rural police force.

What the Republic would do about the church became the question that aroused the most violent passions. Before the Cortes met, the government proclaimed religious liberty and made plans to separate church and state. The bishops protested that the plans violated the Concordat of 1851, which declared Catholicism the official religion of Spain, supported by the state. Nevertheless the Cortes proceeded to write this legislation into the constitution. Article 3 stated, "The Spanish state has no official religion." Article 26 provided that within two years the national and local governments would cease to support the church financially, that religious orders would have to register with the government and give up all property not needed to support their religious activities, and that those orders taking an oath of obedience to an authority other than the state (an indirect way of identifying the Jesuits) would be dissolved and their property nationalized. The debate on this article was bitter. Azaña led its supporters, arguing on principle that Spain was no longer Catholic, since many Spaniards had ceased to be believers, and that the state should no longer be the secular arm of the church. Eventually the article passed, but many deputies abstained from the final vote.

The approval of Article 26 caused the first crisis of the Republic. Alcalá Zamora, the prime minister, a conservative Republican and a Catholic, resigned, forcing the choice of a new leader of the ministry. The choice fell on Azaña, who had gained prestige for his reform of the army and eloquence against the church. As soon as the constitution was approved, in December 1931, Azaña proposed and carried through the election of Alcalá Zamora as president, in a move intended to bind up the wounds of the Republican side.

Subsequent legislation of Azaña's government further embittered staunch Catholics. The Cortes made marriage a civil ceremony, legalized divorce, and put cemeteries under state authority. They made plans to close religious schools. Azaña's government did not deprive Spaniards of religious services, churches, or religious orders, but it deprived the church of those advantages which the Moderados had given it in the nineteenth century to reconcile it to the loss of its lands and to win it to their side. In 1932 the church cried persecution, while Republicans felt they had disarmed the major enemy of the Spanish people. The religious question had become the most heated issue in Spain and was rapidly polarizing public opinion. Symbolic of the tension were numbers of Catholic school children who wore large crucifixes around their necks as a protest against taking down crucifixes in classrooms. Some of the early support of the Republic among middle-class Catholics was evaporating, while liberal priests who had originally welcomed it were disenchanted by this legislation.

The role played by the religious issue in the history of the Second Republic makes it vital to understand why freeing the Republic from the threat of the church became the central concern of the Constituent Cortes of 1931 rather than, say, measures to improve the social structure of Spain and meet the economic crisis. Ever since the Cortes of Cadiz and earlier, reformers had looked upon the church as the strongest bulwark of reaction. It had backed Ferdinand VII, then the Carlists, then the Conservatives, and finally Primo de Rivera. The Republicans of 1931 believed it had an excessive amount of wealth invested, not as formerly in land, but in banks, industries, and public utilities. They laid many of the evils of capitalism in Spain at its door. Many people on the left magnified the church into a vast subterranean conspiracy against the modernization of Spain. It did not occur to them that the clergy were few in number and that they could have little influence unless more numerous groups supported them for reasons of their own. They forgot that the Liberals in the nineteenth century had been able to despoil the church of its property and had defeated the clerical-minded Carlists.

Many of the Republican charges were partly true. The question is why the Republicans let the clerical issue blind them to more real dangers. One can see various reasons. First of all, since the nineteenth century Spaniards had been prone to explain political events by the machinations of secret societies. Thus liberals saw in the clergy, notably the Jesuits, a tightly knit group, with connections in government and high society, pulling strings to obtain their ends. On their side, conservative Catholics believed in a secret international federation of freemasons working to destroy religion. Historians of both sides explained the last hundred and fifty years of Spanish history by such myths. After 1917, conservative clericals believed a secret Communist organization had joined their enemies. To a certain extent both myths were based on truth. Spanish and French Republicans and anticlericals did become freemasons—but it was naive to blame anticlerical legislation on a secret society as it was oversimple to blame the Jesuits for opposition to left-wing policies.

Needless to say, this kind of political mentality is not uniquely Spanish. It has been common in modern democracies. Jews in Germany and France and Catholics in America have been accused of belonging to international groups bent on destroying the values of their societies. It is emotionally easier to blame one's troubles on a convenient but mysterious enemy than to try to understand the complexities of modern society, and political leaders have long known how to make capital out of this penchant.

To this general tendency must be added the strong ideological commitment that was typical of Europe between the world wars. Belief in ideologies as solutions to political problems was another feature of the emergence of democracy after 1789. Political and social doctrines like nationalism, republicanism, Carlism, anarchism, and socialism aroused the kind of devotion that religions had in an earlier age. For Spanish anticlericals, anarchists, and Socialists, the Catholic Church represented not only an organized conspiracy but the bearer of an opposing ideology. Voltaire's cry, "*Ecrasez l'infame!*" could well characterize their spirit.

Moreover, one of the beliefs of the Republicans was in the efficacy of education as a means to remake the country. It was a belief inherited from the Enlightenment and nineteenth-century liberalism. American democrats and French republicans had felt the same way. In Spain most primary and secondary education, especially of the middle and upper classes, was in the hands of the church. Since Spain was backward, the Republicans reasoned, the education given by the church schools must be at fault. As we have seen, Spanish intellectuals and historians of the Generation of '98 blamed Spain's national character for its failures. What force was responsible for this character more than the church, which inspired intolerance and perpetuated obscurantist doctrines?

Finally there was the simple fact that the clergy was conspicuous and different. Priests wore long black cassocks and round black hats. They could never be mistaken for anyone else. Neither could nuns or monks. They took vows of poverty and chastity, which their enemies found unnatural and believed they violated in secret. Like the Jews in Hitler's Germany, they could be easily identified and attacked. More, unlike the Jews, they had consciously chosen to separate themselves from other men. The anticlericals overlooked the fact that for many a younger son or unmarriageable daughter of a middle-class family the church offered a living that was honorable and secure, and that for the son of a peasant to become a priest or monk was often the only way to get an education.

All these reasons help account for the passion with which the Cortes disposed of the question of the church. Heady with joy and satisfaction at having slain the dragon that threatened their beautiful girl (the Second Republic was called affectionately "*la niña bonita*"), the Republican idealists could turn to constructing their new order. Their energies were concentrated in two areas, education and land reform.

3

From Jovellanos through Giner de los Ríos to the founders of the Second Republic, leading Spanish liberals saw in education the greatest hope for the future of the country. A story is told of a conversation between Giner and Joaquín Costa about the problem of Spain. Costa said, "Giner, we want a man." "Joaquín," replied Giner, "what we want is a people." [5] Through the Institución Giner had hoped to help create the people Spain needed. Now his followers could use the power of the state to further his aims. In 1931 it was estimated that 30 to 50 percent of Spaniards were illiterate. First under Marcelino Domingo, a Catalan Republican and an admirer of French lay education, and later under the Socialist professor Fernando de los Ríos, nephew of Giner, the ministry of education drew up plans to provide 7000 schools to replace those of the religious orders and 20,000 more needed to give all

[5] J. B. Trend, *The Origins of Modern Spain* (Cambridge: Cambridge University Press, 1934), p. 168.

children an elementary education. Despite the depression and the desire to reduce expenses, the Cortes voted lavishly the requests of the ministers, while Republican municipal councils donated buildings to the cause. A frantic effort produced 9600 primary schools within a year, while a five-year plan was drawn up to provide the rest. The needed teachers were harder to come by. Despite salary increases and refresher courses, few persons were dedicated enough to move to isolated backward pueblos. Salvador de Madariaga, minister of education in 1934, says that he found "about 10,500 schoolmasters without a school, and about 10,500 schools without a schoolmaster."[6] By then, however, political events had dampened the early ardor.

Enthusiasm for educational improvement also infected the universities, especially that of Madrid. In 1927 the monarchy had undertaken to build a new campus for the university northwest of the city. Known as the Ciudad Universitaria, it came to life under the Republic. The Faculty of Philosophy and Letters opened in the winter of 1932–33, in a modern building described scornfully by Unamuno as "the most luxurious bathhouse I've seen in my life."[7] The next four years saw completed the faculties of medicine and architecture. Within this handsome shell, the faculty, under the guidance of the dean of philosophy and letters, Manuel García Morente, reached the peak toward which it had been climbing for a generation.

Education could not reach all Spaniards as rapidly as the Republicans desired, and they turned to the boundless idealism of youth to fill the gap. This was the objective of the so-called pedagogical missions, a project conceived by Giner's associate Manuel Cossío. Beginning in 1933, organized groups of university and secondary-school students traveled to remote towns carrying movies, copies of works of art, and music. Meanwhile Federico García Lorca directed a group of university students, known as La Barraca ("The Hut"), who went by truck from town to town giving open-air representations of the classic theater of Cervantes, Calderón, and Lope de Vega. For many pueblos this was the first exposure to urban cultural activities, while the students saw a side of Spain that was equally unknown to them. No endeavor ever revealed more clearly the existence of two worlds in Spain, the modern cities that participated in the latest Western culture and the primitive pueblos.

The pedagogical missions were symptomatic of the enthusiasm of many artists and writers for the Republic. Some became deputies in the Cortes; others like Américo Castro consented to represent Spain abroad. Those who continued to write made the next five years a brilliant age

[6] Madariaga, p. 316.

[7] Quoted by Rafael Lapesa Melgar, in Carlos Blanco Aguinada *et al.*, *La Universidad* (Madrid: Ciencia Nueva, 1969), p. 33.

of Spanish letters. Besides directing La Barraca, García Lorca composed his masterpieces for the theater, *Bodas de Sangre* (*Blood Wedding*), *Yerma* (*The Barren Woman*), and *La Casa de Bernarda Alba* (*The House of Bernarda Alba*). Other poets who had matured under the dictatorship, such as Pedro Salinas, Rafael Alberti, Jorge Guillén, Luis Cernuda, and Vicente Aleixandre, wrote some of their finest pieces, letting the excitement of their lives infect their poetry. Luis Buñuel turned from surrealist cinema to make *Tierra sin Pan* (*Land Without Bread*), which depicted in poignant realism the poverty-stricken life of the peasants of Las Hurdes in northern Extremadura. As tensions grew over the next years, Lorca expressed their common attitude: "We (I mean men of intellectual significance brought up in the atmosphere of what we can call the well-to-do classes) are called upon for sacrifice. Let us accept the call. In the world not human forces but telluric are now at grips." [8]

The other passion of the Republic was the reform of the countryside. The land must be made more productive and given to those who needed it. Indalecio Prieto, minister of public works, continued the projects for irrigation and reclamation conceived under the monarchy and begun by Primo. He kept Manuel Lorenzo Pardo in charge, who pushed ahead plans to dam the Guadalquivir, Guadiana, and Tajo river systems to irrigate Andalusia, Extremadura, and Valencia. Besides irrigation, the dams would provide electricity for industry and the countryside. Prieto also planned extensive reforestation of regions that had suffered from centuries of clearing and grazing to stop further erosion and keep the moisture from running off.

The Republic also tackled the problem of land tenure in arid Spain, which reform-minded governments since Charles III had wrestled with in vain. The problem seemed eternal: extensive latifundia, impoverished laborers, exploited tenant farmers. The expropriation of church lands in the nineteenth century had worsened the situation, and the current depression made it acute. Anarchism had spread among the landless laborers of the south and was now keeping them in opposition to the Republic, which they saw simply as another bourgeois regime. The success of the Republic depended heavily on the success of its agrarian policy.

Unfortunately, it was easier and more satisfying to pare down the church and the army than to legislate agrarian reform, a technical question for which neither Republicans nor Socialists were well equipped. They represented the city trying to legislate for a countryside it did not know. The two groups fell back on solutions based less on a study of Spain than on foreign examples. Their reading of

[8] Quoted in José Luis Cano, *García Lorca* (Barcelona: Ediciones Destino, 1962), p. 110.

history had convinced the Republicans that the French Revolution had guaranteed popular support by distributing land to the peasants. Like their Liberal predecessors of the previous century, they wanted to make a loyal class of yeoman farmers. The Socialists, on the other hand, were enamored of the collectivization going on in Russia. They felt Spain needed to collectivize the land, especially if it were to become socialist rather than bourgeois.

The advances in agricultural technology in modern nations depend on exploitation in large units. The Republican plan to divide the land into small holdings, even if it might have been advisable in the eighteenth and nineteenth centuries (and in arid Spain it undoubtedly was not so even then), would have condemned Spain in the twentieth century to backwardness and unnecessary rural poverty. The Socialist plan for large collectives made more sense, but the land must produce more and not simply change hands if the rural standard of living were to rise. Greatly expanded irrigation offered one solution, as Prieto saw, but it could never by itself be sufficient for the magnitude of the problem. Mechanization was another possibility, but gainful occupations would have to be devised for the countless peasants and farm laborers whom machines would throw out of work. Rather than come to grips with such economic dilemmas, the deputies of the Cortes tackled the problem with their different ideological preconceptions.

The Cortes debated at length the rival proposals and finally passed a compromise bill in September 1932 that let the municipalities decide between collectivization and individual ownership. The state was to compensate former owners for expropriated property, except grandees, who were to suffer as a class for presumably plotting to overthrow the Republic. To do the job, the Cortes created an Institute of Agrarian Reform, endowed with an annual budget of 50 million pesetas, far too small to make significant changes. It would provide land for only 5000 peasants per year, and estimates of the number of peasants in urgent need of resettlement ran as high as 75,000. The law offered little to the peasants of the south and was no help at all to the small individual owners of the center and north who were suffering from the collapse of agricultural prices. Certainly it did not produce loyalty to the Republic. Anarchists found wider audiences in the south, where they preached *comunismo libertario*, complete collectivization of the land and an end to central government. Anarchist peasants burned harvests and country estates in Extremadura, and throughout the south the landed classes experienced fear. Many left their estates uncultivated, increasing unemployment.

The realization that the Republic's agrarian policy was not meeting Spain's needs made the Socialists restless within the coalition government by the end of 1932. Since the proclamation of the Republic, the UGT had been organizing peasants with great success, raising the membership of its Federation of Land Workers from 100,000 to nearly 450,000 in one year. Largo Caballero, who was both minister of labor and head of the UGT, feared the effect of the Republic's inactivity on the Socialist following in the countryside. "An aspirin to cure an appendicitis," he called the legislation.[9] It was too easy for the anarchists to blame the Socialists for the ills of Spain and pose as uncorrupted revolutionaries.

4

The uneasiness of the Socialists was symptomatic of the difficulties in which Azaña's government found itself at the end of 1932 and through 1933. One of the major problems facing it was the world depression, which hurt critical areas of the economy. International trade was stagnant; Spain's in 1932–33 was only 30 percent of the 1928 level. World agricultural prices were dropping, affecting three major Spanish products—wheat, citrus fruits, and olive oil. Wheat was the major cash crop of vast areas of Castile and Aragon, and was also important in Andalusia. Valencia depended on the export of citrus fruits and much of Andalusia on that of olive oil. The collapse of prices hit these areas. The Republic continued to protect wheat with high tariffs, but a big harvest in 1932 depressed prices. Unfriendly landowners used the chance to blame the Republic for the rural depression, and a new conservative Agrarian party posed as the champion of the small peasants, who were disappointed at the lack of serious agrarian reform. For citrus and olive growers the government, though concerned, did nothing constructive. In addition, Great Britain, the chief market for Valencia oranges, cut off Spanish imports to give preference to its colonies. The depression also hurt the industrial north, the coal mines of Asturias and the iron industry of the Basques. Unemployment grew, and manufacturers who had welcomed the Republic were becoming critical. To the local workers, mostly organized by the UGT, the Socialists ministers seemed to be cooperating with a regime that was defending capitalism at their expense.

The economic outlook was not all bad. Catalan textile factories were as active as in the twenties (but there had been stagnation in the twenties), and the school construction and public works programs were keeping the building trades active. Spain had a half million unemployed, proportionally only one quarter of the figure of Germany and the United States. But since a much smaller percentage of the total population was industrialized in Spain, the figure indicates severe suffering in certain areas.

[9] Gerald Brenan, *The Spanish Labyrinth* (Cambridge: Cambridge University Press, 1943), p. 263.

In industry, the Socialists obtained the continuation of Primo's *comités paritarios,* renamed *jurados mixtos* (mixed juries), in each industry to decide labor disputes. Each jury consisted of six representatives of labor and six of industry, who would choose a thirteenth man as president. If they could not agree, the ministry of labor would choose the president, which became the usual case. Since Largo Caballero was minister of labor, the law enabled the Socialists to dictate the settlement of labor disputes throughout Spain, and keep wages stable. Employers complained bitterly, while the anarcho-syndicalists found the Republic much more dangerous to their brand of utopianism than the recent dictatorship. If it should satisfy the peasants and workers, the Socialists would get the credit.

These conflicts gave strength to the most militant anarchists of the CNT. They had their base in the semiclandestine FAI founded under Primo de Rivera. In 1932–33 extremists discredited the moderate leaders of the CNT, who had been ready to cooperate with the new Generalitat to create a workable Catalan political system. Militants inspired a series of strikes that made these years resemble 1919–23. The most violent were in Andalusia, with Seville at their center. In 1933 ten times as many days of work were lost through strikes as in 1928, three times as many as in 1931. An analysis of the strikes shows that their purpose was political, to keep the workers in a revolutionary mood, rather than economic, for there was no relation between frequency of strikes and economic distress.[10]

When the government opposed the strikers, it gave the anarchists further ammunition. On two disastrous occasions, government action led to bloodshed. During a period of tension in Extremadura in December 1931, peasants murdered four civil guards who tried to stop a parade at Castilblanco. The government brought the peasants to trial and six were condemned to death, although never executed. The case of Casas Viejas, a small pueblo in the povince of Cadiz, was more serious. In January 1933 several towns in the area proclaimed *comunismo libertario,* under anarchist leadership, and began to put it into effect. Called in to restore order, the Civil Guard besieged the leaders of Casas Viejas, killing five who held out in a house, and later fourteen prisoners in cold blood. Anarchists denounced the Republic as more inhuman than the monarchy, while conservatives also used the occasion to attack Azaña, whom they claimed personally responsible.

It was a shocking event. Azaña could prove that no one in the ministry had given orders to shoot prisoners, but nevertheless Casas Viejas cast an indelible stain on the fair name of the Republic, particularly among the working classes. Within the Socialist leadership,

[10] Gabriel Jackson, *The Spanish Republic and the Civil War, 1931–1939* (Princeton: Princeton University Press, 1965), pp. 96–97.

Largo Caballero demanded that the party leave the ministry, and he began to gain strength against the moderate Prieto. Sensing the disaffection of the largest party in his coalition, Azaña resigned in June 1933, but the Socialists remained loyal and he took office again.

At the same time events strengthened the conservative enemies of the government. The first attack of the monarchists on the Republic was a fiasco. In 1932 several of their number convinced the head of the Civil Guard, General Sanjurjo, who had abandoned Alfonso XIII in April 1931, that the Republic was ruining Spain and no longer represented the wishes of the people. Sanjurjo organized a *pronunciamiento*, but it was badly planned and was betrayed in advance to the authorities. When he struck on August 10, 1932, his attempt was easily crushed everywhere except Seville, where the CNT syndicates took up the defense of the Republic by declaring a general strike. Sanjurjo rapidly lost courage, his movement collapsed, and he went to prison. The government congratulated itself on its triumph, but those opposed to it learned from the experience. Future military plotters would know better than to rely on civilian accomplices, and the workers would not forget that their organizations had been the last defense of the Republic in a crisis.

For the time being, however, opposition to the Republican government was to be much more successful on the political level. The first threat to the Republican-Socialist coalition came from the Radical party under Lerroux, which was second in size to the Socialists within the Cortes. Lerroux had been in the ministry in 1931 and his party had supported the Republican government from the outset, particularly its anticlerical legislation. But he was strongly anti-Socialist, and in December 1931 he withdrew his support from any government that included Socialists. He soon became the leader of the parliamentary opposition. By 1933 the problems facing the Cortes were economic and social rather than constituional, and Radical criticism became more militant. Their deputy Diego Martínez Barrio led the attack on Azaña over the Casas Viejas affair, and Lerroux began to tone down his anticlerical statements. These tactics succeeded in winning support among urban middle-class groups, worried by the extremism of the Socialists, the violence and strikes, and the imminent closing of the Catholic schools to which their children went.

In April 1933 municipal elections, the first since those that had destroyed the monarchy, demonstrated the decline of the Republican parties. The Radicals showed great strength, electing more municipal councilors than the Socialists, while monarchist parties elected almost a third of all the councilors. Azaña's government was clearly in trouble.

During 1933 another party came to the fore on the right. Moderate Catholics, those who supported the church but held no particular brief for the monarchy, had been groping for leadership. In April 1933 many probably voted for the Radical municipal councilors, despite that party's recent anticlericalism. They were grouped around the organization of Catholic Action, led by Angel Herrera, editor of the moderate Catholic newspaper *El Debate*. In 1933 Herrera gave his support to a young deputy from Salamanca, José María Gil Robles, who headed a new party called Acción Popular. Both men stood for liberalizing Spanish Catholicism, furthering social legislation, and working within the framework of the Republic. In this they were following the policies recommended by the Vatican since the 1890's, but strongly opposed by most Spanish prelates, who could see only atheism and freemasonry in the Republic. Gil Robles approached other Catholic groups, including the conservative monarchists, who made up in financial support what they lacked in popular following. He drew these parties together into an alliance known as the CEDA (the initials of Confederación Española de Derechas Autónomas, Spanish Confederation of Autonomous Parties of the Right), so as to be able to present a united front politically. This grouping, achieved while the Socialists were losing faith in the Republican coalition, was to be decisive in the evolution of the Republic.

Azaña reached the height of his popularity in the fall of 1932. The agrarian law had been approved, he had returned from his triumphal tour to Barcelona to deliver the Catalan statute, and the Republic seemed to be settling down to a successful course. All this changed in 1933, beginning with the Casas Viejas affair, and continuing with the municipal elections. During the summer, as labor violence mounted, Alcalá Zamora, president of the Republic, felt called upon to bring in a ministry more in keeping with the spirit of the country. As a good Catholic, he was troubled by the government's commitment to close Catholic secondary schools on October 1, 1933 and primary schools in 1934, according to recent legislation. When the split between the Socialists and Republicans became acute in September, President Alcalá Zamora used his constitutional authority to dismiss Azaña. The Socialists' fear of anarchist gains at their expense had finally shattered the coalition of 1931, with the most serious results imaginable for the Republic.

Alcalá Zamora called on Lerroux to form a government, but without Socialist support, Lerroux was unable to find a majority in the Cortes. Alcalá Zamora thereupon dissolved the Cortes. Elections for new cortes were held in November 1933. On the right, the CEDA provided a united front of Catholic parties, and it campaigned primarily against the anticlerical legislation of the Republicans. In some districts it formed electoral alliances with the Radicals to oppose the Socialists. On the left, the Socialists and Left Republican parties went to the polls independently, split by their recent falling out. The anarchists urged their followers not to vote, not to compromise with the bourgeois state. Although the percentage of votes won by each group did not change much from 1931, because of the nature of the electoral law, the right won a resounding victory. The CEDA obtained 110 seats and other right-wing parties another 102. The Radicals also won 102 seats, while the Socialists got 60 and the left-wing republican parties of Azaña's stamp less than 40. The electoral law was such that a small change in percentage of voters, plus changes in electoral alliances, could cause great shifts in the Cortes. The conservative victory was the result of a return of Catholics and conservatives to active politics and a desire among many middle-class voters to slow down social reforms. It was not the result of a wave of dissatisfaction with the Republic as a form of government. But for the parties of the left, it seemed that reaction was triumphant and that the democratic Republic was in danger. They did not trust Lerroux and they feared Gil Robles.

With the election of November 1933 the halcyon days of the Republic were over; lines were drawn and fears aroused that were to fill the next years with tension and turmoil. What the Republic stood for and what it tried to accomplish must be judged on the basis of the two years of the Constituent Cortes.

12

Spain Splits in Two

1

During the two years of the Constituent Cortes, public opinion had become more and more polarized around the issue of the relation between the state and the church. This was an old issue, as we know, and it was basically a conflict of ideologies. However, alongside the older liberal ideology modeled on 1789 and 1812 and the monarchist Catholic ideology which looked back at "historic" Spain, since the First World War collectivist ideologies on the left had increased their following, and new authoritarian ideologies had appeared on the right. Primo de Rivera had mouthed some of the rightist doctrines, but by and large under him they had not aroused much devotion. By 1934 the twentieth-century versions of left and right found in the rest of Europe were rapidly infecting Spanish politics. Since Mussolini's capture of Italy in 1922, the European democracies that had been created or revitalized in the wave of Wilsonian idealism had been collapsing one by one. The most frightening developments occurred in 1933. In January Hitler became prime minister of Germany at the head of the National Socialist party, and before the year was out he had outlawed other parties and imprisoned many of their leaders. In Austria the Christian Socialist chancellor, Engelbert Dollfuss, suspended parliamentary government in March and later permitted his followers to arrest leading Socialists. When the Socialists fought back in Vienna with a general strike, they were crushed by armed force. Even such an ancient democracy as France did not seem immune. On February 6, 1934 militant right-wing parties attacked the Chamber of Deputies in Paris and the police restrained them only with greatest difficulty and after many casualities.

Little wonder that in Spain Republicans, Socialists, and anarchists viewed Gil Robles, who proclaimed his admiration for Dollfuss, as a fascist and feared that his assumption of power by legitimate means would lead to an overthrow of the parliamentary process and outlawing of the parties that supported the Republic, on the pattern of Mussolini and Hitler. On the other side it is equally understandable that good Catholics, who recalled the Bolshevik suppression of organized religion in Russia and heard of leftist President Lázaro Cárdenas' outlawing of the church in Mexico in 1934, should conceive the Republic as not simply an anticlerical democracy of the nineteenth-century variety but a cloak for the introduction of godless Marxism. World developments —Lorca's clash of "telluric forces"—combined with long-standing domestic antagonisms to exacerbate Spanish hatreds. The story of the next two and a half years is how these tensions grew, despite the energies of sensible leaders on both sides, until they led to the outbreak of a civil war.

The largest group in the new Cortes was the CEDA. By the logic of parliamentary government, President Alcalá Zamora should have asked Gil Robles to form a government, but for sound reasons he did not do so. During the campaign Gil Robles had refused to declare his loyalty to the Republic, although he claimed—honestly, it would appear from later events—that he believed in parliamentary government. Because much of the CEDA's following consisted of monarchists, his unwillingness to state his allegiance to the Republic was understandable, but it led the Socialists and other left-wing parties to argue that for Alcalá Zamora to allow him to form a government would be to turn the Republic over to its enemies.

Alcalá Zamora therefore offered the head of the ministry to Lerroux, whose Radical party was second largest in the Cortes. Many deputies distrusted Lerroux because he had often switched colors, and his recent opposition to social legislation made support from the Socialists impossible. To obtain a majority he turned to the parties on his right and got the backing of the CEDA; without, however, taking members of that party into his cabinet. Gil accepted the arrangement, knowing that the need for CEDA support would force the Radicals to adopt a program that would satisfy it. In this way the Radicals governed during the first session of the new Cortes, which lasted from November 1933 until the summer of 1934.

Lerroux sought to balance his commitment to the Republic and to anticlericalism with his conservative economic views and his need to placate the CEDA. Gil Robles wanted to amend the constitution, ending the separation of church and state. This Lerroux would not do, but he did not enforce the recent laws against the church. He did not close Catholic schools, he allowed the Jesuits to continue teaching, and he maintained the state subsidy of the church in defiance of the constitution. He also acted to gain the favor of other enemies the Azaña regime had made. Over the strong opposition of the left, he put through a bill to amnesty political offenders of the previous two years, of whom the most conspicuous were those involved in General Sanjurjo's abortive *pronunciamiento*. Employers and landowners felt once more the warmth of government blessings. In the mixed juries for labor disputes, the government appointees who cast the deciding vote now leaned toward the employers.

Lerroux had always hated Catalan regionalism, and his courting of the right now gave him additional cause for being a centralist. When local elections in January 1934 again returned an Esquerra majority to the Catalan parliament, a clash between Lerroux and the Generalitat became almost inevitable. Macià had just died, in his seventies, and he was succeeded as president of the Generalitat by Lluís Companys, who was more strongly committed to the Republic and Spain than most Catalan leaders. The clash came over a question of social legislation. The Esquerra majority in the Catalan parliament voted a law which gave the Catalan tenant farmers the right to buy land they had cultivated for fifteen years. Landlords protested and took the case to the national Court of Constitutional Guarantees, which had been elected in September 1933 during the right-wing surge. The court declared the law invalid because it was outside the constitutional scope of the Generalitat, and the Radical ministry upheld the court. Catalanists were furious, and the Catalan parliament challenged the court by enacting another law similar in content.

The conservative attitude of the government also gained it the hatred of the organized proletariat. Feelings ran especially high in the south, where the depression hurt the landless workers. Many large landowners were introducing machinery or leaving their estates uncultivated. Lerroux continued the redistribution of land enacted by the Constituent Cortes, but results were slow and ineffectual. In the spring of 1934 the UGT's Federation of Land Workers formed a united front with the anarchist CNT in southern Spain and threatened to strike just before the harvest. They demanded a decent wage and no reprisals against workers for their political activities. The government met these demands, but nevertheless extremists led local strikes on June 5. The government retaliated violently, deporting peasants and arresting Socialist deputies who had visited the strikers. This vindictiveness sowed anger and frustration among the workers, who turned more and more to the anarchists and new militants belonging to Spain's small Communist party.

If Lerroux had the left against him, the Conservatives were not happy either. Right-wing militants condemned Gil Robles as a compromiser for his support of the Radical government. They looked for a leader with more drive and fire, and their eyes turned to the one-time minister of finance of Primo de Rivera, José Calvo Sotelo. He had been in exile in France since 1931 and had become enamored of the anti-parliamentary doctrines of the Action française. In the new climate of Spain, he was elected to the Cortes in November 1933 and returned from Paris to become the head of a monarchist party called Renovación Española. He immediately began to denounce what he termed Gil's ineffectual leadership of the CEDA.

The Radical government survived until the Cortes adjourned in the summer of 1934. During the next months Gil Robles spoke out aggressively, trying to propitiate right-wing Spaniards. Without CEDA votes, the Radicals would be unable to stay in power when the Cortes reopened in October. Convinced that Gil Robles was out to destroy the Republic, leaders of the left decided that force might be needed to prevent the enemies of the Republic from capturing it by legal means. Largo Caballero, mindful of the frustration and anger among the workers on farms and in industries, threatened an armed rising if the CEDA should enter the cabinet. "Better Vienna than Berlin" became the Socialist motto: Better to die fighting like the Austrian Socialists than without a struggle. Throughout the country the proletarian parties were drawing together against the common enemy. In the Asturias mining region such unity made great progress at the local level, under the slogan "UHP" ("Unión, hermanos proletarios"), and workers clashed frequently with the police. Even the moderate Socialist Prieto foresaw fighting, and he organized the smuggling of arms into Asturias.

When the Cortes reopened on October 1, the CEDA refused further support for a government in which it did not participate. Alcalá Zamora considered dissolving the Cortes, but he finally called on Lerroux to establish a coalition government in which the CEDA would get three ministries, including the critical ones of labor and agriculture. Socialists and Republicans, and some Radicals under Diego Martínez Barrio, cried that Alcalá Zamora was handing the Republic over to its enemies. To prevent the seating of the new government, the UGT on October 5 led general strikes throughout Spain. Workers responded in the major cities: Seville and Cordoba in the South, Valencia and Barcelona in the east, San Sebastián, Bilbao, and Santander in the north, and Madrid. By and large the revolt was a failure. Many syndicates were not prepared, and the Andalusian workers were exhausted from the agitation of the summer. The government proclaimed martial law and crushed the strikes in most places.

The rising had more success in Madrid and Barcelona. Largo Caballero personally led the workers in Madrid, the center of UGT strength, and he kept the strike going for ten days. When it broke, he and many others were arrested. In Barcelona the UGT's declaration of a general strike did not win over the anarchists; however, Catalan anxiety over a CEDA government brought crowds into the streets demonstrating their loyalty to the Generalitat. Companys feared losing the initiative to Catalanist extremists. When Lerroux's government established martial law on October 6, he addressed the crowd from a balcony of the Generalitat palace in a speech carried over the radio and proclaimed a "Catalan State within a Federal Republic." Without anarchist support, however, he had no force to oppose the army when the local captain general remained loyal to central government. The army besieged Companys and the Catalan government in the Generalitat building overnight. Companys surrendered the next morning, and he and his government went to prison, ending Catalonia's brief and hardly glorious bid for autonomy.

From the outset all eyes turned toward Asturias, the only place where the workers had prepared for a conflict. Anarchists and Communists had made recent inroads on the UGT, but all were united by common suffering and the slogan "UHP." Their general strike began on October 4. The next day the workers took over the mining towns, forcing the civil guards and newly created assault guards to surrender. Then they marched down to the provincial capital, Oviedo, which they captured by small-arms fire and dynamite. In the city they set up a kind of republic of virtue, guarded by thelr revolutionary militia, very anarchist in spirit, with equal rations for all and guarantee of personal safety for enemies of the working class, both bourgeois and clerical. Undisciplined groups and individuals, some of them acting out of personal hatred, murdered about forty employers and priests; but given the tensions present, the workers behaved with reasonable self-discipline.

The real bloodletting began when government forces moved in to put down the revolution. The miners held the mountain passes against the army. On the advice of General Franco, who was temporarily on assignment in Madrid, the government shipped in by sea the Foreign Legion and Moorish troops from Morocco, whom it could count on to be merciless. Oviedo fell on October 12, the mining towns were captured house by house during the next week. Prisoners were often shot, but captured rebels were turned over to the Civil Guard, which subjected them to sadistic tortures. A group of observers sent by the British Parliament confirmed the horrors of the repression, and the news sickened European liberals.

The aftermath of the October revolt exasperated the political tensions in Spain. The government clamped censorship on news from Asturias, but tales of atrocities filled the press, each side accusing the other of the most inhuman acts. The right-wing newspapers reported that miners had raped nuns, buried priests and monks alive, and gouged out the eyes of children—atrocities that local residents later denied had occurred, but which were eagerly believed by good Catholics who saw in the left-wing parties the sinister agents of an international masonic-Marxist conspiracy. So strong were Catholic feelings that in March 1935, when Lerroux commuted the death sentence of several leaders of the uprising, Gil Robles and other right-wing deputies violently attacked him and forced a dissolution of the ministry. In the next cabinet the CEDA obtained more seats.

The left had more legitimate grievances. Besides the barbarity of Oviedo there was the imprisonment of over ten thousand people throughout Spain for participating in the general strike, or simply for belonging to left-wing parties. They remained in jail through 1935.[1] Nevertheless, the left also magnified their sufferings. They believed Spain to be in the grip of fascism now that the CEDA was in the government, and failed to consider how closely they were repeating the pattern which had given Primo de Rivera the excuse to become dictator.

The Republican parties had had little share in the October revolt. Nevertheless the right took the opportunity to cast discredit on them, and chose Manuel Azaña as their target. The former prime minister had been in Barcelona on the day of the uprising; and although he had refused to participate in it, he was arrested on suspicion of involvement. Before his trial by the Supreme Court, the monarchists in the Cortes initiated a debate on his case, accusing him of instigating the risings in Asturias and Catalonia. The debate lasted the entire day of March 21, 1935, while crowds gathered outside. The final vote revealed the division of the Cortes on current issues. The CEDA and right-wing parties voted to condemn him, but the Radicals joined the parties of the left to produce a majority in favor of exonerating him. When Azaña left the Cortes, the crowd cheered. Shortly thereafter the Supreme Court found him innocent. Azaña's trial served to draw the Republicans and Socialists together again, for his persecution made him a popular idol among the working classes. With their own leaders in prison, even the anarchists were beginning to see the only hope for their ultimate success in a return to power of the Republicans.

2

Beginning with the trial of Azaña, 1935 was a year of increasing bitterness and tensions. The proportion of Spaniards who took an interest in government was growing, particularly in the cities, and they were becoming ever more sharply divided. On both sides inflamed passions were making impossible rational consideration of each other's grievances and leading to acts that needlessly provoked their oppo-

[1] There is no agreement on the number arrested. Jackson, who is judicious, says 30,000 to 40,000 (p. 161). Éléna de la Souchère, *Explanation of Spain* (New York: Random House, Inc., 1965), a work unfavorable to the Franco regime, says a maximum of 12,500 (p. 248).

nents. Extremist voices stirred the public, but one must ask why the public listened to them.

For one thing, Spain was not unique. The growing tensions throughout Europe contributed to the Spaniards' excitement. Even more, under the Second Republic the reality of free elections and universal suffrage (including the vote for women) made people feel that the actions of ordinary persons could for the first time truly affect their future. Self-government posed a kind of existentialist challenge to each individual to do his duty, to decide and act for himself and for his country. Democracy was a heady brew for a people who had not grown used to it. José María Gironella's historical novel *The Cypresses Believe in God* (1953) depicts the process of polarization and politicization of ordinary people during the years of the Republic in the Catalan provincial capital of Gerona, as individuals and gathering places like cafés took on political identifications they had never had before.

Symptomatic of the tension was the growing activity of extremist youth movements on both the right and the left. Just as Catholics and Republicans felt that authority over education was critical to creating the kind of country they believed in, political parties which demanded a commitment to specific creeds had come to believe in the need to mold the minds of young people. The origin of political youth movements went back to the turn of the century, when European Socialist and Nationalist parties had created them. In Spain Lerroux's Radicals had a youth movement in Barcelona before 1910. Known popularly as the "Young Barbarians," they were more violent than their elders. After 1918 Russian Communists developed a youth movement, a pattern which Italian Fascists and German National Socialists followed. Young people were considered more idealistic, more forceful, less corruptible than their elders, and more malleable. In Spain university students organized the FUE and played a vital role in the overthrow of Primo de Rivera. Under the Republic the right and the left parties established youth movements: Traditionalist (Carlist) Youth, closely tied to the Carlist armed units called Requetés, Socialist Youth, Juventudes de Acción Popular (JAP), which was the movement of the party headed by Gil Robles. The JAP's statements were violent and anti-Semitic and helped give Gil the reputation for being a fascist.

Other groups on the right, though not specifically called youth movements, directed their appeal primarily to young people. In October 1931 Ramiro Ledesma Ramos, a one-time philosophy student who admired Mussolini and Hitler, founded the Juntas de Ofensiva Nacional Sindicalista (JONS), dedicated to opposing Marxism and favoring a popular dictator. In 1933 four hundred Madrid university students joined its syndicate. More important was the founding of the Falange Española (Spanish Phalanx) in October 1933 by José Antonio Primo de Rivera, the dashing and boyish son of the late dictator. Consciously defending the memory of his father, he called his doctrine national syndicalism. He was both anti-Marxist and authoritarian. He condemned political liberalism and economic capitalism, proposing in their place some form of socialism, an abolition of political parties, an authoritarian state, and common devotion to the welfare of the fatherland. Many of these beliefs had origins in the late dictatorship, but they also echoed the current pattern of European fascism. Strangely, he admired the moderate Socialist Prieto and the latter grudgingly admitted that they did have some objectives in common. Both wished to see the government act forcefully to improve the economy by promoting irrigation and industrialization. Young Primo de Rivera was elected to the Cortes in November 1933, at only thirty. In February 1934 the Falange and the JONS merged into one organization, and in January 1935 Primo de Rivera expelled Ledesma, becoming uncontested leader of the Falange.

One of the most fascinating figures to emerge in these years, José Antonio Primo de Rivera became the idol of young persons in their teens and early twenties who opposed the Republic. He aroused them with passionate speeches at mass meetings, sometimes held in theaters, sometimes in romantic open-air settings like the Sierra de Gredos northwest of Madrid. They knew him simply as "José Antonio." Right-wing university students joined the Sindicato Español Universitario (SEU), which he organized in 1933 to oppose the FUE. He also built up a network of cells in all provincial capitals. By 1935 the Falange had between 10,000 and 25,000 members, tiny by comparison with mass movements but a respectable number for an independent new group, and it made up in enthusiasm what it lacked in size.

The youth movements became more militant than the regular parties, except the anarchists, who had always been committed to violence. They formed paramilitary militias, adopted shirts of various colors as their uniforms, had special salutes—the outstretched arm of the Fascists by the Falange, the clenched fist of the Communists by the left—held drills, and at times clashed in street fights, complete with shootings and deaths. After the October 1934 revolt, the youth movements rejected the moderate members of their parent groups. The Socialist Youth called leaders like Prieto, who believed in the parliamentary process, "social fascists," a term used earlier in Germany by the Communists to discredit the moderate Social Democrats. Far from lamenting the violence employed by both sides in Asturias, members of the youth groups glorified it and scorned their elders who were searching for a peaceful solution to Spain's ills, for they were led by men who had lost faith in the parliamentary system. The emergence of youth movements was a central factor in the increasing hatreds of 1935.

Sensing the danger of the situation, Lerroux maintained throughout the year a state of martial law and a close censorship of the press. He prevented municipal *ayuntamientos* and the Catalan parliament from meeting. With the CEDA now participating in the ministry, the government turned against the Republican legislation. It first suspended and then modified the Catalan statute of autonomy. It returned their properties to the Jesuits. The foreign secretary went to the Vatican to negotiate a concordat, a strange procedure for a government whose constitution gave no official recognition to religion. Gil Robles became minister of war in May 1935 and promptly named General Franco chief of staff. Gil favored the promotion of high officers whom Azaña had sidetracked, while discriminating against Azaña's appointees. This meant raising enemies of the Republic to positions of authority in the army. The education program of the Republic also suffered. With Catholic schools operating, the urgent need for new buildings decreased. To save money the government cut back and then abandoned the construction program. The pedagogical missions also had their funds cut, yet such was the enthusiasm of those involved that they continued their activities in the summer of 1935 largely out of their own pockets.

Alcalá Zamora had never been happy about letting the CEDA into the government, but he had no clear democratic alternative until late in 1935. A discovery of graft and corruption among members of the Radical party who were close to Lerroux gave him the opportunity he needed. The public scandal forced Lerroux to resign. Rather than offer the ministry to Gil Robles, Alcalá Zamora dissolved the Cortes on January 7, 1936 and called for new elections. He hoped that dissention among both right- and left-wing parties would produce a majority of the center. He was to be bitterly disillusioned.

The left saw its opportunity for revenge. During 1935 the comradeship of 1931 revived, and the Republican and Socialist parties were able to form an alliance. In this they were helped by the example of France, where in 1935 the middle-class and proletarian parties were drawing together in a "Popular Front" to defend the democratic Republic against the threat from the right. The French Communist party had taken the lead in creating this alliance, for the advent of Hitler had shown the leaders of the Communist International that the policy of attacking the Socialists, as the German Communists had done, could be suicidal. The example was not lost on Spain, and in January 1936 the Republican parties to the left of Lerroux—including some dissident Radicals under Martínez Barrios, the Socialists, and the Spanish Communist party, which since October 1934 had been growing in size and prestige—signed an electoral alliance for a Spanish Popular Front. Largo Caballero agreed to the alliance on the understanding that the Socialists would not participate in the ministry. The Popular Front campaigned on a platform of amnestying the thousands of political prisoners and continuing the reforms of the Constituent Cortes. On the right, meanwhile, the experience of two years in power had produced the same kind of divisions that the left suffered in 1933. The Radicals were discredited and divided. The monarchists were attacking Gil Robles for failing to take over the government by force. Although the center right formed political alliances in many districts, the kind of unity that produced the victory of the CEDA in 1933 was lacking.

The electoral campaign saw press censorship ended for the first time since October 1934. All the hatreds that had built up now burst forth. On both sides the major issue was the October revolt. If one sympathized with it, one favored the Popular Front; those whom it had frightened were on the other side. Emotional posters decorated public places. Large portraits of Gil Robles advertised the CEDA with the suspicious slogan, "All power to the leader." Calvo Sotelo's promonarchist Renovación Española pictured Spain in the grip of Marxism. The Popular Front countered with haggard wives and children pleading for the release of men in prison since the October rising. The hammer and sickle appeared chalked on walls, and in reply "*¡Muera Azaña! ¡Viva Dios!*"

The elections were held on February 16, 1936. They were a victory for the Popular Front, less in total votes than in seats in the Cortes. It received about 4.7 million votes to 4.5 million for the right and center. There had been little switching of votes; what made the difference was the unity of the left, division on the right, and active voting by anarchists who hoped to obtain the release of their friends in prison. The Popular Front parties won 278 seats—99 Socialists, 87 Republican Left headed by Azaña, 39 in Martínez Barrio's Republican Union, 36 Esquerra, and 17 Communists. The right had only 138 seats; nevertheless the CEDA was the second largest party, with 88 seats. The right had by no means been wiped out, in fact its popular vote was larger than in 1933. What had been destroyed was Alcalá Zamora's dream of a strong center. The parties that fitted between the Popular Front and the right got only 40 seats, with only 4 for the Radicals. The working of the electoral law was bringing Spain into a two-party or two-coalition system, more or less as its organizers had intended.[2]

Geographically the strength of the right was in the two Castiles and Navarre. The Popular Front carried the major cities and those

[2] No two historians agree on the number of votes or the number of seats won by each party. My figures on popular vote come from Jackson, p. 193 and pp. 521–24; on seats from Juan J. Linz, "The Party System of Spain: Past and Future," *Party Systems and Voter Alignments*, ed. S. M. Lipset and S. Rokkan (New York: The Free Press, 1967), pp. 260–61, both of whom have analyzed the official returns carefully.

regions which feared centralization or had rebelled in October 1934, Catalonia, the Basque Provinces, Asturias, and Galicia. It also carried Andalusia, showing that five years of active labor organization by the Socialists and anarchists had at last broken *caciquismo* and taken over the cities in this area. Except for Andalusia, however, the elections revealed the old conflict between center and periphery. Spain might be breaking along class and ideological lines, but the break coincided with well-known geographic divisions.

3

Six months after the election, civil war began. The story of this half year can be summed up as the failure of responsible and moderate men on both sides to keep extremists from coming to open conflict. Spirits already tense grew more and more excited as people at each extreme spoke of the danger from the other and the need to resort to force.

Spain was in a state of near anarchy immediately after the election, for the existing ministry and local governments were frightened and discredited. Victory marches in many cities led to violence, attacks on churches, and refusal to obey police orders. Several leaders of the right, convinced of the danger of an immediate social revolution, approached General Francisco Franco, the chief of staff, and urged that the army take over the country, as it had done in 1923. But no plans existed and Franco rejected a futile gesture. In Madrid the old ministry refused to continue in power until final election results were in, as provided by the constitution. Alcalá Zamora had no choice but to call on Azaña to take over the government on February 19. Three days later Azaña amnestied all political prisoners. He also suspended the payment of rents on farm land in southern Spain.

Azaña was the most prestigious person in Spain, enjoying wide popularity on the left and the grudging respect of his opponents. Yet his assumption of power did not bring calm. The militias of the various youth movements kept up street violence after the election, shooting members of opposing groups in what was degenerating into gang warfare. After Falangists attempted to assassinate a socialist professor, Azaña outlawed the Falange and arrested José Antonio Primo de Rivera, but the Falangists simply went underground. Azaña's difficulties were compounded by the attitude of Largo Caballero. He had been responsible for the Socialist decision to leave the cabinet in 1933 and now kept the Socialists from entering the ministry, thus forcing Azaña to include only Republicans in a government that theoretically represented the entire Popular Front. As a result of his imprisonment after October 1934, Largo Caballero was a martyr for many working-class people and the idol of the Socialist Youth. His followers referred to him as the Spanish Lenin (to Azaña's Kerensky), and believed the revolution was at hand. More and more his counsels guided the Socialists rather than those of the moderate Prieto. Largo Caballero began to speak publicly in favor of a proletarian uprising. Although he did not seriously plan one, his demagoguery presented a more serious threat to Azaña's efforts to restore order than the violence of the youth groups.

The new Cortes opened in March. Before Azaña could introduce any legislation, they faced a major constitutional crisis. According to the constitution, after a president dissolved the Cortes for a second time, the first act of the new Cortes was to examine and decide upon the necessity of the decree of dissolution. An unfavorable vote of the Cortes would remove the president. Alcalá Zamora had few friends in the new Cortes. He was known to favor a strong center party and therefore was disliked by both right and left. The Popular Front proposed to condemn him, not for dismissing the previous Cortes, but for not dismissing them in October 1934 instead of allowing CEDA deputies into the ministry. They thus attributed to him the blame for bringing on the revolt in October. The argument was strained but the vote was decisive, since the right abstained. On April 7 Spain was without a president.

The only person on whom the Popular Front could agree for president was Azaña. After some hesitation on his part, he was elected on May 8. He at once asked Prieto to form a ministry. Largo Caballero still opposed Socialist participation in the ministry, however, and the party vetoed such a move. Azaña had to choose another Republican, the Gallegan leader Santiago Casares Quiroga, who accepted out of loyalty although suffering from tuberculosis. The Popular Front, by impeaching Alcalá Zamora and raising Azaña to the presidency, had deprived itself of its most respected leader. From his new position, Azaña could do little to influence policy, and the times were getting increasingly critical.

Cases of public violence multiplied during the spring. A bomb was thrown at the president's stand during a parade in Madrid on April 14 to celebrate the anniversary of the Republic, and in the excitement an assault guard killed a civil guard. Members of the Falange participated in an elaborate funeral for the civil guard, and socialist youths shot at the cortège. A melee developed during which fourteen people were killed. In Andalusia, anarchist peasants, tired of waiting for legal distribution of land, began helping themselves to vacant fields. In June the CNT, which was trying to make inroads into traditional UGT territory, led a long walkout of masons, electricians, and other skilled construction workers in Madrid, against the wishes of the Socialists. This was only the most spectacular of many strikes. The CNT and UGT fought openly in Madrid, and the police strove vainly to prevent such incidents.

The violence was limited enough not to make ordinary citizens fear for their safety, but it frightened employers and landowners and exasperated hatreds on both sides. The press magnified each event, and rightist deputies denounced the situation in speeches aimed at discrediting the government. The most vociferous were Gil Robles and Calvo Sotelo. On June 16, both of them spoke in the Cortes. Gil claimed that since the election there had been 351 general strikes, 269 persons had been assassinated, and 170 churches burned (figures which could only be exaggerated guesses), while Calvo questioned the patriotism of Spanish leftists and accused the government of weakness which was playing into anarchist hands. The prime minister replied that Calvo was exaggerating and his speeches were themselves calls for violence. He could have added that enemies of the Popular Front had hired provocateurs to incite terrorist acts that would convince the moderate classes of the need to end the Republic.[3]

The fact was that whatever effect violence was having on the daily lives of Spaniards, it was preventing the government from proceeding energetically with its reform program. Sane and moderate minds were deeply concerned. Prieto was doing his best to calm the Socialists. On the right Gil Robles accused employers of driving the workers to the extremists by wage cutting and other deliberately hostile acts. Within the church and the government and in the daily press, responsible men sought to end the tensions. The government permitted church schools to remain open, and the Pope received the new ambassador of the Republic. But sane minds were powerless to halt the raging passions, for Gil Robles and Prieto could not be heard over the din made by Calvo Sotelo and Largo Caballero. After five years of the Second Republic, Spain was more bitterly divided than ever. The vision of 1931 of parliamentary democracy legitimized in the hearts of the people had evaporated.

4

In the end, however, not the warring political factions but a calculated military conspiracy destroyed the peace. Within the army, the apparent impotence of the government convinced various generals, as it had so often before in the last century, that it was their duty to save Spain from the evils of parliamentary government. The Popular Front victory had alienated many army officers, not only because they

[3] Stanley G. Payne, *Politics and the Military in Modern Spain* (Stanford: Stanford University Press, 1967), p. 331.

recalled Azaña's military reforms but because the government now planned to subordinate local captains general to civilian authorities in a way never done before. The local influence of the military would decline. In 1933 a conservative, monarchist organization called the Unión Militar Española was founded within the officer corps. It was not secret, but it provided a convenient channel for discovering the political sympathies of the officers. During the spring of 1936, high officers who hated the Republic began to plan an uprising against the government. They turned for leadership to General Sanjurjo, who had been living in exile in Portugal since Lerroux had granted him amnesty.

Azaña was aware that Gil Robles as minister of war in 1935 had placed generals of doubtful loyalty to the Republic in high commands, and he now acted to remove them. He transferred two generals responsible for the repression in Asturias from the war ministry to distant posts, General Manuel Goded to the Balearic Islands and General Franco to the Canary Islands. He brought from Morocco to Navarre General Emilio Mola, known to have kept out of Sanjurjo's uprising in 1932 and therefore believed loyal to the Republic. Mola, however, soon became the plot's leading figure within Spain, acting under the authority of Sanjurjo. Descendants of the Carlists were still strong in Navarre, and he could count on their support. The Carlist armed units known as the Requetés had smuggled in machine guns and had gotten in touch with Mussolini, who had promised them arms to use against the Republic. Mola also approached Calvo Sotelo and José Antonio Primo de Rivera, who was in prison. The latter somewhat hesitantly promised the support of the Falange. Finally Sanjurjo visited Germany and sounded out its government, which proved friendly to the conspirators' aims.

By the end of June the conspirators had worked out their plans, but they still hesitated. The memory of Sanjurjo's failure in 1932 haunted them. They knew many officers were unenthusiastic, and they were not confident of their civilian allies. The key figure was General Franco, for he could count on the loyalty of the Moorish troops and Foreign Legion in Morocco, which he had once commanded. These were the best-trained units in the army, unaffected by Republican and Socialist propaganda. In his new post in the Canary Islands Franco responded amicably to the plotters' feelers but refused to commit himself, evidently willing to count on an eventual legitimate defeat of the Popular Front at the polls. In early July, when it became clear that a rising would occur, he finally pledged himself provided he were given command of the forces in Morocco. He would fly there from the Canary Islands in a plane hired by an agent in England, and the garrisons in Spain would declare their support within twenty-four hours. The date was set for between July 10 and 20.

Despite precautions, such a widely known conspiracy could hardly remain hidden from the government, and it did not. But the long, tense spring had sapped the will of Azaña and Casares Quiroga, and they believed their precautions had been sufficient. The Republic had survived one rising in 1932, the army had not moved in February 1936, and they did not credit the seriousness of the reports they now heard. Prieto was worried, but Largo Caballero dismissed his warnings as a scheme to win back support of the Socialists. To the latter's mind, only the proletariat had the spirit to make a revolution, a conviction probably shared by Azaña, who feared Largo Caballero more than the army. Middle-class Spaniards went off to their summer vacations as usual, looking forward to a rest from political turmoil.

By pure chance, events in Madrid provided the plotters with a perfect occasion. On Sunday, July 12, a Republican lieutenant of the Assault Guard, José Castillo, who had fired on the funeral procession for the civil guard killed on April 14, was himself shot dead by Falangists while taking a stroll in Madrid. Castillo was a leader of the Socialist Youth militia and had devoted friends. Several of these within the Assault Guard determined to exact exemplary vengeance. That same night in their uniforms and with a police car, they sought to assassinate Gil Robles, but he was out of town. They then went to the home of Calvo Sotelo, and announced that he was under arrest. Although suspicious, Calvo was forced to accompany them. The officers shot him and left his body in the morgue.

Next day, the news of the assassination of the most prominent anti-Republican deputy by officers of the Republican police sent a shudder through Spain. Despite the ministry's immediate disclaimer and arrest of the guilty assault guards, many good conservative citizens believed the prime minister personally responsible for the act. For them the Republicans had proved their unfitness to rule. To such an extent had distrust and hatred grown. Spirits were prepared for a desperate act of reprisal.

The murder of Calvo Sotelo incited the generals to act. On Friday afternoon, July 17, the garrison of Melilla in Morocco revolted, caught the local governor and loyal officers by surprise, and rapidly crushed resistance. On July 18 General Franco broadcast from the Canary Islands the reason for the uprising—to reestablish public order and save Spain from anarchy and revolution. On the same day commanding officers of garrisons on the mainland proclaimed their support of the revolt.

13

Civil War

1

For a rising that had been planned with a need for secrecy, the *pronunciamiento* of Saturday, July 18 and Sunday, July 19, 1936 was surprisingly well coordinated. Captains general and other military leaders in each command came out in favor of the rebellion and proclaimed martial law. The Republican government, although warned of the plot, was caught by surprise. Prime minister Casares Quiroga resigned late at night on July 18. President Azaña was torn between various alternatives. On the one hand, he could look for a conservative who might be able to negotiate with the generals in revolt. On the other, he could expand the government to the left to include the Socialists in preparation for forceful resistance. He tried both, but after twenty-four hours of effort, both had failed. The leading generals in Spain, including Mola, reached by telephone, refused to negotiate, and Largo Caballero still vetoed a coalition government. On July 19, José Giral, a close friend of Azaña, formed another all-Republican government.

Since most of the army and the Civil Guard went rapidly over to the uprising, the first reaction of the workers' organizations was to demand that the government open the arsenals and distribute arms to the syndicates and other organized workers' groups. This Azaña and other responsible leaders feared to do, still frightened by Largo Caballero's revolutionary rhetoric. Nevertheless by Sunday militias of the workers' parties in Madrid and Barcelona obtained enough arms, privately or from cooperative military commanders, to attack the buildings held by the armed forces. In both cities they defeated the insurgents. The insurrection also failed in Bilbao and Valencia without much fighting. In Seville, however, where workers also reacted energetically and obtained arms, a daring general, Gonzalo Queipo de Llano, made good use of the radio to sow confusion and fear among the workers and attacked them with the forces at his disposal. By Monday he controlled the city, a vital victory, for its airport was to provide a bridgehead for the troops in Morocco. Following Seville, the other major cities of Andalusia except Jaén and Malaga fell rapidly to the revolt.

By Monday, July 20, it was clear that the generals had failed in their plan to take all Spain without serious opposition. Thanks to the workers' organizations rather than the government, the major cities except Seville and Zaragoza were still in Republican hands. Lines were confused, but the rising had captured Old Castile, Galicia, Navarre, Aragon, and most of Andalusia, while the Republic held the Mediterranean coast, a wide strip running across Spain from the east coast to the frontier of Portugal at Badajoz and including Madrid, and Asturias and the Basque Provinces in the north. Neither side could immediately crush the other; the issue could only be settled by war.

Having succeeded in withstanding the first assault, the Republic could look forward to eventual mastery of the rising. Except for ten thousand well-trained Requetés of the Carlists and thirty thousand civil guards, the generals had few troops in Spain. Their best forces were in Africa, securely controlled by Franco, who had flown to Morocco on July 19. He needed the navy or air force to get his troops to the peninsula, but most of their units had remained loyal to the Republic. Naval seamen had mutinied and murdered the officers who had favored the rising.

At this point foreign intervention became decisive. The generals had been in touch with Hitler and Mussolini, seeking aid. As soon as these heads of government saw that the rising had a chance of success, they sent what the generals most needed: aircraft. Italian bombers and German transports arrived in Morocco before the end of the month. By early August, these planes had taken control of the Strait of Gibraltar from the Spanish navy and were ferrying precious troops into Seville. Some twenty thousand Moorish troops and soldiers of the Foreign Legion thus reached Andalusia. Called the Army of Africa, they were the best-trained forces on either side. Under the command of General Franco, they rapidly assured control of western Andalusia and moved north, capturing Badajoz on August 14. From the outset neither side was giving quarter in the war, and as the Moors advanced they executed all men believed to have borne arms against them. In Badajoz the victorious Moorish troops, after suffering heavy casualties inflicted by a determined Republican militia, herded all men suspected of resistance into the bull ring and shot them down with machine guns. Perhaps two thousand perished. Although different from earlier reprisals only in the numbers involved, the massacre of Badajoz, when reported and exaggerated in the world press, caused anger and horror among the Republicans and roused much of world opinion against the insurgents.

After the fall of Badajoz, Franco's army advancing from the south made a junction with that of the north on September 8, and thereafter western Spain fell rapidly into insurgent hands. The Nationalists, as the insurgents came to be known generally, turned next to the relief of the garrison of Toledo, which, as the world press widely publicized, had been besieged since the outbreak of the war. The workers' militias had here defeated the *pronunciamiento*, but some 1300 soldiers, civil guards, and Falangists together with their families and a hundred hostages had shut themselves into the sixteenth century palace of Charles V, the Alcázar, and were under siege by the workers. A square building with strong walls, it was able to withstand the light artillery available to the militia. The attackers tunneled under it and exploded mines, but the defenders held out. The son of the commander, Colonel José Moscardó, was in Republican hands. The attackers warned Moscardó they would execute his son if he did not surrender. Moscardó refused and they carried out their threat. Finally, on September 28, a column of the Army of Africa drove into Toledo and rescued the garrison. The heroic defense of the Alcázar of Toledo became the outstanding legend of the Nationalist cause.

The Badajoz massacre and the execution of Moscardó's son were but two examples of the ferocious cruelty that marked the Civil War, especially in its opening stages. When Nationalist forces captured cities and towns they systematically hunted out anyone bearing arms against them, those who had belonged to workers' and other leftists organizations, freemasons, anyone who had favored the Popular Front. The numbers of such persons were enormous; and though all of course did not die, vast numbers did, shot without trial, on mere hearsay. In Granada, for instance, gangs of youthful Falangists, including girls, rounded up suspects by the hundreds, drove them in trucks to deserted spots outside the city, and shot them and buried them in shallow graves. Perhaps eight or ten thousand Granadinos died in this way. Among them was its native bard, Federico García Lorca, Spain's most gifted poet of modern times. His support of the Republic in cultural matters was notorious, but who was responsible for his death remains a mystery.[1] Nationalist mass executions, not always so debauched, continued through the war as their troops advanced. How many died will never be known and estimates vary with the viewpoint of the

[1] Gerald Brenan, *The Face of Spain* (London: Turnstile Press, 1950), pp. 127–48.

writer. Gabriel Jackson's carefully thought out estimate is two hundred thousand, almost 1 percent of the population.[2]

On the other side rapidly formed workers' committees took over control of the areas loyal to the Republic and conducted purges of their own. The gruesome task rapidly got out of hand. Each workers' group drew up its own list of suspects, political opponents, unpopular employers, persons whose social class or party affiliation marked them out as enemies of the Republic or the proletariat. Armed representatives of the workers' organizations and even groups of young activists without any formal authorization seized many of these persons in their homes at night, drove them outside city limits, and shot them, leaving their bodies for early risers to discover. Prominent bourgeois and Catholic families in Madrid, Barcelona, and elsewhere in the Republican zone lived in terror during the first weeks of the war, and hundreds of their members were "taken for a ride" (*dar un paseo*); while in small towns local landowners, priests, and civil guards were shot, often by outsiders who came through in gangs. A vast number of churches was also burned and looted, usually by anarchists.

There are no better figures on Republican executions than on Nationalist. After a careful analysis of the claims on both sides and the little available data, Jackson has estimated that 17,000 died at Republican hands in the first three months, and 3000 later.[3] Over a third of these were priests and monks, who were easily identified by their dress. Since there were few mass executions, the figure is reasonable. It contrasts sharply with the claim of 86,000 deaths made later by the Franco government and even more with the ridiculous reports of 300,000 to 400,000 assassinations carried at the time in the foreign press. For various reasons, the number was much smaller than that killed by the Nationalists. The Republican government never condoned the massacres as Nationalist commanders did, so that the *paseos* were never systematic. Members of the upper classes were fewer by far than those of workers' groups, and many had the means to escape or took refuge in foreign embassies. Finally, after the beginning of the war, the Republicans hardly ever advanced into new areas.

The uncontrolled terror on both sides represented an explosion of the tensions and hatreds that had built up since 1934, a form of collective hysteria and momentary intoxication at all levels of authority and society, rather than the product of a national character imbued with violence, as many foreign observers maintained who did not know its background. Fittingly exaggerated by the domestic and foreign press, it was the most sensational news to come out of Spain. Hardly anywhere did the reports find an impartial audience, for world develop-

[2] Jackson, pp. 526–40.
[3] *Ibid.*

ments of the past years had conditioned men's minds to accept congenial stories and discount the uncongenial. Everywhere conservatives and Catholics, both ordinary persons and government leaders, were horrified by tales of the "red" terror, and their sympathies went out to the insurgents. Those who hated Mussolini and Hitler for personal or ideological reasons became incensed at the Nationalist uprising and executions, which they labeled "fascist." Thus almost at once the Spanish Civil War became a major world event, dividing people outside Spain as well as inside.

2

The failure of either side to achieve a rapid victory left both with the problem of establishing a viable wartime government. Within the Republican zone, Giral's ministry had nominal authority, but it lost all control over events. The police had disappeared, and most of the army and civil guards had gone over to the insurgents. Real authority fell to local committees representing the armed workers, which sprang up in the first days after the *pronunciamiento* in the same fashion as municipal juntas had appeared during nineteenth-century revolutions. The most powerful was the committee of Barcelona, called the Central Committee of the Antifascist Militias of Catalonia, established on July 21. It had fifteen members representing eight leftwing groups including the anarchist CNT and FAI, the socialist UGT, the Catalan Esquerra, and two new groups which were to play important roles, the PSUC (Partit Socialist Unificat de Catalunya, a coalition of the Socialist and Communist parties of Catalonia established in the heat of the rising) and the POUM (Partido Obrero de Unificación Marxista, a group of anti-Stalinist Marxists formed in February 1936 under Andrés Nin, one of the original Spanish Communists). Companys, president of the Generalitat, offered to let it replace the Catalan government, since it represented the forces that had put down the rising in the city. The committee allowed him to remain in office to preserve a show of legality, but henceforth real authority belonged to it. Similar committees took over most cities in Republican Spain. Where the *ayuntamiento* was Socialist, the committee usually consisted of its members with the addition of workers' representatives. In Catalonia members of the CNT and FAI dominated the local committees, though the spirit of proletarian brotherhood often brought in the PSUC and POUM as well. Only Madrid avoided a new authority to rival the established government, but even here the militias acted without regard for the ministry.

The committees had three immediate objectives: to create an armed force capable of opposing the armies of the generals, to estabish police authority and end the uncontrolled murder of suspected enemies, and to carry through the social revolution that the anarchists and Largo Caballero Socialists had been preaching. By early August they began to achieve the second aim. They did not end the terror, nor did they intend to, but they set up courts and judges (often workers) who tried the arrested suspects. These courts gained fearful notoriety among their enemies, especially the "*chekas*" of Madrid, yet they acquitted many suspects and occasionally turned on false accusers and condemned them to death.

Dominated as they were by the most radical elements on the Republican side, the committees also carried out a collectivist revolution. Before the uprising Largo Caballero's Socialist followers and the anarchists had inspired widespread belief in the imminence of the proletarian revolution. Now that the "fascists" had attacked the Republic, the revolution would be their just punishment, was the workers' attitude. The revolution took different forms from place to place. In Barcelona *ad hoc* committees representing the CNT and UGT ran public services, hotels, and the major factories. They draped the buildings with red flags or red-and-black anarchist flags. Middle-class people found it wise to dress like workers in blue overalls (the proletarian *mono*) and say "*tu*" instead of "*usted*" and "*¡salud!*" instead of "*¡adiós!*" Madrid, where the UGT was stronger, was less prone to collectivizing and populism, but the authorities confiscated foreign businesses, and workers' committees directed by the ministry of war ran enterprises which could supply military needs. There was much talk of collectivizing farming, but the most suitable region for such a program was Andalusia, and most of it was in insurgent hands. In the Mancha the agrarian laborers collectivized several hundred large estates. Elsewhere the rural revolution meant establishing local cooperatives and confiscating the property of the larger landowners, who had fled or been shot. In sum there was no consistent plan for the revolution, only proliferating attempts to realize the many utopian plans to do away with capitalist exploitation that the different parties had been preaching. That in many instances they worked, and that factories began to turn out arms, can be credited to the tremendous dedication and effort of the workers, who overcame initial confusion and the disappearance of engineers and managers. Eventually, when the enthusiasm waned, unexpected difficulties of unplanned collectivization became apparent.

The third task of the local committees was to create and arm revolutionary militias to oppose the forces of insurrection. On July 24, the Central Committee of Barcelona established the first column of militia under the command of Buenaventura Durruti, a famous anarchist terrorist who had participated in the assassination of the archbishop of Zaragoza in 1923 and had spent years in prison and in exile. When the Durruti column marched toward Aragon to reconquer Zaragoza, it executed priests and landowners on the way and established local agrarian collectives. Other left-wing columns soon followed it to the Aragon front. In Madrid the various labor organizations established their own militias which went north to the Sierra de Guadarrama to stop the troops of Mola. Elsewhere local committees also established their militias who defended their towns or went forward to face the "fascists."

The early militias were a makeshift and ineffectual military force. They were usually commanded by political or union leaders who lacked military training. They did not know how to take cover, fight in open country, or retreat in order. When they met units of the regular army or were strafed by planes, they frequently broke in panic and were mowed down or captured and executed; but they proved courageous and effective as guerrillas in the mountains or in house-to-house fighting in cities. Most of them were organized "democratically," without the usual distinction among ranks. When the Giral government suggested in August drafting men to form a regular army, the CNT of Barcelona replied: "We want to be militias of liberty, not soldiers in uniform. The army has proved a danger to the country; only popular militias protect public liberties. Militias, yes; soldiers, never!" [4]

With revolutionary committees assuming local authority and various militias doing the fighting, one of the most difficult problems facing the Republican government was to establish unity of direction in order to oppose the insurgents effectively. The internal history of the Republican zone during the first year of the war is above all the story of how the constitutional government slowly gathered back into its hands the strands of power. The problem was urgent, for the Republican side desperately needed help from abroad and the apparent disappearance of the central government in face of the triumphant social revolution was discrediting the Republic. Giral's strongest argument for foreign help was his claim to head the legally elected government of Spain. Aware of this, the local committees seldom overtly disregarded his ministry, but he lacked the stature to command their respect.

The only person who could head a government that would be both legitimate and have authority over the militant workers was Largo Caballero. Slowly he abandoned his ideological opposition to a coalition ministry, which had hurt the Popular Front since its beginning. On September 4, Giral resigned and Azaña named Largo Caballero head of a coalition government composed of Socialists—including the moderates Prieto and Juan Negrín—Republicans, Communists, Catalan Esquerra, and a Basque nationalist.

There remained the anarchists, who were supreme in Catalonia,

[4] Quoted in Pierre Broué and Émile Témime, *La Révolution et la guerre d'Espagne* (Paris: Éditions de Minuit, 1961), p. 130.

controlling its Central Committee. The person who managed to tame them was Companys. Since the war began he had worked patiently to bring authority back to the Generalitat, and on September 26 he obtained an anarchist agreement to join a new ministry of the Generalitat and abolish the Central Committee. A little over a month later, on November 4, Largo Caballero succeeded in getting the anarchists to enter his own ministry, taking four positions. The move was urgent, for by now Madrid was in imminent danger, and everyone felt that the fall of Madrid would be a mortal blow for the Republic.

The Nationalist side also experienced confusion and lack of unity, but never to the extent the Republic did, and it found a permanent solution much sooner. Since the military were in control from the outset, the question became which general should be supreme commander. The leading figure of the rising, General Sanjurjo, who was in Lisbon, was killed on July 20 in the crash of a small plane that had been sent to bring him to Spain. Mola in Navarre, Queipo de Llano in Seville, and Franco in Africa and later Andalusia remained to direct the uprising. After Sanjurjo's death Mola took over the direction, for he had inspired the plotting within Spain. On July 24, Mola established a Junta of National Defense at Burgos, consisting of generals headed by the elderly Miguel Cabanellas. It did not include the generals in the south or representatives of the civilian groups that had supported the rising, the Carlists and the Falange. It had as little authority in the next months as Giral had on his side.

After the armies of the north and south had met on September 8, various generals began to call for a single command. Mola and Franco were the logical candidates, but of the two Franco had clearly become the more impressive. He had behind him the best fighting force, the Army of Africa, had reconquered southern and western Spain, and was favored by Germany and Italy, on whom the Nationalists depended for continuing supplies. Nevertheless, personal rivalries held up a final decision until September 29. On that day the Burgos junta and other senior officers accepted Franco as generalísimo and "head of the government." Two days later, the official proclamation appeared, with Franco's title mysteriously changed to "Head of State" (Jefe del Estado) as well as generalísimo, with "the absolute powers of the state." Thus supreme military and civil authority had been joined in one man.

Spain and the world knew little about Franco beyond his name, for unlike many generals he had stayed out of politics until July 1936. The Republicans and many foreign observers felt he was but a tool of Hitler and Mussolini. Not for years would the world realize that Franco never would be subservient to anyone but was one of the most independent and astute figures to come to power in modern times. Nationalist Spain had created a military dictator.

3

The first months of the war had divided Spain in two. The front lines had become clear by October. Despite bitter fighting, they were to change only slowly in the next year. As in July, the Nationalists held most of Andalusia except Jaén and Malaga, all of Old Castile, Galicia, and Navarre, and most of Aragon, and they had added New Castile west of Madrid and Extremadura. The Republicans held Asturias and the Basque Provinces in the north; Catalonia, Valencia, and the Mediterranean coast in the east and south; and a large section stretching inward from the Mediterranean to include eastern Andalusia, eastern New Castile with Madrid, and eastern Aragon. Roughly, arid, agricultural Spain had fallen to the insurgents. The industrial north and east, the bigger cities except Seville and Zaragoza, and the countryside dependent on them were in Republican hands. Spain had divided along lines familiar since the eighteenth century.

Spain had divided along other familiar lines as well, lines solidified by the terror on both sides since the outbreak of the war. Favoring the Republic were those persons who had supported the Popular Front. They included the organized workers of the cities who belonged to the proletarian parties and were caught up in the enthusiasm of their cause. In the countryside many peasants and landless laborers felt the same way. This was especially true in the south, where the anarchists and the UGT had extended their following under the Republic. Large segments of the middle class favored the Republic: a majority of the intellectuals who had experienced the revival of the Generation of '98 and the Institución Libre, including the mass of university professors, many professional people, and those devoted to the autonomy of Catalonia and the Basque Provinces. Essentially the Loyalists, as they came to be known abroad, were the heirs to the groups that had developed in opposition to the established order after 1875, who had been frustrated in 1917, and finally achieved their victory in 1931. Those who had favored the Republic in 1931 out of convenience rather than conviction—members of the former monarchist parties, army officers, moderate Catholics—had fallen away, leaving the convinced hard core of republican support to fight for the Republic.

On the other hand, the groups that had supported the former monarchy—the church, the army, the large landowners—on the whole welcomed the rising. The leading industrialists and bankers joined them, frightened by the revolutionary threats of the left-wing leaders and the armed might of the workers. Middle-class people of Catholic upbringing and sympathy soon desired the victory of Franco, especially if members of their family had suffered in the terror. The most militant Catholics were the Carlists, now known officially as the Traditionalists, whose well-disciplined Requetés provided valuable support in the early battles in the north. Equally committed, though different in outlook, was the Falange, whose principles were not religious or conservative but favored social legislation, cooperation of all classes, and national grandeur. These groups offered as heterogeneous a body of supporters as did those of the Republic, tied together by their fear and hatred of the proletarian parties of the Popular Front.

That the majority of the clergy should support the insurgents was a foregone conclusion, for the polarization of Spaniards had taken place around the religious issue. Churches were closed and priests killed by the thousands in the Republican zone. The hierarchy acclaimed the army's rising as a religious crusade. Cardinal Isidro Gomá, archbishop of Toledo and primate of Spain, proclaimed: "We deny that this is a war of classes. The workers' claims are only a pretext. It is the love of the God of our fathers that has led half of Spain to take up arms. On one side the fields have become temples; on the other side thousands of priests assassinated, churches destroyed, a satanic fury." [5] The church worked to convince Spaniards and the world that the real rebels were the Republicans in the service of international Communism, a myth that was to be maintained officially after the war. Largo Caballero's speeches before the war and the acts of the local committees leant credibility to this story. Typical of the church's statements is a prominent memorial tablet in the Cathedral of Jaén which is dedicated to "The Reverend Diocesan Priests assassinated in the Marxist Revolution, July 1936–March 1939." Beneath this heading are the names of the bishop and 124 priests of the province. Franco, himself a devout Catholic, welcomed the support of the clergy and made the church a partner in the crusade. Catholic youths, Carlists and others, were to fight and die as heroically for the Nationalist cause as did the young idealists on the Republican side.

Only one shadow darkened this alliance. Many Basque priests took the side of the Republic, along with their fellow citizens who were fighting for the autonomy of their homeland. The Nationalists executed about twelve Basque priests whom they captured. Cardinal Gomá interceded with Franco to prevent further executions of this kind, but he condemned their choice: "It is not permitted to divide the Catholic forces in the face of the common enemy. . . . The alliance is monstrous when the enemy is that modern monster, Marxism or Communism, the hydra with seven heads, synthesis of all heresies." [6]

The Falange was a quite different ally. It had grown phenomenally in recent months. In February 1936 it had five thousand members, in

[5] Quoted in F. G. Bruguera, *Histoire contemporaine d'Espagne 1789–1950* (Paris: Éditions Ophrys, 1953), p. 426.

[6] *Ibid.*

August one million, and it was to boast two million members before the end of the war. Many young militants joined its ranks in the early stages of the war, including not a few former anarchists and Communists caught in insurgent territory who were attracted by its philosophy of violence and social reform and by the safety it offered from their past record. Azaña had imprisoned its founder, José Antonio Primo de Rivera, in March 1936 as an enemy of the Republic, and in November the Communist civil governor of Alicante, where José Antonio was imprisoned, acting without approval of Largo Caballero's ministry, had him tried and executed for helping prepare the revolt. Other central figures of the Falange also died. Without its leaders and ideologically opposed to most of the insurgents, the Falange was groping for its proper role in the insurrection. Meanwhile many young Falangists were fighting and dying valiantly in the front lines.

The dominant force in the rising was without question the army. The plotting had been done by high officers who scorned politicians and, like the generals of the nineteenth century, believed it their duty to save the country from disorder. Most military officers supported the generals, and they controlled the professional soldiers beneath them. The new ideologies were anathema to the officers. An extreme example of their spirit was furnished by General Millán Astray, one-time commander of the Foreign Legion and now director of the press and propaganda for the Nationalists. On October 12, 1936 Unamuno, who had been reappointed rector of the university of Salamanca by the Republic, chaired a celebration at which Millán Astray was the main speaker. Unamuno had welcomed the Republic in 1931, but in July 1936 he supported the uprising, which he hoped would end the draft toward violence and confusion. From the audience came repeatedly the Foreign Legion's cry: "Long live death!" Unamuno was horrified, and said that it was insufficient for the generals to conquer; they must also convince. Millán Astray turned on the aged intellectual, screaming, "Down with intelligence!" The next day Unamuno learned he was no longer rector. He died before Christmas in sorrow over the fate of his country.

Although the groups behind the rising included most of the heirs of the Moderado order, they were few in number by comparison with the defenders of the Republic. With many of the middle class and most of the city workers fighting for the Republic and the rural lower classes either hostile to the generals or uncommitted, the advancing insurgent forces felt themselves in a conquered country. They resorted to terror to eliminate all possible enemies, as the Spanish armies had been used to doing in the African Rif. Like Napoleon in 1808, they chose to treat militias as outlaws in revolt, to be executed if caught, not as soldiers entitled to the rules of war. Anyone caught with arms, or showing signs of having fought the advancing armies, was shot. In this way, through mass terror and executions, the insurgents assured themselves of safety behind the lines. When they could, the Republican militias fled before the onslaught.

There remained vast numbers who were still emotionally uncommitted to either side. Many in the cities continued to long for a restoration of peace and tranquility. Many peasants also fell into this group, those who had not been reached by the UGT or the anarchists. The Republic's agrarian policy had not been successful. Except in Andalusia, the Republican cause did not generate wide enthusiasm among peasants. In the Republican zone, many peasants were being forced into collectives they did not appreciate. But throughout the Nationalist zone, farmers were at peace, and the Nationalists promised to protect rural property, provide loans for peasants, and prevent foreclosure of mortgages. Many peasants still loved their priests and were ready to believe that the cities had been infested by dangerous doctrines. Thus the countryside did not actively oppose the Nationalist armies. The number of young men who volunteered to serve Franco was far below that of the volunteers who filled the Republican armies. He was forced to institute conscription early in the war, and by the end of 1937 the draft was general in the Nationalist zone. Through conscription Franco was able to increase his army, which numbered at most 250,000 at the end of 1936, to 500,000 a year later. Once they were drafted, however, the young, mostly apolitical, peasants could be counted on not to desert. Unlike 1808, peasant guerrillas did not appear to fight for the legitimate order. Only in a few instances in Asturias and Andalusia did Loyalists escape to the hills to become guerrillas. The passivity of the peasantry thus became one of the key factors in the eventual Nationalist victory, as it had been earlier in the political control of the *caciques*.

4

The search for a stable central authority on both sides was motivated in large part by the desire to create a favorable impression abroad. The policy of foreign powers was crucial to the Civil War from the outset. While Franco was receiving critical help from Italy and Germany, on July 19 Giral telegraphed Léon Blum, head of the recently elected French Popular Front government, asking for arms and airplanes. Blum, leader of the French Socialists, was immediately sympathetic, but the members of his government who represented the French middle class reacted unfavorably. The British government, in the hands of the Conservative party, when informed, cautioned Blum against getting involved. The attitude of Great Britain affected French policy directly, for France depended on Britain to help it against the threat of Germany, currently rearming under Hitler's National Socialist government. The British Conservatives cared little about the fate of Spanish workers, but the assassination of upper-class Spaniards dismayed them and they were worried over the large British investments in Spain: the copper mines of the Rio Tinto, the sherry vineyards, the iron mines of the north, and the public utilities. Where the Republic was in control, especially in Catalonia under the anarchists, the local committees had collectivized foreign concerns. Six months later Largo Caballero promised to indemnify foreign investors, but by then points of view had hardened that would not change. What the Nationalists would do was not clear, but just as they protected peasant property they could be counted on to leave foreign enterprises alone. Eventually Franco also forced foreign companies to turn over to his war chest all foreign exchange their exports produced. During the war, no profit came to their owners, but the properties were not confiscated. Franco was too smart to frighten foreign investors, and from the outset he had the sympathy of financial circles in England, France, the United States, and elsewhere. The position of the British government echoed the sentiments of persons with interests in Spain. The possibility of a Communist power at the western end of the Mediterranean also disturbed London. Since the British government, by its threat of friendship with Hitler, could determine French policy, its position became the deciding factor in the policy of the democracies toward the war. Indirectly through the Western governments, foreign investors, rather than the church or the large landowners, proved to be the critical supporters of the Nationalists.

Faced with British opposition, Blum backtracked. After allowing some airplanes to reach Spain, he ordered the frontier closed to military shipments on August 8. To salve its conscience, the French government proposed to the major European powers a policy of nonintervention—that no military aid be given to either side, although accepted international policy was not to blockade recognized governments. Britain accepted, and so did Italy and Germany, meanwhile continuing to ship arms to Franco. Russia, as self-appointed leader of the world revolution, was sympathetic to the Republic, but it also agreed. On September 9, an international Non-Intervention Committee met to enforce the agreement. The Republican government promptly presented evidence of German, Italian, and Portuguese aid to the Nationalists, but the commission chose to reject the evidence—the majority of the governments it represented were sympathetic to the insurgents. The Republicans hoped to stir the world against this injustice by an appeal to the League of Nations. The League had virtually abandoned Ethiopia to the Italian conquerors in 1935, however, and the Spanish Republic's appeal was a wasted effort.

The attitude of the Western powers provoked Russia to ignore the nonintervention agreement and begin shipment of arms to Spain in October. Nonintervention was never to work. Hitler and Mussolini sent arms, airplanes, and troops to Franco, in return for much needed minerals. Russia sent arms and technical advisors to the Republic, paid for with the gold reserve of the Spanish government. The only significant effect of the nonintervention policy was to prevent the Republicans from buying arms in Western Europe, thereby placing the Republican government in a position where it had to follow the dictates of Moscow.

While the democratic powers shilly-shallied, private volunteers came from abroad to offer their lives to the Republic. They had been slipping across the Pyrenees since the outset of the war, despite the French closing of the frontier. Throughout Western Europe and America, the war caught the imagination of militant workers and left-wing intellectuals and students. The Spanish people, in their eyes, were rising to crush fascism, the gravest modern threat to freedom and social justice. They could remember that after the bright dawn of 1918–19, the democracies of Europe had collapsed one by one. Mussolini took over Italy in 1922, followed by Primo de Rivera in Spain in 1923 and Pilsudski in Poland in 1926. Yugoslavia fell in 1929, Germany in 1933, Austria in 1934. Mussolini conquered the heroic and independent African people of Ethiopia in 1935. Nowhere in Europe had there been serious resistance. The Italian, German, and Austrian socialist leaders had been imprisoned or murdered or had fled. The proclamation of the Spanish Republic in 1931 had been one of the few causes for hope. Now the Spanish people were the first to stand up and fight for their freedom against the Fasces and the Swastika. Just as Spain had galvanized Europe against Napoleon in 1808, so now it did against the totalitarian menace of the twentieth century. Well-known poets and novelists came and publicized the Loyalist cause. Among them, Ernest Hemingway created *For Whom the Bell Tolls* out of his experiences, André Malraux wrote *Man's Hope*, and George Orwell *Homage to Catalonia*. Large numbers of lovers of democracy and partisans of world social revolution became personally committed to the outcome in Spain. The attitude of their governments angered them, for this was the final betrayal of the democratic idealism of 1918. Their estrangement has continued to this day, only temporarily interrupted by the Second World War.

At first the foreign volunteers joined the workers' militias, but as their numbers grew and the war became the center of world attention, leaders of the Communist International determined to provide direction and support for the volunteers. They organized what they called the International Brigades. They established headquarters for recruitment in Paris, made arrangements for clandestine passage of the volunteers into Spain, and set up a training center at Albacete. Refugees from Mussolini and Hitler, antifascists from central and eastern Europe, militant leftists, idealistic students, and unemployed workers from France, England, and the United States joined the International Brigades and went to Spain. The arrival of their first contingents coincided with the unloading of Russian arms. By the beginning of November they were ready to face the forces of Franco. Compared to the Spanish workers' militias they were an elite corps, many of them veterans, with trained officers at their head. Their first column reached Madrid on November 8, consisting mostly of Germans and Italians, who marched impressively up the main avenues and created a sensation in the now beleaguered city. They were none too soon, for the critical battle of the year had begun that morning.

5

Since the capture of Toledo, the Nationalist forces had been preparing an assault on Madrid. They had not met effective resistance elsewhere, and they counted on its easy fall, which would signal the death of the Republic. Germany and Italy had promised to recognize the Franco government as soon as it captured Madrid. Nor was the fate of Madrid foreseen differently by the Republicans. Despite the strong protest of the anarchists who had just joined his ministry, Largo Caballero moved his government to Valencia on November 6, giving military authority over Madrid to a loyal general, José Miaja, and political authority to a Junta of Defense representing, once again, the proletarian organizations. This time, however, the controlling voice in the Junta belonged to the Spanish Communist Party, whose prestige had been raised by the arrival of Russian arms and by its having created the only effective militia in Madrid, the "Fifth Regiment."

Communist speakers, led by the charismatic Asturian miner's wife, Dolores Ibarruri, known as La Pasionaria, roused Madrileños to a fever of determination. They appealed to the workers of Madrid to imitate those of Petrograd (November 7 was the anniversary of the Russian Revolution), with slogans like "Madrid will be the tomb of the Fascists," and "They shall not pass!" The Madrid militias, stiffened by the International Brigades, withstood the violent assault launched by the Moors and Requetés on November 8, and they continued to do so in succeeding days, dying in the trenches and defending buildings room by room. The attacking forces launched air raids and artillery bombardments on the defenseless city. The bitterest fighting occurred in the Ciudad Universitaria, lying on the northwest outskirts of Madrid, whose modern edifices, the pride of the Republic, soon lay in ruins. During the fighting, Republican troops appeared from elsewhere, notably the Durruti column from Aragon. Slowly, the tenacity of the defenders produced the unexpected miracle. After ten days the attacking forces had made virtually no headway and had to stop exhausted. Madrid had lived through one of the most highly charged emotional experiences in history. In Spain and abroad, a Republican victory suddenly seemed possible. Germany and Italy finally recognized Franco as the legitimate head of Spain on November 18, but his government was still in Burgos.

The Nationalists' failure before Madrid was a blow to their prestige, and they were determined to avenge the insult. Twice more during the ensuing winter, they attempted to take the city. They now counted on hitting it from behind, cutting off the road to Valencia, its only supply line. In February 1937 they attacked southeast of Madrid across the Jarama river. After a week of heroic combat which decimated Republican troops and International Brigades on one side and Moors and Foreign Legionnaires on the other, the Loyalists halted the offensive. Russian planes and tanks and intensive military training had at last built a Republican army that could fight effectively in open country. A month later a Nationalist assault came from the northeast, aimed at Guadalajara. The major force was thirty thousand Italian soldiers, sent by Mussolini, with the latest equipment. Within a week the Italians were in full flight, the laughing stock of the world, routed by a snowstorm and the Republican army and International Brigades. Madrid had proved impregnable, but now Mussolini also had an insult to avenge.

6

The winter 1936–37 produced critical developments on the Republican side. Unity of purpose and spiritual brotherhood among the different parties defending the Republic reached a zenith during the battle of Madrid, when anarchists, independent Marxist POUM militias, Communists, and Socialists fought side by side. Thereafter, however, this unity began to deteriorate. Largo Caballero, despite his earlier calls for revolution, now worked constantly to bring authority back into the hands of the central government and to cooperate with the middle-class supporters of the Republic. He promised indemnities to former owners of nationalized businesses, both foreign and domestic, and he stated that only the expropriation of lands taken from active opponents of the Republic would be recognized. Most important for the military future of the Republic, he gradually forced the workers' militias into a regular army. Officer ranks were established and division numbers appeared. The anarchists resisted stubbornly, but Largo had an unanswerable argument, for his government controlled the supply of weapons and ammunition.

Ever since October the major source of military supplies had been Russia. Cooperation with Russia became essential to the Republican government, with the result that both the Russian ambassador, Marcel Rosenberg, and the Spanish Communist Party had increasing influence over Republican policies. The Communists received credit for the defense of Madrid and they had the prestige of the Russian Revolution behind them. From thirty thousand members in July 1936, the party expanded to over a million a year later. Most of these recruits were from nonrevolutionary groups—peasants, small businessmen, intellectuals, civil servants. For the Communists urged an end to the social revolution in the interest of winning the war. They denounced the separatist activities of the anarchists and the revolutionary élan of the left-wing UGT. The anti-Stalinist POUM were their mortal enemies. They provided Largo Caballero with firm support for his reestablishment of central control, but they went further and extended their own power within the Republican zone. Their main target was the army. To gain control of the army they used the mechanism of political commissars, instituted by the government in October 1936 on the model of those of the Red Army in Russia. They were assigned to military units to instruct the soldiers in political doctrine and to be right-hand men, and watchdogs, of the commanding officers. Not by accident most of the commissars were Communists, and their association with the party and thus with the source of supplies gave them such authority that frequently they rivaled the generals. Largo Caballero had destroyed one threat to the authority of the state only to spawn another, which he resented no less for the Communists' claim to be helping him.

In this way the defenders of the Republic became divided between the partisans of revolution and the partisans of order. Many leaders of the CNT and the UGT still favored immediate revolution, and behind them were the mass of workers who had welcomed Largo Caballero's ministry and were becoming increasingly disillusioned with his policies. Their stronghold was in Barcelona and the Catalan government. The Republicans like Azaña, right-wing Socialists like Prieto, and the Communists represented the partisans of order. They had the support of Russia, which since encouraging the formation of Popular Front governments wanted to appear as the international leader of the defense of parliamentary democracy against fascist totalitarianism. Furthermore the partisans of order argued that only by postponing a social revolution and guaranteeing property could the Republic induce the Western democracies to sell it arms. Reneging on the promise of a social revolution might kill the spirit that had saved Madrid, but the prospect of revolution diminished the chances of help from abroad. The desire to placate foreign investors became as decisive in Republican policies as it was in Franco's.

By early 1937 Largo Caballero was trying desperately to keep the two sides together. He resisted attempts of the Communists to dictate Spanish policy, and he rejected a Russian proposal to unite the Communist and Socialist parties of all Spain as they had been in Catalonia. This independence determined the Communists to get rid of him. A serious incident in Barcelona gave them the opportunity they wanted. On May 3 assault guards, under orders from a Communist member of the Generalitat, tried to take over control of the main telephone building, which the anarchists had occupied and run since the outbreak of the war. Through it passed government communications with Catalonia and the outside world. The anarchists, jittery over the extension of central authority, resisted the guards with gunfire. A running battle rapidly developed in Barcelona between anarchists and anti-Stalinist POUM on one side, and police and assault guards on the other. Eventually government forces from Valencia crushed the anarchists. The Communists in the ministry demanded exemplary punishment of the rising and suppression of the POUM, which they accused of being in the service of Franco's "fascists." Largo Caballero refused to punish any group that had fought the enemies of the Republic, whereupon the Communist ministers resigned on May 13, causing a cabinet crisis. President Azaña urged Largo Caballero to accept a Communist demand to name Prieto minister of war, an office Largo held himself, but Largo refused out of principle to accept their terms, and resigned.

To head the next ministry Azaña selected a moderate Socialist who was acceptable to the Communists, Juan Negrín. His cabinet embodied the triumph of the policy of order. Negrín destroyed the remaining power of the anarchists in Catalonia, and he forced their last militias to enter the regular army. He acceded to the Communist demand to suppress the POUM and arrest its leaders. The revolution that the workers' parties had inaugurated in July and August 1936 had been checked, not by Franco but by the Republic itself. In this development the Communists had played the key role, and behind them stood Russia, striving to gain French and British sympathy against Hitler's Germany. The anarchists of Catalonia and the left-wing Socialists who had followed Largo Caballero in 1936 bitterly resented his fall. They would continue to fight and die for the Republic, but some of their spontaneous enthusiasm was lost.

7

Negrín was to remain at the head of the government until the end of the war. In terms of personnel, his ministry was the most competent the Republic had during the war. Son of a wealthy family, educated in Germany, a professor of medicine at the University of Madrid, he was the polar opposite of the plebian Largo Caballero. He was intelligent, determined, and optimistic by temperament; at forty-seven he was hardly older than Franco. Through the deepest crises of the next years he maintained confidence in ultimate success, and he transmitted this spirit to the Republican soldiers, who performed acts of incredible heroism, both in attack and defense. As war minister he had Prieto, the best organizer the republic had produced. Giral, the former prime minister, acted as foreign minister. In outlook, education, and appearance, the Negrín cabinet would have been at home in Paris or London.

Negrín's policies were motivated by a desire to win the domestic support of the moderate classes and the favor of the foreign democracies. For the first time in the Republican sector he permitted private religious services and gave them protection. Several conservative deputies reappeared at a meeting of the Cortes on October 1, 1937. Except for the fact (a fundamental one) that Negrín promised to preserve the Republican constitution and parliamentary government, to some Loyalists there seemed little difference between the practices of his government and those of the generals they were fighting. When he became too clearly opposed to local autonomy, the Catalan and Basque members of his ministry resigned, in August 1938.

The democracies were not to be impressed by anything the Spanish government did. A new Blum ministry opened the French frontier briefly in 1938, only to have the next prime minister, Edouard Daladier, close it a few months later. Otherwise the nonintervention policy continued, and Germany and Italy continued to supply Franco. Negrín had no alternative but to accept Soviet supplies and accompanying dictates.

Thus to many the Negrín ministry took on the appearance of a Soviet lackey. It silenced criticism in the press of itself or the Russian government. The Communists seemed irresistible. Acting without knowledge of the ministry, Spanish and Russian Communist agents got hold of the arrested leader of the POUM, the well-known anti-Stalinist, Andrés Nin. Unknown to anyone, they tortured and killed him. When their deed came out, the non-Communist left was aghast and Negrín was outraged. In August 1937 he formed a secret police, the Servicio de Investigación Militar (SIM), to centralize counterespionage under his authority. He attempted to keep the SIM out of Communist hands, placing it under Prieto, but by 1938 they had gained control of it. Yet despite appearances, neither Negrín nor Prieto was the kind of person who would become a Russian tool. Maneuvering adroitly, they succeeded in ousting Largo Caballero from the position he had held for almost twenty years as president of the UGT, but they continued his rejection of Russian proposals to merge the Socialist and Communist parties of Spain.

A man of iron determination, Negrín refused to see the Republican armies always on the defensive. He believed they must attack if they were to win domestic and foreign confidence, but he never found the means to match the enemy. Slowly Franco, with his superior armaments from abroad and adequate food supply, wore down and drove back the Republicans. Having found Madrid impregnable and realizing that the war had become one of attrition, he turned to the other fronts. In the spring, summer, and fall of 1937, Nationalist troops, supported by Italian ground forces and German aviation, slowly destroyed the resistance in the north, where the coastal provinces had remained loyal to the Republic, the Basques fighting for their autonomy under Catholic middle-class leadership, and Asturias under revolutionary miners. There was little Negrín could do to help these regions. In the course of the assault, on April 26, 1937, German planes ferociously bombed Guernica, the medieval Basque capital, testing the effect of terror on a civilian population. The experiment horrified world opinion and was the inspiration for Picasso's most powerful painting, "Guernica," which recalled Goya's "Disasters of War." Yet Bilbao fell on June 12. To relieve pressure on the north, the Republicans attacked west of Madrid at Brunete in July under a scorching sun with their best forces, including the International Brigades. After a short advance, they were held and then slowly driven back to their starting lines. The fighting was desperate on both sides, but the Nationalists had more adequate reserves of arms and men. Their advance in the north hardly faltered. Santander fell on August 26, and on October 21 the last Republican troops surrendered in Asturias.

Fighting turned next to the Aragon front, which was henceforth the scene of all important campaigns. In December 1937 the Republicans attacked an enemy salient threatening Valencia. They captured Teruel building by building. But again lack of firepower, airplanes, and reserves prevented them from exploiting their advance. By February 1938 the Nationalists were able to recapture Teruel. Meanwhile the Nationalists had been building up their forces in Aragon, while the Republicans had worn out their best manpower. Generously supplied with German planes and tanks, Franco opened a massive offensive on March 9 down the Ebro River toward the Mediterranean Sea. The Republicans, outmanned and outgunned, were powerless against his armies. Franco's forces reached the coast on April 15, 1938, and the Republican sector was split in two.

By now leading Republicans came to the conclusion that defeat was inevitable. These included Prieto and President Azaña. Negrín, however, was in no mood for defeatism, and the Communists supported his position. On April 5 Prieto and Giral left the cabinet. Negrín was losing the support of the moderates, who began to see in him a possible dictator, closely tied to a Soviet lead string. And yet the war continued, inspired by Negrín's indomitable spirit.

Negrín continued to believe it imperative to regain the initiative if he were to save the Republic, or even to achieve a reasonable peace. On July 24, 1938 fifty thousand well-trained Republican troops with the best available material launched an offensive south across the Ebro River about fifty miles from the sea, hoping to cut a major Nationalist supply line and surround the enemy troops that had reached the coast. The surprise attack was fully successful, despite bitter and heroic resistance on the Nationalist side. But as before, when the Nationalists brought up equipment and reserves they were able to stop the Republicans, this time near Gandesa. The Republicans dug in and held desperately for three months, but their weary soldiers finally evacuated their salient south of the Ebro early in November. Suffering themselves from tremendous losses among their best troops, the Nationalists pled with the Germans to send more equipment to end the war.

8

The final blow to the hopes of the Republic came, not on the Ebro, but from abroad. By 1938 the specter of Hitler's Germany haunted Europe, and international attention shifted from Spain to Germany. In March 1938 German troops occupied and annexed Austria, and Hitler began to demand those parts of Czechoslovakia where the Germans were a majority. The Czechs were prepared to resist, with Russia behind them, but Britain under Neville Chamberlain and France under Daladier wanted to avoid war at all costs. Meeting with Hitler and Mussolini at Munich on September 15, 1938, the two Western leaders agreed to Hitler's dismemberment of Czechoslovakia. Given such a British and French attitude, the Spanish Republicans knew no help would come to them; while Russia, stung by not being consulted, realized she would never win Western support against the German threat. Her aid to Spain virtually stopped after Munich. Hoping to stir the League of Nations to order out the German and Italian troops in Franco's army, Negrín sent home the International Brigades. On November 15, the foreign volunteers who were still alive paraded through Barcelona, while Negrín gave them thanks and La Parisonaria saluted them: "You can go proudly! You are history! You are legend!" [7] Mussolini in response withdrew some Italian soldiers but left the majority in Spain. Hitler heeded Franco's pleas for more arms on condition that Germany get critical Spanish mining rights.

The Republicans at last stood unaided against the Nationalists still well supplied by Germany and Italy. Yet Negrín refused to give in, convinced now that a general European war was inevitable and that when it broke out the democracies would become allies of the Spanish Republic. Now that Russia had abandoned the Republic he moved to reduce Communist influence, hoping to revive Republican unity. His personal courage kept the Republic at war through the winter.

Franco launched his final offensive against the Catalan front on December 23. Negrín sought to resist at all costs, but there was little serious fighting. Franco's superiority in equipment was overwhelming and the Republican troops were exhausted. Behind the lines Barcelona was hungry, cold, continually bombed, and in a defeatist mood. The policies of Negrín and the Communists had weakened its loyalty to the

[7] Quoted in Hugh Thomas, *The Spanish Civil War* (New York: Harper and Brothers, 1961), p. 558.

Republic. There would be no second Madrid. The city which had withstood hopeless sieges in 1652 and 1714 was occupied at the end of January 1939 with hardly a shot in its defense. Many Italian soldiers were among the victors. Barcelona was Mussolini's revenge for Guadalajara. The Republican government and some half million refugees, soldiers and civilians, streamed north across the French frontier. By February 12 the Catalan front had ceased to exist.

The central front remained, including Madrid, Valencia, and much of central and southern Spain. There had been little fighting here since 1937. Negrín flew back to Valencia to continue the war. This time, however, he asked too much. In Toulouse, Azaña resigned as president when he learned that Britain and France had recognized Franco on February 27. In Madrid a junta of civilians and generals, led by the moderate Socialist Julián Besteiro and Colonel Segismundo Casado, an old partisan of Largo Caballero, denied Negrín's authority and opened negotiations with Franco. They sought to gain an honorable surrender and the assurance of no reprisals. Confident now of prompt victory, Franco refused to negotiate with anyone, promising only not to punish soldiers and others who had served the Republican cause without committing crimes. Republican garrisons surrendered between March 28 and 31. General Franco proclaimed complete victory on April 1, 1939, two years and nearly nine months after the war began. Five months later the international war that Negrín had awaited broke out on the Polish-German frontier.

The Republic which had come in with such high hopes eight years earlier had perished after one of the bitterest struggles of modern times. Many were responsible for its death. It had been killed largely by the indifference and hostility of foreign democracies, which in their concern for their own safety in a world apparently gone mad could not worry about the well-being of a second-rate power. Foreign investors, who were one of the groups to establish control over Spain in the nineteenth century, did their part to bring about the policy of nonintervention. When the Second World War began, new Western leaders would denounce the policy of appeasement, too late, however, to undo the sacrifice of the majority of committed Spaniards, who had favored the Republic. But Spaniards too made possible Franco's victory. The Republicans were torn between enacting a social revolution which would inspire the working classes and defending parliamentary democracy and property to reassure the middle classes and foreign powers. They ended by satisfying no one. Furthermore, Franco could count, as conservatives before him had, on the landowners, on most industrialists, and on those who still cherished the Catholic religion. He could also count on most of the countryside, where the population was isolated from modern ideas and for whom the workers in the cities could be painted as atheistic reds, enemies of civilization. To large numbers of peasants, the city workers were "they," not "we," and this alienation went far toward explaining the tranquility that Franco had behind his lines. There was no *maquis* as in France during the Second World War, no guerrilla warfare similar to that of Algeria in the 1950's. The cities, where people were in contact with new ideas, fought virtually alone. Boycotted by most of the world, without food supplies or needed raw materials, with little support in the countryside, they lost.

Nevertheless, the war demonstrated that Spanish society was evolving in a permanent manner. The political authority of the oligarchy had collapsed during the First World War. Primo de Rivera had come in to shore it up with a military dictatorship, and he succeeded without outside help. Under the Republic with a free parliamentary government, modern Spain had been able to dominate the old order, although the match was close. The Civil War showed that the oligarchy and the armed forces could no longer control Spain. Without outside help, they would have lost. The nineteenth century could not be restored, for modern economy and modern ideology had changed Spain too much. A new balance was being created. The Civil War was an attempt to check the natural evolution by force of arms. For more than ten years after his victory, Franco would keep the weaker side in power by terror and military power; but eventually, to prevent the country from dying a slow death, he would have to recognize the forces of modernization.

14

Spain Under Franco: Repression

1

The Civil War ended organized resistance to the Glorioso Movimiento Nacional, as the insurgent side styled itself, but it left Spain exhausted materially and psychologically. Having lived for three years in a state of hypertension, keyed up by wartime propaganda, worried over the fate of loved ones, Spaniards on one side and the other fell into a state of shock. Those who had been in the Republican zone suffered in addition from prolonged malnutrition. Day-to-day living and recovering from the destruction became overwhelming problems. Roads were in ruin from military use, bombing, and lack of repair, bridges were missing, and automobiles and trucks old and lacking spare parts. Rolling stock on the railroads was worn out; rail traffic in 1941 was at the level of 1911, and did not pass the prewar high until 1952. Both sides had received military supplies from abroad during the war; now Spain needed outside help to rebuild its economy and its health. But outside help could not come, for Europe was at war and soon the whole world would be.

Spain also lacked productive manpower. A hundred thousand young men had died fighting. Nearly half a million people, soldiers, civil servants, Republican sympathizers, and their families, had fled the country, most of them to France, where they were crowded into makeshift camps. The majority of the intellectual elite had favored the Republic, and many of them had left, both writers and technicians. Sixty percent of all university professors had been killed in the war or had emigrated.

The war had intensified the hatreds present before it began and turned Spaniards into two irreconcilable peoples. Hatred and fear infected the partisans of Franco, who felt the insecurity of conquerors in an alien country. The supporters of the Republic, especially those who had lost relatives or jobs or property, were alienated from all the new Spain stood for. While few of them desired further bloodshed, most harbored hopes that deliverance would come from abroad. The more indomitable Republicans did not feel the war had ended, they saw the surrender only as another in a long series of defeats. When the Allies had destroyed Hitler and Mussolini they would surely turn on Franco.

Nor did the victors attempt to bind up the wounds of the country. A calculated reign of terror began, aimed at punishing and cowing those who had opposed the Movimiento. Before Madrid surrendered Franco had pledged that those who had committed no crimes would not be punished, but a law of February 9, 1939 declared all persons who had engaged in subversion or opposed the Movimiento even by a "serious passiveness" to be criminals. Franco interned the Republican soldiers in camps where many nearly starved to death awaiting court martial for military rebellion. Members of labor syndicates and of political parties of the Popular Front were also subject to trial. Freemasonry and Communism were considered the most heinous crimes of all.

Perhaps one million persons went to prison. Simple soldiers were eventually freed, but thousands upon thousands of men were condemned to death and executed outside Madrid, Barcelona, and other cities. Count Ciano, Mussolini's son-in-law, visiting Spain in the summer of 1939, reported 200 to 250 executions per day in Madrid, 150 in Barcelona, 80 in Seville. The executions continued at a sustained rate through 1941 and tapered off during the next decade. Jackson's careful attempt to estimate the total number of death sentences reached the figure 200,000, equal in number to the executions carried out by the Nationalists during the heat of the war. Hundreds of thousands of others were condemned to life imprisonment or to sentences of many years' duration, which they could reduce in half by performing hard labor, usually on roads and public works. A large proportion died of disease or malnutrition before their sentences expired. Even after release from prison, many ex-Republicans found themselves "civilly incapacitated," that is without legal rights, unable to hold a job or to enjoy social security, forced to live outside the law, relying on the generosity of friends. To all these people official statements applied the epithet "*rojo*" (red) indiscriminately.

At the end of the war some ex-soldiers and others fled to the mountains, especially in Andalusia, where they took up a life of outlaws and bandits, reminiscent of the nineteenth century. To hold them down and pacify the country, Franco strengthened the Civil Guard. It mounted machine guns at major crossroads, and the famous *parejas* (pairs) of armed civil guards patrolled the highways more conspicuously than ever. The republic's Assault Guard disappeared from the cities, to be replaced by a similar body called the Armed Police, made up of tough veterans. Meanwhile the army was kept up and garrisoned outside Madrid and other cities, ready to crush any sign of an uprising. The most efficient arm of the government was its secret police, centered in the menacing building of "Gobernación" on the Puerta del Sol of Madrid. The building reputedly held files of all persons known or suspected of having disloyal points of view. Spain resembled a conquered land, where the conquerors retained their control by armed might.

2

During the course of the war, Franco had created an authoritarian state with the reins in his hands. The insurgent generals had proclaimed him Generalísimo and Head of State on October 1, 1936. The regular army provided normal channels of authority for its supreme commander, and the officers proved to be loyal and devoted. Control of the state required implementation, however, for the title "Jefe del Estado" was new. The Constitution of the Republic had divided executive power between the president and the ministry headed by the prime minister, the former selected by popularly elected deputies, the latter appointed by the president but needing confirmation by the Cortes. Policy-making was the province of the ministry. The situation had been similar for one hundred years, except that there had been a hereditary king in place of an elected president. Only Primo de Rivera had had a position resembling that of Franco, but he had Alfonso XIII over him. Franco's title was unique, not only in Spain but in Europe. Mussolini and Hitler had come to power through parliamentary channels. Mussolini, like Primo, had a king, and Hitler at first had a president.

Franco moved hesitantly. On the day he became Head of State he established a "Technical Junta of the State," which was an embryo ministry consisting of heads of commissions, some of them civilians (foreign affairs for example), others generals. They were responsible only to him. Since the revolt had been directed at the parliamentary system, Franco did not reestablish the Cortes. The need for traditional political parties disappeared. Those on the Republican side were declared abolished at the outset of the war, and the others withered for lack of *raison d'être*. Lerroux and the Radicals had been disgraced in 1935. Gil Robles was abroad when the war began and he hardly returned to Spain until after 1950. His party, Popular Action, dissolved itself in February 1937, as did the pro-monarchist Renovación Española that Calvo Sotelo had headed.

On the other hand, Franco could not ignore the existence of the

Falange and the Carlist Traditionalists, for both parties had armed forces fighting under him. They stood for vastly different programs: the one Catholic, monarchist, traditional, the other socialistic, anticlerical, quasi-fascist. Neither group had a leader of stature. José Antonio Primo de Rivera had fallen before a Republican firing squad, while the last male descendant of the first Don Carlos had just died in Vienna at eighty-seven, leaving the Carlists groping for a valid pretender. Acting upon the recommendation of his brother-in-law, Ramón Serrano Suñer, Franco decided to regroup the Falange and the Traditionalists into a single party with himself at its head, however incongrous the whole scheme might appear. By creating a civilian political organization, he could avoid the appearance of being only a military dictator. A decree of April 19, 1937 merged the two organizations into a body to be known as the Falange Española Tradicionalista y de las JONS (the Juntas de Ofensiva Nacional Sindicalista, or JONS, had joined the Falange in 1934). "This organization, intermediary between society and state, has for its principal mission to communicate to the state the feelings of the people and to transmit to the people the thought of the state, through the political-moral virtues of service, hierarchy, and brotherhood," the decree stated.[1] It left no room for any other political party. It declared the Head of State to be National Head of the Falange, the title borne earlier by José Antonio, and commander-in-chief of its militias, that is the fighting forces of the Falangists and Carlists. Within the Falange some left-wing militants led by Manuel Hedilla, a close associate of José Antonio, attempted to prevent Franco's seizure of the party. The gesture was futile, and Hedilla received a sentence of life imprisonment. At the same time the Carlist leader Manuel Fal Conde had to flee to Portugal to save his skin, after publicly calling for an immediate restoration of the monarchy. Neither party was to be happy in this marriage of convenience.

On January 30, 1938 Franco finally established a regular ministry. It drew on the main groups of his supporters, Carlist and Alfonsist monarchists, Falangists, and military. Only three of its eleven members were generals. The leading figure was the minister of *gobernación*. Serrano Suñer, a strong partisan of the Falange. The Falange seemed the most powerful force in the state, but Franco was already demonstrating an ability to balance one group against another. Of those that had supported the rising, three were becoming the main pillars of the new regime: the army, the church, and the Falange. By taking control of the army and the Falange into his hands and letting no group obtain commanding influence, Franco maintained authority for himself. By the end of the war he had indeed become undisputed Jefe del Estado and, as he was also called, Caudillo.

[1] Quoted in Broué and Témime, pp. 395–96.

Having united the Carlists and the Falange into the only legal party, Franco proceeded to formulate a policy for Spain that incorporated the ideals of both, incompatible though they were. From the Carlists he took over a glorification of Spain's past and an emphasis on its Catholicism. Conveniently, the Falange had already adopted as its symbol the yoke and arrows of Ferdinand and Isabel. Franco infused his speeches with the theme that, like those two great monarchs, he was uniting Spain, suppressing anarchy, and driving out the heretics. Official pronouncements declared the Movimiento to be the third war in Spanish history in favor of unity and religion (the first was the Reconquest, the second the Carlist War in the nineteenth century). Besides the Carlists, the church hierarchy had placed its full authority behind the Nationalist cause. Since Franco was devoted to the church, dedication of Spain to the Catholic faith became a cardinal feature of the regime. Mass was said regularly in the army, often in the open air, prelates were conspicuous at public functions, civil marriage and divorce were abolished, the crucifix returned to the classroom, and the Jesuits were restored to their property and position.

To the official Catholicism of the state Franco joined the social ideals of the Falange. Capitalist exploitation of workers was to give way to a society in which each group would work for the good of the whole and receive its due. Society was to be hierarchical and moral. On March 9, 1938 Franco proclaimed the first "fundamental law" of the state, the Fuero del Trabajo or Labor Charter (*fuero* was a suitably traditional term). Spelling out the social policy of the regime, it declared that all Spaniards had the duty to work, and in return the state had the "mission" to guarantee the right to work. (One is reminded that the Constitution of 1931 had established a "Republic of workers of all categories.") The Fuero condemned capitalism as a liberal doctrine and materialism as Marxist. Without being specific, it called for adequate wages to support family life, a limit on the hours of work, paid vacations for all workers, and rest on Sunday and holidays. But it declared treasonous any actions taken to disturb production—a euphemism for strikes. While industry was to remain in private hands and small producers were guaranteed protection, the Fuero declared managers and owners responsible for the welfare of their employees. In agriculture it promised higher wages, protection from foreclosures, and eventual distribution of private plots to all families. It specified that the various productive sectors of the economy would be incorporated into vertical syndicates to which both owners and workers would belong, on the pattern already introduced by Primo de Rivera. Directors of the syndicates would "necessarily" be members of the Falange, and the state would implement its economic policies through the syndicates. In this way Franco made the Falange his instrument for running the economy and policing labor. On paper he had joined the social aims of the

Republicans and Socialists to the Falange ideal of hierarchy and authority. It remained to be seen how the Fuero would work in practice.

To celebrate the victory, the regime carried out a symbolic pageant in the fall of 1939. The Falange exhumed the body of their founder, José Antonio Primo de Rivera, from his burial place beside the sea in Alicante and transferred it to the Escorial in the hills above Madrid. Members of different local units carried the casket on their shoulders in one continuous funeral procession of five hundred kilometers, which lasted ten days and nights, halting only to change the men honored with the task. At the Escorial a solemn military and religious ceremony laid the body to rest before the high altar at which Philip II had worshiped, above the crypt where the kings of Spain lie buried. On the tomb were placed monumental wreaths sent by Hitler and Mussolini. The anniversary of José Antonio's execution, November 20, would henceforth be a national festival. Meanwhile, on the outside walls of churches throughout Spain the name "José Antonio" was painted, above those of the local men who had died "for God and for country," almost as if he were a saint. Thus tradition, religion, monarchy, and twentieth-century national syndicalist ideology were drawn together in pageantry and public life.

3

The authoritarian state took shape as the war progressed. By and large Franco kept the traditional administrative structure, but he eliminated the local election of officials introduced by the Republic. Behind the lines military authority gave way progressively to civilian rule with appointed provincial civil governors and municipal *alcades*. There was a strict investigation of civil servants and high officials to remove any suspected of Republican sympathies who had escaped the early purges. (Those who passed muster were so few that sometimes army officers had to be assigned to civilian posts. The civil governor of Malaga, for instance, was an army captain.)

In April 1938 the government established regular censorship of the press. The text of newspapers and books had to be approved in advance; furthermore, authors and editors remained liable to prosecution if what they published turned out later to be offensive. Understandable in wartime, censorship would continue until after 1960.

The army, Falange, and monarchists had never been sympathetic to the federalist aspect of the Republican constitution. On April 5, 1938 Franco abolished the Catalan statute of 1932 with its provisions for an autonomous government, the Generalitat. Subsequent decrees prohibited the use of the Catalan language in school, in government, or in the press, and abolished all laws passed by the Generalitat. After the defeat of France by Hitler in 1940, Franco obtained from the head of the

French state, General Pétain, the extradition of Lluis Companys, president of Catalonia during the Civil War, and executed him for military rebellion, the most notorious case of Franco's vengeance against his Republican adversaries. Henceforth Castilians and docile Catalans would hold the offices of civil governors, captain general, and *alcaldes* of the major cities of Catalonia, while the Catalan people would be barred from reading their language in the press, hearing it on the radio, or using it in the classroom or even the playing fields. The Basques too, who had set up a virtually independent government during the Civil War, Catholic and conservative, which fought for the Republic because it desired autonomy, saw it disappear, along with the public use of the Basque language. The new Spain would be unitary—"Una, Grande, Libre" was its motto, and the first term had been accomplished on the surface if not in the hearts of Basques and Catalans.

The greatest structural innovation in Franco's state was the single political party, the Falange, and the syndicates under its control. Neither was a new concept, for they existed in other authoritarian regimes and had been anticipated in Spain by General Primo de Rivera in his Unión Patriótica and corporations. Through a tight hierarchy, the Falange gave obedience to the Head of State. The Jefe Nacional (National Head) of the Falange, Franco, appointed the *jefes provinciales,* who appointed the *jefes locales,* who controlled the local units. Franco also appointed the National Council of the Falange. The structure thus paralleled the civil government and administration, and not entirely by accident government and Falange officials were often the same person. By 1941 civil governors were in practice also the provincial heads of the Falange. Since all army officers had been made members of the Falange and at times also were civil officials, the military, the state bureaucracy, and the single party became closely intertwined.

The Falange developed various auxiliary bodies. During the war several young Falangists, dismayed at Franco's taming of their party, proposed to create a youth organization, a Frente de Juventudes. They saw it as a radical, uncorrupted body, patterned after the prewar youth movements. The proposal horrified army officers and the new leaders of the party. Franco finally approved the Frente late in 1940, but only after it had been reworked into a safe organization, useful in regimenting young Spaniards. For the next twenty years, its Falanges Juveniles could be seen drilling in parks and fields, dressed in the blue shirt of the Falange and red beret of the Carlists.

Much more constructive was the women's auxiliary of the Falange, the Sección Femenina, which was founded in 1934 by José Antonio's sister Pilar and has since been directed by her. With Franco's support it expanded rapidly during the war, and by its end had half a million members. It helped administer the Auxilio Social, another Falange institution whose main job was to feed starving poor, especially children. Young unmarried women were required to serve the state for six months, and many went into the Auxilio Social. By 1939 Auxilio Social was feeding nearly a million people, mostly in conquered cities like Barcelona, and was remarkable for its impartiality between friend and foe. In a world where corruption and favoritism were rampant, Pilar Primo de Rivera offered a model of generous service to society.

None of the activities of the Falange compared in importance with its monopoly of the syndicates. It was some time, however, before the ambitious structure promised by the Fuero del Trabajo took on life. Before the war almost all organized workers were in the socialist UGT or anarchist CNT. Both of these were labor associations, aimed at combatting employers and government to obtain their objectives. The Falange had founded some "national syndicates," but it organized workingmen and employers in separate syndicates. Although the Republic's *jurados mixtos* had brought together representatives of labor and management to settle disputes, no one had joined the two in the same syndicate.

The Falange's syndicate for university students, the SEU, the only one that achieved any success before the war, was revived in 1937 and two years later all other student groups were abolished. Before other syndicates could materialize, decisions had to be taken about their nature and purpose. Many committed Falangists of prewar days, who were known as "old shirts" in contrast to those who joined under Franco, wanted to establish syndicates that would effectively fight for workers' rights. The proposal was frightening to other sectors of Franco's following, the army and industrialists, which conceived of the syndicates as a means to implement state control of the proletariat. Franco's first ministry, set up in January 1938, included a Minister of Syndical Organization and Action, a new office. To fill it Franco appointed Pedro González Bueno, a Falangist old shirt and one of the authors of the Fuero del Trabajo. For a year González Bueno worked to establish the syndicates, but both he and his office disappeared from the ministry in August 1939 without anything positive having been accomplished. The task went next to the first man Franco selected for National Delegate of the Syndicates, the highest office in their organization. This was Gerardo Salvador Merino, another old shirt, appointed in September 1939. He was strongly committed to creating a militant workers' organization, but he tried to move cautiously and not alarm the opponents of such a program. In January 1940 Franco issued a Law of Sindical Unity which prohibited any labor or management associations except those of the Falange. Merino worked to give concrete reality to the syndicates. A decree of June 1941 finally confirmed his efforts by dividing the economic life of the country into twenty-three spheres, each with a syndicate. Already, however, influential people were anxious over the potential strength and the aims of his organization. High army officers especially distrusted Salvador Merino's intentions after he included several thousand workers in a military parade on March 31, 1940 in Madrid celebrating the first anniversary of the victory. The generals prevailed upon Franco to dismiss him in July. With him vanished the dream of the old shirts of establishing syndicates to represent proletarian desires. In the next years the skeleton he had created took on flesh, with compulsory membership for all workers and employers and a vast bureaucracy of appointed officers, loyal and subservient members of the Falange. The syndicates served the state to collect insurance premiums, distribute social welfare, regiment the workers, and inform the authorities of any who might voice dangerous ideas.

The years from 1938 to 1941 saw the Falange at the peak of its authority. During these years the person with most apparent influence on Franco was his brother-in-law, Serrano Suñer, who was minister of *gobernación*. He was an admirer of the German and Italian regimes and hoped to see Spain fashion a similar political and economic structure. The Falange was his chosen instrument for the task. He was responsible for uniting the Carlists to the original body, and he could have become party secretary, but he preferred to see a member with more seniority in the job while he accepted for himself that of Press and Propaganda Chief of the Falange. With his support the Falange became a mammoth organization with thousands of jobs for loyal supporters and dazzling white uniforms that stood out at all public functions.

Even in its heyday, however, the party never obtained a position of command. Insofar as policy was made by anyone besides Franco, it was done by the ministry, and in the ministry the Falange had few voices. The army and state bureaucracy had more authority than the Falange hierarchy. Franco was authoritarian but not doctrinaire. He sympathized with his officers and trusted them, while the Falangist old shirts represented an alien world to him. He sincerely wished to improve Spain, but he had no mind for social revolution, even of the controlled variety envisaged by committed Falangists. He found the Falange a useful façade for his dictatorship, but he would never grant it independent authority. Time and again his attitude was to frustrate the old-shirt Falangists who recalled the enthusiastic idealism of José Antonio.

4

In France, it has been noted, while one revolution after another has altered the political regime, the administration has continued intact, with the same functionaries performing the same tasks from one government to the next. A comparable statement can be made about

Spain. While functionaries have been purged along with regimes, especially in 1939, the objectives of the governments have remained surprisingly constant beneath the appearance of radical alterations. The physical and social realities of the country in the long run have determined policy more than the clashing ideologies. Primo de Rivera continued the plans of the parliamentary monarchy. The Republic picked up many of them. Now Franco was to carry on the projects of the Republic, and of the regimes before it, however much he might wrap them in a different ideological mantle.

Republican social legislation had concentrated on agriculture, but its troubled life had prevented noteworthy achievements. The failure had been instrumental in the Republican defeat in the war. Franco had the canny insight to realize the need to keep the peasants on his side, although his outlook and the nature of his support meant he would not, like Republicans and Socialists, attack the position of the large landowners directly. For a long time, his government's efforts resulted less in improving the life of peasants and agricultural workers than of bringing them under state authority.

In August 1938 Franco created a National Wheat Service to manage the marketing of grain. Farmers were required to sell their grain harvests directly to the service at fixed prices, while the service distributed wheat to bakers and other consumers. It established prices and administered bread rationing, which became necessary when Franco had to feed the cities after the end of the war. The decree creating the service described it as a measure to protect peasants from exploitation by grain speculators; what it did was to bring production and distribution of Spain's most vital foodstuff under government control.

As soon as the war was over, the government developed plans for rural reconstruction. From the outset it saw the problem as primarily one of increasing production through the extension of irrigation and the resettlement of farmers, ideas that were centuries old. In October 1939 it established a National Institute of Colonization. In an endeavor that recalled the colonies of Charles III in the eighteenth century, the Institute projected new settlements to open up undeveloped areas. The first ones were built in the forties to replace towns like Brunete that had been destroyed in the war. For the rest, the Institute accomplished little else in this decade, partly because of lack of funds and partly because it did not develop a coherent program. Meanwhile the ministry of public works laboriously pushed ahead plans inherited from earlier eras for the construction of dams. Throughout the forties the capacity of Spain's dams increased gradually. From 3.9 billion cubic meters in 1940 (about 140 billion cubic feet), it rose to 6.7 billion in 1954, not quite double in fifteen years.

The government, like the Republic before it, also worried about the destruction of Spain's forests. In 1940 60 percent of the regions officially labeled forests were without trees and half the remainder were depleted. The state forestry service undertook a program of "forest repopulation" (*repoblación forestal*), but little was done until it drew up an overall plan in 1951.

The Falange, through the syndicates, was mainly responsible for the beginnings of a different kind of agricultural reform. A law of 1942 provided the necessary regulations for founding cooperatives. Under it the syndicates initiated industrial, consumer, and agricultural cooperatives, but their only marked success came in the last field. By 1948 half the members and five sixths of the capital involved in cooperatives were in agriculture. The most important were the National Rice Cooperative, which, like the National Wheat Service, monopolized the entire Spanish output, and cooperative wine cellars and olive oil factories. These rural cooperatives were bound together by the National Union of Rural Cooperatives. The National Union created a chain of *cajas rurales*, rural banks, one of whose main purposes was to offer farmers credit for improvement and the purchase of machinery. In 1948 there were three hundred *cajas*.

The revolution of 1936 behind the Republican lines had featured cooperatives. A revival of the movement now offered the Falange the solace of appearing to encourage socialistic objectives in what had remained an essentially capitalist economy. Cooperatives would have significant repercussions after 1950, but in the forties they had little effect. On the whole the decade was one of stagnation for agriculture. Despite the National Wheat Service, wheat production was only 70 percent of that under the Republic. Harvests suffered from a lack of fertilizers going back to the beginning of the war. Plans for agricultural reform existed more on paper than in fact. The government's resources were extremely limited, and it chose to use what it had first of all to industrialize the nation.

The government early decided to run Spain as a planned autarky, hoping to free its economy from dependence on foreign countries. To make the country self-sufficient, it determined to build up industry. The man largely responsible for this decision was Juan Antonio Suanzes, a childhood friend of Franco. Before the war he had been an engineer, a naval officer, and an industrial entrepreneur. During the war he became one of Franco's most trusted advisers and was his first minister of industry in 1938. Following Suanzes' advice, in 1941 Franco established an agency called the Instituto Nacional de Industria (INI) to foster and finance industrial growth. Suanzes became its director and remained at its head until 1963. For two decades he was the most powerful individual in the Spanish economy.

The INI had unique characteristics. It was an executive agency, that is, it was directly responsible to the Head of State rather than to any ministry. It received a handsome government budget which it used to invest in those corporations it chose to establish or support for the good of the national economy. In theory, the INI would sell its stock and get out when a corporation was able to stand alone, except in cases of vital national interest. In fact over the next decades it had great difficulty in abandoning any of its chosen enterprises, some of which never became profitable. Private industrialists and bankers resented it, arguing that its protégés enjoyed an unfair competitive advantage. Creation of the INI meant that the limited government subsidies and scarce investment capital flowed into those sectors and geographical regions that the state decided to favor. Franco's government did not attack private property, but it created a vast organization to direct industrial development and compete with those enterprises that did not enjoy its favor.

The INI supported industries in a variety of fields. In 1957 it had a controlling interest in almost fifty firms, which among them dominated critical sectors of the economy. Mostly they were basic industries prerequisite to the development of production in the consumer goods field. It helped industries of cellulose products, cement, chemicals, aluminum, naval construction, and merchant shipping. It took over and has since held all stock in the Spanish national airline, Iberia. Its greatest undertaking was the Empresa Nacional Siderúrgica, S. A., founded in 1950, established to build a modern steel plant to bring Spain abreast of current methods of world steel production. The plant was located at Avilés, a coastal town in Asturias. It involved a tremendous investment of capital over the next decade, to the outrage of the private Basque steel firms, but by 1960 banks which had an interest in the older plants were beginning to place capital in the Avilés corporation.

One of the objectives of the regime, which derived partly from the nationalism of the Falange, was to eliminate foreign influence in the Spanish economy. Franco understood well enough the importance of keeping on the good side of foreign investors, and he did not harm those already present. However, his government early placed a limit of 25 percent on the share of stock in new enterprises that could be owned by foreigners. Near the end of the war, when he needed arms to conquer Catalonia, he succumbed to Hitler's pressure and allowed Germans to obtain controlling interest in three major mining companies. But the limit on foreign investment in Spanish corporations remained the rule.

There was one industry that Franco decided to nationalize, even though foreigners would be hurt in the process. This was the railroads. The war had damaged them seriously. Roadbeds and bridges had been blown up, and rolling stock was worn out or destroyed. The companies had insufficient capital to rebuild them without asking help from abroad, and World War II prevented foreign investors from coming to their aid even if they had wanted to. Primo de Rivera had considered nationalizing the railroads as he did petroleum distribution, but he let them be. Franco's government studied the problem for two years, then in 1941 it took over all wide-gauge railroads as state property (some local narrow-gauge railroads remained in private hands). To run them, it created a state organization entitled Red Nacional de los Ferrocarriles Españoles (National Network of Spanish Railroads), or RENFE. The decree compensated the former owners with state bonds, what amounted to legalized confiscation so far as foreign stockholders were concerned. It freed Spanish railroads after a hundred years from foreign exploitation, but the fear of reprisals hung on. In 1948 the administration of the RENFE was divided into seven geographic zones different from those of the former companies, thus rendering virtually impossible any restitution of property to them.

5

The Republic had dedicated itself more than anything to educational reform, confident that good schools could eliminate the dead hand of the past. Understandably, Franco's reaction was most violent in this sector. His government began at once to extirpate Republican influences and make the schools serve the new state. Almost the first act of the Nationalist forces after occupying Madrid was to close the Institución Libre de Enseñanza, accused of nurturing the spirit that had animated the Republic. The semi-official bodies associated with it also disappeared, the Junta para Ampliación de Estudios and the Institutos Escuela. University students had been among the keenest devotees of the Republic, and their organization, the FUE, had become militantly Marxist. It was abolished, and in its place all students were required to join the Falange's SEU. At all levels teachers were screened to eliminate those suspected of Republican, Marxist, and anticlerical beliefs.

The guiding figure of the educational program was José Ibáñez Martín, minister of education from 1939 to 1951. A one-time supporter of Primo de Rivera and a CEDA deputy under the Republic, he was strongly Catholic in outlook. Under his aegis, Catholic doctrine replaced the hated beliefs of the Republicans as the basis of educational philosophy, along with nationalist doctrines of the Falange in a modest second place. The government made religion a required and central subject at all levels of schooling. It gave active encouragement to the schools of the religious orders, which the Republic had tried to close. The Republic had established coeducation at all levels. A Law of Primary Education of 1945 declared school attendance obligatory from six to twelve years of age, with free education available in state schools, but prohibited join classes for boys and girls, except where the state could not yet afford to provide the necessary teachers and buildings to separate the sexes.

This law made universal elementary education the objective of the new regime, as it had been the Republic's (and indeed every government's since 1856). Since the schools of the religious orders could never handle all the children of Spain, the law was an implicit promise to continue the Republic's school-building program, which the war had halted. However, in the forties the promise remained on paper, for there were no funds for so massive an undertaking. According to official figures, by 1950 about 8000 new elementary schoolrooms had been built, adding 16 percent to the number at the end of the Republic. (The Republic had built about 10,000 rooms in five years.)[2]

Franco chose instead to concentrate on the University of Madrid, where improvement was less costly and results more conspicuous. The Ciudad Universitaria housing the university had been one of the prides of the Republic. The war had destroyed it, for the most bitter battle for Madrid took place in its grounds and buildings northwest of the city. Almost at once the government undertook to rebuild it. Reconstruction began in 1940 with generous budgets. Three years later the Caudillo dedicated the new building of the Faculty of Philosophy and Letters, and in 1945 that of the Faculty of Science. By 1950 few wartime scars remained. The regime was so proud of the university that it continued active construction for the next two decades and in the sixties crowned the Ciudad Universitaria with a massive triumphal arch as its gateway from Madrid.

Besides the instructional buildings, the government projected new residences for university students, which were a definite need. Before the war there had been only the famous Residencia de Estudiantes and a Residencia de Señoritas. In 1942 the regime introduced a new form of student housing called *colegios mayores,* a name taken from collegial residences located at the main universities before the nineteenth century. Run by the religious orders, they had dominated the university politics, but Charles III weakened them in the name of enlightenment and they had died out. Their revival now seemed to evoke the days of traditional Spain, although in form the new ones resembled more the residential colleges of Anglo-Saxon countries. Students would live in them and attend classes in the university. However, the objective went further than to provide adequate housing. The Residencia de Estudiantes had spread the ideals of the Institución Libre; the *colegios mayores* offered a structure within which to provide religious and political supervision and indoctrination. Being new,

[2] Figures derived from data in Spain, Junta Interministerial Conmemoradora de los 25 Años de Paz Española, *El Gobierno informa: la educación nacional* (Madrid, 1964).

they could be molded by the forces in control of Spain. By 1950 ten were in operation in the country, mostly in converted buildings. Many were built thereafter, some sponsored by religious orders, others by the Falange through the SEU, but most were run by the state. Taking students out of rooming houses and providing for communal living, they revolutionized university life. They made it easier to supervise the students, but they also brought them together where they could share their grievances and formulate opposition to the regime.

Ibáñez Martín had long opposed the Institución Libre and was determined to root out its influence. Nowhere, however, was Franco's heritage from recent regimes more evident than in the means Ibáñez Martín chose to accomplish this aim; for beneath the new ideology the old forms reappeared. Besides the university, the other great educational achievement of the early part of the century had been the Junta para Ampliación de Estudios e Investigaciones Científicas. Through it the influence of the Institución had penetrated the official world. Franco decreed its death, but on November 24, 1939 a law established a Consejo Superior de Investigaciones Científicas (Superior Council of Scientific Research) to be an autonomous entity under nominal supervision of the minister of education. It moved into the buildings of the former Junta. Nearby, the Residencia de Estudiantes, no longer needed for students, became the Residencia del Consejo Superior, to house its personnel and visitors. Next door were the buildings of the Instituto Escuela, also declared defunct. The Consejo took them over and operated them as a new *instituto* (secondary school), christened Ramiro de Maeztu, after a conservative essayist assassinated by workers in 1936. It became the model and pride of official secondary education, as the Instituto Escuela had been in its day.

The activities of the Consejo Superior were divided among eight *patronatos*, covering subjects from chemistry and biology to history and theology. Ibáñez Martín dedicated it to "stripping our culture of its past servility to foreign models," and to bringing that culture in line with "our religion and our science." [3] Its emblem was the *arbor scientiae*, which depicted all forms of knowledge as branches of the same tree, the unity of Truth, a modern version of the medieval view of knowledge and science.

Ibáñez Martín found ready support for his war on the Institución in a new group being formed within the church. It owed its life to an Argonese priest named José María Escrivá de Balaguer. After taking orders in 1925, he went to Madrid, where he entered the circles of Catholic Action and right-wing university groups. Here he learned to hate the Institucióninistas. After the outbreak of the Civil War he fled

[3] Dedication speech quoted in José Ibáñez Martín, *Diez años de servicios a la cultura española* (Madrid, 1950), p. 9.

to Burgos and organized a following dedicated to rooting out the evil influences of the Institución and strengthening the Catholic faith in Spain. He wrote a book entitled *Camino* (*The Road*), which he published in 1939, calling on Catholics to gird themselves to fight for their faith. It reflected the passions of the Civil War, urging its readers to become commanders or disciplined followers in a crusade for religion. But it also told them to strive for material and professional success the better to be able to influence others. At some point Escrivá conceived of founding a religious order dedicated to these objectives. He called it Opus Dei and dated its origin in 1928, although one investigator has been able to find no mention of it in any publication before 1939, which is the date when Escrivá began to transform his small group of associates into a formal order.[4] In 1941 the bishop of Madrid recognized Opus Dei as a diocesan association.

Five years later Escrivá's society had grown so far as to attract foreign members, and he went to Rome. In 1947 Pope Pius XII created a category of "secular institutes" within the Catholic Church and established Opus Dei as the first such institute. Since its founding, Escrivá has been its president general. It has never published its statutes or made known its membership except for its highest officers, with the result that information about it is mostly secondhand and an air of mystery envelopes it. Both priests and laymen (and women) can be members, but the lay members are by far the most numerous.

Escrivá was in awe of intellectuals, and he gave them preeminence in the order. The highest rank, the numeraries, could only be reached after advanced philosophic and theological studies and taking a university degree at the doctorate level. The numeraries formed a small elite within the order, normally living in its houses. Below them were the oblates, who came from a lower social and educational background, lived in their own families, and worked like ordinary people. Both these groups took vows of poverty, chastity, and obedience, like members of the older religious orders, but they did so in private and continued to wear ordinary clothes. Probably the largest number of members were neither of these, but the supernumeraries, who might be married, have families, and outwardly lead normal lives, but otherwise accepted the vows and rules of the order.

Opus Dei was essentially an association of dedicated laymen under the direction of priestly members. They performed God's work by seeking success in their chosen professions and thus helping extend the influence of the church into places where it had long been in decline. Through their associations within the order many advanced rapidly in their personal careers and enjoyed high economic rewards that seemed

[4] Daniel Artigues, *El Opus Dei en España, I, 1928–1957* (Paris: Ruedo Ibérico, 1968), 16–25.

out of keeping with their vow of poverty. By 1950 Opus Dei had branches in various countries, and since then its fortunes have continued to prosper. Like the Jesuits in the sixteenth century, it has sought to achieve its aims primarily by infiltrating social, political, and intellectual elites; but it differs from older religious orders in that most of its members lead ordinary lives and may never divulge their membership.

Nowhere has the success of Opus Dei equaled that in Spain. Here the destruction of scholarly institutions and the flight of intellectual leaders at the end of the war left a vacuum easily exploited by an aggressive movement of its kind. Its fortune was made when Ibáñez Martín appointed Escrivá's closest collaborator, José María Albareda, head of the Consejo Superior de Investigaciones Científicas. Albareda's position in the virtually autonomous Consejo allowed him to reward members and sympathizers of Opus with university fellowships and research grants and thus to attract promising young scholars into its fold. When the Consejo founded an official journal called *Arbor*, its editor was Rafael Calvo Serer, who in time became the main theorist of Opus Dei in Spain.

From the Consejo the influence of Opus spread to the universities and other seats of learning. New legislation under Franco empowered the minister of education to appoint the members of the juries which judged the public competitions or *oposiciones* for university chairs. Ibáñez Martín's sympathy for Opus led him to name juries which selected its candidates, often, it was said, passing over more competent scholars. Opus concentrated on obtaining the chairs of history and philosophy. (Calvo Serer won a chair of philosophy at Madrid.) It also used the religious exercises of the *colegios mayores* to extend its influence to university students. After 1950 it would found its own *colegios*. A professor of history, Vicente Rodríguez Casado, of Opus, became president of the Ateneo de Madrid, once a liberal stronghold. Within a decade Opus Dei had moved into the official institutions of letters and science more effectively than the Institucionistas had before the war.

By the end of the forties not only enemies of the regime but friends as well began to fear and suspect the new order. The obvious favoritism in fellowship and university appointments angered those students who could not bring themselves to join Opus Dei. (They referred cynically to the *oposiciones* as "*opusiciones*.") It clashed with the Falange, which remained chauvinist and intellectually isolationist, while Opus worked to open contacts with the outside world, especially the Catholic powers of Europe: France, West Germany, and Italy. Even traditional Catholic groups like Acción Católica and the Jesuits felt their noses out of joint. The true extent of its power became a much mooted question, for the secrecy of its membership encouraged wild speculation. Many observers felt it was becoming the strongest force in Franco's Spain. However, its only undisputed conquest was the Consejo Superior, and it appears never to have captured more than one quarter of the university faculties. Many who joined it to obtain a position later dropped out. Spain's culture has long been sympathetic to belief in the machinations of secret societies. While there is no question that Opus Dei became powerful, especially after 1950, its enemies magnified its unity and strength beyond plausible reality. In popular fancy it came to replace the Jesuits and Masons as the occult power running the country.

Ibáñez Martín's attempt to re-create the structures inspired by the Institución was involuntary recognition of the vision of Giner de los Ríos. It proved easier to rebaptize Giner's institutions than to breathe new life into them. The result of the campaign to remake Spain's intellectual world was mediocrity. The university faculties, the work of the Consejo Superior, the articles in *Arbor*, remained dull and second rate, a great falling off from the twenties and thirties. The demand for ideological conformity and rampant favoritism meant that true intellectual creativity went into other areas. Most inellectual leaders of the previous decades were dead or absent, and the official orthodoxy was not conducive to attracting their disciples who were still in Spain. The old ideals of the Institución found echoes in the Falange's youth movement, which encouraged sports and outdoor life. They were stronger in the Falange's Sección Femenina, which took up the labor of collecting and preserving popular songs, dances, and costumes. But even more, the spark of Giner lived on in private hearths and hearts, which shut themselves off from the new official Spain to remain true to their loyalties. Some sent their children to the schools maintained in Spain by the French, British, and German governments. Few publicized their views in the forties, but one of Giner's pupils, Jimena Menéndez Pidal, daughter of the great medievalists whose stature kept him above reprisals, founded a small school in Madrid to continue the Institución's educational philosophy. Within the limits of the law, her Colegio Estudio taught Giner's "positive tolerance" of all viewpoints to the children of his followers. Confined at first to a building offered by an American foundation, it moved in the late sixties into an edifice of its own, an architecturally exciting structure facing the sierras north of the city. The school's alumni made it possible, for by then they were reaching top positions in all fields of endeavor. The hated seed had not been extirpated.

6

With Europe at war in the early forties and again divided shortly after the peace by the iron curtain that fell between East and West,

Franco's regime was no more independent than the Republic had been from the impact of international developments. Since the Nationalists owed their victory to German and Italian help, many anticipated Spain's entrance into the Second World War on the Axis side. Franco kept his own counsel, however, and guided his nation acutely around the maelstrom. At the outbreak of the war, he declared Spain's non-belligerence. Although he recognized his debt to Hitler and Mussolini, Spain was in no position to enter a new war. After the fall of France in June 1940, Franco's principal adviser, Serrano Suñer, encouraged cooperation with Germany and Italy, and Franco publicized Spain's friendship with them. In October 1940 he met Hitler at the Pyrenees, and in February 1941 Mussolini. The leaders discussed a joint effort in North Africa. Franco demurred, but he allowed German submarines to use Spanish ports. When Germany invaded Russia in the summer of 1941, Serrano Suñer, who was now foreign minister, organized the "Blue Division" of Spanish soldiers euphemistically called "volunteers" to fight on the Russian front, avenging Russia's aid to the Loyalists. This proved to be the high point of Franco's commitment to the Axis powers. Spain never entered the war, for Franco was determined to become no one's satellite.

In 1942 Franco's policies began to reflect the turning tide in Europe. The United States entered the war at the end of 1941, and in 1942 British and American troops landed in French North Africa. Franco began to doubt an Axis victory, and he took steps to propitiate the Allied powers, although both countries assured him they had no hostile intentions. He dropped Serrano Suñer from the cabinet on September 3, 1942. Serrano had been the Caudillo's closest adviser. He was both pro-Axis and pro-Falange, and his disappearance from Franco's councils signified a major change in the orientation of the regime. On July 17, 1942, six years after the generals' rebellion, Franco proclaimed the second fundamental law of the state—the first was the Fuero del Trabajo of 1938—a Law of the Cortes which revived that body in order to provide "the participation of the Spanish people in the tasks of the State." Most of the five hundred-odd Cortes deputies were to be *ex officio:* cabinet ministers, mayors of the provincial capitals and a representative from each province chosen by the municipal councils, rectors of the universities, and representatives of the leading educational, professional, and cultural associations, all of them directly or indirectly owing their position to the Head of State. In addition one hundred and fifty were to be representatives of the syndicates (and thus of the Falange), and fifty were to be personally named by the Head of State from among ecclesiastics, military officers, and others qualified by their "exceptional services to Spain." The Cortes could only approve legislation presented by the executive. Spain was no closer to a free parliamentary regime than it had been before, but

Franco had cast a sop to the Western democracies with a name that recalled freer ages.

Three years later Franco reacted to the Allied victory in Europe by issuing another fundamental law on July 17, 1945, the Fuero de los Españoles. Worked out by the Cortes and approved by the Head of State, it was ostensibly a declaration of rights, but it stressed the duties of Spaniards and the authoritarian structure of Spain more than the rights of citizens. The second article read, "All Spaniards owe faithful service to their country, loyalty to the Head of State, and obedience to the laws." The Fuero granted Spaniards the right to participate in public functions; not as individuals, however, but through their families, their municipalities, and their syndicates. It gave official protection to the Catholic religion and declared the family to be "the natural and fundamental institution of society,"[5] and pronounced marriage indissoluble. Non-Catholic Spaniards would not be molested for their private religious beliefs (a promise the regime violated regularly in the next decades), but only Catholic ceremonies could be conducted in public (as under Cánovas). The Fuero de los Españoles incorporated various features of the 1938 Fuero del Trabajo: it guaranteed workers social security and a share in profits, and it made all economic activity subservient to the needs of the nation and the common welfare. It also promised Spaniards freedom of speech, "so long as they do not attack the fundamental principles of the state,"[6] privacy of correspondence, guarantee of their homes from search, and presentation of charges against arrested persons within seventy-two hours. But the Fuero specifically stated that all these rights could be "temporarily suspended by the government" without specifying the length of "temporary" suspension or stating the reasons which might justify suspension. The Fuero was timed to win support of the victorious Allies, and many foreign observers were taken in by it. A keen American historian has called it "an ostensible guarantee of personal rights and immunities that Thomas Jefferson would himself have applauded."[7] In fact it provided for an authoritarian, strongly religious political system with conditional rights for those who did not oppose the regime.

Franco made other gestures to impress the democracies in this year. A law reestablished elections for municipal councils. A third of the councilors were to be elected by the heads of families, a third by the syndicates, and a third by those two thirds combined. But *alcaldes* were still appointed by the state, as under the Moderado system. Franco also granted pardons to those in prison for minor crimes during the Civil War, and reduced the terms of others. He invited back the

[5] Article 22.

[6] Article 12.

[7] A. P. Whitaker, *Spain and the Defense of the West* (New York: Harper & Row, Publishers, 1961), p. 122.

refugees, and those who returned were not molested if they did not engage in political activities.

The fact was, Franco and his advisers were worried by the victory of the Allies over the Axis powers. Would they consider Franco another enemy, and force him out by diplomatic pressure or by aiding a Republican invasion of Spain? Many thought so inside and outside Spain. In the fall and winter 1945–46 Communist and anarchist guerrillas crossed the Pyrenees to attack the Spanish armed forces directly and foment a popular rising. Some got within one hundred kilometers of Madrid, but they failed in their mission, for they were unable to provoke a response and the Allies did not aid them.

Nevertheless, world opinion was generally opposed to the Franco regime, partly out of a sense of guilt for failure to aid the Republic. After 1945 both France and Great Britain had left-wing governments, and in the United States President Truman was no admirer of Franco. The three countries were attempting to work with Russia, and Russia pictured Franco as an unrepentant fascist. The conference of San Francisco that established the United Nations in 1945 adopted a resolution excluding Spain from the new world organization. In December 1946 the United Nations General Assembly resolved that all members recall their ambassadors from Madrid. The few powers with ambassadors there did so. In the same month France closed the Spanish border to commerce. These gestures indicated Spain's political and ideological isolation, but they did not help the opponents of Franco. The Republicans in exile were sadly divided, between Communists and non-Communists, between partisans of Negrín and of Prieto. There was no government in exile the Allies could unequivocably support even if they wanted to.

Franco continued in power. Judging carefully the tenor of the postwar world, he adopted two policies aimed to counteract his isolation. His first was to warn the world loudly of the Communist danger and point out Spain's role as what he called the first country successfully to crush the Communists. The second was to stress Spain's Catholicism and to seek ties with other Catholic countries. In July 1945 he formed a new ministry in which the role of the Falange declined in favor of representatives of Spain's Catholics. The leader of the lay society Catholic Action, Alberto Martín Artajo, became foreign minister. In the next years he worked to strengthen ties with Latin American countries through stressing the doctrine of Hispanidad—the spiritual and cultural unity of all Spanish-speaking peoples, which, Spaniards argued, the political separation of the nineteenth century had not destroyed. A doctrine kept alive through the nineteenth and early twentieth centuries in opposition to United States influence in Latin America, it now received official support through programs of cultural exchange.

These policies would have their reward in the future. More immediately, Franco had to make his government look less arbitrary and less temporary. To this end, in July 1947 he proposed a fourth fundamental law, known as the Law of Succession. It declared Spain to be a "Catholic, social representative state . . . constituted as a monarchy." No king or future king was named (following his typical policy, Franco would not commit himself to the partisans of Alfonso XIII's son Juan or the Carlists), but the law confirmed Franco's position as the Jefe del Estado. It gave him authority to name the next king at his pleasure, and even to revoke his nomination later if he should wish to. The Cortes had to approve his decisions, but the Cortes as they existed could be only a rubber stamp. The law established a Council of Regency, consisting of the president of the Cortes (who would normally be a Falangist), the highest prelate of the Spanish church, and the highest military officer, in other words the leading representatives of the three pillars of the regime. Should Franco die before naming a king, the Council of Regency would meet with the ministry and the Council of the Realm, which the law also established to be a select body of advisers to the Head of State, and the three groups would together name Franco's successor as king or regent. No provision was made for another Head of State; Franco was *sui generis.* The law was submitted to a "referendum" which recalled Primo de Rivera's plebiscite. Over 90 percent of the 15 million voters said "yes." The whole undertaking was cleverly conceived. While appearing to reestablish the monarchy, Franco had legitimized his position as Head of State by popular suffrage, with the power to designate his successor. Spain became a monarchy on paper, but the future monarch became the creature of Franco. Yet the monarchists were in no position to protest openly, though for over twenty years Franco named no king.

Not Franco's legislation, but world developments, brought about Spain's eventual reentry into the family of nations. In the winter of 1946–47 the cold war began; in 1948 American airplanes saved West Berlin from a Soviet blockade. The next year, the United States, Canada, and the Western European democracies founded the North Atlantic Treaty Organization. Henceforth the confrontation between the United States and Russia became the overriding international issue. Communist North Korean troops invaded South Korea in June 1950 and the United States sent in an army. At once the specter of a Soviet attack on a demilitarized Western Europe while America was busy in the Orient haunted Western statesmen. The new atmosphere rapidly changed the international position of Spain. In May 1948 France had reopened the Spanish frontier. Spain, with its anti-Communist government and its strategic location controlling the entrance to the Mediterranean Sea while entrenched behind the wall of the Pyrenees, became more and more attractive to American military planners. Franco's oft-repeated boast of being the only country to put down Communism began to find credulous listeners in North and South America, especially among Catholic leaders. In November 1950 a coalition of Latin American countries together with the United States obtained the repeal of the United Nations resolution to withdraw ambassadors from Spain. Spanish newspapers carried the exultant headline, "The blockade is broken!" A month later the United States announced a loan to Spain of 62.5 million dollars.

7

Spain's bill of good health arrived in a moment of need, for its domestic situation was becoming desperate. The critical factor was the failure of the economy to recover from the Civil War. Both internal and world conditions were at fault. The government's fear of allowing Spaniards free rein choked activities of every kind. Most of Spain's best trained personnel were in disfavor for their activities in the war. Highly qualified engineers, doctors, and other professionals whose abilities were vitally needed languished in secondary positions because of their political backgrounds. Censorship of the press and terror of being reported to the secret police prevented criticism of incompetence and disclosure of graft and dishonesty. The Second World War and the subsequent boycott also hampered recovery. The country was unable to import machinery and transportation equipment, needed in part to replace worn-out material. Furthermore Spain lacked foreign exchange. During the Second World War it built up its gold reserves by sales of minerals and other poducts to the warring nations, above all Germany, but this balance rapidly evaporated after 1945. Beginning in that year, a series of bad harvests due to drought and lack of fertilizers forced Spain to use its foreign exchange to buy grain. One example will illustrate the difficult situation. By 1950 the government had completed various dams for hydroelectric power and irrigation, but generators and other equipment were lacking. The drought years depleted the water in those dams that could produce electricity. Despite official figures showing a growth in electrical output since 1940 from 3.6 to 6.9 billion kilowatt hours, in 1950 Madrid had electricity only after seven in the evening, so that machinery in small shops could not be used during the day. In Barcelona textile factories could function only one day a week unless they could generate their own power. Yet under orders from the syndicates, employers were required to pay their workers in full for their regular hours.

The controlled economy so proudly introduced at the end of the war seemed created on purpose to prevent all classes from making a living. A major activity of the syndicates was to provide for the welfare of the workers through an extensive system of social insurance promised in the Fuero of Labor. The trouble was that social security cost too much. An employer had to deduct so much from the wages of his workers to pay the syndicates for health, retirement, and other social insurance that it was impossible for workers to support a family on the take-home wages. To make matters worse, prices were going up. By 1948 the price index was five times its level in 1936, and for foodstuffs about ten times higher. Yet wages had only increased threefold. Even persons who considered themselves in the middle class were living near the subsistence level, and doing so only by holding two or three jobs at each of which they could work only a portion of the normal hours. The whole economy had become geared to subterfuge.

Two words that were on everyone's lips characterized the economic system: *estraperlo*, the black market, and *enchufe*, the connection. There were shortages of every type of commodity. Rationing of food, gasoline, and other scarce goods which had been instituted during the war was still in effect. The syndicates and professional associations controlled distribution. They determined how much of a product each store would get, which doctors would get supplies and desperately needed automobiles, and made other such decisions that could determine individual well-being or financial ruin. Such a system of controlled shortage lent itself to favoritism and corruption, and both were rampant. Supplies allotted by the government for housing projects were sold under cover by contractors to private builders at exorbitant prices; wheat bought from Argentina to alleviate the food shortage turned up in Italy. Farmers hid their harvests from the government wheat service to sell on the black market, and women openly offered bread on street corners at black-market prices while bakers were unable to supply the legal rations at the official prices which workers could afford. Poverty, undernourishment, and tuberculosis stalked the cities, yet many were migrating to them from the countryside seeking work. For lack of housing the poor lived in caves or in shacks, *chabolas*, which they built on the outskirts of cities from scraps of wood or stolen bricks. Above them the black market, bribes, and favoritism were producing a class of ostentatious new rich, drawing their income from illegal or immoral sources.

Under such conditions Spain was demoralized, discouraged, cynical, a country rife with misery and hatred held down by the fear of the army and the police. Former Loyalists, stigmatized publicly as "*rojos*," felt prisoners in an alien state, discriminated against in schools and jobs, scared of expressing their true thoughts even in the presence of their children lest they be unintentionally betrayed. Many who had favored the Nationalists in the war were now open critics. Within the church and the army, disenchantment was widespread. Falangist old shirts mourned the death of the Utopia they had fought for. Capitalists hated a controlled economy which kept them from making a profit unless they could bribe the proper officials. Agricultural conditions were worse than ever, and the INI's industries were not prospering. On the left, a few die-hard young rebels had kept opposition alive within Spain, encouraged by the existence of Republican groups abroad. Small underground movements, one called the Socialist and Republican Libertarian Youth, another the left-wing student association FUE, which remained alive in spite of its official abolition, tried to proselytize among workers and students. They printed and distributed sheets denouncing the regime in 1946–47, but the police discovered them, and their leaders were sentenced to prison.

The acceptance of Franco in international society in 1950 was a mortal blow to the hopes of most Republican die-hards. Now indeed the Civil War seemed over, the Western powers had at last dealt the Republic its *coup de grâce*. Yet organized opposition did not die. A dramatic expression of it occurred in the spring of 1951. Workers were excited by the Korean War and the possibility of a Russian invasion of Western Europe. Should the Russians reach the Pyrenees, they assured each other, "Uncle Whiskers," as they fondly called Stalin, would find Spain rising *en masse* to welcome his soldiers. In Barcelona pamphlets circulated clandestinely calling for a general strike. The strike took place on March 12. Possibly three hundred thousand workers left their jobs and many paraded down the main avenues. Next day civil guards and police took over the city, ending the strike. But now strikes spread to the Basque cities, where Catholic organizers took the lead. Since strikes were illegal, the government threatened strikers with loss of jobs and social security benefits. The opposition in Madrid decided on a safer way to demonstrate its strength. No one would buy in a store or ride public transportation for one day, May 22. The plan proved effective. Despite orders of the government to the Falange and government officials to ride buses and fill the stores, subways and markets remained empty. At sundown the streets leading to the workers' suburbs were crowded with men in blue overalls, the famous proletarian *monos* of the war years, carrying their lunch pails and walking long kilometers home in order to demonstrate their hatred of the regime. In workers' districts the boycott was perhaps 90 percent successful.

Twelve years after the end of the Civil War Spain remained deeply divided, and the opposition was once again ready to show itself. The balance sheet of official policies was negative, for they had failed to overcome the ravages of the war. Spain's international isolation was partly responsible, but mostly the inherent weakness of the regime. It had existed by crushing the forces that had threatened the established classes since the beginning of the century; in so doing it stifled the economy, for at mid-century the country could not get along without the help of these forces—technicians, intelligentsia, urban workers. Halfhearted attempts to placate them through the Fuero del Trabajo, the syndicates, and the official research of the Consejo Superior had been vitiated by fear of the consequences if these efforts should get out of hand.

Beyond creating an authoritarian state and economic autarky, Franco's regime had followed no consistent policy. Except for his deep Catholicism, Franco was not doctrinaire. In the forties fear guided him and his advisers more than constructive thinking, for fear was not the monopoly of the vanquished. Fear of the forces defeated in the war maintained Spain as a police state, probably the cruellest regime it has ever known, with strict censorship, an enforced ideology, countless thousands in prison, and many of the best minds in disgrace. Fear of being discredited and weakened prevented the regime from unmasking wrongdoers among its partisans. Fear of falling into the hands of any of the groups supporting him led Franco to favor first one and then another and keep them all in a turmoil of uncertainty. Fear that foreign powers would decide to reestablish the Republic went far to determine the evolving image Franco presented through the fundamental laws.

In one sense this pragmatic response to the dangers besetting the regime had succeeded, for Franco was still in power. By 1951 things were beginning to change. Persons with good minds were beginning to forge ahead in industry, the professions, and government service, whatever their political background. But the workers' demonstrations of that spring revealed the bankruptcy of the official policies. Franco was in the most serious trouble he had known since the war, for it was now manifest that he had not mastered the forces of this century. He had, however, two major factors in his favor: the army and police remained loyal, preventing open organization of the opposition, and the United States had decided to seek Spanish friendship. Once again foreign developments were to be decisive in determining Spain's evolution.

15

Spain Under Franco: Transformation

1

Although they appeared to accomplish little, the spring demonstrations of 1951 marked a major turning point in Franco's regime. Hitherto his policy had been to run the state as a regimented economy and to hold a lid on all opposition by police methods. He had made changes in his government usually in response to outside events, seeking the favor of the foreign powers most likely to help his regime become legitimate in the eyes of Spain and the world. He had achieved a limited success abroad, but the spring of 1951 showed the bankruptcy of his domestic policy, for the economy was in crisis and his unpopularity was great, even among one-time supporters. Franco realized he would have to pay more attention to the image of his government held by Spaniards.

In Western democracies, including Spain under the Republic, political crises have led to changes in the cabinet in response to shifting alignments of political parties and their strength in the legislature, determined ultimately by the electorate. In Spain under Franco the ministry has changed at the will of the Head of State, almost as absolute kings once changed their councilors. The composition of the ministry has reflected his current appreciation of the groups supporting him and the policies for which they stand. After the spring troubles of 1951 he decided to use more carrot and less stick on his subjects—although he always kept the stick handy in case of need—and he embodied the decision in a new ministry in July 1951.

Franco's choice of ministers indicated that he now favored a revival of the early socially oriented doctrines of the Falange and a relaxation of religious authoritarianism. By replacing conservative monarchists and Catholics, he hoped to pacify the workers and also the university students and faculties angered by the growing power of Opus Dei. The relatively liberal Catholic Martín Artajo, who could claim credit for ending Spain's international ostracism, remained foreign minister. Raimundo Fernández Cuesta, José Antonio's right-hand man before the war, had entered the ministry in 1948 as secretary general of the Movimiento (that is, the Falange), filling a position that Franco had left vacant since 1945. Franco also kept him on, but he changed most other ministers. A newly created ministry of information and tourism took over censorship of the press. It went to another Falangist, Gabriel Arias Salgado. Ibáñez Martín disappeared after twelve years as minister of education, and in his place Franco appointed Joaquín Ruiz Giménez, like Martín Artajo a member of Catholic Action. Ruiz Giménez promptly obtained a law making *oposiciones* for university professorships more impartial, thereby serving notice to Opus Dei that the universities were not all theirs. Two Falangist old shirts, both now more social democratic than national syndicalist in outlook, Pedro Laín Entralgo and Antonio Tóvar, became rectors of the universities of Madrid and Salamanca. Nothing could properly be done, however, to deprive members of Opus of their achieved positions on the faculties.

With diplomatic recognition and an American loan, Franco was in a position to relax some of his controls. The best wheat crop since the war and the purchase of grain abroad enabled the government to end rationing of foodstuffs in the summer of 1952. For the first time since the war Spaniards were free to buy the food they could afford. Continuing inflation meant, however, that most families of the lower classes could afford little more than bread, potatoes, soup, and occasional sardines and fruit. The price index in 1952 was seven times higher than before the war, almost 50 percent higher than in 1948. The great advantage derived from the end of rationing was the disappearance of the black market in food items, with all the corruption it involved. The government also made an attempt to placate the workers by providing for direct election of the employees' representatives, the *enlaces*, on the national syndicates. The move was largely window dressing, for candidates received official approval in advance. Nonetheless it was a step in the direction of letting the syndicates express the grievances of labor instead of being merely an instrument to keep the workers in line. In the countryside the Civil Guard began to withdraw from obvious public sight into newly built barracks, although it continued to patrol in out-of-the-way places. The change in climate was slow, but it meant that Spain seemed less a dictatorship, at least to the casual observer. The large number of prisoners still serving sentences for political crimes prior to 1951 could testify that it was a police state, nevertheless. Courts martial continued to try those accused of political crimes, where the legal rights guaranteed by the Fuero de los Españoles did not apply.

While Franco sought to quiet the opposition by modest concessions, he continued to win influential friends abroad. The first was in Rome. The Republic had abrogated the Concordat of 1851, and since the war the Vatican and Spanish government had been working out a replacement for it. A covenant of 1941 gave Franco the right formerly held by the king to nominate candidates for bishoprics, and the Fuero de los Españoles of 1945 responded with explicit recognition of the Catholic basis of the Spanish state. Now Franco pushed for the conclusion of a formal treaty that would seal these agreements. Such a concordat was signed on August 21, 1953. It proclaimed, "The Catholic religion continues to be the only religion of the Spanish nation," [1] confirmed the church's supervision of education, and provided for state financial support of the clergy. The Vatican in return restated Franco's right to nominate to bishoprics. None of these stipulations were innovations; the importance of the concordat was that it gave papal sanction to the regime and provided Franco with a weapon to use against conservative clerics who claimed that his new ministry was threatening Spain's Catholicism.

What particularly troubled conservative Catholics like Cardinal Segura, who was now almost as violent a critic of Franco as he had been of the Republic, was the likelihood of an alliance with the United States. Since July 1951 the United States had been negotiating for military bases in Spain in return for military and economic aid. The Spanish press publicized the talks, but few people in Spain or abroad welcomed them. Arch-Catholics feared the effect of Protestant soldiers among the Spanish populace; Cardinal Segura accused Franco of trading Spain's "Catholic conscience" for "heretical dollars." [2] Falangists and other nationalists objected to the appearance of foreign troops on Spanish soil—they warned of new Gibraltars—while opponents of the regime felt betrayed once again by the leading democratic power. Outside Spain, the liberal and left-wing parties of Western Europe raised cries of dismay, and American liberals and Protestants also protested. Nevertheless negotiations continued, pushed by American strategists eager to strengthen the United States hold over the Mediterranean Sea. They culminated in the Pact of Madrid of September 26, 1953, a ten-year military and economic agreement for the two powers to build and maintain joint naval and air bases in Spain and for the United States to supply Spain with dollars and armaments. With the United States behind him, Franco became virtually unassailable at home and abroad.

[1] Quoted in Éléna de la Souchère, *An Explanation of Spain*, p. 275.
[2] Arthur P. Whitaker, *Spain and the Defense of the West*, p. 41.

Coming one month after the concordat, the pact guaranteed the continuation of the regime, which appeared shaky indeed in 1951.

Two years later, in 1955, the United Nations voted to admit Spain to membership along with various other nations. Thanks to his keen reading of the world pulse and his sense of the possible, Franco had ceased to be a pariah. Only the blocking of Spain's entry into the North Atlantic Treaty Organization by its European members, the refusal of some well-known hispanists to set foot in Spain, and the periodical publications of various groups of Spanish exiles preserved the memory of the anti-Franco crusade of the thirties.

2

In the more relaxed atmosphere of the fifties, a new generation of writers and painters showed that the artistic spirit of Spain was still alive. The Civil War had occupied the efforts and emotions of writers and artists as well as of ordinary men, and they had had little time for creativity. After the war, the memory of its passions and the suffering, hope, and hatreds of the postwar years offered obvious themes for novelists; but fear and discouragement silenced most of those who could have risen to the occasion. They hid what they wrote or destroyed their manuscripts to avoid detection.

Even in the forties, however, the seeds of previous decades sprouted; but they did so in relatively safe fields like poetry and painting. The poetic flowering of the thirties never died completely, even in the war. García Lorca had been assassinated, but most of his contemporaries lived on. Some, like Salinas, Guillén, Cernuda, and Alberti, had emigrated; others remained in Spain, notably Vicente Aleixandre, who became the inspiration of young poets after 1940. A landmark was the publication in 1944 of a collection of poems called *Hijos de la ira* (*Children of Wrath*) by Dámaso Alonso, a poet of the twenties who was driven by the sorrow of his country to take up the pen again. His work depicted the personal anguish of an intellectual who had chosen to stay in Spain. By then new voices had joined those of the older poets. They included Miguel Hernández, who died in a Franco prison in 1942, Blas de Otero, and León Felipe in Mexico. Despite their physical separation, the poets in exile and those in Spain remained spiritually united. Given Franco's strict censorship and police surveillance, poetry could be a stronger bond than politics, for exiles could communicate with Spaniards more safely in this medium than through underground political movements. In 1946 Enrique Canito and José Luís Cano, the latter a young friend of the poets of the thirties, inaugurated in Madrid a monthly literary review called *Insula,* dedicated to keeping Spanish men of letters at home and abroad informed of each other's activities. In the more encouraging atmosphere of the next decade émigrés began to return for visits and meet their new colleagues, spurring artistic production.

Inside and outside Spain, the war had the effect on poets of turning their writing to current issues. Rather than evoking eternal passions and problems of man, they now portrayed the suffering of their contemporaries and of themselves as individuals. A common theme to run through the poetry of the forties and fifties was an invocation of Spain by her sons who loved her deeply and wept for her suffering. Blas de Otero wrote:

> Madre y maestra mia, triste, espaciosa España.
> He aquí a tu hijo. Ungenos, madre. Haz
> habitable tu ámbito. Respirable tu extraña
> paz. Para el hombre. Paz. Para el aire. Madre, paz.[3]

In 1951 Camilo José Cela published *La Colmena* (*The Hive*), an episodic novel depicting the miserable life of Madrid in the postwar years. It marked the reappearance of good prose writers. By general agreement Cela is the best of a new generation of Spanish novelists, which includes Miguel Delibes and Ana María Matute. Since 1951 Cela has divided his work between other novels and accounts of travels through the country, excelling in descriptions of human situations and the environment in which men live. So far the new figures have not achieved the stature of their predecessors of the first part of the century. The fear of censorship and reprisal has remained to inhibit them, since their dedication to contemporary problems, which they share with the poets, drives them to write about what they see, and much of what they see is not pleasing to the men who have controlled the country.

Even more than poets, painters could work in relative freedom from attack, or at least chose to do so by abandoning representational art almost entirely. In the first third of the century the Catalans Picasso, Dalí, and Miró and the Castilian Juan Gris figured at the head of the cubist and surrealist movements, but they left Spain for France and became part of a wider art world. In the fifties their heirs made the art salons of Barcelona and Madrid among the most exciting anywhere, and established Spanish painters as leaders in abstract art. The new movement can be dated from 1948, when Antoní Tapiés, Joan Josep Tharrats,

> [3] Mother and teacher mine, my sad and spacious Spain.
> Behold your son. Anoint us, Mother. Grant surcease
> of anguish in your bounds. Make breathable again
> your strange peace. For man. Peace. For the air. Mother, peace.

From Blas de Otero, "Hija de Yago", in *Pido la paz y la palabra* (Santander: Canta la piedra, 1955). Translation by Geoffrey Connell in *Texas Quarterly* 4, no. 1 (Spring 1961), special issue "Image of Spain," 274–75. Reprinted by permission of the publisher.

and Modest Cuixart founded a group in Barcelona calling itself the Dau al Set (the Seventh Side of the Die, a surrealist concept). Ten years later another group appeared in Madrid with the name El Paso (The Step), headed by Luis Feito, Manuel Millares, and Rafael Canoger. All were members of a new generation of artists (the oldest, Tharrats, was born in 1918; the youngest, Canoger, in 1935). They experimented radically with unorthodox materials that were attracting artists elsewhere in the Western world—sand, burlap, wood, metal. Although they were part of an international movement that looked back to nonrepresentational painters like Kandinsky and Mondrian, they created a peculiarly Spanish art. They used strong but not garish color contrasts that seemed to revive the palettes of El Greco and Goya, who had in their day responded to the hues of the Spanish landscape. In 1959 the Spanish government, long sensitive to the charge of stultifying intellect, gathered their work together in an exhibit that toured the galleries of Europe and America. Its reception abroad established the international reputation of Spaniards in the realm of abstract art.

3

More than the easing restrictions on public expression, the first stages of a profound social transformation showed that the fifties were the beginning of a new era. The economy, sick since the depression and the Civil War, at last began to mend. The fifties was an age of economic expansion in all Western Europe. Since 1948 the Marshall Plan had dispensed United States aid to its European allies and facilitated their recovery from the ravages of the Second World War. Although American help to Spain after 1951 was modest by comparison, it had much the same effect on the Spanish economy. It provided the margin to purchase needed imports and finance long-term projects.

During the decade Spanish industrial potential expanded rapidly. Between 1950 and 1958 the index of total industrial production almost doubled, but it rose even faster in certain basic industries.[4] Steel output went from 815,000 tons to 1,480,000 (in 1913 it was 392,000). Encouraged by the Instituto Nacional de Industria (INI), the production of chemicals more than tripled, and factories for the first time turned out Spanish automobiles and trucks. Following fifteen years of slow growth, the completion of new dams after 1954 dramatically increased the country's water storage capacity. By 1960 it was 18.4 billion cubic meters, nearly three times the 1954 level. The production of electricity went from 6.9 billion kilowatt hours in 1950 to 18.6 ten years later.

The government also paid attention to communications. During the forties the national railroad network, the RENFE, was able to do little

[4] See table in Whitaker, p. 225.

but keep the trains running with ancient, exhausted equipment. In 1950, amid much publicity, it introduced a rapid lightweight passenger train, known as the Talgo, between Madrid and the French border. Conceived and built on radical principles, very low slung to compensate for the poor state of the roadbeds, it almost halved travel time and was a tourist attraction. In 1958 the RENFE initiated a ten-year program to modernize its system, helped by a fifteen-million-dollar loan from the United States. The plan included replacing worn track, substituting diesel and electric engines for steam locomotives, and introducing Talgos on all main lines. The RENFE also completed a direct line from Madrid to Burgos which had been under construction for decades and cut over one hundred kilometers from the distance by rail to France. Despite the new automobile age, the RENFE managed to keep the railways a going concern.

In the fifties the state at last began to extend the highway network beyond the stage where Primo de Rivera had left it. The official statistics do not tell the whole story. They list 110,000 kilometers of highways in 1950, of which 84,000 were paved, and 130,000 in 1962 of which 85,000 were paved. However, any traveler could see improvement in the quality of pavement and ease of communication in rural areas, where the 20,000 kilometers of new unimproved roads opened many small towns for the first time to trucks and cars. Accompanying this improvement—indeed, making it peremptory—was a rapid increase in motorized vehicles. In 1950 there were about 9000 interurban buses and 60,000 trucks, largely of prewar vintage. Ten years later the figures were 12,000 and 150,000, and most of these were of recent manufacture. Passenger cars multiplied from less than 90,000 to over 300,000.

Industrial expansion and better communications were to have a major impact on society. They went a long way to explain the acceleration in the growth of cities, which was described in the opening chapter.[5] They also laid the basis for the revolution in consumer production that began at the end of the decade. But the cost of this expansion was high. By putting its impetus behind the development of basic industries, the government upset the normal balance of the economy without taking proper precautions to prevent the harm that might occur. It took the paths of least resistance and by the end of the decade found itself in almost as serious a crisis as at the beginning. The immediate difficulty arose from a shortage of foreign exchange. To proceed with industrialization, Spain needed to import machinery and raw materials like steel, petroleum, and high-grade coal. The hydroelectric installations required advanced equipment, and so did the INI's steel plant at Avilés, planned to be among the most modern in the world. Until the latter began to produce steel at the end of the decade, it represented a heavy

[5] See pp. 20–22.

drain on state resources. Spain had few manufactured goods to sell abroad. Despite its agricultural and mineral exports, the country had a continually unfavorable balance of payments. Running between 100 and 200 million dollars per year from 1952 to 1955, the deficit in foreign exchange jumped to almost 400 million in the next three years. Only American economic aid enabled the government to continue such a spendthrift policy; during the decade the United States furnished almost one billion dollars in nonmilitary loans and aid and another 400 million in military aid.

Industrial expansion affected the social classes and geographic areas of the country very unevenly. To finance its projects, the government issued credits through its agencies, like the INI. Since this spending was not backed by corresponding government income, it multiplied the currency in circulation and led to a rapid inflation. Control of imports and high tariffs to protect the nascent industries also raised consumer prices. The government maintained restrictions on wages and salaries, however, so that the middle and lower classes were forced to suffer to make possible the expansion. In their case, the cause was partly lack of official foresight. More deliberate was the decision to hold back the industrial areas traditionally opposed to the regime: Catalonia and the Basque Provinces. The Avilés plant was located in Asturias, although it competed directly with the older Basque steel furnaces. The building of dams was concentrated in central and western Spain, and new power lines did not at once reach Catalonia, retarding the expansion of its industries. Barcelona continued to suffer from shortages of electricity throughout the fifties.[6] The emphasis on basic industries also placed the older consumer goods industries of Catalonia at a disadvantage. The relative stagnation of Barcelona was evident from the census. It had been even with Madrid in 1940 with just over a million people each. By 1960 Barcelona had one and a half million, whereas Madrid, where the government had concentrated much of the automotive and other new industries, had risen to two and a quarter million.

On the other hand certain sectors of society benefited inordinately. Because the government controlled the distribution of scarce resources and imports, its favor meant the difference between rapid expansion and austerity for an enterprise. As in the forties, bribery and corruption continued to mark the relations between official agencies and entrepreneurs. Permission to import materials and machinery was given in return for gratuities; one quarter of Spain's imports was contraband, and this would not have been possible without official conniving.[7] The situation was geared to encouraging subterfuge and double dealing. Those

[6] Souchère, p. 323.
[7] Whitaker, *op. cit.*, p. 237.

who succeeded were rewarded with high profits, which they were free to invest or spend on conspicuous extravagance: foreign cars, luxury apartments, summer houses in the mountains or at the seaside.

Rising above the expanding economy were the large private banks, which dated from previous eras. From the outset Franco showed great concern for them, and they responded with their support. From 1936 to 1962 the founding of new banks was prohibited, and during this period the "five great banks" of the early century absorbed seventy-three smaller institutions, over one third of those in existence.[8] The power of the large banks, *la banca* as Spaniards called them collectively, became highly concentrated; the eight largest handled almost two thirds of the banking business.[9] The periodical reports on the state of the economy of the Banco Hispano-Americano, the Banco de Bilbao, and others were influential with the authorities. A Superior Banking Council established in 1946 brought together representatives of the private banks, the Bank of Spain, and the government to formulate credit policies. The large banks thus collaborated with the ministry and the INI in directing the economic expansion.

But the banks, since the founding of the first ones in the nineteenth century, represented private capital. Because they were the main agents for floating stock, they had always pushed the development of corporate industry. Their search for influence and profits led them to encourage the multiplication of corporations under Franco. In 1950 there were about eight thousand corporations with 55 billion pesetas in stock; by 1960 there were twelve thousand, with 184 billion pesetas in stock. Using their authority to borrow from the government-controlled Bank of Spain, the private banks bought up stock in rapidly expanding corporations in fields like the metallurgical and electrical industries, and what they did not take they distributed to the public. Like the INI, which also acquired stock of private corporations, they held the power to make or break business enterprises. At the beginning of the century family firms had dominated Spanish manufacturing everywhere except in the Basque Provinces. Corporate enterprise had grown steadily during the century, but never so fast as under Franco. Private firms withered beside corporations, *sociedades anónimas* as they are aptly called in Spanish, with anagrammatic names like UNESA (Unidad Eléctrica, S.A.) and CEISA (Construcciones e Inmuebles, S.A.).

Since the beginning of the century Madrid had been the financial center of the nation, but under Franco its power increased markedly. In 1940 the capital investments of businesses incorporated in Madrid represented 42 percent of the national total. By 1966 it had risen to 50

[8] Ramón Tamames, *Estructura económica de España* (3rd ed., Madrid: Sociedad de Estudios y Publicaciones, 1965), p. 664.

[9] Whitaker, p. 230.

percent. During this same period Barcelona's share declined from 24 to 21 percent, much of it in small family concerns of a previous era, and Bilbao's from 13 to 11 percent. The same pattern held true in banking. In 1965 Madrid banks had 60 percent of the national total of capital and reserves, Bilbao banks followed with 20 percent, and Barcelona's were a poor third with 4 percent. So attractive was Madrid as a financial capital that many businesses had their headquarters there whose productive activities were carried on elsewhere in the country.[10] Even though the Basque Provinces and Catalonia remained the most highly industrialized regions of Spain, the evolution of the financial structure was centralizing control of the national economy in Madrid.

During the fifties the investment of capital turned from the public to the private sectors of the economy. Of 4 billion pesetas of obligations issued in 1950, 69 percent represented government bonds, 10 percent the bonds of private companies, and 21 percent private stocks. By 1959 there was a revolution in the pattern. The obligations issued that year reached 25 billion pesetas, of which government obligations took only 12 percent while 34 percent went into private bonds and 58 percent into stocks.[11] Part of this stock was bought by the INI, part by the banks, but when the banks floated the issues they gratified their preferred clients with inside information and distribution of stock in ventures that were guaranteed handsome profits by the favor of the government.

In this way the development of corporate industry was bringing about a profund change in the pattern of private savings. Since early modern times Spaniards had been suspicious of investment in business. In the nineteenth century real property in land and buildings was the ideal place to put one's savings, and the disentail of church and public lands catered to this penchant. The middle class also invested in family businesses, usually their own. Already before the war the stocks and bonds of corporations were attracting some investors, but under Franco they became generally accepted as a source of security and income for the family with savings. The practice began with the upper layers of society who were close to the banks, many of them descendants of the old Moderado oligarchy. In the sixties the fashion spread downward, and ordinary middle-class people who had never dreamed of owning stock, *acciones*, used their savings to become *accionistas* in *sociedades anónimas*. Thus the regime through its investment policies spread the acceptance of a corporate capitalist economy through the influential sectors of society.

The entire process was also creating a more centralized and unified

[10] José L. García Delgado and Arturo López Muñoz, "Analisis de la banca privada española," *Cuadernos para el diálogo*, VIII extraordinario (April 1968), 35–38.

[11] *Anuario financiero y de sociedades económicas*, 1964–1965, p. xxxix.

national economy, transforming the structure inherited from the Moderado period. In place of several diverse ruling groups—landowners, Basque steel industrialists, Asturian mining interests, and Catalan cloth manufacturers—a more modern, more concentrated, and less personal ruling elite was appearing. The Moderado oligarchy was not despoiled, it was simply deposed from its ruling position. Many individual members, including landed aristocrats and army generals, found places in the new elite, often on the governing boards of banks and corporations.[12] Just as roads, telephones, and electric power lines were welding the separate geographic regions into one interconnected economic unit, and migrations were filling the cities with workers from all parts of the country, government agencies, banks, and corporations were producing a single interlocking elite of state officials, bankers, and corporation executives, highly concentrated in Madrid. In a very real sense the regionalism which had marked Spain since medieval times was under mortal attack.

4

In Spain today three types of manmade structure break the horizon of the countryside and indicate to the traveler that he is approaching a settlement. Two, centuries old, represent an artistic inheritance from the Middle Ages and the absolute monarchy—castles and church towers. Beside them in the grain-bearing regions now rise square windowless tan and white concrete buildings. They are modern grain elevators, *silos* in Spanish, standing near railway sidings or highways. The National Wheat Service has erected them to store the wheat it purchases from the farmers. The first large *silo* was inaugurated in Cordoba in 1951, and by 1964 there were 262 in all Spain. The tall *silos* are a superficial manifestation of a profound transformation going on in the countryside since 1950. Government action has accounted for much of it, but its full depth has been the outgrowth of the myriad changes, planned and unplanned, in process in all areas of Spanish life.

As to other sectors of the economy, the military agreement with the United States gave an impetus to agricultural reform. The two countries exchanged agricultural experts, and the United States furnished farm machinery and gave grants and loans to the Spanish agencies furthering agricultural improvement. By 1963 Spain had received 90 million dollars for this purpose. The sum was not large, but it offered the marginal outlay the country needed. With greater resources at its disposal the government could bring to fruition some of the ambitious plans of the forties.

[12] Whitaker, pp. 140–41, 146–47; García Delgado and López Muñoz, "Analisis de la banca privada española," pp. 39–47.

The Institute of Colonization was the primary agency for reform. It had achieved little since its founding, but a law of 1949 drawn up after a decade of indecision gave it clear objectives. With authority to expropriate large landholdings for improvement and redistribution in small parcels, it now undertook to populate and irrigate major regions of arid Spain. The most important were in the upper Guadalquivir basin in eastern Andalusia, the Guadiana valley near Badajoz, and the northern tributaries of the Ebro River in Aragon. The construction of dams was arranged to provide for irrigation as well as hydroelectric power. By 1958 300,000 hectares (1200 square miles) had been placed under irrigation. Ten years later the offical figure was 800,00 hectares (over 3000 square miles).

Irrigation involved the resettlement of farmers. Those living in the valleys flooded by dams had to be indemnified and relocated, while people had to be brought in to cultivate newly irrigated areas. By 1962 the Institute of Colonization had built two hundred new towns with 17,500 dwelling units. Half were in Extremadura and Andalusia. The institute claimed to have resettled 50,000 families, of which 8000 had acquired full title to their fields. Another 20,000 families had benefited through irrigation of lands they already owned.

The most publicized of the projects was the Badajoz Plan. The valley of the Guadiana above this city on the Portuguese frontier was flat and fertile but virtually barren for lack of water. Development plans went back to the twenties. The new undertaking called for the eventual irrigation of 130,000 hectares (500 square miles). The institute would take over the lands, leaving former owners a maximum of 125 hectares and distributing the rest in family plots of four to five hectares. It planned new towns to house 9500 families. To the INI was assigned the task of developing processing industries for the crops. By 1964 five dams were completed, 50,000 hectares already under irrigation, and 4000 families of colonists established. Smaller but similar undertakings were meanwhile taking shape in many other places.

An integral part of the program of water conservation and use involved reforestation. The planting of trees had also made little progress in the years after the war, and in 1951 the forestry service drew up an overall plan. It was directed largely at replanting the watersheds of the dams to stop erosion and slow down water runoff. By the sixties small evergreens could be seen growing in regular rows on the hillsides of arid Spain, promising to transform the landscape within a few decades from the barren appearance it had had for centuries.

Irrigation and colonization were only one way to increase the output of individuals engaged in agriculture and thereby to raise their standard of living. It could never affect more than a minority of Spanish farmers. There was no single solution to the ill-rewarded primitive toil of the other millions of small peasants, but in these years a number of developments joined together to bring a profound change to their lot as well. One of the achievements of the fifties was the introduction of countless peasants to the use of artificial fertilizers. Before the Civil War the use of chemical fertilizers was a practice of large landowners, but it had declined drastically during the war for lack of supplies. It rose again between 1940 and 1962 from less than one million tons per year to almost four million. The INI made possible this advance by developing the domestic manufacture of fertilizers, for Spain could not afford the foreign exchange needed to import them as it had done before the war. Small farmers who learned the economic benefits of fertilizers accounted for much of the increased use.

The cooperative movement that had gotten under way in the forties also contributed to the well-being and effectiveness of peasant farmers. Marketing cooperatives were the most successful, especially for crops that needed elaboration. Hitherto the small producer of grapes or olives had to deliver his harvest to private wine cellars and oil mills, where he had no choice but to accept the prices offered him for his highly perishable crops. Only the larger producers had the economic strength to build their own mills or demand a fair price. By the end of the fifties, and more especially in the sixties, in the grape and olive regions new wine and oil mills proudly labeled "*cooperativas*" arose beside aging private mills. Farmers would discuss with the visitor the success of "their" cooperatives, exuding a new dignity at being able to stand off their former exploiters.

Agricultural credit became more accessible in these years. The number of *cajas rurales* of the National Union of Rural Cooperatives doubled between 1948 and 1964, offering loans to finance improvements and the purchase of machinery. The state also intervened directly to offer credit to peasants through the National Service of Agricultural Credit, set up in 1946 and rebaptized the National Bank of Agricultural Credit in 1962. Its outstanding loans rose from 400 million pesetas in 1952 to 4.6 billion in 1963.

The cooperative movement, easier credit, domestic industry, and American aid all contributed to the mechanization of the countryside. Farm machinery began to appear in places that had never known it. To cite only the most common type of machine, Spain had 4000 agricultural tractors in 1940, 114,000 in 1963. No doubt the majority of farm machines were purchased by farmers whose lands were extensive enough to justify the investment. Less well-to-do peasants could rent the tractors and threshers of their wealthier neighbors or pay to have their lands plowed and harvested. The cooperative movement offered a more dignified solution adopted by many. Groups of small farmers associated to buy and share machinery, using the credit offered by the *cajas rurales* and the National Bank.

One of the greatest hindrances to improving and mechanizing agriculture was the large number of tiny plots of land dating back for centuries, the result of dividing inheritances without concern for the unproductive labor such division entailed. Throughout most of Spain individual peasants had to work many minuscule fields in different parts of the town limits. Before 1950 in ten provinces located in the central plateau and Galicia, the average number of plots per owner was over ten, and in Soria it reached twenty-six! Reformers had long worried about the problem, but they had achieved virtually nothing. The minister of agriculture in the 1951 cabinet, Rafael Cavestany, took up the challenge with determination. In 1952 he obtained the creation of a technical staff known as the Service of Parcelary Concentration. It received the authority, on petition of a majority of the landowners of a town, to survey and reallocate the land so that each owner would get as few tracts as possible while preserving the quality and extent of his former holdings. The activities of the service began slowly, since it had to train teams of experts, but it gained momentum at the end of the fifties and continued to accelerate in the sixties. The peasants needed little encouragement to undertake the change. As one told me, "We can all see the advantage, but we could never carry it out by ourselves. It has to be the state who does it." Petitions for "concentration" poured in from towns faster than the service could deal with them. By 1963 145,000 hectares had been concentrated; nearly 500,000 plots had been reduced to 60,000.

That all these campaigns were having an effect was evident in production figures. Perhaps the most significant was the growth of the wheat crop. From 1939 to 1954 there had been little change in it, averaging about 33 million quintals per year. In the next decade it rose sharply and in the early sixties averaged nearly 45 million, more than before the war. Spain was able to reduce its imports of grain despite a growing population, a vital saving in foreign exchange. Furthermore, the growth in grain output occurred while land was being taken out of wheat and put into more specialized crops like olives, cotton, and sugar beets. The production of olive oil increased by a third from the late forties to the early sixties. Much of the land put under irrigation went into sugar beets and cotton, especially in Andalusia. Sugar beet output rose 60 percent from the early fifties to the early sixties; while the cotton crop multiplied twenty-five times from 1944 to 1963, from 20,000 bales to 500,000. Again these figures meant fewer purchases abroad.

Besides being initiated to modern agricultural methods, peasant life was changing in more indirect ways. The effect of the improvement of communications was more noticeable than in the cities. The telephone network spread deeper and deeper into remote areas, and so did electricity. There had been a limited number of radios in the small towns before the war, but not until their price declined and electricity reached throughout the rural areas could they become commonplace.

This occurred after the war, and especially in the fifties. The radio brought news of the outside world, even if censored, sporting events, and advertisements of the latest in cosmetics and household appliances. Although most of the increase in automotive transportation involved interurban freight and passengers, it also invaded the small towns. Trucks began to circulate along minor roads that had hardly been passable before, while the *alcaldes* of the smallest *pueblos* petitioned for bus service and often obtained it. Peasants could now ship out their produce by truck, and they could take their families for the day to the provincial capital on the *coche de linea* and return with the latest style printed cottons and ready-made clothes. The young men and women of the *pueblos* on the traditional Sunday promenade along the main street now looked no different from those who were parading at the same hour in the avenues of the cities. Only middle-aged and older persons hung on to the dark clothes they had always worn.

Schooling was another innovative force. From the outset, universal education had been one of the objectives of the regime. Since illiteracy was a greater plague in rural areas than in the cities, the campaign had to be directed primarily at the small towns. The forties had seen vast plans but little achievement. The decade of the fifties began to see the projects materialize. In 1953 the government approved a general plan for school construction, and after 1956 building began in earnest. It was estimated that 18,000 new elementary school rooms were needed (about a third again as many as those in existence) and another 7000 had to be rebuilt. By 1964 the government claimed to have completed almost all of these, and however inexact these figures might be, the achievement was no vain boast. By the mid-sixties new elementary schools were visible throughout the *pueblos*, one for boys and one for girls, or else a common building carefully divided to separate the sexes. Often there was also a new house for the *maestro* to attract him from the city. Slowly illiteracy was receding. The Republic had found 32 percent of Spaniards illiterate and left 23 percent. By 1960 the figure was down to 12 percent, mostly of an older generation.

The ideal of the rulers was to open all levels of education to the lower classes, both urban and rural, aware that a technological society needs more trained persons than Spain's traditional elitist education could provide. A law of 1957 established a new plan for technical education, projecting a larger number of schools and reducing the entrance requirements. To make university education more accessible, the government pushed the building of *colegios mayores*. By 1963 there were 124 in the twelve universities, 38 of them in Madrid. In 1956 the state began to offer scholarships for secondary and technical education, giving to a limited number of working class and peasant youths the opportunity to pursue schooling beyond the elementary level. The scholarship program became one of the central concerns of the ministry of education.

In 1966 150,000 students received state aid; a relatively small number, but it meant that the son of a peasant no longer needed to enter the clergy to get an education.

The government tended to lag in the field of secondary education, however. It continued to allow private schools to do the job, and this meant above all those of the religious orders. The number of students at the secondary level per 10,000 population rose from 60 in 1940 to 150 in 1960, but less than one fifth of these were in state *institutos*. Rather than build new *institutos*, the government licensed private schools under a law of 1938 to give official secondary degrees, the *bachillerato*, provided they had properly qualified teachers and met other standards.

The picture had other dark sides. More attention had been paid to extending education than to improving its quality. At all levels schools suffered from backward pedagogical methods. Textbooks had to be approved by the state, and those that got by were dismally dull and uninspiring. Even at the university students were expected to memorize rather than question, and teachers remained distant and infallible. Nevertheless, specialized training was ceasing to be the monopoly of the middle classes. For the first time laboring class and peasant families could encourage their children to study with the expectation of social and economic rewards. The spread of education, like so many other changes, was working to end the division of the country into alien rural and urban worlds.

Rural life had never stood completely still, although the visitor from the city might feel that peasants were living and working as they had under the Romans. In the fifties, however, it began to change so rapidly that it transformed the mentality of the peasants, especially the young ones. Parcelary concentration and mechanized farming destroyed the monopoly of mules, burros, Roman plows, and the town threshing field. Roads, buses, and trucks brought the city nearer to the village, while telephones, radios, and new schools made the villagers feel that they were really part of a larger world. The drab backbreaking labor of all members of the family that had been the lot of their ancestors from time immemorial no longer seemed the preordained way of life for those born to till the land. Even small farmers and agricultural laborers who could not afford the improvements or who lived in towns not yet touched by the changes determined at least that their children, if not they, would enjoy easier lives.[13]

For thousands and thousands of men and women under forty the easiest and fastest way to throw off the old life was to abandon the *pueblos* and go to the cities, where unskilled labor was in demand.

[13] See Victor Pérez Díaz, *Estructura social del campo y éxodo rural* (Madrid: Editorial Tecnos, 1966), a sociological study of a town in Guadalajara province.

Since the nineteenth century young people had left the countryside for the cities or for Spanish America, but restrictions had reduced the flow to America since the First World War. Those who continued to go there came from the Canary Islands, Galicia, and other places near the sea. The interior rural areas sent their excess people to Madrid, Barcelona, and other Spanish cities in the north and east. This was still the pattern after the Civil War, but after 1955 the flow increased; a quarter of a million people went to Madrid in the second half of the decade, twice as many as in the first half. By and large the migrants were adult males from rural areas where the number of landless laborers was high, Andalusia and New Castile.[14]

The rural exodus became a flood about 1960 and its pattern changed. Over two hundred thousand workers moved their residence within Spain that year, nearly one fiftieth of the total active population. They went from the agricultural areas to Madrid and the industrial centers of the north and east, as before, but now many also began to go to north European countries which needed cheap labor, above all to France, Germany, and Switzerland. Seven hundred thousand people from all parts of Spain were to cross the Pyrenees seeking jobs between 1959 and 1963—half again as many as fled at the end of the Civil War. Eighty-five percent were adult males, and of these perhaps nine tenths were from the countryside, although some had gone first to Madrid or Barcelona before leaving the country.[15] No longer were they all landless emigrants, for peasants who owned land or expected to inherit it began to leave their homes. Tired of eking out barren lives on too small farms, they began to sell their fields, or when there were no buyers simply abandon them, and move to the city. Married couples left their children with their grandparents, hoping to be reunited with them in the near future. Most of the migrants to the cities ended up in slums or in temporary hovels on the outskirts, but they could find unskilled jobs in construction or the services and had the satisfaction of being where the action was.[16]

Thus began, without advance planning, what one Spaniard has called "the most singular agrarian reform of all time." [17] Emigration

[14] Angel Cabo Alonso, "Valor de la inmigración madrileña," *Estudios geográficos*, XXII (1961), 353–74, and Jesús García Fernández, "El movimiento migratorio de trabajadores en España," *ibid.*, XXV (1964), 139–74.

[15] Jesús García Fernández, *La emigración exterior de España* (Barcelona: Ediciones Ariel, 1965), pp. 76, 100, 228–32, 269.

[16] See Juan Anlló, *Estructura y problemas del campo español* (Madrid: Editorial Cudernos para le Diálogo, 1967), pp. 96–103, and the moving article by Julio Caro Baroja, "La despoblación de los campos," *Revista de Occidente*, No. 40 (July 1966), pp. 19–36.

[17] Quoted by Angel Martínez Bosque, *Colonización agrícola* (Ministerio de Agricultura, Instituto Nacional de Colonizatión, *Estudios*, Vol. VI, No. 30), 13. The author of the phrase is not named.

was the most effective, indeed the indispensable, way to raise the standard of living of rural Spaniards. So long as masses of peasants weighed down the rural economy, forcing the use of inefficient, outdated forms of production to keep them all busy, they were condemned to poverty. Even with new methods agricultural production could never rise fast enough to bring up to modern standards the level of income of all the people in the countryside. In 1940 4.8 million Spaniards were actively engaged in agriculture. In 1960 the number was the same, although the proportion of the total population had declined from 52 to 41 percent. Only large scale emigration could reduce the absolute number of agricultural workers and make possible a solution to the centuries old agrarian problem. The changes of the fifties laid the groundwork, both material and psychological, for this to begin in the sixties.

5

Spain might be changing, but Spaniards were far from happy. During most of the fifties the transformation did not benefit the ordinary city dweller, while inflation, shortages, corruption, favoritism, and police rule were not calculated to endear the rulers to him. After the first demonstration of labor solidarity in the spring of 1951, however intangible its success, the regime was unable to stifle further opposition. Spanish workers seemed to realize that they had to take their fate in their own hands, since all hope had vanished of the regime being toppled from abroad; while Franco, fearful of paralyzing the economy and needing American and western European friends, could no longer resort to the same mass brutality that he had used after the war. In October 1952 the police discovered plans of anarchists acting in the name of the former CNT to organize a general strike in Barcelona protesting government corruption and rising prices. Junior army officers were reported to be sympathetic. While the government arrested the leaders, it sought to pacify the workers by decreeing an extraordinary bonus of one month's salary for state and industrial employees. Labor unrest continued. In December 1953 several thousand workers in Bilbao went on strike to protest insufficient wages, organized by Socialists and Basque nationalists. And in March 1954 workers rioted in Seville.

After a decade of smouldering, the unrest in the universities also flamed into open revolt. In January 1954 police broke up a student rally in Madrid ostensibly organized to denounce British occupation of Gibraltar. The next day three thousand university students demonstrated against police brutality in the Puerta del Sol and stormed the nearby Madrid radio station. The students were not the only aggrieved group. On the other side the members of Opus Dei were not happy with their fall from grace in 1951. The Consejo Superior de Investigaciones Científicas, which Opus dominated, in December 1965 released the results of a poll taken among students at the University of Madrid which revealed overwhelming opposition to the regime. Seventy-five percent believed the government to be incompetent. Even more accused it of immorality and said Spain was rent by class hatred brought on by its capitalistic economic system. In his annual New Year's Day speech, Franco denounced what he called the "venom of materialism" infiltrating the universities. Students responded by challenging official control of higher learning. On February 1, 1956 students of the University of Madrid, led by Dionisio Ridruejo, a radical Falange leader of the thirties, petitioned for changes in the SEU. They stated that the Falange's control of the SEU prevented it from voicing student grievances, and asked to have it run democratically. Several days later the law students challenged the rules by electing non-Falangist delegates to the SEU. Fighting ensued between radical students and loyal members of the Falange that mushroomed into mass demonstrations and clashes with the police in central Madrid. Rioting spread to Seville and other university cities, and the crisis became so serious that the government gave the police arbitrary powers of arrest.

In April the government brought to trial four young intellectuals, two of them university students, accused of inciting the disturbances. To everyone's amazement they obtained as their defense attorney José María Gil Robles. Gil had hardly been heard of since his brilliant political career under the Republic as leader of the rightist CEDA. About 1954 he returned from Portugal, where he had been an adviser to the pretender Don Juan. Now he stepped forward as champion of the opponents of the regime. His eloquent defense pilloried the government for denying the right of free expression promised in the Fuero de los Españoles. Witnesses for the accused included Ridruejo and Laín Entralgo, the liberal Falangist rector of the University of Madrid. The Spanish intellectual world followed the trial eagerly, and when the judges decreed token sentences of six to twelve months in jail for the accused young men, it rejoiced at what it felt was a moral victory.

In the next years Gil Robles was to remain in public sight, at times defending others accused by the regime. Around him he built a movement called the Christian Democrats, a name taken from left-wing Catholic parties in other countries. Laín Entralgo was in the same camp. Ridruejo, on the other hand, remained aloof from the church and founded a group called the Social Party of Democratic Action.[18] Neither of these or other similar groups that appeared could be more than informal associations, for the law prohibited all parties except

[18] Benjamin Welles, *Spain, the Gentle Anarchy* (New York: Frederick A. Praeger, Inc., 1965), pp. 190, 204.

the Falange; yet the willingness of university students to challenge Franco's rule had incited respected figures within Spain for the first time to oppose the regime openly. Those who did so had all fought the Popular Front in 1936. In speaking out now against the government, they declared that the Civil War was a thing of the past and new issues were at stake, giving the lie to official statements that the student disturbances were the work of Communists and other agents of the defeated Republicans. Because of their respected names and impeccable backgrounds, they offered relatively safe rallying points for dissatisfied middle-class persons and intellectuals. Political opposition was still illegal, but it was no longer all clandestine or led only by the former Popular Front parties.

The workers, loyal to the memories of the war, were hardly attracted by Gil Robles and Ridruejo, but they used the student agitation to urge their own grievances. Trying to head off labor disturbances, the government decreed a 20 percent wage increase in March 1956. The workers again rejected what they considered token satisfaction, and in April they conducted strikes in Barcelona and other Catalan cities, in Bilbao, San Sebastián, and even conservative Pamplona. They protested worsening economic conditions as well as the dictatorial nature of the regime. The government granted further across-the-board wage increases of 40 to 50 percent in November, but agitation continued. In the winter of 1956–57 activity centered in Barcelona, where both students and workers staged public protests. Henceforth Franco could not face opposition from one of these sources without anticipating trouble from the other.

Thanks to his hold on the police and army, Franco rode out the unrest, but he decided to entrust his government in the future to harder headed men than the Falangist old shirts and liberal Catholics. The crisis opened the door for the enemies of both groups who had been biding their time since 1951: the Opus Dei.

The leaders of Opus Dei had not been idle since their setback. With their conquest of the universities stimied, they decided to establish one of their own. In 1952 Opus founded a private school of higher studies at Pamplona, in the heart of the most Catholic part of Spain. Known as the General Studies of Navarre, it was similar to existing institutions of the Jesuits at Deusto and the Augustinians in the Escorial. By long tradition none but state universities could grant higher degrees. (Primo de Rivera's concession of the right to the Jesuits in 1928 was instrumental in his downfall.) Opus worked to end this monopoly, citing an article in the recent concordat giving the church the right to found schools at all levels of instruction. The General Studies of Navarre was at last empowered to grant university degrees in 1962, but not until long after the fortunes of Opus Dei had revived.

Meanwhile Opus was extending its interest in other directions. In 1947 it founded a publishing house which devoted itself to works on philosophical and contemporary topics presented at a popular level. Opus also gained control of three newspapers in Madrid and others in Barcelona, Valladolid, and León. It acquired a strong interest in the Banco Popular, one of the major banks of Madrid.[19] All of these undertakings began on a modest scale and did not rival the leaders in their fields, but they gave Opus a foothold in the banking, publishing, and other business worlds where it could taste the spirit of Spain's new capitalism.

In the fifties certain of its members turned to politics to achieve their ends. The leader of this group was Calvo Serer, already recognized as the spokesman for the order. He published an open attack on the ministry in 1953 in the French periodical *Ecrits de Paris.* In it he denounced both the Falangists and the liberal Catholics, scornfully calling the latter Christian democrats, the name that they later took up. He accused the two groups of being totalitarian and at the same time opening Spain to the leftists and anticlericals defeated in the Civil War. In their stead he called for a "Third Force" which would loosen economic regimentation and political centralization under a popular monarchy—the last item an appeal for the support of the monarchists disappointed at the failure of Franco to name the next king.

Although Calvo Serer presumably spoke only for himself, his article turned Opus into a political force. The ministry reacted energetically. Calvo Serer lost his editorship of the Consejo Superior's journal *Arbor,* but he remained a professor at the University of Madrid. A muted war developed in the next years between the politically inclined members of Opus and the minister of education Ruíz Giménez. Student troubles provided ammunition for the former, who blamed them on the dictatorial methods of the government and urged more emphasis on religious education. "The dilemma is this," Calvo Serer wrote, "either catechism and culture or the Civil Guard." [20] Thus the spokesmen of Opus Dei offered its philosophy as an alternative to the increasingly discredited policies of the ministry.

The student uprising in the spring of 1956 and continuing unrest gave the political leaders of Opus Dei their opportunity. Franco at once eliminated the men who represented the liberalization of 1951. Ruíz Giménez lost his job as minister of education, Fernández Cuesta his as secretary general of the Movimiento, while Laín Entralgo stepped down as rector of the University of Madrid. A year later, in February

[19] Whitaker, pp. 275–77, and Artigues, pp. 131–32 and 157–58.

[20] Rafael Calvo Serer, *España después de los tratados* (1954), quoted in Artigues, p. 153.

1957, Franco announced the appointment of a new ministry. Martín Artajo, moderate Catholic foreign minister since 1945, also disappeared. The men to enter the ministry stood for maintaining order while reducing economic regimentation. Franco placed a general at the head of *gobernación* who could be counted on to crush opposition. His new foreign minister was Fernando María Castiella, a loyal servant of the regime who had fought in Russia in the Blue Division, had negotiated the Concordat of 1953 in Rome, and now favored rapprochement with Western Europe. But the most significant appointments brought known members of Opus Dei for the first time into the government. The new minister of commerce, Alberto Ullastres, was an Opus numerary, and the minister of finance, Mariano Navarro Rubio, a supernumerary. Admiral Carrero Blanco, one of the closest advisers of Franco, who remained in the cabinet as subsecretary to him, took on as his technical secretary another member of Opus, Laureano López Rodó.

Whether Opus Dei had a concrete political policy, as its enemies claimed, or only religious objectives, as its spokesmen maintained, Franco had decided to turn to its men to fill the most sensitive positions in his ministry. Ever since the forties the belief had grown in the mysterious and irresistible power of Opus Dei. To the enemies of both Franco and the order, the appearance of two of its members in the cabinet and rumors of its influence with others like Carrero Blanco confirmed the reality of its occult power. They tended to forget that Franco had never let himself become ensnared by any group.

The economic doctrines of the Opus Dei ministers were to have more impact on the future of Spain than their religious connections, however. More than anyone else Navarro Rubio, Ullastres, and López Rodó were to determine the course of Spain's economy in the next decade. Navarro Rubio had been a director of Opus's Banco Popular, Ullastres was a professor of economics and vice-governor of another bank, and López Rodó, only thirty-seven, was a professor of administrative law. The three represented Opus Dei's infiltration of the university and business worlds. In spirit and associations they belonged to the circle of the large banks and corporate entrepreneurs, and as such they would throw their weight in favor of fewer economic restrictions and Spain's integration with the rest of Europe.

The new government faced a difficult economic situation. Wage increases granted in 1956 to curtail strikes only accelerated the inflationary spiral. By 1958 the price index was nearly eleven times the prewar level, 56 percent higher than in 1952, wiping out the workers' recent gains, and inflation seemed out of control. Imports were running farther ahead of exports than ever. One reason was that the government kept the peseta pegged so high (42 to the dollar) that Spanish goods were pricing themselves out of the export market. The unrealistic rate of exchange also discouraged tourists and fostered a flourishing black market in foreign currencies. American aid no longer could match the balance of payments deficit. Between 1956 and the end of 1958 Spain's gold and dollar reserves dropped from 220 million dollars to 65 million, 3 million less than its foreign liabilities.

During 1958, the government, inspired by Castiella, Ullastres, and Navarro Rubio, moved to end Spain's economic isolation. It became an associate member of the Organization for European Economic Cooperation, originally made up of the countries receiving Marshall Plan aid. It also entered the International Monetary Fund and the International Bank for Reconstruction and Development (World Bank), bodies established by the Allies in 1944–45 to stabilize world currencies and help war-torn and underdeveloped countries.

In the winter of 1958–59 the public discovered that highly placed Spaniards had been illegally sending their capital to Swiss banks to protect themselves in case of a crash. The scandal forced the government to take vigorous action to save Spain's credit. Experts from the United States and the International Monetary Fund visited the country to analyze its economic condition. Desperately needing further foreign aid, Franco had no alternative but to agree to the terms imposed by the United States and the International Monetary Fund, although they meant dismantling the cherished state-regulated economy created at the end of the Civil War to implement a corporate autarky. On the whole the recommendations agreed with the ideas of Ullastres, Navarro Rubio, and the leading bankers. Spain must devalue the peseta and it must curtail government spending. It must abandon its economic controls and free foreign trade, especially with European countries. It must attract private capital from abroad to share in the development of industry. It should aim toward eventual association with the European Common Market, which had just been established by six Western European countries.

The Stabilization Plan, as these measures were called, was published in July 1959. The plan ended many domestic economic controls —eighteen government agencies disappeared, but not the INI, which was too well entrenched—and it tightened domestic credit. It devalued the peseta to sixty to the dollar, abolished import licenses for the most common items, and raised to 50 percent the share of stock in Spanish corporations that could be owned by foreigners. In return the United States, the International Monetary Fund, and private banks promised Spain 420 million dollars to support it through a period of readjustment to the new conditions. Spain also became a full-fledged member of the Organization for European Economic Cooperation, seen as a step toward its eventual inclusion in the Western European economic community. The pill was hard for Franco to swallow, since it reversed the accepted economic doctrines of the regime and meant outside supervision of his administration, but it was the price he had to pay for continuing support by the United States. Once again he showed that he was a tough unsentimental pragmatist rather than a doctrinaire.

After years of reckless government spending and soaring inflation, the Stabilization Plan committed Spain to enforced austerity. The immediate effect of devaluation was further price increases. Those who suffered most were the urban workers, for austerity measures deprived them of overtime pay while the credit squeeze on business almost doubled unemployment. The year 1960 was a hard one for the lower classes. In the countryside a disastrous harvest raised rural unemployment and encouraged peasants to abandon the land. It was no accident that this year saw a sudden increase in internal migration and the beginning of large-scale emigration to north Europe. On the other hand, the plan saved Spain's international economic position. By the end of 1959 its gold reserves had risen for the first time in years and stood at 100 million dollars. After the initial period of readjustment, the economy quickened in all areas. The Stabilization Plan laid the basis for the remarkable economic transformation of the next decade, with which we began our story, far more rapid even than that of the fifties.

The Moderado order had at last expired, after a long-drawn-out agony that began with the collapse of *caciquismo* in the second decade of the century. Despite the defeat of its opponents in the Civil War, it never regained control of the country. Like Primo de Rivera, Franco protected the entrenched groups, but he did not give them authority. Both dictators preferred to rely on the army and the church rather than the old wealthy classes. By 1950 Franco discovered that he must relax his punitive rule and revive the economy if he were not to strangle the country. For him and his advisers economic revival meant first of all industrialization. Though his enemies criticized him for neglecting agriculture, it was the proper choice, for agricultural reform could never by itself raise Spain's standard of living to European levels. Industrialization was carried out by large corporations sponsored by the state through the Instituto Nacional de Industria and through the larger banks. The result was the appearance of a new elite, made up of high government officials, bankers, technocrats, and corporation managers, similar to that of Germany, France, and other industrial countries. Franco had not attacked the old Moderado oligarchy in frontal assault, he had simply reduced its importance. Large landowners and industrialists merged with the new elite in a subordinate role, just as more than a century before the former owners of *mayorazgos* and *señoríos,* which the liberals abolished, had joined the Moderado oligarchy. Franco's early laws had also placed foreign investors in a secondary role, but the Stabilization Plan, which both Spanish bankers and foreign lenders demanded, reopened the door to them as partners with the new Spanish elite.

Under Franco the forces of the twentieth century which had opposed the Moderado order demonstrated that they were indispensable. The country could not industrialize and treat its workers like convicts, or the university students, who would be its future professionals, technocrats, and scientists, like children. Tacitly if not legally, Franco recognized their right to press their demands, and this meant giving their due to the forces he had defeated in the war. Indeed, he had no alternative. The rural half of Spain that had furnished votes for the Moderados and soldiers for Franco's army was joining the cities, either physically by migration or spiritually by imitation. Moreover, the dominant foreign powers, which had made possible his victory, now condemned a vindictive attitude toward workers and intellectuals. The Moderado order had welcomed Franco as its savior. In twenty years of rule he had had to forsake it in order to survive himself.

16

Conclusion

1

In seeking to disentangle the history of Spain since the eighteenth century, I have followed the evolution of three tensions that have been central to the whole period. The first and most obvious was ideological or temperamental, between those who championed parliamentary government and economic progress and sought to learn from the contemporary experiences of other nations and those who defended accepted beliefs and practices. Conservative clergymen were long the most vocal spokesmen of the second group, with the result that the two contending parties frequently appeared simply as clericals ad anticlericals. This was true at the Cortes of Cadiz (although some of their "anticlericals" were Jansenist monks and priests), it was true in the Carlist War, in the Revolution of 1868, in the Tragic Week of 1909, and in the Second Republic and the Civil War. The clerical issue tended to cover the fact that differing political philosophies or ideologies were essentially rationalizations to defend or attack entrenched institutions and privileged social positions. So prominent was this struggle in the whole period that it led many observers and historians to accept the existence of "two Spains," as if the country had become divided into two different peoples.

The second tension sprang from the unequal division of land in vast areas of central and southern Spain, where a struggling peasantry dug their existence from tiny overworked plots and an opulent landowning oligarchy lorded it over downtrodden agricultural workers. From Charles III to the Second Republic reformers who sought to aid the rural poor failed before the immensity of the task and the power of the oligarchy. The only attempt that produced results, the disentail of church and municipal lands in the nineteenth century, ended in strengthening the class of large owners.

The third tension was geographic, between the arid, depopulated rural central plateau and the urban, watered periphery of the north and east—between Old and New Castile, supported usually by Andalusia, on the one hand, and the Basque Provinces and Catalonia, joined at times by Galicia, Asturias, Navarre, and Valencia, on the other. The Carlist War took this form, as did the conflicts of the First Republic (except that here Andalusia acted against Castile). In one guise the tension appeared as the resentment of industrial entrepreneurs against agrarian partisans of low tariffs, and in another as Basque and Catalan nationalist movements against Castilian centralism. The Civil War was its most violent manifestation, for by this time it also involved the conflict between industrial proletariat and capitalist class typical of a budding industrial society. As on this occasion, the city of Madrid was often aligned with the periphery.

All three issues emerged in the eighteenth century and, although their form evolved, continued through the nineteenth century and were at the heart of the cataclysm of the 1930's. Since then, however, the first two have lost much of their virulence, while the third has taken new form. Ideologies have not disappeared from Spain, but as in other parts of the world they no longer inspire the blind following they once enjoyed. Although Franco has continued to evoke the red specter of the war years in his attacks on his opponents, he has always been a pragmatist and the actions of his governments have belied his words. Spain has opened trade with eastern Europe and continued cultural and economic relations with the Cuba of Fidel Castro despite the displeasure of its North American ally.

On the other side, students and workers still like to think that they are inspired by some form of Marxism or other collectivist doctrine, but too many changes have taken place in Spain and the rest of Europe since the Civil War for Spanish revolutionaries to convince a wide audience that any specific doctrine offers the only solution to the nation's injustices. What is more significant, the new generation of rebels no longer finds its principal enemy in the clergy. They may fear Opus Dei and dislike certain conservative prelates, but the new tone of the church since the time of Pope John XXIII, and the appearance of revolutionary young priests encouraging militant Catholic labor unions and cooperating with illegal workers' commissions, have convinced the rebels that they have friends within the church. One would find scant acceptance among younger Spaniards of the argument that Spain's problems could be solved if the Jesuits were expelled and the crucifix removed from the classroom. This fact alone means that the ideological conflict that raged from the Cortes of Cadiz to the Civil War has lost its strength. Like Franco, his opposition has become more pragmatic.

Franco never attacked the rural oligarchy directly—after all, they were one of the sources of his strength—but his governments did try to improve the lot of the small farmer with irrigation, parcelary concentration, credit for farm machinery, and other programs. None of these measures would have brought the good life to the masses of Spain's rural poor, especially the myriads of landless workers in New Castile and Andalusia for whom they did little. Independent developments, however, began to reduce the age-old problem. The great rural exodus of the late fifties and sixties offered a solution that reformers of two centuries had been unable to find. It did not provide land for the landless, as liberals and Republicans wanted to do, nor did it create cooperative farms such as the socialists proposed. It began instead to remove excess hands and mouths from the countryside. In the sixties the peasants who remained in the towns which had been cursed for generations with small holdings were buying tractors or going into grazing, either way turning agriculture into a business enterprise. Meanwhile Andalusian *latifundistas* began to complain that the scarcity of labor was forcing them to pay more than they could afford. They were ceasing to be lords of their local subjects and having to bargain with them as business associates. Spanish agriculture still had plenty of ills, and the unplanned exodus was bringing new ones, but the classic problems of a vast impoverished proletariat and marginal peasant farmers were becoming things of the past. When the national economy suffered a recession in 1967–68, some recent emigrants found the new rural conditions encouraging enough to return.

Of the three conflicts, the one between center and periphery has remained the most tenacious. Catalans and Basques fought Franco more bitterly than any ruler since Isabel II, and he retaliated with oppressive measures against their culture and self-government. The regime sought steadily to strengthen central Spain vis-à-vis these regions. It cooperated with the major banks to unify the financial structure of the country and make Madrid the center of it. It encouraged the development of heavy industry in Madrid and other cities of the center and south. Except for two in Franco's native Galicia, the seven "poles of development" established by the four-year Development Plan of 1963 were all in this area.[1]

So far these policies have not destroyed the human and economic potential behind Catalan and Basque regionalism. The momentum from earlier periods and the better location of these two zones have kept their population growing faster than that of the center. Between 1941 and 1955 Barcelona province accounted for 44 percent of the

[1] See p. 21.

net immigration registered by all Spanish provinces, and Madrid was second with 35 percent. In 1960 thirteen peninsular provinces showed a net balance of immigration of workers. All but Madrid and Zaragoza were in the periphery of the north and east, and the highest was Barcelona.[2] The percent of the population located in each of the major areas of the peninsula at various dates in the twentieth century is as follows:

DISTRIBUTION OF POPULATION, 1900–1967

(excluding Balearic and Canary Islands)

	Percent of Total Population				Percent of
	1900	1950	1960	1967*	Area
East	24.4%	25.0%	26.1%	26.7%	16.5%
South	19.9	20.9	20.3	19.8	17.7
North	21.8†	20.0	20.0	20.0	12.8†
Center	33.9†	34.1	33.6	33.5	53.0†
	100.0	100.0	100.0	100.0	100.0
4 Catalan Provinces	11.0	12.1	13.5	14.7	6.5
3 Basque Provinces	3.4	4.0	4.7	6.9	1.5
Madrid Province	4.3	7.2	9.0	10.3	1.6
Totals	17,937,000	26,761,000	29,043,000	30,365,000	492,454 km.^{2}

* According to estimates in Instituto Nacional de Estadística, *Anuario estadístico*, 1968, pp. 466–67.

† These figures differ from those in the table on page 116. In that table Santander province was included in the center although it is located on the northern coast. In 1797 it was part of Burgos Province, and its population for that date could not be separated from that of the rest of the province, which belongs in the center. For purposes of comparison, its population had to be included in the center in 1900 as well.

The eastern seaboard steadily gained a greater share of the total population, until in 1967 it reached almost 27 percent, while the remaining

[2] Angel Cabo Alonso, "Valor de la inmigración madrileña," *Estudios geográficos*, XXII (1961), 361, and Jesús García Fernández, "El movimiento migratorio de trabajadores en España, *ibid.*, XXV (1964), 144.

areas showed little relative change after 1900. Although the demographic evolution appears at first sight to continue the pattern of peripheral growth initiated in the seventeenth century, there is an important difference from previous periods.[3] In the twentieth century the growth of the north and east has been concentrated in the industrial Basque and Catalan regions. Between 1900 and 1967 Catalonia rose from 11 to almost 15 percent of the total population of the peninsula, and the Basque Provinces doubled their share from 3.4 to 6.9 percent. Without the growth of these two regions, both the north and the east would have registered declines since 1900 relative to the rest of the peninsula. After 1950 industrialization and the flight from the countryside became the main factors behind the evolution of the demographic pattern. Aided by government-inspired industrialization, cities of the center like Zaragoza and Valladolid were growing as fast as Barcelona, but their growth could not offset the thousands of rural emigrants from the central area, many of whom by the logic of the situation ended up in Basque and Catalan cities. Only Madrid acted as a demographic counterpoise. Because of its position as national political and financial capital, official pressure for its industrialization, and its attraction for tourists, its province grew faster than any other, rising between 1900 and 1967 from 4.3 to 10.3 percent of the total population of the peninsula. Politically, however, its expansion was a doubtful counterpoise, since in the Civil War and earlier it had sided with the periphery.

After 1950 the government tried to placate the Basques and Catalans by relaxing the antiregionalist measures taken during the Civil War, allowing publication of works in their languages. These measures did not calm their hatred of Franco. Local nationalism remained very much alive, encouraged by young priests who used their languages in church services and participated in underground movements. The University of Barcelona was second only to Madrid's in the daring of its student protests. Catalan and Basque factory workers and Asturian miners led the opposition to wage control and syndicalist regimentation with strikes and violent demonstrations. All of these types of activity, however, revealed an evolution in the nature of the conflict between these regions and the central government that had been foreshadowed in the Civil War. More than a geographic division between zones of different economic activities, or even a drive for the rights of local nationalities, the conflict was now a struggle of the employed groups, industrial workers and future technicians, against a centralized state bent on preventing economic disruption and thus in effect protecting the interests of the corporate financial elite.

The fact that all three historic tensions have been changing rapidly

[3] Compare the table on p. 116.

under Franco suggests that one might profitably look for some common factor involved in their current evolution.

2

When Unamuno sought to explain what was wrong with Spain at the end of the nineteenth century, he drew a contrast between the political classes who were divided between the partisans of Europeanization and the defenders of Hispanic purity, on the one hand, and on the other, the masses of the common people, the bearers of the true Spanish tradition. The first, who made the news and were the subject of written history, according to Unamuno were merely the frothy waves on the surface of the deep and silent sea of the real Spain. He mocked General Prim who in 1868 spoke of "destroying the obstacles in the midst of the storm" and the men of the Restoration of 1875 who claimed to be tying together the broken strands of Spain's history.

> It was not the Restoration of 1875 that reunited the thread of Spanish history, it was the millions of men who continued performing the same activities as always, those millions for whom the sun was the same after September 29, 1868 as it was before, for whom the tasks were the same, and the songs the same with which they followed the furrow of the plow. And in truth they did not tie anything together, for nothing had been broken.[4]

Unamuno recognized that there were two profoundly different levels of life in Spain, which he called the historical and the intrahistorical—we might say the political and the apolitical. Reading deeper, we could also call them the urban and the rural. When he asserted that the eternal Spanish tradition lived in the depths of the peasantry and rose out of it to save the nation in times of crisis, like 1808, he was himself inspired by a romantic urban view of the purity of the rural people.

Some persons soon began to study the nature of the peasantry, Unamuno's intrahistory, but they were ethnographers or social anthropologists, not historians. Since his day the study of peasant life in various parts of the world has become one of the principal activities of anthropologists. They distinguish peasants from the primitive tribes which had earlier attracted them, in that primitive peoples have virtually no frame of reference outside their own society, whereas peasants are part of a society that is greater than their own. To quote a leading American anthropologist, A. L. Kroeber: "Peasants are definitely rural

[4] Miguel de Unamuno, *En torno al casticismo* ("Colección austral," Madrid: Espasa–Calpe, 1943), p. 28.

—yet live in relation to market towns; they form a class segment of a larger population which usually contains urban centers, sometimes metropolitan capitals. They constitute part-societies with part-cultures." [5] Their inclusion in a society whose authority is beyond their control places them in a state of tension with the outside world. To determine the nature and effects of this tension has been one of the quests of the social anthropologists.

The scholar who has dealt most brilliantly with this question in Spain is Julian Pitt-Rivers, whose *The People of the Sierra* is the product of a period spent living in a *pueblo* in the mountains of the province of Cadiz in the early 1950's. His observation of the patterns of life of Alcalá de la Sierra, as he calls the town in his book, led him to conclude that its society was basically egalitarian. The only essential differences recognized among themselves by the people of the *pueblo* consisted of age and sex and characteristics derived from them, such as marital status and ability to support a family. Occupation, insofar as it was carried on within the economic unit of the *pueblo*, had little bearing on one's social status. The common people of Alcalá were not its only inhabitants, however. There was another group whose wealth, profession, or official position brought them into direct relation with the outside world. State appointees like the *alcalde*, the schoolteachers, the doctor, and the civil guards mostly came from other places and thus did not belong fully to the society of the *pueblo*, and this was true also of the priest. The larger landowners, whose income permitted them to reside in Malaga or Jerez and return only for vacations, had chosen to escape from the cultural limitations of the *pueblo* and enter the large world of Andalusia or Spain. Because of the existence of this varied group of people who did not fit into the society of the town, the term "*pueblo*," besides meaning the town as a physical entity, had a second meaning, which was the common people, those who had only local interests and stood united in face of the upper group which represented outside authority.

The culture of the *pueblo*, in both senses of the word, reflected the tension between the egalitarian local community and the authoritarian state.

> The formally constituted institutions controlled by the ruling group or the state and the activities wherein the pueblo avoids them stand in opposition to one another. The latter spring from the network of interpersonal relations within the community and depend upon the memories and cultural traditions of the pueblo rather than on the written word. The former owe their existence to authority delegated by a central

[5] Quoted in Robert Redfield, *Peasant Society and Culture, an Anthropological Approach to Civilization* (Chicago: University of Chicago Press, 1956), pp. 29–30.

power. . . . The two systems are, at the same time, interdependent and in opposition. They are both part of the same structure. If a tension exists between the two, it is as much a condition of one as of the other.[6]

Through a study of historical sources, notably the *catastro* of the Marquis de la Ensenada of the 1750's,[7] Pitt-Rivers sought the origins and causes of the tension between *pueblo* and state. In the eighteenth century superior authority was represented by the church and the seigneurial lord more than by the state (that is, the king), and it was administered by local men. Presumably the people of the *pueblo*, feeling little outside interference in their lives, did not experience the state of tension of their descendants. In the nineteenth century much of the basis for the *pueblo's* political independence disappeared with the sale of its municipal and church lands, and under the Restoration of 1875 officials appointed by the state came in to administer it. "Authority no longer comes from God but from Madrid." [8] The modern conflict between *pueblo* and state became manifest in the appearance of the anarchist movement about 1880. Andalusian anarchism represented the defense of the rights of the *pueblo* against outside encroachment. "The concept of the pueblo as the unique political unit was so deeply embedded in the outlook of the peasants that it became a corner-stone in Anarchist policy. The Anarchists sought, in fact, not to break this political monopoly, but rather to become empowered with it and to eliminate the governing class which represented external influences." [9]

In his search for the causes of the structural tensions in Alcalá, Pitt-Rivers concentrates on the relations between the egalitarian *pueblo* and the authoritarian state. That is, he sees the tensions arising out of a political and economic conflict. There is another side of the explanation that he tends to lose sight of, although he gives many examples of it; the accompanying tension between the culture of the *pueblo* and that of the city. In Kroeber's words, peasants are not only a part-society, they are a part-culture, and the ruling group of Alcalá represented not only the state but a different way of life, one based on education and the written word. The larger landowners who could afford to move their families to the city spoke condescendingly of the *pueblo*. "This place is dead," "Nothing ever happens here." [10] The common people responded by referring to such persons as *señoritos*, a term which

[6] J. A. Pitt-Rivers, *The People of the Sierra* (Chicago: University of Chicago Press, 1961), pp. 200–201. This and following quotations from Pitt-Rivers are reprinted by permission of the author and S. G. Phillips, Inc., Publisher.

[7] See p. 58.

[8] *Ibid.*, p. 220.

[9] *Ibid.*, p. 17.

[10] *Ibid.*, p. 16.

implied a curious mixture of respect and scorn at their inability to do a hard day's work. The *señoritos* had joined the wider social group of the urban middle classes and as a result escaped the moral sanctions of the *pueblo*. The common people imagined the city as a place where one went to do things that he could not do in the *pueblo* without loss of reputation—keep a mistress, become a prostitute.[11]

Other anthropologists have attached more importance than Pitt-Rivers to the cultural distinction between city and town. Robert Redfield, an American scholar who did much to establish the study of peasantry as a discipline, sought to define the nature of the distinction. He called the intellectual frames of reference of educated men and of common people respectively the "great tradition" and the "little tradition."

> In a civilization there is a great tradition of the reflective few, and there is a little tradition of the largely unreflective many. The great tradition is cultivated in schools or temples; the little tradition works itself out and keeps itself going in the lives of the unlettered in their village communities. The tradition of the philosopher, theologian, and literary man is a tradition consciously cultivated and handed down; that of the little people is for the most part taken for granted and not submitted to much scrutiny or considered refinement and improvement.
>
> If we enter a village within a civilization we see at once that the culture there has been flowing into it from teachers and exemplars who never saw that village, who did their work in intellectual circles perhaps far away in space and time.[12]

The two traditions belong to the urban upper classes and the rural common people. Because it is outside his subject, Redfield does not consider which tradition the common people of the cities adopt.

There is a striking similarity between Redfield's great and little traditions and Unamuno's history and intrahistory. Both were trying to put into words a reality that they had perceived in societies with peasant masses: two distinct levels of culture existing side by side and to a certain extent interdependent. Whereas Redfield concluded that most innovation came from above, Unamuno believed that any initiative leading to national achievements would come from below, from the uncorrupted peasantry. The two views are not strictly incompatible, but Unamuno did add a refinement to the concept which is essential to a full understanding of the relationship between the two levels in

[11] *Ibid.*, pp. 70–81. See also Julian Pitt-Rivers, "Honour and Social Status," in *Honour and Shame: the Values of Mediterranean Society*, ed. J. G. Peristiany (Chicago: University of Chicago Press, 1966), pp. 19–77, esp. 50–51 and 61–73.

[12] Redfield, p. 70.

Spain. He pointed out that at the historical or great tradition level a conflict was in progress between Europeanizers and defenders of *casticismo*. The barrenness of their controversy explains why he looked to the common people to save the country. With this additional feature, the concept of two traditions helps to bring to light much of the motive force behind the last two centuries of Spanish history.

One suspects that for some time before the eighteenth century, probably during most of the period of Habsburg rule, Redfield's model of two unified traditions describes fairly accurately the relationship between the Spanish countryside and the cultural centers. In the eighteenth century, however, the great tradition split in two—in the fashion Unamuno pointed out. This was the meaning of the Enlightenment and the ideological conflict of the next two centuries. Although the Enlightenment derived much of its structure and content from medieval and classical thought, it made its appearance in conflict with the dominant religious culture. The Enlightenment and the doctrines that later evolved out of it, liberalism, socialism, and anarchism, struck at the roots of the old great tradition, for to doubt the teachings of the church and demand free expression was no superficial matter. We can therefore alter the model and describe Spain's subsequent history as involving a conflict between the bearers of two great traditions, who struggled for control of the instruments of political authority. Because of the constant interaction between great tradition and little tradition, the conflict affected the latter and in so doing turned the relation between the two levels into a factor in political life. More properly speaking, those who were involved in the conflict exploited the relation between the great and little traditions as best they could for their own ends. From time to time in the course of our story we have observed the political effects of the separation between the educated political classes and the unsophisticated common people, especially the divorce between cities and countryside. It will be helpful to review the story briefly, using the concepts just introduced.

In the eighteenth century the bearers of the great tradition were a small minority inhabiting urban islands in a great rural ocean. Only about 10 percent of the population lived in cities, and most of these were uneducated. Because at the outset the little tradition reflected the earlier form of the great tradition, the conservative Catholic view of the universe and society, it was easy for those defending the old great tradition to mobilize large sections of the common people, both urban and rural, against the new forms of thought. They presented them as something alien and wicked, a threat to the bases of Spanish society, to monarchy, and particularly to religion. This happened most clearly during the Napoleonic war, when the clergy aroused the lower classes first against the French and then against the Cadiz Liberals, whom they depicted as bearers of the French poison. The restoration of Ferdinand in 1814 rested on the loyalty of the common people to the older tradition.

During the first half of the nineteenth century, however, the urban lower classes, who had welcomed Ferdinand back and excoriated the Liberals as eagerly as did the peasants, slowly adopted ideas from the new, rational, Europeanizing great tradition. They were in a position to hear the arguments of the Liberals, Progresistas, and Democrats. During the Carlist War, the urban proletariat joined the radical elements of the shopkeeper class in sacking monasteries and murdering monks and friars, and after 1840 factory workers in Barcelona began to follow socialist leaders. Carlist strength lay in the north, where economically independent Basque, Navarrese, and Catalan peasants under clerical inspiration fought for the old order, for the intransigent Church and the absolute monarchy. The active persons in the cities of these regions, like Bilbao and Barcelona, including the working classes, supported the cause of Isabel, and they successfully withstood Carlist sieges. Most of the urban lower classes, however, could receive only a rudimentary view of the new political philosophies in the form of slogans and catch phrases. One could say that beneath the two great traditions there were now two little traditions, one urban and one rural. Their opposing conceptions of the nature of the good life and the correct source for knowledge of social organization—revealed and traditional, as opposed to rational and empirical—made them distinct traditions.

The rural people of arid Spain did not become involved in the civil struggles of the nineteenth century in the same way as the Carlist peasants, but they too had their role in politics. While there were Carlists in these areas, there was also a rural oligarchy that benefited from the confiscation and sale of church lands, and it kept the countryside quiet during the Carlist War. The oligarchy rejected most radical doctrines, but it was not in its interest to arouse the peasants and landless *jornaleros* with an appeal to traditional beliefs, and it evidently managed to control the local clergy as well. Later in the century, when the landowners had become a pillar of the Moderado regime and had to defend it against Progresistas and Republicans, who were urban and peripheral, they discovered in the peasants a precious resource. Besides furnishing the manpower for their exploitation of the land, the rural masses provided docile recruits for the army, and by the end of the century they could also vote.

The techniques used to keep the peasantry on the conservative side of the ideological conflict have not received much attention. Historians have tended to see *caciquismo* as the use of local patronage, stiffened when needed by recourse to economic reprisals and the Civil Guard, but this is surely not the whole story. In one way, *caciquismo* seems so natural as hardly to need an explanation. The rural people were

imbued with the older tradition and looked with suspicion on those who believed in new ways. Although peasants' sons and daughters migrated to the cities throughout the nineteenth century, there was insufficient interchange between the two worlds for the cities to seem near and familiar. It is true that there were intermediate places, like many *cabezas de partido*, whose affinities were in some ways with the cities and in others with the *pueblos*. Nevertheless, when a peasant arrived at the provincial or national capital in his rural dress on business or to seek employment, he felt conspicuous and ill at ease. He knew that city dwellers applied the contemptuous term *paleto* (hick) to him, and he sought the company of people from his own town or region for protection and reassurance. Peasants were alienated from the city and what it stood for.

There may seem little connection between such alienation and the political arena, for there was no direct reason for it to make the peasants support the political objectives of the Moderado oligarchy. This was not how it worked. All that was necessary was to keep the rural masses away from the influence of the urban reformers. Commitment to the oligarchy was not a prerequisite for *caciquismo*, nor was a strong religious conviction, only passivity and estrangement from the city, so that, in Unamuno's image, the peasants would remain the deep silent sea beneath the frothy waves. The rest of the process can be imagined. Priests, *alcaldes*, and reliable schoolteachers appointed from outside, as in Pitt-Rivers' Alcalá, could paint the cities as morally evil, where radical movements attacked God and property. As late as 1964 in a small town in the province of Avila in Old Castile, the *alcalde*, who was also the boys' schoolteacher, summed up for me in two brief sentences what he considered the essential features of the nearby mill town of Béjar. "It has many factories," he said. "There there are *rojos* (reds)." He and his wife, who taught the girls, had both come from the city, but they were much loved by the *pueblo* for their dedication to the local children. I visited the town with an elderly priest, no friend of *rojos* either, who had once served that parish but had been transferred to a larger town nearby. As we walked down the only street of the town, women and children, surprised at his presence, came out of the doorways to greet him fondly and kiss his hand. Their reaction reflected an age now rapidly disappearing. The corollary would have been, in time of elections, to vote as the priest and *alcalde* suggested, in a time of civil strife to send their sons to the army that the town leaders favored. "When they ask me to vote," an old farmer of Alcalá said to Pitt-Rivers, "I ask who for, and when they tell me who for, I vote. And if they don't ask me to vote I stay at home and mind my own business." [13]

[13] Pitt-Rivers, p. 159.

Two cases stand out where by the end of the nineteenth century the rural people came under the influence of urban doctrines. The first was in the original centers of Carlist strength. Navarre, where there were no major cities, remained true to the Carlist faith, but the Basque and Catalan peasantry joined urban middle classes behind the demand for local autonomy. Ideologically the change was not abrupt, because the new nationalisms continued the Carlist hatred of centralization and glorified local *fueros* and traditions much as the Carlists had done. Taking their cue from Romantic writers and poets, Catalan and Basque merchants and industrialists discovered how to gain support among the rural classes for their struggles with Madrid. The movements glorified the speech and customs of the countryside, where Castilian language and modern ways were still foreign, and in this way tied the peasants to what was basically an urban struggle against the centralist, agrarian policies of the national government. What had happened was that the urban middle classes had discovered how to appear to be the defenders of the old tradition. After 1900 they used the peasants against their own workers, who were becoming anarchist and socialist and could be painted as radicals infested with foreign ideas, just as the Carlist clergy had once done with the liberals. The whole process was a variation of the *caciquismo* of central Spain in an area where the peasantry had become politically aware. Catalan nationalism had an ambiguous career as a result. Until after the First World War it was used by the local dominant groups alternately against the central government and in alliance with the central government against the urban proletariat. Their case was not unique. Propertied classes in France and Germany were using nationalism in the form of rural populism in much the same way.

The other case, the spread of anarchism through rural Andalusia at the end of the nineteenth century, is almost the reverse. Pitt-Rivers explains it as a natural defense of the rights of the *pueblo* against the encroachment of the state, but the phenomenon was more complex. It did not occur in the central *meseta,* although the state was also encroaching on local affairs. One of the reasons was certainly the difference in size of towns, far larger on the average in Andalusia than in central Spain. Even though the Andalusian economy was based on agriculture, its towns had distinctly urban characteristics, with merchants, craftsmen, and a ruling group, which as Pitt-Rivers shows in Alcalá was not part of the egalitarian *pueblo* society. The *latifundistas* also belonged to this group, even if they lived in the capitals and appeared only for vacations. To the common people this group was responsible for their economic hardships and was the bearer of an alien culture. Because of its proximity and visibility, the ruling group could not maintain the fiction before the *pueblo* that the common enemy was someone in the cities with new ideas. Instead, when wandering anarchist missionaries came preaching their new doctrines against the local rulers, they found willing listeners, both among the agricultural workers and the artisans. Like Catalan and Basque nationalism in the north, anarchist doctrines echoed the accepted norms of the local common people: in this case social equality, self-rule, and distribution of land to all. But unlike the north, in Andalusia the lower classes were adopting a little tradition derived from the new great tradition. Their millenarian visions of the future—*comunismo libertario* was one of the terms—were related to the sophisticated doctrines of proletarian revolutionary leaders much as the religious beliefs of the rural masses were to the lessons taught in theological seminaries. The working classes of Andalusian towns, in effect, were experiencing the same process as those of the more industrialized cities of the north had done earlier in the century.

Andalusian anarchists ceased to be part of the silent sea, but they did not become reliable legions for progressive Spaniards. They only mobilized for action sporadically, in outbursts of frenzy, which usually did not coincide with a national struggle. They did not believe in voting, so they were no help against *caciquismo*. Indeed, they remained fundamentally suspicious of the cities, which for them embodied the sins of their ruling oligarchy, and this suspicion hindered their effective organization.[14] The gifted English observer and historian of Spain Gerald Brenan has recounted an experience at the beginning of the Civil War:

> I was standing on a hill watching the smoke and flames of some two hundred houses in Malaga mount into the sky. An old Anarchist of my acquaintance was standing beside me.
>
> "What do you think of that?" he asked.
>
> I said: "They are burning down Malaga."
>
> "Yes," he said: "they are burning it down. And I tell you—not one stone will be left on another stone—no, not a plant nor even a cabbage will grow there, so that there may be no more wickedness in the world." [15]

Anarchism made little headway in the vast central area of Spain, running from Extremadura in the southwest through the plateau of the two Castiles to Aragon in the northeast, where population was sparse and grouped in small units and the proportion of landowning peasants was higher than in the south. Here there were only eight cities in 1900 of over 20,000 people, compared with nineteen in Andalusia; for although the area comprised twenty provinces, most of the provincial capitals did not reach that figure. Discounting Madrid, which

[14] *Ibid.*, pp. 17–18.

[15] Gerald Brenan, *Spanish Labyrinth*, p. 189.

belonged to another world, only one twentieth of the population of the area lived in these cities. At the other extreme, a third of the total population was in towns of less than one thousand persons, which could hardly have had a ruling group with outside interests and where the priest would have represented the bearer of the great tradition. Even in larger towns most of the people remained loyal to the old beliefs, as late as the Civil War. Much the same could be said for the rural areas of the rest of Spain, except among the Basque, Navarrese, Catalan, and Andalusian towns, where Carlism, local nationalism, or anarchism were making headway. In the silent rural areas lay the hidden strength of the traditionalists in their fight against the reform programs of the modernizers. Without this apolitical but reliable mass to fall back on for votes, soldiers, and labor, the oligarchy would have had to compromise with progressive Spain long before the middle of the twentieth century.

3

At the very end of his book, Pitt-Rivers writes:

> Yet today the divergence between the national rulers and the pueblo grows less. State education, the radio, the cinema, easy communications and the experience of military service all in their different ways carry the culture of urban society to Alcalá.[16]

The cultural integration he describes had begun at least half a century earlier. Two related developments are involved. The first is simply the urbanization of Spain, which has made it less and less a rural country. Urban population began to assume a larger share of the total population in the second half of the nineteenth century, and it continued at a faster pace in the twentieth.[17] In 1900 cities of over 20,000 population accounted for 21 percent of the population, double the figure for 1800. In 1930 the proportion was 31 percent; in 1950, 40 percent; in 1960, 45 percent. In 1970 it was about 50 percent. The massive rural exodus of the last fifteen years has depopulated vast regions of the countryside.

At the same time the towns have been coming into closer contact with urban culture. I have described some of the means by which the city has invaded the town: the appearance of motor transport and the extension of the highway network, the spread of electricity and the telephone. First colorful local costumes disappeared in the face of cheaper factory made dark cottons and corduroys; then the radio began

[16] Pitt-Rivers, p. 223.
[17] See above, pp. 20–22 and 116.

to drive out folk songs and dances. About the time Pitt-Rivers was in Alcalá the process suddenly accelerated as a result of the burgeoning economic transformation of the country. An example from my own experience will illustrate the point.

In 1951 I spent two weeks with my wife and son in a small town in the Alcarria, a poor rough region about one hundred kilometers northeast of Madrid. The trip had been arranged in advance by mail, for there was no public transportation into Jaranda, as I shall call the town. After changing buses in the provincial capital of Guadalajara and taking one of prewar vintage which rattled and shook for what seemed an interminable time along an unpaved country road, we descended at Masegoso, the stop nearest to our destination. Here we were met by a man of advanced age who had come from Jaranda with his mule to fetch us. We walked for eight to ten kilometers over fragrant hills of thyme and rosemary and through narrow gorges past small grain fields set between rocky outcroppings, while our guide described to whom each field belonged and how some owners were planting vines on a trial basis. During the Civil War the front line had run just south of Jaranda, and we passed first the Republican trenches and then on a hill opposite those of the Nationalists, both makeshift shallow affairs in front of which the soldiers had piled occasional mounds of loose rock to protect snipers. Italian troops had occupied Jaranda, and they had built a temporary road of some twelve kilometers in from the north to supply themselves, but since the war no motor transport had used it and it had fallen into disrepair.

The town was perched on the side of a narrow valley, at a place where an abundant natural spring had been turned into a town fountain. The settlement consisted of some sixty houses, with a population of less than 250 people. Its life could have changed little in the past century. There was no telephone or electricity. Lighting was by *candiles*, the simplest of metal oil lamps, which were hung from the wall or on the chimney. The central room of the houses was the kitchen, which had a vast fireplace whose fires served both for cooking and heat, burning wood gathered in the hills. The only public building was a church dating from the absolute monarchy. One house served as the town hall, and the second floor of another was both schoolhouse and residence of the teacher, but no schoolmistress had ever stayed more than a few months and we were able to live in her residence.

The economy was purely agricultural and largely self-sufficient. The townspeople owned sheep, which shepherds watched day and night in the hills except during the worst weather, and goats, which were taken out daily to pasture by a goatherd and slept along with the mules in the stables on the lowest level of the houses. The people raised vegetables for their consumption in the flat bottom of the valley on small irrigated plots called *huertas*. The basic market crop, however, was wheat, sown and harvested individually by each farmer on tiny strips of land scattered wherever feasible on the rolling hills above the town. The men plowed with mules and wooden plows, and everyone of both sexes who was old enough and strong enough shared in harvesting the wheat by hand with sickles, under the hot July sun. Later they used their mules to drag wooden sledges over the grain stalks on a stone-paved threshing ground, or *era,* above the town. When the kernels had been dislodged by this process, the men and women would winnow the grain by tossing it in the wind with wooden pitchforks.

In their official relations with the state, the townspeople carried on a stubborn defense of their independent economy. According to the regulations introduced by Franco, the entire wheat crop had to be sold to the National Wheat Service at controlled prices, and it all had to be taken to the city to be ground. The peasants obeyed the regulations only so far as they had to in order not to shock the authorities. Part of their harvest they kept for themselves, and part ended up in the black market. There were two mills on the stream, both officially closed. One was in ruin, but the other was inhabited by a miller and his family, and he kept it going clandestinely and ground the wheat needed by the town for its own consumption. When civil guards approached the town he was warned, and cleaned off the millstones, replaced the official seal on them, and shut off the water at the dam. There was also a town baker, a Catalan veteran of the Loyalist armies who had appeared after the war with his wife and children looking for a living. Once or twice a week he rose before dawn and built a fire in the town's old stone oven with wood he had collected. When the oven was hot, the peasant wives appeared with round loaves they had prepared the day before, letting them stand overnight to leaven, and the baker baked them, keeping one for every twelve he baked.

While we were there a peddlar came through with his mule loaded with dishes, pots, pans, cloth, and notions, which he spread out before the church. For such staples as olive oil and wine the men drove their mules to Masegoso or another town on the highway, and they picked up any mail that might be waiting. The young men did their military service, and some girls went off to be maids in Madrid in households that were properly recommended, and usually returned to marry. The girls who came back might wear printed cottons, but most women still dressed in black, and the men in dark corduroy. The town was too small to have a priest of its own; one came from time to time on foot or by mule from a nearby parish to say mass. Except for the experience of the Civil War, the outside world had never impinged much on the life of Jaranda. The townspeople could easily have kept the road open, if they had had any motivation to do so.

We returned to Jaranda thirteen years later. This time we drove into it by car, for the road had been repaired and extended so that it went through the town and out to another road. After repeated petitions to the civil governor of the province, Jaranda had recently obtained regular bus service on alternate days, joining it and the other towns on its road to the provincial capital. Although the older generation continued to wear dark clothes, the marriageable girls sported colored skirts and blouses. Little girls and boys were decked out for their first communion in white frilly dresses and formal suits, just as in the city. The baker and his oven had disappeared and the mill was abandoned, its dam empty and overgrown with reeds. All the harvest now went out by truck, and a regular delivery service brought in bread baked in a larger town and distributed it to the housewives according to prearranged orders. Jaranda even boasted an automobile, a Seat 600, the smallest car manufactured in Spain. It belonged to a tailor, who used it to market his suits to the surrounding territory. He kept in touch with his customers by telephone. A small, fresh, windowless building stood by the town fountain. It housed transformers to step down the electrical current coming into Jaranda for distribution to the houses. A television set had been installed in the building that served as town hall for the benefit of the community, and one enterprising peasant had turned his house into a bar, where he had a refrigerator and sold cold beer and soft drinks. There was now a regular schoolteacher for the children. The outside world now not only existed for Jaranda, it had invaded the town, and the younger people in particular were doing all within their power to become indistinct from it.

Only the agriculture had changed little. The town was waiting for parcelary concentration, and until such time the fields were too small and the soil too poor for anything but mule-drawn plows and hand harvesting. The more enterprising men were becoming impatient with the slow rate of economic change. Some were leaving their fields untilled and going to work in the cities, especially Madrid. Between 1950 and 1960 the population fell by a dozen people, but by 1964 the decline was more marked, although there was no census count. Even the largest landowner of all, the *alcalde*, had decided to abandon his lands and escape to the national capital to be a mason. Later we visited one family that had gone to Madrid, to a small apartment in a working-class suburb. The husband had a regular job and they were happy as urban proletariat, having exchanged the hot summers, freezing winters, and ceaseless drudgery of rural life for urban civilization, fixed working hours, and better schooling for their children. It did not matter to them that prosperous residents of Madrid were seeking ways to escape from urban crowding and air pollution to the open countryside, at least in summer.

The experience of Jaranda could be multiplied thousands of times through the remote regions of Spain. Roads and television were transforming life in the countryside. When Franco was celebrating twenty-five years of peace, my research took me through the rural areas of western Spain and Andalusia. I did not find a town which could not be reached by car and truck, although some of the roads were primitive beyond belief. Everywhere the story was of the penetration of urban culture and emigration. The large proportion of elderly people and children bore eloquent evidence of the depletion of young adults. The traditional rivalry between neighboring towns now took the form of boasting which had more television sets. They were in the town halls, bars, and wealthier homes, and everyone was free to gather around them and watch. The passion for spectator sports, formerly limited perforce to the cities, had spread throughout the country, and elderly men and women in tiny towns, who had probably never been inside a city bull ring, would discuss knowingly the latest *corrida* in Madrid. Spanish radio and television are commercial, so that any sporting event, movie, news broadcast, or other program is interspersed with advertisements for beer, cosmetics, banks, butane gas stoves, refrigerators, and more television sets. Electricity and highways were making all these products of modern civilization seem relevant and accessible to the peasant, even if he could not at present afford them. One observer found the people of a town in Guadalajara Province criticizing a radio program called "Agricultural Spain," which featured a peasant discussing rural problems. They felt that the speaker's use of rural mannerisms, which the producers had intended to appeal to his audience, served only to ridicule them. "He is too *paleto*," they said, unconsciously repeating the slur they had suffered from.[18] The dichotomy between the city and the *pueblo* had not disappeared—this is why so massive a rural exodus was in progress—but the city was fast losing its distance and hostility.

This transformation marks a profound break in the evolution of Spain. For over a century, between the war against Napoleon and the Civil War, the privileged groups cultivated support among the rural population by painting the bearers of progressive doctrines as enemies of a tradition which they claimed to share with the peasants. The common people of the countryside were culturally unprepared to look beyond these sermons to the real issues involved. By the time of the Second Republic, however, the proportion of the population living in cities was growing rapidly and peasant alienation was breaking down. Socialist and anarchist organizers were attracting rural support, although one suspects still mostly in the larger towns. Franco had to rely on outside help as well as peasant alienation to achieve his victory. The tremendous changes that have taken place since 1950 have completed the destruction of the social structure on which the Moderado order was based. The privileged sectors can no longer fall back on the

[18] Pérez Díaz, pp. 136–37.

countryside, for it no longer has the will or the strength to oppose the cities.

In this transformation one can see a basic reason why the three tensions that marked Spain's history for nearly two centuries have evolved sharply under Franco. The improving condition of the men who labor on the land in arid Spain is a central feature of breakdown of rural isolation, an effect of this "most singular agrarian reform of all time," as it has been called. The displacement of the church from the center of ideological controversy has resulted from the decision of young priests to support the urban proletariat. Unlike the majority of clergy of previous generations, who were more at home in rural parishes, young priests, like young peasants, no longer feel alien to the common people of the cities, and therefore join in their struggles. They believe, as did Pope Leo XIII seventy years earlier, that the future of the church lies in winning the new industrial proletariat, not in mobilizing the middle classes and peasantry against it. This decision, along with the changing outlook throughout Western Europe, has been instrumental in reducing ideological tensions in Spain since the Second World War. Finally, the end of rural alienation has been central to altering the nature of the conflict between center and periphery. As indicated earlier, the struggle of the peripheral areas now represents that of the employed groups against the forces in control of industry. The Civil War already had strong overtones of this conflict, but it also still represented the older conflicts between industrial and agricultural zones and between urban and rural Spain, which have since been outmoded.

The most persistent historical conundrum of Spain's recent history has been the reason for its inability to settle on a stable form of government once the French Revolution and Napoleonic invasion had destroyed the aura of absolute monarchy. As we saw in the second chapter, for over half a century the most popular answer was that the experience of Spaniards as a people in earlier ages endowed them with a collective character that was violent and incompatible with parliamentary government. Not all historians have been so gloomy, and other reasons besides national character have been proposed. One is the lack of a strong middle class, which presumably would have understood the workings and benefits of representative government and defended it before the rest of the country. Some, like Americo Castro, believe Spain's character, adverse to economic activity, precluded the growth of a bourgeoisie; others, like Sánchez Albornoz, believe it was stifled by the policies of the Habsburg rulers. Another answer is Spain's strong particularism, the loyalty to the culture and interests of local regions. For Ortega y Gasset, particularism, not only of regions but of interest groups, was an effect of Spain's historic lack of a guiding elite.[19] Recently the

[19] See above, pp. 30–32.

English historian Raymond Carr has argued that both regionalism and the weakness of the middle class stemmed from the poverty of the country, which prevented the development of a flourishing integrated economy. It also made impossible the mass education needed to create an enlightened electorate.[20]

Except for national character, whose effects have never been concretely demonstrated, all these explanations of instability have validity. But they all, in one way or another, indicate that the causes lie outside the history of the last two hundred years. They all see Spain suffering from a kind of original sin from which it had no escape. A different explanation, one that comes out of the life of the Spanish people during this period, is the lack of cultural integration between rural and urban Spaniards. It is obviously true that once the French Revolution and the Napoleonic invasion destroyed the aura of absolute monarchy, Spain did not have a class committed to parliamentary government that was strong enough to make it function on a permanent basis. Stated simply, however, this explanation implies that there was a stronger class opposed to parliamentary government. This was not the case, at least numerically. The progressive groups had facing them an enigmatic foe. It seemed small in numbers, unjustly privileged, and easily overthrown if the progressives could mobilize their forces. Yet, whenever the progressives appeared to have won the contest, their foe always turned out to have unexpected strength and managed to dislodge them. Partly the fault lay with the progressive groups. The middle and working classes could unite to overthrow the oligarchy, but they regularly fell out after victory. This occurred after the revolutions of 1854 and 1868, in 1917, and in the Second Republic and Civil War. However, these conflicts were typical of all industrializing European societies, and everywhere they contributed to political instability. The defeat of the progressives was also partly due to outside intervention, aimed at silencing dangerous doctrines or protecting foreign investments—1823 represented the first reason, 1936 both. Spain became a second-rate power after the loss of its empire, and suffered the fate of such countries.

More reasons than these account for the defeat of Spanish progressives, however. When pushed to the wall, the privileged groups, who did not want the Cortes to develop into a forum where all classes could claim their due, called on the countryside for help. Their intermittent recourse to the rural masses meant that the relative strength of the contending parties varied wildly and goes far to explain the violent swings of the political pendulum. The *pueblo*, instead of rising as Unamuno hoped to drive out the ruling classes of both persuasions

[20] Raymond Carr, *Spain 1808–1939* (Oxford: Clarendon Press, 1966). For a discussion of his interpretation, which is broader than stated here, see my review in *The English Historical Review*, LXXXII (1967), 580–85.

and purify the nation, appeared on the scene only when the traditionalists called on it in their times of need.

I conclude that the alienation of the common people of rural Spain from the urban groups holding progressive doctrines, brought about by the process described above, was the most important cause for Spain's political instability in the last two centuries. This alienation arose after the Enlightenment introduced an ideological schism into the ruling groups, and it is disappearing with the integration of the countryside into modern urban culture. Accompanying this process was the rise and fall of the Moderado order, which rested on this alienation. If this is the case, it means that Spain is emerging from the era that it entered in the eighteenth century, from what we might call the age of rural-urban disjuncture.

4

This is not to argue naïvely that conflict will cease; only that it will take a different form. What seems likely is that henceforth Spain will experience the divisions of an industrial society, between an interconnected elite that controls industrial, and to a lesser extent agricultural, production and the more numerous groups that are employed at various levels in these activities. Whether their conflicts can be kept from open fighting and attacks on the constitutional structure will depend largely on whether the opponents of the government are willing to solve the issues within the present structure by becoming a loyal opposition; in other words, on how far Franco's regime has become legitimate.

Before Franco all rulers since 1808 sought in vain to revive the legitimacy once enjoyed by the absolute kings. They all failed largely because they were unable to establish a form of government that did not represent the victory of one of the contending parties. The restoration monarchy under Cánovas' constitution came the closest, but when the opposition threatened to upset the Moderado order by legal means, the king and the army overthrew the constitution, showing that they did not accept its legitimacy. Despite his plebiscite, Primo de Rivera did not solve the problem, for he never dared convoke freely elected cortes, where his opponents could speak out. The Second Republic also failed to stand above the fray. By writing anticlerical legislation into the constitution, the Republicans turned it into a partisan program rather than a document that could win the loyalty of all major groups. In the terms of the sociologist Max Weber, once the traditional basis for legitimacy had been destroyed, there remained only the possibilities of a charismatic leader reestablishing it or of the general acceptance of a new legal structure and constitution because they were believed to be impartial in their working. Spain found no charismatic leader, and the bitter ideological division within the political classes and its repercussion on the common people produced a situation where every new constitution seemed to large numbers of Spaniards an arbitrary instrument for protecting their opponents' position.

How to establish his legitimacy was thus one of the most serious challenges facing Franco. At the outset the task might seem hopeless. He was too cold and inhibited to become a charismatic leader. Although he called his cause a crusade and national movement, half the Spanish people, more than half of those politically committed, had fought him and could see in him only a military dictator who had been forced on the country by outside powers. Abroad in 1945 the United Nations read his regime out of the family of civilized nations.

For a quarter of a century Franco struggled to gain acceptance. Like Primo de Rivera, in 1947 he resorted to a plebiscite so that he could base his rule on more than the force of arms, and he sought to attach to himself what remained of the aura of the former monarchy. After 1950 his alliance with the Catholic church and his boasted reputation as a successful anti-Communist finally won him official acceptance in America, if not in Europe. Legitimacy at home was much harder to come by. Defense of privilege, police rule, corruption, and favoritism meant the regime was not impartial. So long as Franco denied his opponents freedom of expression and organization, he clearly did not believe a loyal opposition had developed. Nevertheless, the simple fact of remaining in power for decades while a new generation matured that had not been involved in the Civil War gave his regime stability, and the social and economic transformation in progress made people at all levels apprehensive of any change that might deprive them of their material gains. By the time of the celebrations of twenty-five years of peace, few Spaniards any longer dreamed of overthrowing Franco as head of state.

The success of the celebrations and the booming economy encouraged the government to give the opposition greater freedom of action. The reform of the Cortes in 1967 created the first directly elected members of that body. In the same year, spurred on by a spirited minister of information, Manuel Fraga Iribarne, Franco at last modified the censorship law of 1938. Compulsory prior censorship of books and newspapers was abolished, but publishers and editors would still be held responsible for any attacks on the state and morality and could be punished with heavy fines, confiscation of objectionable books, and suspension of periodicals. On paper the change did not seem profound, but in the next years considerably wider expression of opinion developed. Newspapers began to report candidly domestic news, books by and about Marx and other revolutionary leaders were published, and periodicals like *Cuadernos para el diálogo* discussed controversial issues frankly.

The euphoria was brought up short in 1967. The rapid economic expansion gave way to a recession, which, while part of a general European development, was particularly severe in Spain. Reports began to circulate that Franco's health was declining and that he no longer controlled his ministers with his usual firm hand. The recent reforms did not calm agitation: illegal workers' commissions disrupted industrial production and students continued refractory. The year 1968 was no better. The economy continued to stagnate, and the government was unable to start its second four-year development plan on time.[21] In the summer Basque nationalists flouted the regime with acts of sabotage, armed robbery, and assassinations. The government responded by proclaiming a "state of exception" in the Basque province of Guipuzcoa, on August 5, 1968. The decree suspended various articles of the Fuero de los Españoles of 1945, thereby permitting the police to arrest or deport hundreds of suspects, including at least fifteen priests. With the beginning of the new school year, students began to insult the Head of State directly. On October 31 demonstrators at the University of Madrid burned Franco's portrait, and on January 18, 1969 others at the University of Barcelona threw a bust of Franco out of the window of the rector's office into the street. Freedom of the press to report these events magnified their audacity.

The opposition found a subject they could exploit with telling effect in the treatment accorded the new wave of political prisoners. Although they were spared the terror of the postwar years, those accused of political crimes still faced special courts and received different treatment from ordinary criminals. During the months of December 1968 and January 1969 small groups of women relatives of men in prison for participation in workers' commissions staged sit-ins in churches in Madrid, Bilbao, and San Sebastián, for days at a time. Thirteen hundred intellectuals signed a petition in January asking for the investigation of alleged police tortures, and the associations of lawyers of Madrid and Barcelona petitioned the ministry to abolish the special military and civil courts for the trial of political prisoners. All these acts publicized the hypocrisy of a government that pretended to liberalize the press and Cortes while maintaining a police state. When a student of the University of Madrid died during a police interrogation on January 20, 1969—a suicide, according to official statements—the campus exploded in a virtual rebellion. Mass meetings and demonstrations of students rocked the Ciudad Universitaria, complete with red flags bearing the hammer and sickle, and angry groups spread out through the city blocking traffic and shouting insults at the authorities.

Although Franco had survived worse disturbances, the full publicity given these events threw into a panic certain generals and ministers, who had before them the image of the violent student disorders in Paris in May 1968 which had almost toppled de Gaulle. On January 24,

[21] See above, pp. 14–16 and 21–22.

hearkening to their demand for forceful measures, Franco proclaimed a state of exception for three months throughout the country. The decree suspended freedom of expression and assembly, the right to choose one's residence, immunity of private homes from search without a warrant, and the right of an arrested person to have charges presented against him within seventy-two hours, all of which were guaranteed by the Fuero de los Españoles. With the press safely muzzled, in the next weeks the police acted against persons suspected of subversive activities in labor organizations, the universities, and the Catalan and Basque nationalist movements. A score of professors of the University of Madrid were deported to small towns, and student leaders were arrested or confined to their homes. Perhaps 700 persons went to prison throughout all Spain.

The numbers were tiny by comparison with the mass arrests that followed the Civil War, but the significance of the measure lay elsewhere. At one blow, and without protest, all the liberal advances of recent years suddenly evaporated, and Spain returned to the conditions of the forties. Franco's government had proved far more dramatically than the opposition that the country was still a police dictatorship. Although the government subsequently tried to convince the public that the measure was only a normal reaction to the attempt of a small minority of Spaniards to threaten the peace, the state of exception was a catastrophic blow to the long efforts to achieve legitimacy. Once again the rulers themselves had shown that they did not believe the public accepted their rule.

The disastrous effects of the measure rapidly became evident abroad. Spanish exiles and foreign enemies of Franco mounted demonstrations against his regime, and his revived reputation as a military dictator threatened Spain's application for membership in the European Common Market. Worse, Franco's best friend appeared about to desert him. Since 1968 the United States and Spain had been negotiating without success a renewal of the military bases agreement, and the state of exception gave ammunition to American congressmen who wished to force an end to the alliance. These developments enabled the saner heads in Franco's ministry to convince him of his mistake. On March 21, while the state of exception still had more than a month to run, Franco lifted it as suddenly as he had imposed it.

The shock and uncertainty felt by Spaniards in the wake of the state of exception demonstrated the need to provide for the continuity of the regime once Franco should disappear, especially since rumors of his declining health could not be silenced. Franco's appreciation of the seriousness of the situation at last overcame his long aversion to naming a successor. On July 22, 1969 he appeared before a special session of the Cortes, and in accordance with the Law of Succession of 1947 he nominated Juan Carlos of Bourbon, grandson of Alfonso XIII, to be the future king of Spain, succeeding Franco as head of state. He would ascend the throne when Franco should die or be incapacitated, and until such time his title would be Prince of Spain. In a brief speech Franco asserted that the monarchy he had established "with the consent of the nation" was "traditional, Catholic, social, and representative." It did not, however, he insisted, represent a restoration of the previous monarchy. It was a "monarchy of the Movimiento Nacional," and arose out of "the decisive act of July 18 [1936]." [22] Thus indirectly he justified passing over Alfonso XIII's son Don Juan, who had steadfastly refused to become Franco's creature by swearing loyalty to the Movimiento and was now in Portugal, betrayed, he felt, by his son. The Cortes approved the nomination at once, although nineteen deputies, Carlists, supporters of Don Juan, and angry Falangists, voted No.

Thirty years after the end of the Civil War, twenty-two after the plebiscite restoring the monarchy, Franco finally played his best card by ending speculation over his choice of successor. His choice surprised no one—what was surprising was his decision at last to name someone to stand with him at the summit of the state. By subordinating his vanity to the needs of the hour, he had once more shown his pragmatic approach to ruling. Nevertheless, he had no intention of letting the untried young prince actually replace him. Under the structure established by the fundamental laws, the authority held by Franco would fall to no single person. According to the Organic Law of State of 1967, besides the king as next head of state, there would be a president of the government or prime minister, a position which Franco also occupied. The Council of the Realm, of seventeen members, ten of them deputies of the Cortes, would advise the king and sanction his decisions. On the other hand, effective sovereignty, which was denied to the king, would not fall to the president of the government or the Cortes either. The president of the government and the other ministers would be responsible to the king, appointed and dismissed by him with the approval of the Council of the Realm. The Cortes could not by an adverse vote overthrow the ministry if the king should choose to preserve it. The total result was a strange division of powers, which by giving final authority to no one, king, or ministry, or Cortes, left the future working of the system a matter of doubt.[23]

Naming Franco's successor hardly appeared to solve the problem of legitimacy. By calling the monarchy a product of the Movimiento, Franco perpetuated the partisan role of the crown, which had been its greatest weakness from Ferdinand VII to Alfonso XIII. References to the Catholic, traditional nature of the Movimiento could not hide the fact that Franco's claim for its legitimacy rested originally on victory by arms and thereafter on police rule, a reality that the state of exception

[22] *ABC* (Madrid), July 23, 1969; *The New York Times,* July 23, 1969, pp. 1, 16.

[23] See Rodrigo Fernández-Carvajal, *La Constitución española* (Madrid: Editora Nacional, 1969).

had brutally recalled. Tying the crown to the Movimiento was a serious gamble, which appeared to prejudice the position of the future king before he reached the throne, but one that the logic of Franco's career rendered inevitable. His pragmatism never went so far as to recognize in his foes anything but anti-Spanish usurpers of the national authority. Thus, although the social change under Franco was altering the tensions that plagued the country for two centuries, he missed the opportunity to make the new constitution appear impartial. There remained the possibility, however, that the social and economic gains of the past two decades would persuade the conflicting parties to carry on their struggle within the established framework rather than risk the loss through civil turmoil of the style of life they had achieved.

The following day Franco brought the prince to the Cortes to be invested. Juan Carlos was thirty-one, a tall, handsome blond of whom the public knew little except that he was married to a Greek princess and had two daughters and an infant son named Philip. In the streets a small crowd applauded politely when the Head of State and his heir arrived. Both wore military uniforms. The old general looked bent and frail beside Juan Carlos, who was a full foot taller than he. Now seventy-seven, Franco had aged visibly since the triumphal celebrations of twenty-five years of peace in 1964. On the podium of the Cortes, where Isabel II as a young queen had inaugurated the building a hundred and nineteen years before, her great-great-grandson Juan Carlos kneeled and swore loyalty to the Head of State and to the principles of the Movimiento Nacional. Then he rose and addressed the body. The deputies, many of them middle-aged men in Falange uniforms, cheered when he promised not to shrink from any act needed to uphold the principles to which he had just pledged his word, but they remained almost silent when he said:

> I am close indeed to youth. I admire and share its desire to seek a better and more genuine world. I know that within the rebellion which worries so many persons there lives the fine generosity of those who want an open future, often in the form of unattainable dreams, but always with the noble desire for the best for the people.[24]

Juan Carlos seemed to say that he would not let the oath he had been obliged to take prevent him from being king also of rebellious workers, priests, and students. During the speech, Franco turned stiffly from time to time to smile at the new Prince of Spain, but otherwise, in his customary fashion, he betrayed no emotion. After the ceremony he left first. Juan Carlos, standing alone, saluted the deputies before going out.

[24] Speech quoted in *ABC,* July 24, 1969; see *The New York Times,* July 24, 1969, pp. 1, 3.

Suggested Readings

The following list of writings on Spanish history concentrates on those in English on the period since the eighteenth century. Fortunately much of the best work on Spain in this period has been published in English. A few recent studies in other languages are included because of their importance. Many books provide comprehensive bibliographies, and those with bibliographies that seem most useful are marked with an asterisk (*). Those available in paperback editions are marked with a dagger (†).

General

There are two recent brief histories of Spain written by the leading French and Spanish historians of Spain. †* Jaime Vicens Vives, *Approaches to the History of Spain*, trans. Joan Connelly Ullman (Berkeley: University of California Press, 1967), is an extended essay on the dominant questions of Spanish history, stressing the period before 1500, with a critical discussion of the major interpretations. † Pierre Vilar, *Spain, a Brief History*, trans. Brian Tate (Oxford: Pergamon Press, 1967), originally written for the "Que sais-je?" series, is excessively brief, but it is an excellent survey, especially of the period since 1814. Older but more readable than either of these is † J. B. Trend, *The Civilization of Spain* (London: Oxford University Press, 1944), most of which deals with the period before 1700. The author was professor of Spanish literature at Cambridge University.

A longer one-volume study by Jaime Vicens Vives is * *An Economic History of Spain*, trans. Frances López-Morillas (Princeton: Princeton University Press, 1969), which covers Spain's history from prehistoric times to 1900. It was first published in 1955; this is a translation of the third edition of 1964, revised by Jorge Nadal Oller, one of Vicens' best pupils. Despite its title it is a broad social history, and it is good on the eighteenth and nineteenth centuries. To supplement it, Jorge Nadal Oller has summarized current knowledge of Spanish demographic history in *La Población española: siglos XVI a XX* (Barcelona: Ediciones Ariel, 1966).

Spanish historians and publishing houses delight in elaborately illustrated multi-volume histories of Spain. Vicens Vives headed the group that has produced the best one to date: * Jaime Vicens Vives *et al.*, *Historia social y económica de España y América* (4 vols. in 5, Barcelona: Editorial Teide, 1957–59; reissued in 1961 in five vols. as *Historia de España y América*). It covers Spain and Spanish America down to 1936 and includes good sections on recent Spanish political history, written by Vicens himself. A good part of its value lies in its maps, graphs, and illustrations. Ramón Menéndez Pidal, ed., *Historia de España* (Madrid, Espasa-Calpe, 1947–) is planned to be the most inclusive and authoritative history of the country. How much the great medievalist had to do with the enterprise beyond lending his name and writing the introduction is hard to tell. Twelve *tomos* have appeared, some in more than one unwieldy volume, but the only one past 1600 is Vol. XXVI, *La España de Fernando VII*, by Miguel Artola Gallego (1968). Menéndez Pidal's introductory essay to Vol. 1 on the nature of Spaniards and their historical evolution, written in the tradition of the Generation of 1898, has been translated: † *The Spaniards in Their History*, trans. Walter Starkie (New York: W. W. Norton & Company, Inc., 1950). Starkie gives a biographical sketch of Menéndez Pidal and a bibliography of his writings.

Medieval and Habsburg Spain

Early in this century Roger Begelow Merriman wrote what is still the only work to treat the domestic history of Spain from the Middle Ages to the end of the sixteenth century systematically in its setting as the center of a vast empire in America and central Europe: *The Rise of the Spanish Empire in the Old World and the New* (New York: The Macmillan Company, 1918–1934, reprinted New York: Cooper Square Publishers, 1962). Merriman is a good raconteur, and his volumes still bear reading, although they are out of date for social and economic history.

There is no recent history in English devoted to the Spanish Middle Ages. One can use Vol. I of Merriman's *Rise of the Spanish Empire* for the narrative and institutions and Vicens Vives' *Approaches* for a brief interpretive account. Américo Castro has given a controversial but now classic interpretation of the Spanish Middle Ages in his *The Structure of Spanish History*, trans. E. L. King (Princeton: Princeton University Press, 1954), which traces the origin of the Spanish character to this period (see above, page 31). It is heavy going, but he has summarized his ideas in an article: "The Spanish People," in *Image of Spain* (see below), pp. 1–14.

For the Moslems in Spain there is † W. Montgomery Watt and Pierre Cachia, *A History of Islamic Spain* (New York: Doubleday Anchor Books, 1967).

Two English scholars have recently written good surveys of the Habsburg period. †* J. H. Elliott, *Imperial Spain, 1469–1716* (New York: St. Martin's Press, 1964) is an unusually broad and penetrating brief history. John Lynch, *Spain Under the Habsburgs* (2 vols., Oxford: Basil Blackwell, 1965–69), provides a fuller treatment especially of the seventeenth century and the empire.

Spain's decline in the seventeenth century has long intrigued historians. Summaries of the various explanations are in Vicens Vives, *Economic History*, pp. 411–55 (see above), and J. H. Elliott, "The Decline of Spain," *Past and Present*, no. 20 (Nov. 1961), pp. 52–75, reprinted in † Trevor Aston, ed., *Crisis in Europe, 1560–1660* (New York: Doubleday Anchor Books, 1967), 177–205. John Elliott looked more closely at the domestic aspects of the crisis in *The Revolt of the Catalans: a Study in the Decline of Spain (1598–1640)* (Cambridge: Cambridge University Press, 1963). How much the Inquisition was at fault has long been argued. The latest book in English on the Inquisition, † Henry Kamen, *The Spanish Inquisition* (London: Weidenfeld and Nicolson, 1965), reviews the question. Kamen's view that that body served to uphold the power of the aristocracy is both novel and debatable.

Eighteenth Century

Unlike Habsburg Spain, Bourbon Spain of the Old Regime lacks a brief comprehensive history. One must be content with studies of specific aspects. Henry Kamen, *The War of Succession in Spain 1700–1715* (Bloomington: University of Indiana Press, 1969) describes the political, social, and economic structure of Spain and shows how the war transformed it. My own * *The Eighteenth Century Revolution in Spain* (Princeton: Princeton University Press, 1958) deals with the apogee of the Enlightenment and economic advance under Charles III and the disruptive effects of the French Revolution. Two stimulating articles are Raymond Carr, "Spain," (i.e., the nobility of Spain) in † A. Goodwin, ed., *The European Nobility in the Eighteenth Century* (London: Adam and Charles Black, 1953), pp. 43–59, and David R. Ringrose, "Transportation and Economic Stagnation in Eighteenth Century Castile," *Journal of Economic History*, XXVIII (1968), 51–79. The full development of Ringrose's argument appears in his *Transportation and Economic Stagnation in Spain, 1750–1850* (Durham, N. C.: Duke University Press, 1970), which provides a new understanding of the prerequisites in transportation for an industrial revolution. The first two chapters of Carr's *Spain 1808–1939* (see below) survey the structure of eighteenth-century Spain.

One must turn to other languages for the major recent works on this century. * Jean Sarrailh, *L'Espagne eclairée de la seconde moitié du XVIIIe siècle* (Paris: Imprimerie Nationale, 1954; Spanish trans., Mexico: Fondo de Cultura Económica, 1957) is the outstanding study of the thought and organizations of enlightened Spaniards. The last two volumes of * Pierre Vilar, *La Catalogne dans l'Espagne moderne* (3 vols., Paris: S.E.V.P.E.N., 1962) deal with the eighteenth century. The second, on population and agriculture, is especially rewarding. (Vol. I has a good essay on Catalan-Castilian relations since 1814, as well as a survey of Catalan history before 1700.) I have reviewed this and Elliott, *The Revolt of the Catalans* (see above) in *Revista de Occidente,* No. 26, May 1965, 207–28. Antonio Domínguez Ortiz, one of Spain's finest contemporary historians, in *La Sociedad española en el siglo XVIII* (Madrid: Consejo Superior de Investigaciones Científicas, 1955) gives an excellent picture of the towns and countryside of Castile but is weaker on the prosperous north and east. Marcelin Defourneaux, *Pablo de Olavide ou l'Afrancesado (1725–1803)* (Paris: Presses Universitaires de France, 1959), a biography of one of Charles III's most radical servants, includes the best account of that ruler's first period of reforms, 1766–73. *Trasmundo de Goya* (Madrid: Revista de Occidente, 1963), by the American scholar Edith Helman, is a unique form of intellectual history built around the literary inspirations for Goya's "Caprichos" of 1799. On this subject she has published in English "The Elder Moratín and Goya," *Hispanic Review,* XXIII (1955), 219–30; "The Younger Moratín and Goya: on *Duendes and Brujas,*" *ibid.,* XXVII (1959), 103–122; and "Padre Isla and Goya," *Hispania,* XXXVIII (1955), 150–58.

Two eye-witness accounts of Spain at the end of the century are still capable of bringing it to life for today's reader. One is by an English clergyman, Joseph Townsend, *A Journey through Spain in the Years 1786 and 1787* (3 vols., London: C. Dilly, 1791). The author of the other, Joseph Blanco White (pseud. Don Leucadio Doblado), *Letters from Spain* (London: H. Colburn, 1822), was a Spanish priest who abjured his faith and fled to England in 1809. He gives an inside picture of both provincial and enlightened society highly spiced with anticlerical sentiments. Letter III is an autobiography of his youth.

1800–1939

Most histories of the nineteenth and early twentieth centuries in Spain have been written to explain the background and causes of the Civil War. They stress those aspects that are important for the final outcome rather than for the period itself, and as a result there has been no adequate account in English of the period until the recent publication of * Raymond Carr, *Spain, 1808–1939* (Oxford: Clarendon Press, 1966). While still dominated by the vision of the Civil War, it explains the confusing political history of the preceding century and a quarter in a comprehensible manner and gives extensive original descriptions of social and economic evolution, but it fails to integrate political and social history satisfactorily. (See my review cited in note 20, p. 282.) The bibliographical essay is excellent. C. A. M. Hennessy's short †* *Modern Spain* (Historical Association pamphlet No. 59, London, 1965) provides a rundown of major events since 1868 and a good bibliography. An older work that still can be read with pleasure and profit is Salvador de Madariaga, *Spain* (first published New York: Charles Scribner's Sons, 1930; enlarged to cover the Republic and Civil War, London, 1942 and again brought up to date, New York: Frederick Praeger, Inc., 1958). By a minister of the Second Republic who later became a professor at Oxford, it is a classic study of the end of the constitutional monarchy and the Republic. Madariaga, a follower of Giner de los Ríos, blames the extremist parties of both sides, and also King Alfonso XIII, for Spain's sorrows. Another witness of the Civil War to search for its origins is A. Ramos Oliveira in *Politics, Economics and Men of Modern Spain, 1808–1946*, trans. Teener Hall (London: Victor Gollancz Ltd., 1946). He is a partisan of the Socialists, and his later sections become a defense of that party in the 1930's. He has a forceful interpretation of the nineteenth century, suggestive but to be read with caution and in conjunction with Carr and the last volume of Vicens Vives, *Historia ecónomica y social*, which is one of the finest accounts of the period.

The one book that all persons interested in contemporary Spain should read is †* Gerald Brenan, *The Spanish Labyrinth: an Account of The Social and Political Background of the Civil War* (Cambridge: Cambridge University Press, 1943). An Englishman long resident in Spain, Brenan describes the different social problems and political movements of the half-century before the war so perceptively that most later studies, including this book, have been under his pervasive influence.

Foreigners have left vivid descriptions of the country, and Thomas F. McGann has shown how revealing they can be, even when colored by their own predispositions, by collecting some of their best passages in *Portrait of Spain* (New York, Alfred A. Knopf, Inc., 1963). Of the authors whom McGann has selected, I recommend full reading of * Washington Irving, *The Alhambra* (1832), George Borrow, *The Bible in Spain* (1843), and John Hay, *Castilian Days* (1871); and I would add to his list Richard Ford, *Gatherings in Spain* (1846).

Priceless for following the political evolution of this period is Arnold R. Verduin, ed. and trans., *Manual of Spanish Constitutions, 1808–1931, Translations and Introductions* (Ypsilanti, Mich.: University Lithoprinters, 1941). It gives the full text of all constitutions in English, but it appears to have been published in a small edition and may be hard to come by.

Nineteenth Century

A number of works have come out in recent years in English on various aspects of nineteenth-century Spanish history. They vary in quality, but they are as comprehensive as those in any language. Gabriel H. Lovett, *Napoleon and the Birth of Modern Spain* (2 vols., New York: New York University Press, 1965) covers the military events of Spain's war with Napoleon and the political and ideological conflicts around Joseph Bonaparte and the Cortes of Cadiz. It is well written but fails to look at the social structure of Spain which makes the conflicts understandable. My own "Good, Evil, and Spain's Rising against Napoleon," in Richard Herr and Harold T. Parker, eds., *Ideas in History* (Durham, N.C.: Duke University Press, 1965), pp. 157–81, describes the last years of Charles IV's reign and gives a new explanation of Spain's revolt. The Spanish authority on the period is Miguel Artola, who has written the volume on Ferdinand VII in Menéndez Pidal's *Historia de España* (see above).

At the time of the Revolution of 1854 Karl Marx wrote a series of newspaper articles on Spain during the first half of the century which can still be read with interest, both because of the author and for their information. They are included in Karl Marx and Friedrich Engels, *Revolution in Spain* (New York: International Publishers, 1939). Eric Christiansen, *The Origins of Military Power in Spain, 1800–1854* (London: Oxford University Press, 1967) and Raymond Carr's earlier article "Spain, Rule by Generals," in *Soldiers and Governments*, ed. Michael Howard (London: Eyre & Spottiswoode, 1957), both treat a central aspect of nineteenth-century history (Carr goes to 1931). Edgar Holt, *The Carlist Wars in Spain* (Chester Springs, Pa.: Dufour Editions, 1967) is by a devotee of nineteenth-century wars rather than of Spain, but it provides a useful and pleasant account of both the Carlists and the intrigues around Isabel II. John Fagg, "Isabel II and the Cause of Constitutional Monarchy," in Herr and Parker, *Ideas in History* (see above), pp. 239–65, deals with the causes of her failure as a queen. V. G. Kiernan, *The Revolution of 1854 in Spanish History* (Oxford: Clarendon Press, 1966), is adequate but uninspired.

The Revolution of 1868 and the First Republic have received better treatment. C. A. M. Hennessy, *The Federal Republic in Spain: Pi y Margall and the Federal Republican Movement, 1868–1874* (Oxford: Clarendon Press, 1962) paints Pi y Margall as the intellectual and political leader of the period. Joseph A. Brandt, *Toward the New Spain* (Chicago: University of Chicago Press, 1933), studies the same years but defends the centralist Republican Castelar as the only person capable of saving the Republic from the confusion introduced by Pi and the federalists. Both books concentrate on political history.

The various other political and cultural movements have received uneven treatment. A delightful work on the founders of the Institución Libre de Enseñanza and their circle is J. B. Trend, *The Origins of Modern Spain* (Cambridge: Cambridge University Press, 1934; reprinted New York: Russell & Russell, 1965). Alberto Jiménez-Fraud, "The 'Residencia de Estudiantes,'" in *Image of Spain* (see below), pp. 48–54, gives an eyewitness account of the atmosphere in which they lived. Gabriel Jackson's article "Joaquín Costa: Prophet of Spanish National Recovery," *The South Atlantic Quarterly*, LIII (1954), 182–92, is the result of extensive study of this attractive figure. John Lynch has written on the intellectual leader of the Catholic opposition, "Menéndez Pelayo as a Historian," *Bulletin of Hispanic Studies*, XXXIII (1956), 187–201. The Andalusian anarchists have a romantic attraction for many lovers of Spain. The chapter on them in †E. J. Hobsbawm, *Primitive Rebels: Studies in Archaic Forms of Social Movement in the 19th and 20th Centuries* (New York: Frederick A. Praeger, 1963), pp. 74–92, is largely drawn from Brenan's *Spanish Labyrinth* (see above) but sets the anarchists into a wider European pattern. In marked contrast is Gabriel Jackson's article "The Origins of Spanish Anarchism," which is hidden in *The Southwestern Social Science Quarterly*, XXXVI (1955–56), 135–47. He makes a fine case for Andalusian anarchism being a quasi-religious movement growing out of Spain's past.

Except for the work of Vicens Vives and Carr, there is little good social or economic history of nineteenth-century Spain. Rondo E. Cameron, *France and the Economic Development of Europe, 1800–1914* (Princeton: Princeton University Press, 1961), is informative on foreign investment (especially pp. 248–75 on Spanish railroads). S. G. Checkland, *The Mines of Tharsis: Roman, French and British Enterprise in Spain* (London: George Allen and Unwin Ltd., 1967), is a case study of foreign exploitation since ancient times, but the emphasis is on the nineteenth century. David R. Ringrose, *Transportation and Economic Stagnation in Spain, 1750–1850* (see above) deals in part with the first half of the century.

Early Twentieth Century

The last decades of the constitutional monarchy and the dictatoship of Primo de Rivera receive good treatment in the books listed above under 1800–1939, notably Brenan's. The period also is central to several specialized studies. *Stanley G. Payne, *Politics and the Military in Modern Spain* (Stanford: Stanford University Press, 1967), goes from 1814 to the present but centers on the period 1898–1939, and provides about the only study in depth of the years 1917–1931. E. Allison Peers, *Catalonia Infelix* (London: Methuen & Co. Ltd., 1937) is a history of Catalonia since the Middle Ages, and it is best on the Catalan nationalist movement in the late nineteenth and early twentieth centuries. (Vilar offers a more profound analysis in *La Catalogne dans l'Espagne moderne*, I, 131–65; see above.) *Juan Linz, "The Party System of Spain: Past and Future," in S. M. Lipset and Stein Rokkan, eds., *Party Systems and Voter Alignments* (New York: The Free Press, 1967), pp. 197–282, covers roughly from 1910 to 1936. Its detailed analysis of elections offers a key to the politics of the period.

The turn of the century, with which Brenan opens his account, has found its historian in Joan Connelly Ullman, whose *The Tragic Week: a Study of Anticlericalism in Spain, 1875–1912* (Cambridge, Mass.: Harvard University Press, 1968), is a study not only of anticlericalism, but of the Barcelona proletariat and the causes for the failure of the constitutional monarchy. She makes a strong case for 1909, the year of the Tragic Week, being the critical turning point. Dillwyn F. Ratcliffe, *Prelude to Franco: Political Aspects of the Dictatorship of General Miguel Primo de Rivera* (New York: Las Americas Pub. Co., 1957), is brief and fully as limited as the subtitle suggests.

Before leaving the period it is a pleasure to point to a recent Spanish study which, if a harbinger of the future, promises exciting work by Spaniards on the constitutional period: Miguel M. Cuadrado, *Elecciones y partidos políticos de España (1868–1931)* (2 vols., Madrid: Taurus, 1969).

Second Republic and Civil War

During and shortly after the Civil War a flood of books, pamphlets, and articles appeared on the Republic and the war in all Western languages. After a lull, writing on these topics has revived in the past decade. Much of this work deals with the Republican side in the Civil War, because its internal struggles and foreign relations roused strong passions at the time and have since become the object of bitter and romantic memories. The sober historian must recognize, however, that since the Republicans lost the war, unraveling the intricacies of their wartime history contributes relatively little to our understanding of contemporary Spain. I shall point out only the best-known studies, and the interested reader can turn to them for detailed bibliographies.

It is hard for historians to be impartial on the period and their critics are even less so. Thus there is no agreement on the relative value of the histories of the period. To my mind †*Gabriel Jackson, *The Spanish Republic and the Civil War, 1931–1939* (Princeton: Princeton University Press, 1965), is the best general account. It has the advantage of being written by a trained historian who had worked on earlier periods of Spanish history before turning to the 1930's. While partial to the Republicans, he weighs his evidence and judgments carefully. It has little on the evolution of the Nationalist side, and its lengthy bibliography is skimpy on critical comments. †*Stanley G. Payne, *Falange: a History of Spanish Fascism* (Stanford: Stanford University Press, 1961), also by a historian, though its topic is limited, provides the other side of the picture missing in Jackson. It goes back to the origins of the Falange under the Republic. †*Hugh Thomas, *The Spanish Civil War* (New York: Harper and Brothers, 1961) is more specifically on the war, with a great amount of information (some of it self-contradictory). It struggles to be impartial, but I find it marred by an insufficient knowledge of historical background and a marked lack of sympathy for Spaniards of any persuasion. Pierre Broué and Emile Témime, *La Révolution et la Guerre d'Espagne* (Paris: Éditions de Minuit, 1961) deals more analytically with developments on both sides of the war than any of the above studies. As the title indicates, the authors believe the Civil War represented the crushing of a proletarian revolution, with which they sympathize.

Two of the best works written during and after the war have already been cited: Brenan, *Spanish Labyrinth* and Madariaga, *Spain*. One should add the account of a leading English hispanist: E. Allison Peers, *The Spanish Tragedy, 1930–1937: Dictatorship, Republic, Chaos, Rebellion, War* (London: Methuen & Co., Ltd., 1936, revised 1937), moderately favorable to the Nationalists. Frank E. Manuel, who is far better known as an intellectual historian of Europe, wrote *The Politics of Modern Spain* (New York: McGraw-Hill Book Company, 1938). It covers the period from the First World War to the Civil War and still deserves reading for its insights into Spanish politics.

There were many eye-witness accounts of the war; the following three are especially noteworthy. †Franz Borkenau, *The Spanish Cockpit* (London, 1937, reprinted Ann Arbor: University of Michigan Press, 1963) is by an Austrian sociologist who traveled widely in Republican Spain during the first year of the war. His introductory historical sketch sets down much of the analytic pattern later followed by Brenan. Elliot Paul, an American correspondent, wrote *The Life and Death of a Spanish Town* (New York: Modern Library, 1937) a moving portrayal of life on the Mediterranean island of Ibiza before the war and of the leftist "revolution" between the outbreak of the war and the Italian occupation of the island. †George Orwell, *Homage to Catalonia* (London: Secker and Warburg, 1938), is this novelist's account of his participation in the POUM militia on the Aragon front and in the May 1937 uprising in Barcelona. He combines memoir with analysis and makes reality read like a macabre novel. I know of no account of the Nationalist side to rank with these.

Under Franco

There has as yet been little serious historical work on the Franco regime. One must rely mostly on the accounts of contemporary observers, frequently newspaper correspondents, and a few biographers of Franco. Almost all such books cover the Civil War rapidly and then emphasize Franco's international relations and the institutions and political groupings in Spain that support or oppose him. Despite the inevitable chapter on economics, these works tend to ignore the situation of the people and the changes going on in society.

Several American scholars have studied the nature of the regime. The Council on Foreign Relations commissioned Arthur P. Whitaker, a noted historian of Spain and Latin America, to review Spain's international and military position, but his book, †**Spain and the Defense of the West* (New York: Harper and Brothers, 1961), also provides a perceptive look at domestic evolution during the first two decades of Franco's rule.

The sociologist Juan J. Linz has used Spain as his prime example for a theoretical study of contemporary authoritarianism: "An Authoritarian Regime: the Case of Spain," in Erik Allardt and Yrjö Littunen, eds., *Cleavages, Ideologies and Party Systems* (Transactions of the Westermarck Society, Vol. 10, Helsinki: Academic Bookstore, 1964), pp. 291–341. In collaboration with Amando de Miguel, Linz has analyzed social structure and social mobility under Franco: "Within Nation Differences and Comparisons: the Eight Spains," in Richard L. Merritt and Stein Rokkan, eds., *Comparing Nations* (New Haven: Yale University Press, 1966), pp. 267–319. †*Stanley G. Payne has written a brief history, *Franco Spain* (New York: Thomas Y. Crowell, 1967), but it is uneven and not up to his other books, which deserve reading on this as on earlier periods (see above). Entirely different in approach and objective is Gabriel Jackson's fascinating autobiographical account of writing the history of the Republic and Civil War: *Historian's Quest* (New York: Alfred A. Knopf, 1969). It provides a unique picture of the atmosphere in Spain in 1960 and the persistent political divisions inherited from the past.

There are two recent carefully prepared biographies of Franco, both by sympathetic Englishmen: George Hills, *Franco, the Man and the Nation* (London: Hale 1967), and Brian Crozier, *Franco* (Boston: Little, Brown and Company, 1967). Both men interviewed Franco and had access to government sources. They concentrate on his military activities before 1939 and his diplomatic relations thereafter, and they have little on internal developments except at the level of ministerial intrigue.

Works of an earlier date can still be read with interest and profit. During the Second World War E. Allison Peers published *Spain in Eclipse, 1937–1943* (London: Methuen & Company, Ltd., 1943) as a sequel to his *Spanish Tragedy*. Besides describing the end of the war and Franco's diplomacy, it shows how his regime took shape. Peers visited Spain in 1939 and gives an eyewitness account of the immediate postwar days, relatively favorable to Franco. Although Gerald Brenan's *The Face of Spain* (London: Turnstile Press, 1950) gives a gloomy picture, nothing on this period can equal it for sheer joy of reading. It recounts his impressions on returning to Spain in 1949 for the first time since the war. His tale of searching for the burial place of García Lorca has a classic quality (it is included in McGann, *Portrait of Spain*; above). The second half of Richard Pattee, *This Is Spain* (Milwaukee: Bruce, 1951) provides a fund of information on the structure of the state and domestic conditions in the 1940's. The author, an American Catholic, wrote in defense of Franco, whose government was currently boycotted. A more recent book, this one critical, is †Eléna de la Souchère, *An Explanation of Spain*, trans. from the French by E. R. Levieux (New York, Random House, Inc., 1964), an unusual book in that it deals at length with the institutions and the conditions of the people.

Three correspondents of *The New York Times* have published books on their observations while assigned to Spain. Thomas J. Hamilton wrote

Appeasement's Child, the Franco Regime in Spain (New York: Alfred A. Knopf, 1943). As the title suggests, Franco was for Hamilton still the tool of Hitler and Mussolini, but his direct picture of Spain after the Civil War conveys a graphic sense of those days. Herbert L. Matthews was in Spain during the Civil War and at various times thereafter before writing his *The Yoke and the Arrows, a Report on Spain* (New York: George Braziller, Inc., 1957, revised 1961). The account is chatty and readable but not profound or incisive. Matthews was highly opposed to Franco, whom he made out as all powerful within Spain. He grudgingly recognizes the social advances being made, but in a strange way he fails to appreciate the potential of Spaniards as a people. Benjamin Welles covered Spain in the early sixties. His *Spain, the Gentle Anarchy* (New York: Frederick A. Praeger, 1965) is a balanced account, well disposed but critical. Unfortunately Welles' interest was caught by the personalities heading the government and the opposition, and he gives little impression of having left Madrid except to interview dignitaries.

Two collections of writings about contemporary Spain came out in 1961. *The Atlantic Monthly*, January 1961, has a supplement on "Spain Today" (pp. 74–134) which covers politics, art, and literature, with articles by leading Spanish intellectuals and selections from recent writers. More important is the volume of articles by Spaniards and foreigners about Spain's recent cultural life, with translations from the best poets and authors and reproductions of paintings and sculpture, edited by Ramón Martínez-Lopez: *Image of Spain* (a special issue of *The Texas Quarterly*, Austin, 1961). Several selections from it have been noted above.

Literature and Art

Since the study of Spanish literature is more developed among English and American scholars than the study of Spanish history, it would be out of place to offer extensive suggestions in this field. The following works can provide an introduction to the subject and to Spanish art as well. †*Gerald Brenan, *The Literature of the Spanish People: from Roman Times to the Present Day* (Cambridge: Cambridge University Press, 1951) is especially helpful to the novice because it comes at the literature fresh from the point of view of the nonspecialist. Nicholson B. Adams, *The Heritage of Spain: an Introduction to Spanish Civilization* (rev. ed., New York: Holt, Rinehart & Winston, Inc., 1959) is a survey of Spanish history, literature, and art, and has adequate sections on arts and letters in the nineteenth and twentieth centuries. In the same style but older is E. Allison Peers, ed., *Spain, a Companion to Spanish Studies* (5th ed., London: Methuen & Co. Ltd., 1956). It is sketchy on recent times, but its chapters are written by specialists. The best accounts of literature and art since the Civil War are in *The Atlantic Monthly*, January 1961, and *Image of Spain* (both listed above). They also have articles on Unamuno, Ortega y Gasset, Picasso, and others who flourished before the war. I have discussed the attitude of the Generation of 1898 toward their national history in "The Twentieth Century Spaniard Views the Spanish Enlightenment," *Hispania,* XLV (1962), 183–93.

The standard Spanish works on literature are Angel Valbuena Prat, *Historia de la literature española* (3 vols., Barcelona: G. Gili, 1960–62) for the full extent of the subject, and *Gonzalo Torrente Ballester, *Panorama de la literatura española contemporanea* (Madrid: Ediciones Guadarrama, 1965) on the last hundred years. Both are more suitable for reference than for extended reading.

Contemporary Society

The conclusion has shown the importance of studies of social anthropologists for understanding the nature of Spanish society. The most readable and most informative work is *J. A. Pitt-Rivers, *The People of the Sierra* (Chicago: University of Chicago Press, 1961) discussed above pp. 268–70). *Michael Kenny, A *Spanish Tapestry, Town and Country in Castile* (Bloomington: Indiana University Press, 1962), contrasts life in a pueblo in Soria (Old Castile) with that of a parish of Madrid; while Susan Tax Freeman, in *Neighbors, the Social Contract in a Castilian Hamlet* (Chicago: University of Chicago Press, 1970), provides a sensitive examination of an *aldea* in the high country between New Castile and Aragon. Carmelo Lisón-Tolosana, *Belmonte de los Caballeros, a Sociological Study of a Spanish Town* (Oxford: Clarendon Press, 1966) is written by a Spaniard about a town in Aragon on the main Madrid-Barcelona highway. Less static than any of the above, it discusses both the historical past and the changes going on at the present time. Two valuable short studies are included in J. G. Peristiany, ed., *Honour and Shame: the Values of Mediterranean Society* (Chicago: University of Chicago Press, 1966). Julian Pitt-Rivers' "Honour and Social Status" (pp. 19–77) deals with all levels of Andalusian society, and Julio Caro Baroja, "Honour and Shame: a Historical Account of Several Conflicts" (pp. 79–137) studies the evolution of the concept of honor among the top sectors of Spanish society since the Middle Ages.

Index